"IT FEELS LIKE A HUMAN ARM!"

From under the back door of the stolen rental truck parked in the driveway, a thick orange extension cord snaked out, looped over the wooden fence, and across the backyard of the adjacent property. Inside the truck a locked, large, off-white chest-type freezer bound with a dozen wide strips of heavy masking tape was running to keep its contents frozen in the hot Arizona sun.

Wearing protective clothing police investigators opened the freezer's lid and a foul odor emanated. They could see frost on the inside walls and a large object completely covered with black plastic bags resting on the bottom.

Detective Garcia tentatively reached in and felt along the top section of the plastic. His face grim, he withdrew his hand and said, "It feels like a human arm!"

The investigators carefully sliced through the rigid layers of plastic, peeling them back one by one, and gradually exposing icy, whitish flesh. A pair of well-manicured frozen hands came into view, in the middle of the body's back.

They were bound together by steel handcuffs.

BOOK YOUR PLACE ON OUR WEBSITE AND MAKE THE READING CONNECTION!

We've created a customized website just for our very special readers, where you can get the inside scoop on everything that's going on with Zebra, Pinnacle and Kensington books.

When you come online, you'll have the exciting opportunity to:

- View covers of upcoming books
- Read sample chapters
- Learn about our future publishing schedule (listed by publication month *and author*)
- Find out when your favorite authors will be visiting a city near you
- Search for and order backlist books from our online catalog
- Check out author bios and background information
- Send e-mail to your favorite authors
- Meet the Kensington staff online
- Join us in weekly chats with authors, readers and other guests
- Get writing guidelines
- AND MUCH MORE!

**Visit our website at
http://www.pinnaclebooks.com**

Cold Storage

Don Lasseter

Pinnacle Books
Kensington Publishing Corp.
http://www.pinnaclebooks.com

Some names have been changed to protect the privacy of individuals connected to this story.

PINNACLE BOOKS are published by

Kensington Publishing Corp.
850 Third Avenue
New York, NY 10022

Pinnacle and the P logo Reg. U.S. Pat. & TM Off.

First Printing: September, 1998
10 9 8 7 6 5 4 3 2

Printed in the United States of America

PART I

DENISE

Foreword

Cones of bright light from hundreds of passing cars and trucks pierced holes in the night, illuminating the long curve of concrete pavement at the freeway's dividing point. Sparse traffic wooshed by in the darkness, with drivers' eyes aimed high at two overhead freeways signs. Forty feet above the left lanes, white letters on a green background instructed State Highway 73 motorists headed toward Coronal Del Mar to continue straight ahead. Over the right lanes, two arrows, pointing oblique right, guided drivers into a broad sweeping turn for the 55 freeway to Newport Beach. Perhaps nocturnal travelers' concentration on the two signs kept them from paying much attention to the stranded, silver-blue, 1988 Honda Accord parked in lonely solitude on the right shoulder, emergency lights blinking, the right rear tire flat.

Or perhaps a natural urge of self-preservation, a fearful rationalization, overcame the automobile occupants who roared by and vanished into the distance. Nearly everyone has, at one time or another, thought, *Someone's in trouble. I'm sure glad it isn't me. I've got my own problems.* Fear can be a powerful influence on personal behavior. It is certainly possible that fear kept potential Samaritans from braking to a halt to see if someone needed help.

After all, no one stood outside the Honda. It would be easy to assume that the driver had walked to the emergency telephone, just a hundred paces forward of the car, and called for assistance. With that flat tire, the Honda owner was lucky not to have lost control and rolled over the deep slope at the side of the freeway, down into the blackness sixty feet below. So the poor, unlucky soul had felt the bumping and heard the flapping of a flat tire, then pulled over to the side of the road, parked, probably called for help, and no doubt had already been rescued from any danger lurking in the predawn hours. Maybe even a California Highway Patrol cruiser had stopped and given the unfortunate Honda driver a ride to safety.

In the protective cocoon of a traveler's automobile, it is easy to find many reasons not to become involved in someone else's problems. Why take the risk of stopping on a freeway shoulder in those lonely hours preceding dawn, before the rays of sun peeped over nearby Saddleback Mountain? Drivers headed home from Sunday night parties certainly wouldn't be inclined to delay their trips, especially if they had tilted a few too many beers or cocktails. Truckers hauling payloads wouldn't gamble on making late deliveries. Early June vacationers arriving in the southland would be concentrating on visions of Disneyland, sunny beaches, surfing, fishing, and the thousand other delights of southern California. They would not be concerned with a stalled, stranded car.

As Monday morning dawned and commuters began jamming the freeways en route to millions of jobs, the Honda continued to sit silently, alone, buffeted by the roar and gusts of rushing vehicles, most of them exceeding the 55-miles-per-hour speed limit. Its red emergency blinkers continued to flash, weakening as the battery gradually drained, but still attracting no attention. Golden brown grass, two feet high, carpeting the steep slope next to the car, waved in the turbulent wake of southbound trucks.

At the bottom of the slope, a chain link fence separated Bear Street from freeway property. On the south side of the four-lane street, an apartment complex housed late sleepers, none of whom noticed the parked Honda sitting across the divide, up on the raised highway shoulder.

Typical of a June morning, cloudy overcast burned off as the sun ascended, gradually elevating spring temperatures toward the mid-seventies. Radio stations blared news stories of June 3,

1991, along with traffic bulletins and weather reports. Early traffic dominoed with congestion, crept along at a stop-and-go pace, then regained normal velocity as the workforce reached their destinations and settled into a multiplicity of jobs. At midday, the cacophony peaked again as scrambling lunch crowds filled roads, sidewalks, and restaurants. The thunderous blur of various hued automobiles and trucks ebbed and flowed in a continuous roar along the 73 freeway.

So they passed. On an average Monday in June, approximately fifty thousand southbound vehicles regularly traveled by that spot on the freeway. No one stopped. Not even a California Highway Patrol officer.

As the warm day slipped by, and the Honda's shadow grew long, tired workers threading their paths toward home shot past the car. A different fleet of vehicles zoomed by; people who had been on the northbound side of the freeway that morning. Thousands of pairs of eyes saw, but did not see. Just as their counterparts had done earlier, they found no reason to stop and inspect a stalled car with a flat tire. Too much trouble. Too dangerous. Someone else's job. That's for the police to take care of.

The sun dropped into the Pacific, lights sparkled in Costa Mesa, Newport Beach, and all across south Orange County. The Honda sat, stone still, doors unlocked, windows down a couple of inches, blinkers still weakly flashing.

Somewhere, the driver had been swallowed into a morass. People who loved her had already spent hours making panicky, desperate, heartsick phone calls.

Not until 9:30 Monday night, after more than nineteen hours, would anyone brake to a halt to check out the Honda. Incredibly, the person who stopped happened to be the missing driver's best friend.

Chapter 1

Twelve hours before the Honda first appeared on the freeway shoulder, Denise Huber braked it to a stop in front of Rob Calvert's Huntington Beach home. She had been eagerly anticipating that Sunday evening, thrilled from the moment another man, Jason Snyder, had invited her to attend a Morrissey concert. On Saturday, though, Snyder found that he could not be excused from his bartending job at the Old Spaghetti Factory restaurant, and had asked his buddy, Rob Calvert, to accompany Denise to the event. Denise would provide the transportation in her Honda.

Calvert happily accepted. "She was beautiful," he proclaimed. "A terrific dresser, with classy clothes. I would love to have had a close, or romantic, relationship with her." But he recognized that Denise Huber, age twenty-three, had avoided romantic entanglements, and chose to keep it that way. Even her relationship with Jason Snyder, who had invited her to the concert, was strictly platonic.

Standing five feet, nine inches, and weighing a trim 130 pounds, with long, perfect legs and a dazzling smile, Denise Huber rattled the libido of more than one young man. "She was everyone's fantasy date," Calvert said. Her shiny, dark brown hair cascaded past her shoulders, and her blue eyes could light up a dark room. All of that combined with athletic grace, superior intellect, and an effervescent sense of humor, made men's pulses quicken and other women's envy rise like a thermometer on summer sand. "She sure had a lot of guys scamming her," Calvert would recall.

On previous occasions, during the four years of their friendship, Calvert had the pleasure of escorting Denise to several movies and concerts. Music, Calvert said, formed the most important common ground between them. They spent hours discussing it, and learned they both liked a wide variety of rhythms, beats, and melodies, especially older songs. Movies Rob and Denise attended together included *The Silence of the Lambs.* "There was a part in it," Calvert said, "where the murderer is dancing in his lair, with weird music. We were both entranced by the sound, and wanted a record of it. We really liked the soundtrack," Calvert reminisced, recalling that they searched every music store in the county. He finally found a recorded rendition, but it was "an orchestral version" which he didn't especially like. "So I warned her not to bother buying it."

"We could talk about everything." With a grin, Rob described the sense of humor Denise often displayed. "You remember that movie, *Splash,* with Tom Hanks? Daryl Hannah did this funny little squeak with her voice, and Denise could imitate that perfectly. When you least expected it, Denise would come up with that squeak. As soon as I heard her do it, I immediately recognized it. It would really tickle me." The grin disappeared from Calvert's face, replaced by a somber look. "Gosh," he said, "she is so cute doing that."

In mid-May, Rob took Denise to a club called Bogart's. They danced together and had a few drinks. He felt very close to her, but respected her wishes not to become involved. "I knew, also, that she had religious beliefs. They never really became an issue with us, though. She just liked to have fun. I am a Christian, too, but don't attend church regularly. I think she was just a very moral person."

A native of Orange County, Rob Calvert came within one week of being born on Denise Huber's birthday, but one year earlier. She entered the world on November 22, 1967, and Rob was born on November 15, 1966. During his life, he would have some interesting corollary brushes with notorious crimes. Just four months before Calvert's birth, Richard Speck slaughtered eight nurses in Chicago. A couple of weeks later, Charles Whitman climbed a tower on the campus of the University of Texas, in Austin, and used a telescopic rifle to pick off forty-five people, twelve of whom died from the wounds. One day after Calvert's arrival in the world, a jury in Cleveland, Ohio, found Dr. Samuel Sheppard not guilty of murdering his wife twelve years earlier, a crime for which he had already served a dozen years in prison. While attending Huntington Beach High School, in Orange County, Rob Calvert befriended a classmate named Lynel Murray. On November 12, 1986, three days before Rob's twentieth birthday, a hell-bent couple kidnapped Lynel from the Huntington Beach cleaners where she worked, took her to a motel, sexually assaulted her, and savagely strangled the bound and gagged young woman. The killers, James Gregory Marlow and Cynthia Lynn Coffman, are both imprisoned on California's death row. And in 1994 Calvert happened to be at an Orange County night club on the same night another young woman was beaten to death. Her killer is also on death row. These bizarre coincidences bother Calvert, a gentle, sensitive man whose interests are along the lines of music, history, and astronomy.

But he didn't have any idea, on Sunday night, June 2, 1991, that his worries were just beginning.

When he'd first learned that he would take Denise Huber out that Sunday, Rob Calvert could not have been more delighted. Early that evening, after arriving home from work, he checked his telephone answering machine and found a message from his buddy, Jason Snyder. "Hey, Rob. I have a couple of tickets for the Morrissey concert at the Forum, but I have to work tonight. I was gonna take Denise. I need you to go with her. Okay, man? She'll drive."

The second message on the machine warmed Calvert's heart. Denise Huber's bubbly voice confirmed the arrangements, and told Rob that she would pick him up about 7:30 that evening.

She arrived promptly, and looked stunning to Calvert in her short black dress with spaghetti shoulder straps, a matching black jacket, hose, and black high heel pumps. Her shiny, long, dark hair and perfect makeup made her one of the most beautiful sights he'd ever seen.

With Rob in the passenger seat, they drove north on Brookhurst Street, chattering in happy anticipation about the concert. After pulling into a station for gas, they agreed to stop at a liquor store near Garfield Street. Neither Rob nor Denise consumed large amounts of alcohol, but thought a few drinks might enhance the concert fun. Rob recalled, "Denise and I purchased a small bottle of vodka, some orange juice, and some pretzels."

Denise wove west through Sunday traffic along the I-405, locally called the San Diego Freeway, followed the South Bay curve that swept them northward, and after traveling about three-quarters of an hour, exited near Inglewood. The congestion increased as they closed the distance to the Great Western Forum, home of basketball's Los Angeles Lakers and the ice hockey L.A. Kings. A fan of the Kings, Denise had attended several games there with her best girlfriend, Tammy Brown. She had written a fan letter to one the team members, and flushed with excitement when she received a warm response.

With half an hour to spare before the concert, the couple found a parking place in the crowded lot. They sat in the car, chatting about Morrissey while sipping vodka with orange juice and munching on pretzels. Rob characterized it as, "Getting a little partied up before the concert."

On foot, following the flow of fans into the interior of the vast arena, Denise and Rob found their assigned seats, but would stand through most of the evening.

Perhaps one of the reasons Denise liked Morrissey related to the singer's self-proclaimed lifestyle of celibacy. She didn't rush the stage, though, as many fans of both sexes often did at his performances, ostensibly to become the only person able to seduce the rock star. Morrissey probably wouldn't qualify as a sex symbol to most people, as judged by his personal appearance. With sharp facial features, and wearing his dark hair in a high pompadour close-cropped at the temples, black shirts which usually came off during the performance as he sang lyrics questioning many social institutions, he usually bared a distinctly undernourished chest. His fans appeared to number more frail young men than women. But the words of his iconoclastic songs, accompanied by a four-piece band, obviously appealed to both sexes, as measured by the constant noise level from the crowd.

Denise and Rob joined in chanting "MORRISSEEE, MORRISSEEE," at the start of the evening, and sang along with, "(I'm) The End of My Family Line" and a full program of the popular entertainer's other hits.

Said Rob, "I bought a twenty-ounce beer. Just one for both of us to share. It was rather, you know, a large cup. So there was a long line to get the beer, and I just grabbed one."

Fortified by vodka and beer, Rob worked up enough nerve to put his arm around Denise's waist during the remaining sets of songs. "It was such a joyous occasion. We were standing during most of the concert, and moving together to the music." It would be three unforgettable hours for Calvert.

As the couple exited, Denise found a public telephone and stopped to make a call. She'd had such a good time at the event, she didn't want the night to end. So she dialed Jason Snyder's number and invited him to meet her and Rob in a restaurant bar near Marina Pacifica in Long Beach, about a forty-five-minute drive from the Forum en route to Orange County.

There are few traffic jams anywhere worse than those preceding and following public events in the Los Angeles region, especially at night, with headlights pointing in all directions, and everyone trying to edge the other driver out. But with her infinite humor and patience, Denise Huber managed to slide through the tangle of cars, find her way back to the I-405, and drive toward Long Beach.

After midnight, the couple entered El Paso Cantina, a Mexican-food restaurant/bar situated a few miles up the highway from Rob's home. Rob bought a glass of beer for each of them to sip while they waited for Jason Snyder to arrive. They danced to a couple of jukebox tunes, talked, and Denise bought another beer for each of them. A mutual friend named Ross showed up and joined them at their table. But Jason never made it.

A little after 1:30, the bar announced last call. Monday would be a work day for Rob and Denise's part-time job might also require her services, so they finally decided to call it a night. It

had been delightfully pleasurable for both of them. On the way
back to his place, they made one last stop to buy a pack of ciga-
rettes.

A few minutes later, Denise once again parked her Honda in
front of Rob's home. He would recall with a touch of chagrin
that when he reached to unbuckle his seat belt, it jammed. No
matter how hard he tried, he couldn't unsnap the stubborn latch.
"I wrestled with it at least five or six minutes." Finally, Denise,
with her usual aplomb, reached over and disconnected the
buckle. They both laughed. He wanted to kiss her goodnight,
but refrained from the attempt. They chatted amiably for a few
minutes before Rob promised he would give her a call within
the next few days. Denise flashed one of her brilliant smiles,
waved, and drove away just a few minutes after two in the morning. She should have arrived at her parent's Newport Beach
home within thirty to forty minutes.

Rob Calvert had no idea at that moment that he would never
see Denise Huber again.

When the Honda's right rear tire went flat, and Denise Huber
steered to the freeway's right shoulder in the dark, wee hours,
no one heard what she may have said. It would be easy to imagine
her initial alarm, perhaps fright, as she voiced the predicament
with, "Oh no! What am I going to do now?"

Chapter 2

"Oh, no, what am I going to do now?" little Denise Huber squealed. The pretty strawberry blond angel, not yet three years old and wearing her new red boots, had just completed a joyous stomp through a sidewalk puddle of water, perhaps two inches deep, and had managed to splatter water all over her clothing.

From a vantage point out of Denise's view, her parents watched the exuberant romp, and covered their mouths to keep from laughing out loud. Ione Huber rushed across the yard and stood with her hands on her hips trying to assume an expression of motherly disapproval, but couldn't hold back the chuckles as she swept her soaked daughter up into her arms. Father Dennis, after whom the baby had been named, shook his head in amusement.

No parents beamed more proudly at a child than Ione and Dennis Huber, and with good reason. The cherubic youngster had already learned the entire alphabet at age two, having regularly and faithfully watched *Sesame Street* on television. Holding a newspaper open, Denise would point her tiny fingers to each letter and call out its identification. She spoke with more articulation than many adults who lived near the Huber family in the outskirts of California's capital, Sacramento. When Denise grew more sophisticated, at age five, she made the transition from *Sesame Street* to *I Love Lucy,* and would ultimately own a huge collection of video taped copies of the show, which she wore out by watching them repeatedly. Lucille Ball helped hone the youngster's sense of humor, and the Three Stooges gave her a deeper appreciation of riotous slapstick comedy.

From television, her interest would turn to books, especially those written by Dr. James Herriot, who eloquently penned tales of caring for animals among the moorlands of Yorkshire, England; each book bearing a title taken from the poems of Cecil F. Alexander: "All things bright and beautiful, All creatures great and small, All things wise and wonderful. . . ." Those stories, her parents recalled, instilled in young Denise a lifelong love of animals. She would collect a complete set of hardcover editions, and in her preteen years announce that someday she planned to become a veterinarian.

During their second year in the suburbs of Sacramento, Ione produced a little blue-eyed, blond brother for Denise. Jeff Huber made his entry on May Day, May 1, 1970. His earliest memories were of a plastic wading pool Dennis had installed in the backyard for his kids. "I loved splashing around in it and I can remember the berry vines back there too. Boysenberries, I think. Denise and I picked them in the summer and really liked eating them. But once, when I was trying to pick a handful, and avoid getting scratched by the thorny stems, I upset a bee, and got a painful sting for my trouble." His father explained that Jeff had an allergy to bee stings.

"That was a beautiful house we had in Fair Oaks, outside Sacramento," Dennis would recall. "It was on a quiet cul-de-sac. We had two almond trees in the front yard and one in the back." A memory flashed in Dennis's mind as he spoke. "I built a patio in the back. A big, difficult job. I had just finished smoothing out the cement floor, when guess who went stomping right through it. Yep, and she wore those same little red boots." Dennis chuckled at the thought, but tears formed in his eyes.

Reaching again into his memory, Dennis said, "Hey, in the crotch of one of those almond trees, I cultivated the nicest vines. I thought they were really pretty. But I couldn't figure out why the kids kept breaking out in a rash. Finally figured out I was raising poison oak!"

* * *

Whenever *The Wizard of Oz* showed up on television, both kids would watch it. Later, when it became available on videotape, Denise purchased a copy and kept it among her personal treasures. Both children loved all kinds of music. It would eventually play a major role in both of their lives. Dennis and Ione provided piano lessons for them while they were still toddlers. Their daughter learned as a hobby, but young Jeff took it more seriously. By the time he reached the sixth grade, he had learned to play the saxophone as well and had already shown interest in the guitar. According to Jeff, "We were taught to play the traditional stuff, but we both liked listening to' sixties and 'seventies rock and roll. Among our favorites were Credence Clearwater Revival, The Who, Three Dog Night, and Led Zeppelin."

"My sister," Jeff recalled, "was kind of a tomboy when she was a kid. That included her clothing, right up until she went to college. She always wore jeans and t-shirts. And she was very athletic; really good at baseball."

A lot of the time, said Jeff, "Denise was sort of authoritarian over me. She was only two and a half years older, but tried to act like it was a lot more." Admitting to a tendency to "push the limits a little bit" in his behavior, which meant that he'd sometimes hang out with his friends and fail to notify his family of his whereabouts, Jeff recalled that Denise would reproach him.

She'd say, "I'm older than you and I know better."

"It was probably true most of the time," Jeff said, years later, "But I didn't want to hear it." Usually, though, Denise would not snitch on him, preferring to keep his transgressions between them. If his father did learn of misbehavior, "he would give me a spanking." Jeff smiled at the memory, acknowledging that he probably deserved it at the time.

As the two siblings reached their preteen years, Denise's hair changed to a shiny, sable-brown color, while Jeff's remained blond.

When their paternal grandfather died, Jeff said, Denise was broken-hearted and cried for hours. "Denise was his favorite. He was kind of a typical German, had an accent, and wore a crew cut. But he was really a good guy. In my earliest memories, he was already old and frail. Denise loved him. When we would visit him at his home in Herreid, South Dakota, he would take us fishing on the Missouri River. I remember we would catch catfish, and walleye, and northern pike. When he died in 1986, we got a call at two or three in the morning. Dad had already gone back to South Dakota because Grandpa was sick. So I knew when the call came that early in the morning, exactly what it meant. Grandpa was gone. Denise was so shocked, and couldn't stop crying." The funeral, he said, was very painful for her.

Herreid, South Dakota, where the paternal grandfather of Denise and Jeff died, and where Dennis Huber entered the world on May 16, 1939, sits just below the northern border of the state about fifteen miles east of the Missouri River. A tiny community of fewer than 600 citizens, it occupies land where millions of bison once thundered across the grassy plains and stopped to drink in the wide river. On the other side of the Missouri from Herreid, the site of Chief Sitting Bull's death is commemorated by a marker. He is buried a few miles to the south, not far from the western bank of the river. Dennis's father, Edward, lies in the small, tranquil cemetery at Herreid.

Edward Huber, a native of South Dakota, indeed spoke with a German accent, because his parents had immigrated from a German colony in Russia near the turn of the century. He married a woman who came from the same background. Dennis remembered that his parents often spoke in their native language when they didn't want the children to know the subject of their conversations. But Dennis understood "about ninety-eight percent of it." He recalls, "When I grew up in Herreid, the old guys with long beards would sit around on benches and talk in German." He still likes to try out his skills in it when the opportunity presents itself.

The Huber family descended from farmers, and adapted quickly to tilling the soil in South Dakota. They lived in primitive conditions. Dennis's younger sister was born in a house constructed of sod, part of which still stands today. They later moved to a farm with no electricity or indoor plumbing, and that's where Dennis Huber grew up. "It was a rough life. Can you imagine working outdoors in temperatures thirty or forty degrees below zero? Our only heat was a wood-burning stove. The wind chill factor sometimes dropped to eighty degrees below. No electricity. I milked cows by kerosene lantern light, and sometimes had difficulty finding my way back to the house due to white-out blizzard conditions."

Dennis felt relief when his family finally moved into town and built a ten-unit motel at the time he started the sixth grade. The Huber motel sat within a block of the Herreid school in which students from the first to the twelfth grade attended.

The town is a place of peace and mid-American values. Dennis grew up there learning the importance of personal responsibility, religion, and moral ethics, regularly attending a Lutheran Church. With two sisters, one younger and one older, he continued through high school in Herreid and graduated with twenty-five other seniors. By that time, his parents had added six more units to the prospering motel and rented some of them out as apartments.

Few professional opportunities exist for young men in the county of his birth, so Dennis left in 1957 to join the U.S. Air Force. After a tour of duty in England, the USAF transferred him back to the United States where he accepted his discharge not too long before the struggle in Vietnam heated up.

Still wondering what to do with his future, Huber worked in construction for a while, then enrolled at Northern State University, Aberdeen, South Dakota. He majored in business administration. At night, he worked as a janitor in a grade school for "a buck-ten an hour."

Not long after leaving the Air Force, Dennis busied himself with chores around his parent's motel one afternoon when he spotted a young woman who shared a room with her sister, renting it on a monthly basis. He soon learned her name.

Ione Mae Vandenburg came from Flasher, North Dakota, about 150 miles from the home of Dennis Huber. Her family exceeded the size of his, though, by seven children. Born on February 16, 1943, she was the youngest of ten brothers and sisters. The entire brood grew up on a farm, which had electricity and added indoor plumbing when she reached the age of five.

Religion was an extremely important factor in Ione's life. She, along with her gang of siblings, dutifully attended the Presbyterian Sunday school every week. The small church building, the only place of worship in the town of Lark, became a symbol of faith to them.

Being the last born of a large family, Ione didn't realize until later that her parents were necessarily older than the average child-bearers. Her mom was forty-six and her dad sixty-one. She attended high school in the town of her birth, graduating with a class of twenty-seven, then moved on to junior college in Bismarck. In 1962, while Ione studied at Dickinson State Teacher's College, her father passed away. True to the family traditions, an older brother took over the farm, and still operates it today.

At Dickinson, Ione received a certificate that allowed her to begin teaching, on the condition that she would continue her education. She and a sister, Darlene, found jobs at a small school in Herreid, just below the border in South Dakota. Their daily commute would be very short, walking the few steps from and to the Huber Motel where they arranged to pay monthly rental for an apartment unit.

When Dennis spotted her at his parent's establishment, with her sister-roommate, he felt an immediate attraction. He liked her statuesque five-eight height, her dark hair, and especially those soft-yet-mischievous brown eyes, which matched his own. With all the persuasive skill Dennis and his buddy could muster, they arranged a double date that night with the sisters.

As the low October sun stretched long shadows over the rolling Dakota plains, reflecting red and coral in the leisurely drifting current of the wide Missouri River, in a world of peace and harmony, Dennis and his pal arrived at the motel in his white, two-door '57 Chevy. The pair of young women weren't quite sure which of the two guys they were supposed to be matched with. When Dennis's buddy climbed into the backseat, Darlene followed and Ione sat in the front passenger seat. They rode around listening to Fats Domino, Elvis, Buddy Holly, and Johnny Mathis. Romance bloomed.

Dennis and Ione exchanged wedding vows in her little Presbyterian church at Lark on June 13, 1964. From that time forward, Dennis Huber adopted the Presbyterian faith, "and began to take religion and faith in God very seriously."

In 1967, Ione experienced the first discomforts of pregnancy. The couple decided to move to California to establish better professional futures. They selected the agricultural flatlands of the central San Joaquin Valley, in Modesto. There, Dennis found a job in the pricing department of one of the world's largest makers of wine, the E & J Gallo Company. Ione had no difficulty at all resuming employment in education as a substitute teacher. They bought a green ranch-style house, 1,400 square feet, in a clean suburban tract on the north side of town, for $17,250.

Nothing could have made the couple happier than the arrival of Denise Anette Huber on November 22, 1967. Dennis recalled that the baby, at a little over eight pounds, was "pretty-beat up looking" in the first few minutes as the result of a "tough birth." But within a couple of hours, she "was the most beautiful thing I had ever seen." As soon as she opened her blue eyes, Ione and Dennis could see the light of perfection. But both parents wondered just how they, with their brown eyes, could produce a baby with eyes the color of a tropical ocean.

After a short tenure with the Gallo Winery, Dennis accepted a position as a mortgage banker with the Lomas and Nettleton Firm. The job would turn into a long-term career which would last almost two decades.

Before the baby's second birthday, in August 1969, Dennis accepted a transfer with his firm to Sacramento, eighty miles north of Modesto, as a mortgage company loan officer. He moved his wife and baby to the home where little Denise would stomp through puddles and fresh cement while wearing her tiny red boots, and where the new and final addition, Jeff, rounded out the family the next in May, in 1970.

* * *

Another job transfer materialized for Dennis in 1973, taking him to southern California's sprawling San Fernando Valley. He bought a home in Northridge and settled into the urban tangle of traffic, smog, crowds, malls, and crime, continuing as a mortgage banker.

Both children, Denise and Jeff, attended Valley Presbyterian School, and Ione joined the institution's faculty as a full-time teacher. Jeff, his hazel eyes sparkling with amusement, remembered: "Denise did very well, and I got passing marks. We couldn't get away with very much with Mom teaching there."

When Denise reached the seventh grade, she transferred to Los Angeles Baptist, a grade seven through twelve school. According to Jeff, she continued to wear "tomboy" clothing all through high school, and he couldn't remember her associating with any boys. "She really didn't date or anything. She wasn't popular with guys until after high school, not until she got to college."

Andrea Ludden, Denise's closest friend at L.A. Baptist, would have different memories about her companion, recalling a love of flowers, music, sports, frogs, pizza, dogs, the beach, and a profound enthusiasm for life. Years later, the woman with long, thick blonde hair and soft, friendly features, would smile and say, "I'll never forget the time we spent at summer camp, and how she always managed to step in the stinging nettles."

Soon after moving to the San Fernando Valley, the Huber family joined a Presbyterian church group in Calabasas, a tiny rustic community at the western end of the valley. The town, which has been used in motion pictures as a setting for the Old West, contains authentic buildings from the mid-19th century, and at that time boasted a Catholic college, St. Thomas Aquinas. The Presbyterian congregation, with no actual church in which to meet, used a school building on weekends.

A soft-spoken young woman at the Presbyterian church became the Sunday school teacher for Denise and Jeff, and a good friend of their parents. Nancy Streza and her husband Dick also served as volunteer youth leaders and counselors for congregation children, often accompanying them on outings. Streza recalls a day at the world-famous theme park, Magic Mountain, where Denise, as a seventh grader, impressed Nancy with her ability to repeatedly endure the bone-rattling, stomach-hollowing, hair-raising thrill rides. "She had a stomach of iron," said Nancy. "It made me sick just to watch."

"Denise and the other youngsters in our youth group," Streza later said, "were our kids, until Dick and I had our own children."

Another woman the Hubers met upon their settlement in southern California in 1973, also through the Valley Presbyterian church, was Claudia Moreland, who began baby-sitting little Jeff and Denise, and later became Denise's teacher. Moreland, a gentle, diminutive woman with strawberry blond hair, would never forget her association with Denise. "She was an adorable little girl at six, with her hair cut short and big blue eyes. I often baby-sat her and her brother. Denise was quiet, sweet, and well-behaved, and loved to be read to while snuggling up close to me. She also loved to play games, and it seemed as though I always lost. Denise never wanted to hurt my feelings, so she always assured me that I would get better at game playing, and that, of course, she just had more practice. As Denise went through elementary school, I had the privilege of becoming her teacher in both the fourth and sixth grades. An excellent student and avid reader, well liked by her peers, she had a deep love for the Lord, even at this age. She had a tremendous devotion to animals, especially dogs, and for a time, said she wanted to be a veterinarian. I encouraged her because she was really bright and had the potential to be whatever she chose.

"I also remember her cute little sense of humor; she loved frogs and for several years her room was decorated with images of them, ceramic, stuffed, anything related to the frogs."

During the summer of Denise's fifteenth year, Ione and Dennis treated their children to a trip to Hawaii. In Ione's photo album, she keeps a photo of Denise standing upright on a surf-board at Waikiki Beach, gracefully riding toward the sand on a three-foot wave. She demonstrated a remarkable grasp of the sport in her first few attempts.

Surfing, water skiing, swimming, or dolphins and frogs, virtually anything associated with water, became favorite parts of Denise's life. The backyard of the house in Northridge contained a swimming pool, so Denise became an expert swimmer and kept her slim body in perfect shape. The pool also attracted visitors, even relatives from northern California. A cousin from Modesto would one day reflect on how nice it was to visit his kin so he could use the pool and be with his favorite relative, the upbeat, always smiling Denise.

Her father recalls that she performed well in most sports, especially basketball and softball. Whatever she tried, she usually did well, including her first attempts at driving an automobile. When she reached the age of sixteen, and obtained her driver's license, Denise desperately wanted a car. Ione had been commuting to work during that year in a little white Datsun stick shift. It didn't take long for the parents to succumb to their daughter's pleading. How could they not reward her hard work in school and her exemplary behavior as a teenager? Ione gave her the Datsun.

Jeff remembers Denise as being very quiet and shy during this period. Being far more gregarious and outspoken, he took delight in making fun of her, particularly in public places. He said, "In a restaurant we went to, I worked hard to embarrass her. I didn't really intend to be mean. It was just the typical younger brother and older sister competition. We would butt heads and even had a few physical fights. She gave me a good whipping a couple of times." Their musical tastes, once quite similar, became disparate. "She liked new pop stuff, and I liked older material, with country influence. She called my music 'hick garbage.' " The siblings, as many brother-sister relationships tend to do, began a slow drift apart.

Excelling in academics, and deeply involved in extra-curricular activities, Denise immersed herself in school. "She wouldn't help me with my homework," Jeff complained. The gulf of misunderstanding between them grew even deeper. "When we were younger, we often went to movies together. We saw *Airplane* twice in two days." But, Jeff said, as their differences escalated, they seldom liked the same music, television, movies, food, or anything else, so they stopped going anywhere together.

Dennis Huber's job took him all over the country. He would eventually visit every state in the union, racking up over 600,000 miles on American Airlines. Business became so active in Texas that his firm asked him to relocate to Richardson, near Dallas, in January, 1985. Jeff went with them, but Denise couldn't face the trauma of leaving her high school and companions during her senior year. Her friend and teacher Claudia Moreland remembered: "About the time Denise entered her senior year in high school, her father Dennis was transferred to Texas. We offered to have Denise live with us so she could complete high school at L.A. Baptist." With her parents' reluctant permission, the vivacious teenager gratefully accepted. The teacher's eyes gleamed with love, and suppressed tears, as she reminisced about the happy time, recalling Denise's hearty appetite for pizza, her dedication to the Kings hockey team, the beach, dolphins, and her crush on Steve Sax of the L.A. Dodgers. Denise, she said, was not fanatically religious, but had strong Christian convictions and deep faith.

Proudly wearing her red cap and gown with white collar, Denise marched with her senior classmates to the stirring "Pomp and Circumstance" in June 1985. Mom and Dad made the trip from Dallas to sit with shining, proud faces in the audience.

After she rejoined her parents in Texas, Denise completed two semesters at a junior college. Jeff began the ninth grade in high school at Plano, Texas where he went out for the football team but played sporadically. Having developed an upbeat personality, he bonded with a solid circle of friends and finally felt at home in the school. To keep him company at home, he decided he wanted a dog. They found a little black Lab puppy, born on St. Patrick's Day, and named it Sam. Ostensibly, Sam belonged to Jeff, but Denise, with her affinity for animals, became his *de facto* owner. The frisky pup returned her affection and became her constant companion.

Searching for a suitable four-year school, Denise found the perfect one for her needs. She had grown up in the Presbyterian faith and discovered a college in Tennessee affiliated with the Presbyterian Church of America. In the fall, she applied for acceptance at Covenant College, located close to the Civil War battle site of Lookout Mountain, near Chattanooga. There she met Debbie Detar, a young woman whose facial features and long brown hair resembled Denise's. But that's where the similarity stopped. Denise towered over Debbie, who stood just a little over five feet tall.

Years later, Debbie fondly recalled her best pal. "I met Denise in 1987 at Covenant College. It was very easy becoming friends with her because she had such a bubbly personality and everyone liked her. I considered myself lucky to be her best friend. People were always asking if we were sisters. We were close enough to be, but there was always that height difference that gave it away. We became inseparable roommates. Whenever I needed her, she would always be there . . . she could always make me laugh. I knew she had a happy and loving childhood 'cause she called home every week and I really respected her for that. She was always so compassionate, she would even get teary-eyed watching a commercial. We shared our innermost secrets . . . and adventures. Once we even ditched school for a few days to visit New Orleans." At spring break, Debbie accepted Denise's invitation to go with her to California. "We went everywhere. She even got me interested in hockey, her absolute favorite sport."

One weekend, while his daughter was still in college, Dennis flew to Tennessee on business. Naturally, he paid a visit to Denise, who insisted on driving her father back to Dallas. "We left in the afternoon," he recalled. "We were crossing the Mississippi River at Memphis, when the transmission on the Datsun locked in third gear. We drove all night in third gear. When we'd stop, we would try to do it on a down slope so we could get started again without destroying what was left of the transmission." They made it, but Denise gave up on the little white Datsun.

As had happened several times before, another move loomed when Dennis accepted a position with different firm and relocated back to California in 1987. The pending move unsettled Jeff, who had established strong ties to his school and buddies. Reluctantly, he accompanied his family and enrolled at Costa Mesa High School in Orange County, but felt miserable. At last, he convinced his parents that he really would like to complete the twelfth grade in Texas among his pals and with teachers he liked. After all, Denise had done the same thing and hadn't been forced to move during her last year of high school. Overcoming their misgivings, Dennis and Ione agreed that Jeff could stay with friends they had made in Richardson until he earned his diploma the following June.

Jeff reunited with his family that summer and began serious pursuit of a career in the music he loved. He honed his guitar skills, developed a mellifluous voice with a touch of the Bruce Springsteen sound, and made some contacts in the right circles. Until he could establish his independence, though, he continued to live with his parents. Jeff felt impressed with the new home Dennis and Ione had acquired. In affluent Newport Beach, where yachts and Mercedes-Benzes proliferated, just a few steps from the bluffs overlooking Upper Newport Bay, the spacious two-story condominium selected by the Hubers would be regarded as a dream home to millions of Orange County residents. Under a roof of red Spanish tiles, the second-floor living area and bedrooms opened onto a veranda extending the full-length of the building. Two eucalyptus trees dominated the small lawn in the front, where a low, black wrought-iron fence divided the yard from the entry. Painted in pastel earth-tones, the inviting home occupied a lot surrounded by equally prestigious structures along Vista Grande Street. Outside, ocean breezes swept away southern California smog, leaving a fresh aroma of salt air and eucalyptus leaves.

Denise also rejoined Ione, Dennis, Jeff, and the overjoyed dog, Sam. She adapted easily to the South Orange County lifestyle, but still hadn't made up her mind what to do with her future.

So many possibilities existed for a bright, beautiful young woman with her positive outlook. Like selecting a great meal from a five-page menu of gourmet delights, the decision was a tough one. In the fall of 1988, Denise enrolled at University of California, Irvine (UCI), a twenty-minute drive from home. She still loved animals, but had abandoned the childhood dream of being a veterinarian. In the interim, still pondering future professions, she took a job as a waitress at the Old Spaghetti Factory restaurant, where she befriended two co-workers, Rob Calvert and Jason Snyder. They became great pals, and could be frequently seen together at concerts, dances, movies, and a variety of social events.

One Sunday, soon after their return to California, the family attended the Aliso Creek Presbyterian church in Orange County, and were elated to find their good friends from Calabasas, Nancy Streza and her husband, Dick. Dick Streza had earned his law degree and started a successful business as a tax attorney. He and Nancy had moved to Mission Viejo in southern Orange County. They and the Hubers celebrated a joyous reunion, and would once more begin socializing together. The Strezas, including their two young daughters, spent an afternoon with Denise at the Balboa fun zone, on the Newport Peninsula. Little Calee, age six, would never forget that bright day in the harbor, sun glittering on the water, laughing, music filling the air, and taking her first ferris wheel ride with the young woman she would always admire.

By coincidence, the two families would see Hawaii together. The Hubers had already planned another trip to the Pacific paradise and mentioned it one day to the Strezas. "No kidding," they said. "When are you going?" Both families were astonished to find that they had independently arranged for a Hawaiian vacation at the same time. They flew on separate airlines, but met in Kona on the big island. Nancy, wanting to learn golf, joined the two men on the greens. She found it too difficult. "So Dick and Dennis played golf, while Ione, Denise, and I laid on the beach. Denise got that wonderful golden suntan. One afternoon, Dick took time away from golf long enough to take

Denise snorkeling. She came back so excited, describing all the tropical fish she had seen."

The golden glow of Denise's smooth, perfect skin would one day inspire Nancy Streza to write a beautiful song.

Needing another car to commute both to school and to work, Denise found and fell in love with a new silver-blue Honda Accord. Her father agreed that it would be perfect for her, and helped with the transaction by trading in an Oldsmobile he had been driving. Denise accepted the responsibility of paying the monthly payments and insurance costs. To augment her income from the restaurant, she found an additional part-time job at the Broadway department store in Newport Beach's Fashion Island mall.

A reunion took place when Denise's companion from Covenant College, Debbie Detar, accepted her invitation to stay at the Huber home for a while. Detar recalled, "She convinced me to move to California, and didn't even think twice about sharing her bedroom with me. Even before I arrived, she had been searching for jobs for me. She welcomed me into the family, and I always felt I belonged. She helped me get the job where I met my husband." Denise worked her charm to convince the restaurant manager to add Debbie to the payroll. "She saw the best in everyone," Debbie said.

Jeff's expanding interest in music led him to choose it as his career. He let his blond hair grow to shoulder length and worked endlessly to perfect his voice and guitar playing. In 1991, he moved to Covina and connected with a band. Demand for their performances grew steadily, and Jeff felt he had found his niche in life. When he visited his parents and sister in Newport Beach, he found them fully supportive. Even the differences he and Denise had experienced began to fade away. They grew closer, rehabilitating the bond they'd shared as children. "She was more accepting of my rebel outlook," he would recall. "She even came and heard my band play at a gig in Fountain Valley, and really seemed to enjoy it." Denise helped him celebrate his twenty-first birthday on May 1, 1991. "It was a Friday night," said Jeff "She said, 'Let's go out.' There were some places on the Balboa Peninsula she liked, and she invited me to go with her. Just the two of us, together."

With the family spending time together again, and Denise living with her parents in a beautiful neighborhood, isolated from poverty, crime, and the grimy underworld of urban life, nothing but a utopian future loomed in front of them.

Chapter 4

Tammy Brown dreaded the "communal weekend" arranged by her sociology class instructor at UCI in late November 1988. Shy and introspective, despite her extraordinary good looks, large green eyes, dark brown shoulder-length hair, and golden-girl tan, Tammy didn't believe that she was pretty, even though people told her she bore a startling resemblance to actress Suzanne Pleshette. She often became embarrassed when men flirted with her because she saw herself more as a lonely wallflower with few friends. So the communal weekend, an experiment in socializing with peers by staying overnight with a group and sharing a variety of activities, after which each student would be required to submit a written report describing the experience, worried Tammy.

Among rows of homes, most of which would carry seven-figure price tags, Tammy arrived at the selected house on the Newport Peninsula, which separates the open Pacific Ocean from Newport Bay. On a Friday afternoon, she joined several other students, all female, to begin the ordeal. It turned out to be great fun, and a life-changing event.

The young women played games, talked, cooked meals together, chatted, walked on the beach, laughed, played some more, and learned. As Tammy recalled it, "Much of the conversation centered on how we value money, about the influence on us of material wealth, and on morals. The most important thing was getting to know each other and sharing our experiences."

Tammy frequently found herself pairing off with a tall, slim, attractive, blue-eyed, athletic woman named Denise Huber. "I'm five-four, and I admired her height so much. And her friendly personality. Denise had celebrated her twenty-first birthday just two days before the session. She talked a lot about the birthday party and a Newport restaurant where she had celebrated. She was so full of life and laughter." Denise described to Tammy her work at the Old Spaghetti Factory, and suggested Tammy might want to come in and apply for a job, too.

While the two women seemed to "really hit it off" at the communal weekend, their deep friendship wouldn't develop until a year later when they attended classes together at UCI. Tammy lived with a roommate on the Peninsula, while Denise stayed with her parents. "Besides the classes," Tammy said, "it got to a point where we ate lunch together almost every day." When Tammy took Denise's advice and landed a job at the Old Spaghetti Factory, too, they became even closer. "Our friendship really took off in full swing in about December of 'eighty-nine. I had felt kind of alone. Denise really helped me a lot. I was struggling through college, and she offered me her friendship. That meant a lot to me."

Sharing mutual tastes in music and movies, the two women started socializing. "We'd go to El Paso Cantina in Long Beach and listen to music for hours. It was really a nice crowd there; people in their early twenties. We met quite a few of them."

A frequent customer at the Old Spaghetti Factory would say, years later, that he was certain Denise Huber had served his table, probably more than once. Chris Evans, a prosecutor with the Orange County District Attorney's Office, stopped by the restaurant at least weekly for several years, including the period of Denise's tenure. Often, after a day of sailing his thirty-two-foot sloop up and down the coastline, and into Newport Harbor where he kept it moored, Evans enjoyed dining at the popular restaurant which offered good food, a convivial crowd, and excellent service by attractive table servers.

* * *

As Tammy recalled the times with Denise, her huge green eyes sparkled, and her full lips curved into a smile. "One night," she said, "I was at her house, in Denise's bedroom, typing up a school paper on her old typewriter. I was concentrating really hard on it when Denise walked by. It startled me and I accidentally hit the carriage return, which snapped over to the left, and banged against a big thirty-two-ounce fast-food plastic cup filled with water. Denise saw it, and lunged over me to catch the cup before it spilled water all over our work. I can still see her, parallel to the floor, in mid-air, and she caught that cup! When she came down, we both stared at each other and started laughing hysterically. We were holding our stomachs, laughing so hard." Tammy's eyes glazed with moisture as she told the story.

Other people in their circle of friends, Tammy said, also were drawn like magnets to Denise. "Jason Snyder worked at the restaurant, too. He was a waiter at first, then I think he started tending bar. He really had a crush on Denise, and may have wanted a real relationship with her. But she regarded it as just a good friendship. Denise didn't want to get romantically involved with anyone at that time. She just hadn't found the right guy yet. Guys hit on her. I think Denise was a very trusting person, but she was also quite aware of what was going on. Sometimes, she seemed to pretend to be a lot more naive than she actually was. She was very intelligent." Observing the main difference in their personalities, Tammy said, "I always tend to look at the dark side of people, and Denise always saw the bright side." They complemented each other to arrive at balanced outlooks.

While Tammy focused her college education on becoming adept in the financial world, with a specific professional goal, she felt that Denise hadn't yet decided what her life's work would be. "Denise expressed the idea that she was still young, that there was plenty of time to have some fun before buckling down to any specific objectives." The one thing they both decided quite early was that they weren't ready to have any children, for a long time, if ever. And the idea of aging horrified Denise. "She *didn't* want to get old. And she thought *thirty* was old."

The twosome filled their lives with fun. They attended concerts, movies, and sports events. Being an exceptionally orga-

nized and tidy person, Tammy saved ticket stubs. Both women
thrilled at watching slam-bang action while attending sports
events, as well as rocking to music at concerts. On March 8, 1990,
they drove over to the Great Western Forum in Inglewood to
see an ice hockey game between the Los Angeles Kings and the
Montreal Canadiens. Denise ardently admired the Kings, often
staying after the game to chat with players. She met Jimmy Car-
son, Jim Fox, Dave Taylor, and Wayne Gretsky. One of her most
prized possessions would be a hockey stick autographed by Gary
Laskowski, with whom she often spoke. A couple of the players
corresponded with her during her college years.

Another ticket stub in Tammy's collection reflects their attendance at The Los Angeles Sports Arena in May that year, $38
each, for a David Bowie performance. In August, they joined a
sold-out crowd of 50,000 screaming fans at Dodger Stadium for
a Depeche Mode concert. The musicians wouldn't take the stage
until after a group of rowdies in the upper decks caused a near
riot by tossing paper cups full of liquid onto the fans below.
When lead singer Dave Gahan finally opened the performance,
amid wild lighting and smoke, the crowd chanted along with his
lyrics, "Everything counts in large amounts." Tammy and Denise
swayed and shouted along with them.

These outings, Tammy said, represented only a sample of the
fun the two women shared. "We went to a lot of concerts . . .
[and] to lots of movies, too . . . Gosh, we went to movies once
or twice each week." Sometimes they went with guys, but often
it was just Tammy and Denise.

The beach also attracted the pair, all year round. "We went
all the time. Denise had this really cool black bikini, and looked
so good in it. We usually preferred a stretch of sand off 35th
Street in Newport. I think we went every day in the summer of
1990. We'd sit in the sun, talk, laugh, watch guys, and girls. Of
course, we got catty in criticizing them. But we could be honest
in our admiration of people who kept themselves in good
shape." Both Tammy and Denise tanned beautifully, and attracted an infinite number of admiring glances from the beach
crowd. Despite frequent trips to fast food joints where they
munched on pizza, tacos, and subway sandwiches, both women

somehow maintained terrific figures. "Denise always liked ice tea, too, with *real* sugar, none of the fake stuff."

Now and then, at clubs such as El Paso Cantina, they would sip alcoholic drinks. "Girly drinks," Tammy giggled. "Maybe some Long Island iced tea, or margaritas, or Polynesian style cocktails. No whiskey or Scotch. Yuck!"

On outings, Denise usually drove. Tammy respected Denise's skills behind the wheel. "She was a good driver, paid attention to the laws. I trusted her driving and felt very comfortable. She was always very alert."

When Denise joined the table serving staff at The Cannery restaurant in Newport Beach, she couldn't wait to tell Tammy about the popular lunch and dinner spot for boaters and yacht owners, which offered its own slip in the harbor. Patrons vied for outside tables overlooking the water and a view of the restaurant owned yacht which was available for chartering. For Denise, with her love of the ocean, it would be a great place to work part time while deciding what to do with her life.

On Saturday, June 1, 1991, Tammy journeyed to Santa Barbara, 120 miles up the coast, with another friend. The next day, she called Denise at about 4 P.M. "I wanted to tell her about the dolphins and porpoises I'd seen at the beach. They were so delightful and I knew Denise would like hearing about them."

Tammy also knew that Denise was excited about the concert she would attend Sunday night and would be eagerly anticipating the live performance of Morrissey. "Denise wondered how she should wear her hair, so we talked about that for a while. She said, 'I don't know what to wear.' So we mulled that over and decided she should wear the black dress. She had some really cute 9West shoes that would match her outfit. I told her about a new bikini I had bought. It was white with little purple and blue flowers. But I wasn't happy with the way it fit. Denise convinced me to take it back and exchange it. I did later, for a purple one."

"Have a great time," Tammy told Denise. She had no idea it would the last words she'd ever say to her best friend.

* * *

Gillian Fay, a native of London, speaks with a cultured English accent, and has that dry wit, accompanied by marvelous Anglo-Saxon laughter, the kind heard throughout England. Middle-aged, she has the fair skin of her ancestors along with the light hair. Her husband, Pat, who ran a financial consulting business, stands a little over six feet tall with a physique mindful of Gary Cooper, and dignified speech more like Charlton Heston's. His thin, sculptured face is topped by perfect waves of white hair. Their daughter, Teri, was born in 1970.

The Fays met Ione and Dennis shortly after the Hubers returned from Texas. Through mutual acquaintances at the firm, Pat and Gillian became acquainted with Dennis Huber, and began socializing off duty with him and Ione. They became close friends, meeting for dinners, hosting them at their spacious residence in Huntington Harbor, attending the Christmas boat parade in the Marina, and taking short trips together. Denise, enchanted by Pat and Gillian, also liked spending time with them and treated their daughter Teri like a beloved cousin.

Dennis and Ione had long planned to make a return visit to the Hawaiian Islands, so the two families arranged to make it a joint vacation in the summer of 1988. Denise couldn't have been happier. At Kona, on the big island, the group rented a large condominium for two weeks. During a luau one night, the parents coaxed Denise and Teri to get up on the stage and do a hula dance, which they performed with surprising skill. Gillian recalled, "The kids were very good sports about it."

Even though Denise was twenty years old, she still asked and received permission from her parents to take Teri out one evening. Gillian later described it: "Dennis was looking at his watch all evening. But the girls faithfully reported back in by 11:30 that night. I remember they came in trying to be quiet, but giggling the whole way. Denise whispered to Gillian, 'Are we in trouble?' No. They weren't. They were ideal girls."

At some time during the trip, Denise bought a keychain imprinted with the word *Maui*. She proudly showed it to her parents as she slipped the Honda key on the ring.

* * *

Denise became like a second daughter to Gillian. "She was such a lovely girl. Outgoing, bubbly, always laughing. She had a great outlook on life."

On New Year's Eve, Gillian felt like celebrating. But the guests in her home, including the Hubers, were "awfully quiet." With a touch of petulance, she explained, "In England, we make noise and celebrate the coming of the new year. No one goes to sleep." Her guests, she said, didn't respond. So Gillian invited Denise and Teri to accompany her to the adjacent restaurant where they might have some fun celebrating. "C'mon," she shouted, "I'm going to the restaurant next door."

Pointing out that her purpose was simply to join in on some excitement, but not to drink, she noted, "There was very little drinking in either of our families. We didn't need it. Denise, Teri, and I had a jolly time."

Pat Fay added, "That New Year's Eve was not long after the night we flew to London. Denise stayed overnight with us because she was going to England at the same time. A different airline, but leaving the same time we were. So, she went with Gillian to the restaurant, and stayed out quite late."

The two-week trip to London in 1990 came about for Denise as a result of Teri being involved in a student exchange program which took her to Oxford University for six months. Pat and Gillian announced plans to visit their daughter, and Denise cried, "Oh, I want to go!" She could travel free of charge because Dennis Huber had earned more than enough frequent flyer mileage on American Airlines. The Fays traveled on Delta, but Denise's flight on American would arrive in London at the same time.

Denise asked permission to stay out with some friends the night before the planned departure. Gillian granted it, but warned, "Don't forget, the car is leaving at 4:30 in the morning, and is going with or without you."

Laughing, Denise said, "Okay." She went out, and the Fays

didn't know what time she came in. But she was in bed at 3 A.M., still dressed, when Gillian went to the bedroom to wake her.

Years later, Gillian would recall it. "I can see her now, coming out of that bedroom, sleepy as anything. As soon as she climbed into the car, she was instantly sound asleep again. But she was smiling when she woke up. Denise was always like that, ready with a dazzling smile."

Also reminiscing about her, Pat Fay said, "She was still wrapped up in making up her mind what to do with her life. Still employed as a waitress and part time in a department store. She had no time for any serious romance. Just enjoying her life. And music was a big part of it."

Dennis and Pat understood all of the intricacies of the mortgage banking business, and talked often about starting their own firm. By 1991, they had made the decision. Dennis would leave the company where he had been employed, and start an independent operation, with the help of Pat Fay.

On Saturday evening, June 1, 1991, Dennis and Ione Huber paid a visit to Pat and Gillian Fay to join them, along with another couple, for some of Pat's "famous" barbecued ribs served with corn on the cob and garlic bread. The two men also planned to talk about the business they would launch on the following Monday morning.

Before the guests arrived, the Fay's phone rang. Gillian answered and heard the voice of Denise. "Do you mind if I come over with Mom and Dad? I'm going to a concert tomorrow night."

"You know you don't have to ask," replied Gillian.

Recalling that night, Jillian said, "We spent the evening talking and laughing. Denise was very excited about the upcoming concert on Sunday night, and talked about the singer, Morrissey. It was a nice evening, and a great dinner. Afterwards, we sat around and chatted."

Pat and Dennis planned to start the new business. Denise apparently didn't know about it. Her father asked her if she would be interested in helping him with the preparation of some labels on the computer, then added that he would talk to her about it on Monday.

Denise asked, "How can we talk about it Monday? Won't you be at work?"

"No," said Dennis, "My last day there was yesterday." His daughter nodded.

The guests prepared to leave. Pat and Gillian planned to depart Sunday for Las Vegas to attend a memorial service for an old friend who had recently passed away. Pat spoke to Dennis. "So, we'll call you Monday from Las Vegas. We'll be back on Wednesday, but will call you Monday." Everyone commented on the great dinner, bid their good-nights, and filed down the outside stairs to depart. Denise was the last one out.

As she reached the first landing of the stairs, Denise stopped, turned and spoke to Gillian. "Oh, by the way, tell Teri I'm going to give her a call."

"Oh, sure," said Gillian with a patronizing smile.

"No," Denise laughed. "Really. Tell her I'm going to call."

"You always say that. Sure, sure." Gillian found herself chuckling, too. Denise affected people that way.

Still laughing in her charming way, Denise waved and disappeared into the night.

On Sunday evening, in Newport Beach, on Vista Grande, Denise dressed for the concert. She wore the outfit she'd talked about with Tammy, a black above-the-knee spaghetti strap dress, black jacket, matching 9-West black pumps, dark thigh-high hose, silver hoop earrings, a topaz birthstone ring on her right ring finger, a silver ring bearing a tiny dolphin on her left little finger, and a gold chain necklace with a heart-shaped, diamond-mounted pendant.

As Denise walked out of the house, she turned toward her parents, gave them one of her dazzling smiles, and said, "I love you Mom and Dad."

PART II
VANISHED

Chapter 4

When Ione and Dennis Huber awoke on Monday morning, June 3, 1991, they both felt an unidentifiable sense of something being not quite right. At first, Dennis mentally attributed the discomfort to the pressure of starting a new business that day, perhaps experiencing stomach butterflies such as an athlete feels on game day. But that wasn't it.

The hours slipped by, and both parents performed normal duties. Dennis puttered around with some details of the new enterprise. Neither of them, though, could shake the feeling of something ominous.

Ordinarily, Dennis didn't check on his daughter or try to keep track of her activities. At age twenty-three, Denise could certainly make her own decisions, which meant that she could come and go as she pleased. But both parents had grown accustomed to their daughter's considerate habit of telling them in advance if she planned to stay overnight with Tammy Brown, or elsewhere. If she'd arranged for a weekend trip, they would be the first to know. And if some unexpected activity delayed her return home, without fail she would telephone them to avert any worry. There would seldom be any need for Dennis to look into her bedroom. But on that Monday, the restless feeling guided him.

The parents knew that Denise had planned to attend the Morrissey concert at the Forum. The site, near the Hollywood Park race track, sat not far from an area of urban blight in which crime was commonplace. Unless Denise had lost her way, though, she would probably use the freeway to return home and wouldn't be exposed to any extraordinary danger. They also knew that she planned to work at The Cannery restaurant Monday afternoon. Her other part-time job, at the Broadway department store, usually required her services only on weekends. But now and then she might be asked to work evenings.

If she had returned home in the early morning hours after the concert, and left the house again, she probably would not have made her bed. Dennis wondered, and felt a compulsion to check. She hadn't called on Sunday night. And something felt different on that empty Monday morning

Uneasy, Dennis knocked on her bedroom door. No answer. He twisted the knob, and gently pushed the door open, trying to be as quiet as possible. Their dog Sam looked in, too, a wistful sadness in his eyes.

No one had slept in Denise's bed.

Trying not to reveal any particular tension in his voice, Dennis told Ione that Denise had not returned home from the Morrissey concert. Probably no need to worry, though. Rob Calvert had gone with her, and they felt confident in her safety with him. She might very well have visited Tammy Brown afterwards, and stayed the night with her. That had to be it. Ione picked up the phone and punched in the numbers to reach Tammy.

When she re-cradled the handset, Ione's eyes met her husband's. "Tammy didn't see her last night." A knot developed in each of their stomachs.

Forcing herself not to hurry, Ione keyed in Rob Calvert's number. She listened as Rob explained that Denise had dropped him off a little after two in the morning. As far as he knew, she drove straight home afterwards. Ione thanked Rob, told him that Denise hadn't arrived, and asked him to call her back if he heard anything about where she might be.

As the knot of worry within each parent grew and tightened, they tried not to panic. There could be several explanations why Denise hadn't come home. Perhaps she simply fell asleep at another friend's house. Or even pulled over to the side of the road somewhere because she was too drowsy to drive any farther, and napped in her Honda. No, she would have called to tell them.

Maybe not. Maybe she was too sleepy to call. That wasn't like her, but it could have happened.

When Ione checked messages on the answering machine, she found only two, both from Tammy. One asked Denise to let her know how the concert was, and the second one said, "You should be home by now. Call me as soon as you can."

With her hands beginning to tremble, Ione called several more telephone numbers. First she reached her son Jeff, where he now lived in Covina, fifty miles north in the foothills of the San Gabriel mountains. Her voice betraying the worry, she asked, "Jeff, have you seen Denise?"

Jeff's new band had been booked for a gig that night at the El Toro Marine Base in Orange County, and he had to shift his concentration from preparing for that. He responded, "No, Mom. Why?"

Ione explained and Jeff felt the first twinge of concern. "Maybe she just stayed somewhere." He knew the suggestion offered little comfort, and that his parents had probably already checked that out. "Okay, Mom. I've got a gig tonight. If I hear anything, I'll let you know right away. I'll call you back during our break at ten tonight. Don't worry." He felt that his last comment rang hollow.

Now becoming nearly frantic, Ione called The Cannery Restaurant. No, they hadn't heard from her all day, and she had never been absent before without advance notice.

Yet another call to the Broadway department store yielded the same answer, but they hadn't scheduled Denise to work on Monday. None of the hospitals Ione dialed had any emergency patients by that name. Neither the Costa Mesa Police Department nor the Newport Beach P.D. had any record of accidents involving Denise Huber or a silver-blue Honda. The Costa Mesa P.D. emergency operator, as Ione would later recall, was "very nice" and said, "We will call you and keep you advised if there is any news."

Even Sam, the black Labrador Retriever, who always spent every possible moment with Denise, trying to be her shadow when she was at home, seemed restless, and kept checking in her room.

The business matters Dennis had anticipated handling during his first day as an independent entrepreneur, which might normally have occupied him into the late evening, would have to wait. They lost all meaning and importance in comparison to his developing fears. Concentrating on work would be impossible until he knew that his daughter was safe.

With each fruitless phone call, the tension in the bodies and minds of Ione and Dennis twisted and tightened. He would always compare the feeling to "being kicked in the stomach."

Every time the phone rang, one or the other parent would instantly seize it, desperately hoping that it was Denise, or someone calling with good news about her. They tried to curtail long conversations and to quickly curb the inquiries of casual callers in order to keep the line open. Now, as the torment deepened, all they could focus on was their missing daughter.

When Tammy Brown received the call from Ione, she felt alarmed at first, but figured there must be a reasonable explanation. She hurriedly punched the keypad numbers of her own telephone, first to Jason Snyder, then to Rob Calvert. Calvert told her how he and Denise had stopped at El Paso Cantina hoping to meet Jason, but Jason never showed up. They had chatted with several casual acquaintances at the bar, but Rob felt sure none of them would know anything about where Denise might be. No, he was quite sure she hadn't gone back to meet any of them. Jason said he had no information at all about the previous night.

Feeling the gradual invasion of fright and worry, but trying to rationalize it, Tammy called her boyfriend, who asked her to come to his office in Huntington Beach. She drove the eight miles via Pacific Coast Highway, along the shortest route Denise might have taken, keeping her eyes peeled at each intersection, the beach parking lots, the roadside, and at all business establishments, looking for the silver-blue Honda. She accompanied her boyfriend on a few of his business appointments, but stayed in his car while he visited clients. She wanted to watch passers-by and pedestrians. Maybe her missing friend would magically appear. Worried sick, Tammy used the mobile telephone in the car to call Ione. No, they hadn't heard anything yet.

Rob Calvert couldn't believe it when he heard that Denise hadn't made it home. He wracked his brain—did she mention that she might go somewhere else after she dropped him off? No. He was positive that she intended to return directly to her parents' home, with no stops en route. Anyway, it had been much too late for her to visit anyone else, other than Tammy. Rob, too, called everyone he could think of who knew Denise, on the outside chance that one of them had heard of her whereabouts.

The phone rang again at the Huber residence. Before it had completed one full ring, Ione snatched it up. "Hello?"

"Hi, luv. This is Gillian. I just wanted to let you know we are in Las Vegas, and will start home tomorrow. How are you?"

"Oh, Gill! Denise didn't come home last night from that concert, and we are so worried. We haven't any idea where she is."

Stunned, Gillian Fay fought down her own rising sense of alarm. There must be some logical reason. In the most soothing voice she could summon, Gillian said, "Oh, don't worry, dear. Maybe she stayed with a friend somewhere. Or maybe she fell asleep."

"I know, but that's not Denise. She is so good about calling us so we won't worry."

"Were there no messages on the answering machine?"

"No, just earlier ones from Tammy."

"Well, surely everything will be all right. I'll tell Pat. Please don't worry . . . I will call you back shortly, and I'm sure you will have good news."

True to her word, Gillian called several times, and understood the pain Ione and Dennis suffered each time they answered and had their hopes dashed. Both Pat and Gillian Fay felt torn between their loyalties. The memorial service for their departed friend was scheduled for later that afternoon. Should they stay for it, or drive home immediately to help the Hubers? But what could they do there? They would stay in Las Vegas a little longer to see what developed.

In Newport Beach, each minute seemed like an eternity for Dennis and Ione.

Jeff arrived at the El Toro Marine base. During the previous dragging hours, his confidence that Denise would suddenly turn up safely had eroded. "This is serious," flashed through his thoughts. Images of Denise filled his mind. He and his sister had grown so much closer during the past few months. They'd shared laughter, a new camaraderie, and mutual understanding. Jeff's fears for her safety pushed the music out of his consciousness and he announced cancellation of his group's segment in the program that night. Another band took their place.

Jeff had told his mother he would call at ten, and he didn't want to sound overly anxious by bothering her earlier than that. Maybe by that time, there would be some good news. He waited. He downed some beer in a Mexican food restaurant near the military base. When he made the call, exactly on the hour, and heard the trembling anxiety in Ione's voice, he knew that he belonged with his parents during this crisis.

Time lost all meaning for Dennis and Ione. The police had been informed, and had agreed to watch for her. All of the telephone calls imaginable had been made. What to do now? Wait. Hope. Wait some more. Try to think. What can we do? Dennis made several short stabs at driving around to search for her, but knew that in the vast megalopolis of Orange County, his chances of seeing anything useful were infinitely small. Excruciating tension gripped them as time crawled by.

* * *

In the home of Nancy and Dick Streza, the phone rang while they were out. Carol Harbach, who worked with Denise at the Broadway, socialized with both the Hubers and the Strezas as a fellow Presbyterian church member, and was part of their "prayer chain" (organized to pass important information from one member to another in an orderly manner), left a message. "Call me when you get home, no matter how late it is."

That kind of a message usually sends a jolt of adrenalin racing through the recipient, suggesting an urgency and signalling bad news. When Nancy returned the call that evening, she felt herself shaking even before Harbach spoke. "Nancy, Denise is missing!" Stunned and heartsick, Nancy wanted to call the Hubers, but felt reluctant to bother them so late. She couldn't sleep at all. When she arose before dawn and learned by telephone that Denise was still missing, she and Dick left immediately. They drove from the isolated mountaintop home they'd recently purchased to the Vista Grande house where they joined hands with the Hubers in fervent prayer for the safe return of their beloved Denise.

Tammy Brown left her boyfriend's office at about 9:30 that Monday night. Trying to avoid becoming an emotional wreck after hours of worrying about Denise, she knew she had to make some effort to find her. Maybe, Tammy hoped, retracing the northern route Denise could have taken from Rob's house in Huntington Beach, would reveal some clue along the way. Even though it was slightly farther, the use of freeways, instead of Pacific Coast Highway, might have appealed to Denise in the early morning hours because it would probably get her home faster. The two friends had previously agreed that there was a greater chance of being stopped by a traffic cop along PCH. Tammy plotted the alternative route: Denise would probably have driven north on Brookhurst, approximately six miles, to the San Diego Freeway. After entering the freeway, she would have headed east three miles and made the southeast transition to the 73, crossed the 55, and exited south on Jamboree. The total distance to her home would be no more than eleven or twelve miles.

Scanning both sides of the road in the dark, Tammy wasn't quite sure just what to look for, other than the silver-blue Honda. But she had to try. It took nearly twenty minutes along Brookhurst to reach the San Diego freeway, and she found nothing helpful. Entering the fast flow of night traffic, Tammy quickly reached the turnoff to the 73, Corona Del Mar Freeway, and steered right. In the distance, she could see the two over-head signs, one guiding drivers to the left lanes to continue on the 73, the direction Denise would have taken, and one with directional arrows to the right lanes for the 55, Costa Mesa Freeway. At that moment, something on the right shoulder caught Tammy's attention.

The silver-blue Honda sat there in lonely silence.

"My stomach turned inside out and I had this awful dropping, sinking feeling," Tammy would later say. "I started screaming and crying . . . 'Oh my God, Denise, where are you? Please come home.' "

Because Tammy had merged into the number one lane to continue on the 73, she couldn't pull over in time to park behind the Honda. She managed to swerve far enough to the right to enter the south 55. "I passed the Honda and pulled off at the next ramp, Del Mar Avenue. I crossed over the freeway and went to a liquor store with a pay phone." Trembling as she never had before, Tammy inserted the coins, and called the Hubers. "I found her car!" She gave directions find to the Honda and heard Ione say she and Dennis would be right there.

Still hoping that Denise might have been trying to contact her, Tammy again called her own number to check for messages, only to be disappointed. After making one more call, to her boyfriend, she circled back to the site where she'd seen the Honda. This time, she stayed in the far right lane, and slowed to a halt behind the familiar silver-blue car. Tammy focused at first on the license plate, which she knew started with "2JVV," and the distinctive Newport Beach frame, which reflected Tammy's headlights. And she noticed that the right rear tire on the Honda was flat. Nervous, she stepped outside, into the bright beams and noxious exhaust fumes of noisy, passing cars. Trucks roared by, creating a breeze which rippled her clothing and hair.

Frightened at what she might encounter, Tammy cautiously approached the passenger side of the Honda. As it became obvious that she wouldn't find Denise, it occurred to Tammy that she should touch nothing. She tried to peer inside but could see very little without opening a door, and couldn't force herself to do that. A nostalgic jolt of pain shot through her as she recalled riding with Denise in the car, on previous occasions, and how Huber would remove her thigh-high stockings to be more comfortable before driving.

Feeling depressed and even more worried now, Tammy returned to her own car, started it, and flipped the turn signal switch to re-enter traffic. As she pulled away, the car behind her began flashing high beams in her rearview window. She wondered if she had pulled out too soon and irritated the approaching driver.

Tammy wouldn't know until later that the driver flashing his high beams behind her was Dennis Huber.

Ione Huber grabbed the phone when it rang close to ten o'clock Monday night. She heard Tammy's voice say "I found her car."

Ione's heart pounded as if trying to rip right through her chest. But Tammy had given precious little information. The frantic mother heard Tammy say that she'd seen the Honda parked on the shoulder of the 73 freeway just south of the 55 turnoff, and that she'd been unable to stop in time, so had hurried to a pay phone to call.

Thanking Tammy, and making sure she understood the exact location of the Honda, Ione hung up to tell Dennis about the distressing call. They immediately raced out to drive to the scene.

As Dennis approached on the freeway, he saw Tammy's car pull out into traffic. He flashed his high beams several times to alert her that he and Ione had arrived, but she apparently didn't understand his signal, and drove away. Dennis wheeled to the right, and halted behind the Honda.

Both parents jumped out and walked to their daughter's abandoned car. Ione approached on the passenger side, noticing that the window had been rolled down about an inch or two. She opened the unlocked door. When questioned later, Ione wouldn't be able to recall whether the interior light went on or not. But street lamps and the headlights of passing cars provided plenty of illumination for her to see inside the Honda. Ione saw the stockings on the passenger seat, and observed that the ignition keys had been taken out. Nothing else seemed unusual.

Dennis Huber opened the driver's door. He would later say, "I was afraid to look in." But he entered, seating himself behind the steering wheel. He, too, noticed the wadded thigh-high stockings on the passenger seat. No clue could be found inside the car to suggest what might have happened. Obviously, the right rear tire had gone flat, and Denise had pulled over to the shoulder. Whatever had taken place afterwards could only be the subject of vague speculation.

Because Denise's keys were missing, and the parents had no spare ones, they saw no choice but to leave the Honda where they found it. With hearts feeling like lead, and tears in their eyes, they left the Honda and returned home.

As soon as they arrived back on Vista Grande, Dennis telephoned the Newport Beach Police Department. The night emergency operator advised him to call a towing service and have the car taken to a repair facility or to his home.

The Hubers had known a Costa Mesa police officer named Tom Curtis for several years. He attended the same Presbyterian church. Dennis called him at his home to ask, "What should we do?" Curtis sympathetically advised the parents, in considerable detail, about filing a missing person report and letting the police take custody of the vehicle for evidence purposes.

Following the instructions, in what seemed an unbearable nightmare, Dennis gave the police the details of what had happened, a description of his daughter, and how the Honda had been found. He did his best to answer all their questions. The sympathetic officers advised him and Ione to refrain from talking to the media until the initial investigative steps could be taken.

Remembering that their dear friends, Pat and Gillian Fay, still in Las Vegas, must be waiting on pins and needles for any news, Dennis made the call. When Pat answered, Dennis whispered,

"They found her car." He filled in the sparse details, and heard the heartfelt consolation from Pat, who said he would be back in California as soon as possible.

Dennis could not sleep the rest of Monday night. He and Ione heard helicopters whirling overhead and, with raw nerves, wondered if it meant something or someone had been sighted in the neighborhood. They knew they were grasping at straws, drowning in the sea of doubt and worry. In the wee, early morning hours, Ione finally took some sleeping pills, mostly to escape the unimaginable, heart-ripping pain.

Pat and Gillian, torn and worried about the Hubers, met their Las Vegas hosts at a restaurant for breakfast early Tuesday morning, but could not eat. They empathized with the Hubers' pain, and wanted to be with them to do anything they could to lighten the burden. Grabbing some take-out coffee, and explaining to their friends, the Fays left immediately for the eight-hour drive to Newport Beach. They arrived at the Huber home on Tuesday afternoon, and would stay the following two days and nights, and then many nights over the next few weeks.

Officer Thomas Coute, Costa Mesa Police Department, arrived at the scene of the abandoned Honda shortly after one o'clock, Tuesday morning. Even though traffic had thinned considerably, the noise level of trucks and cars whizzing past still forced the officer to shout to other arrivals. The uniformed cops used flashlights, along with the ambient light of apartments, overhead lamps, and moving headlights to search the area. Coute could see black marks on the concrete pavement where the Honda's shredded right rear tire had left a trail of neoprene and rubber until it reached the asphalt shoulder. The trail would be painted on both highway surfaces to preserve it for investigative purposes.

To assist in the search for a possible crime victim, Officer Jane Walker, assigned to the K9 unit, brought her police dog and gripped the leash as the alert shepherd, ears high, followed his nose on a zig-zag path. He pulled hard, almost dragging Walker along, approximately seventy-five yards in front of the Honda, then circled and came to a stop. The dog lifted his face and eyes, letting his handler know that the scent ended there.

Glancing back and forth, a few members of the search team climbed down the slope to the right of the vehicle, and tramped along the bottom, next to a chain link fence. Fully realizing the improbability of finding the missing driver dead or injured in the immediate surroundings, the officers nevertheless carried out the routine procedures. They would spend nearly two hours combing over the scene, searching for any clue to shed some light on the earlier events. Nothing turned up to even hint at what might have happened. No bodies, no weapons, no rope, tape, or other tools of abduction, no identifiable signs of a struggle. A strobe camera light periodically flashed as one of the investigators snapped photographic records of the scene and the Honda, before a tow truck transported it to a police storage yard. It had been nearly twenty-four hours since Denise Huber had vanished into the night.

Sergeant Ronald Allen Smith, twelve-year veteran of law enforcement, arrived at the site before the car was towed. He'd been awakened at his home by a phone call during the night to check out a missing woman report and to oversee the investigation of a possible homicide.

Shortly after Dennis Huber had left his daughter's abandoned car, he'd called the Newport Beach P.D. A watch officer there had relayed the call to the Costa Mesa P.D pointing out that the car had been found in their jurisdiction, and a CMPD detective had accepted responsibility for investigating the case. After he and a group of uniformed officers visited the scene, he called Sergeant Smith at home that night.

When Smith arrived, he examined the car's interior. The thigh-high stockings remained undisturbed on the passenger seat. He asked that they be collected and bagged as possible evidence. Smith also spotted a beach towel and a backpack inside the back compartment. Nothing unusual about them, but he ordered them to be collected anyway. He checked the Honda's gas tank, and found it nearly full. But the battery had gone dead, drained by the emergency blinkers.

Kneeling at the right rear corner of the car, Smith scrutinized the mangled flat tire. He could see no apparent sign that anyone had tried to remove it and mount the spare, which remained in the trunk. "The flat tire was an enigma," Smith would later say. "It was shredded in a manner that usually happens when a tire is low to start with. I had to consider the possibility of sabotage. Or maybe it was just badly under-inflated, and blew out. Maybe the valve stem was tampered with, or damaged, causing a slow leak. There were so many possibilities. I did call in a special unit from the California Highway Patrol, who are experts in such matters. It turned out that there was no damage to the valve stem."

If Denise Huber, frightened and alone, had tried to seek assistance, what would she have done first? Smith answered the question for himself. She probably would have looked for a telephone to call for help. He scanned the area, and saw that it would have been relatively easy to locate an available phone, even in the dark early morning hours. She had passed an emergency call box a short distance from the spot where she stopped her car. If, for some reason, she overlooked that one, several alternatives were available. If Denise had wanted to walk forward on the freeway shoulder a short distance, she would probably have seen an opening in the six-foot-high chain link fence. She could have descended the slope to Bear Street and walked southeast, parallel with the freeway, about two-tenths of a mile to the easily visible intersection of Bear and Bristol Streets. A standalone pay phone was there. If she had missed that, she could have made a left turn and walked another four-tenths of a mile. This would have taken her to some well-lighted fast food restaurants and a gas station, with telephones available. Another option would have been to turn right on Bear Street at the bottom of the slope, and walk about a quarter of a mile, past an apartment complex. Potentially, she could have knocked on a door at the complex to ask for assistance. If she considered that too risky, she could have continued along Bear Street a few more yards where she would have found an all-night desk clerk at a motel, or a couple of pay phones at an adjacent strip mall.

Or she could have continued to walk along the shoulder of the freeway, around the transition curve, where she would have found another emergency call box.

Certainly, Smith realized, a young woman all alone, with a flat tire on the freeway after two in the morning, would probably be terribly frightened. The prospect of walking away from her car might have been awfully intimidating. The search dog had led his handler about seventy-five yards from the car, suggesting that Denise may have embarked on such a walk. If that's what she had done, Smith asked himself, what had probably happened next?

The answer was not a pleasant one. He'd heard the description of what the missing woman had worn. Smith had little doubt that another motorist had seen a beautiful young woman, in a tight black dress, walking alone on the freeway, and had stopped within a close proximity to her. Perhaps he, or they, had offered Denise a ride. From that point, it was anyone's guess. Thinking as a police investigator, Smith had to consider the possibility that Denise had done one of two things, if she had been offered a ride. One: she accepted, and entered the driver's vehicle willingly. Or two: she had been forced into the vehicle. Smith could only hope, in either scenario, that no harm had come to her and she would soon return home. His instincts, though, told him not to be too optimistic.

Denise Huber was not the only woman to disappear from that same area within twenty-four hours. Another thirty-four-year-old woman had paid a visit to her estranged husband and left her two young daughters with him, then vanished. At first, police had to consider the possibility that the two cases could be linked. They issued APBs (all points bulletins) for both women. In the case of the missing mother, events developed quickly. The very next day, her father discovered her car in a Newport Beach strip mall parking lot. He and the two children would experience the grinding, heart-sickening pain of worrying and wondering for a short time. By Wednesday night, the missing mother turned up. From Riverside, eighty miles away, she telephoned her parents and said, "Mom, I'm okay." She said that she had made a conscious decision to leave for personal reasons.

It was the type of phone call the Hubers prayed for. They would not be so lucky.

For Dennis, Ione, and Jeff Huber, the nightmare continued to deepen on Tuesday morning. Through the minds of each of them ran a mixture of hope, despair, emptiness, and excruciating mental pain. They couldn't allow themselves to contemplate the possibility that Denise might never return to them.

When Pat and Gillian Fay arrived that evening, they gave the Hubers a cathartic outlet for expressing the agony of waiting, hoping, and trying not to let despair blind them. The Fays understood. They did not attend the same church as the Hubers, but both families would find solace in their respective faith in God.

The media descended on the Huber residence on Wednesday morning anxious to explore the details of a potentially gripping news event. A beautiful young woman from affluent Newport Beach had mysteriously vanished; it was the kind of story that would interest readers and television watchers all across the southland and, eventually, the nation.

"We'd been advised by the police not to say much to the reporters," said Dennis Huber. "But, on the other hand, the expansive coverage might cause someone to come forward and reveal a clue to her whereabouts. We would have done anything to help locate our daughter." He found the reporters cooperative and sympathetic, nothing like they are often portrayed in movies, as an insensitive flock of vultures on a feeding frenzy. "They were really nice," Dennis recalled.

One of the reporters would become a virtual part of the family through a remarkable link.

Jonathan Volzke had never heard of the Hubers until Denise vanished. A native of New London, Connecticut, he had been transplanted to southern California as a child and had grown up in the San Gabriel Valley. L.A. Pierce College and Cal State Fullerton provided his college degrees, and he began his journalism career with City News Service in Los Angeles. It didn't take him long to master the crime beat by using police scanners, calling LAPD and the sheriff's office every two hours, and just listening to the lingo and procedures. At age twenty-three, in 1988, he moved to Costa Mesa with *The Daily Pilot,* and met Sergeant Ron Smith, Detective Lynda Giesler, and their colleagues. Early the next year, Volzke joined the *Orange County Register,* the twenty-fifth largest paper in the country, and became a regular reporter three years later.

When Denise vanished in early June, Volzke read the brief article by another reporter, chatted with her, and learned more of the case. He saw potential in the story for follow-up pieces, and asked the editor for permission to pursue it. When he got the green light, Volzke dropped in at the Spaghetti Factory to see what he could learn from Denise's friends who worked there. One of them gave Jonathan the Hubers' address.

On June 13, Volzke had his first telephone contact with Dennis Huber, and met him in person at the Vista Grande home one week later. When he walked in, Dennis' words nearly floored Volzke. "By golly," Dennis said, grabbing Jonathan's hand in a firm grip, "you must be related to old Tuffy Volzke." Jonathan recognized the nickname of his grandfather. Puzzled, he asked Dennis how he knew that.

Well, explained Huber, the resemblance was certainly there. Volzke had the same clear eyes, and the Cary Grant dimple in the chin. But mostly, the unusual name told him. Tuffy Volzke had owned and operated a hardware and lumber store diagonally across the street from the Huber Motel in Herreid, South Dakota, where Dennis grew up. Jonathan's aunt Louise had gone to school just up the block from the motel with Dennis. In a town of fewer than 600, everyone knew each other.

Eventually, Volzke would learn more about his family history through conversations with Dennis than he had ever learned from his own relatives. A bond between the reporter and the grieving family developed from the first day, and would continue to grow. At times, as Volzke covered the story, and wrote from personal knowledge of the Huber family, he would struggle with journalistic objectivity, working hard to assure that he wrote with his head, not his heart.

At the Aliso Creek Presbyterian church in nearby Laguna Niguel, Pastor Walter D. Shepard Jr. informed the congregation of Denise Huber's disappearance. Their prayer chain, including Nancy and Dick Streza, offered pleas to the Almighty, calling for the safe delivery of Denise, who was a faithful believer in Him.

Hoping that any reluctant witnesses might be motivated by money, Dennis offered a personal reward of $5,000 on Thursday, June 6, for any information leading to the safe return of Denise. Other contributors soon raised it to $10,000.

Jason Snyder, Denise's friend who couldn't take her to the Morrissey concert, wanted to help. "I just know foul play is involved," he said. He explained to reporters that he hadn't accepted Denise's invitation to join her and Rob at El Paso Cantina late Sunday night for a very simple reason. He needed to watch his budget very closely, and couldn't afford to spend what little money he had. About Denise, he said "She wouldn't have taken a ride from anybody. I think she's being held against her will, but she's resourceful."

Asked about his feelings for Denise, Snyder explained that they were good friends. "I don't know anybody who didn't like her. She's . . . outgoing. I just want everybody to hold out hope . . . It's hard, but I love her and a lot of people do. I can't imagine anything bad happening to her." Feeling deep personal grief from her disappearance, Snyder volunteered to help distribute police fliers containing a photograph of Denise and a printed request for information. Within a short time, more than 15,000 of the leaflets found their way to local shopping malls, flea markets, sporting events, and various public functions. Versions printed in Spanish were distributed in the region of the freeway intersection. Snyder explained. "We thought a lot of people might not have been able to understand them in English and a lot of Mexican nationals are restaurant workers in that area." He planned to take a few bundles 125 miles south, to the Mexican border city, Tijuana, just in case the abductor held her as a captive down there. Rejecting rumors that Denise might be voluntarily hiding out somewhere, he commented, "I know that lots of people have said that she probably just took off. But she would have called her parents and let them know where she was, or she would have called me." Snyder scoffed at the possibility that she had voluntarily accepted a ride from a total stranger in the middle of the night. "No way." As he spoke, Snyder posed for newspaper photographers on the Corona Del Mar Freeway where the Honda had been abandoned.

A vacation trip to Colorado would take Nancy Streza, the woman who had known Denise since Sunday school days in the San Fernando Valley, away from Orange County for a week. But it wouldn't keep her from lending a hand in the search. Streza took a thick stack of fliers with her. "My girls and I stopped at every truck stop and rest area along the way to put up fliers." The trip would become a regular pilgrimage, taking on the secondary purpose of posting the notices. Streza hoped that just one other traveler might see them and break the silence with some new information.

Other sympathetic acquaintances arranged to send copies of the fliers across the nation. Jeff Huber took several bundles to be hand-distributed by him and his friends where they congregated for music events.

A side effect of the publicity made Snyder and his pal Rob Calvert uncomfortable. They both felt an oppressive sense that people regarded them with some suspicion. The emotional wave that swept the county, swelled by the media coverage, aroused sympathy and anger among millions of residents. How can this happen? Why? Why can't we rid ourselves of the bloodsucking scum who abduct women? What has happened to our society when a young woman has a flat tire on the freeway, and then just vanishes? There was a time when a Samaritan would have stopped to help her get home safely. Now, the night is crowded with predators who can't wait for the opportunity to prey upon such a vulnerable victim.

News watchers wanted quick action to find Denise Huber and to crucify the person who might be holding her captive. Or worse. Were those two men who last had contact with her somehow involved? When hysteria grips the population, suspicions are not always based on reason.

"The worst part," Calvert said, "is not knowing what happened to her. As the days go by, I'm getting less and less optimistic." He added that he wanted to think she would be okay. "I just wish that her tire could have blown out before she dropped me off. But you can't really have hindsight . . . I guess there was nothing I could do."

Sergeant Ron Smith, giving the Huber case top priority, arranged for a group of Explorer Scouts, sponsored by the Costa Mesa PD, to scour every inch of the area adjacent to the freeway where the Honda had been abandoned. They found nothing useful. Just to be sure, he invited them to try it again. The second sweep produced no better results.

Smith wrestled with another question: Just exactly when was the Honda parked on that freeway shoulder and abandoned? Rob Calvert had told him that Denise left his house around two in the morning. Tammy Brown had spotted the car nearly twenty hours later. Any number of things could have taken place during that stretch of time. If Denise had been abducted, or met with dreaded violence, it might have happened anywhere along her route. The car could have been stolen and left there by the perpetrators. That problem would bother Smith for several weeks.

Cynthia Brown liked her early morning job delivering newspapers for the *Orange County Register* in Costa Mesa. And she liked the newspaper itself; she read it daily. One of the ongoing stories had captured her attention, the sad case of the missing woman, Denise Huber. Brown felt a special affinity for the missing woman because each morning she passed the freeway spot where Denise had vanished.

Scanning the news one day, Brown noticed something wrong. The article said that a private investigator had suggested that someone may have abducted Denise, then abandoned her car several hours later on the freeway.

"Wait a minute," Brown thought. "That can't be. Surely the police know the Honda was on the 73 freeway shoulder, where they found it, somewhere around 2:30 in the morning. I know it was. I saw it there." Cynthia Brown had assumed that the police had long since verified that fact. She didn't know yet that no other witness had come forward to corroborate that critical bit of information. "Gosh," she said to herself. "I sure don't want them going off on the wrong foot." Brown telephoned the Costa Mesa Police Department.

Sergeant Smith courteously greeted Cynthia Brown, who reported that she had some information to offer about the case of Denise Huber. No, Cynthia said, she was not related or acquainted with Tammy Brown, Huber's best friend.

Speaking with calm clarity, Cynthia informed the sergeant that she delivered newspapers for the *Orange County Register,* and that she routinely left her house in Westminster at 2:14 A.M. to reach the Costa Mesa warehouse. "I like to get there first so I can get a good parking place to pick up my daily bundles of papers." She always arrived by 2:30. Her route took her along the 405, to the 73.

With renewed interest, Smith asked Brown if she usually passed the section just north of the turnoff to the 55.

"Oh yeah," Brown chirped. "I pass it every morning."

"On the particular morning of June 3, did you notice anything along there?"

"I sure did. As I got on the 73, I saw some lights blinking up the road a ways, in the distance. I couldn't really tell, you know, very much about it. But I knew it was a car with the hazard lights on."

"And what did you do as you approached the blinking lights?"

"Drove right past 'em."

"Could you tell what kind of an automobile it was?"

"Sure. It was a blue Honda."

"Did you see anyone around the Honda?"

"No." Nor could she see the flat tire.

"How fast were you going when you passed the car?"

"About that time, I probably laid off my accelerator a little bit. So I was probably going forty-five to fifty."

Smith's next question would be critical to the case. "What time, as close as you can recall, was it when you went past the car?"

Without a hint of hesitation, Cynthia Brown answered, "It had to have been around 2:25 in the morning."

Smith asked, "Did you see anyone walking along the freeway, on either side, as you approached the car or as you passed it?" He already knew the answer.

"No, I took a long look, checking to see if someone was in trouble. But I didn't see anyone."

While she hadn't seen anyone, Denise or possible suspects, the cheerful newspaper delivery woman provided an important bit of information by establishing that Denise Huber's Honda had already been abandoned within approximately twenty-five minutes of her departure from Ron Calvert. It would help Sergeant Smith narrow the investigation.

Pain and restlessness marked every hour of Ione and Dennis Huber's endless days and sleepless nights. Their missing daughter's presence echoed through every minute of their existence.

No matter what they tried to do, the specter of Denise, perhaps injured, possibly bound and held captive, flooded their thoughts. If they tried to escape by reading newspapers, it became worse. Headlines in the *Orange County Register* blared in the parents' faces: "Man tells how he killed 2 Florida women" and "Judge sentences rapist to 47 years in prison." Images too horrible to contemplate flashed in their minds. Even advertisements alerting shoppers that Father's Day was coming soon pained the two parents. Denise would have already been trying to find the perfect gift for her dad. Dennis found himself choking back tears at the reminder and increasingly turning to his faith in God.

Neither parent could work. Dennis suspended his efforts to start a new business, and Ione took a leave from her teaching duties. Even the preparation of meals became hopeless drudgery. But they always had plenty of food available, brought by sympathetic, loving members of the Presbyterian church. Pastor Walter Shepard had told his congregation about the crisis in the Huber family. Many of them already knew, having been well acquainted with Dennis, Ione, and Denise. The moral support they brought with the food provided a sustenance even more important to survival.

Each hour, though, took its toll on the distressed couple. Wracking his brain, trying to think of something he could personally do, Dennis had an idea. He put a leash on Sam, the black Lab who also loved Denise, and loaded him into the car. Fifteen minutes later, in the dusky evening, Dennis parked at the spot where her car had been found. Holding the leash so Sam couldn't run into the traffic, Dennis let him jump down to the pavement.

"Find Denise," Dennis commanded. "Find Denise." The dog looked up, made alert eye contact with the hopeful father, and seemed to understand. He put his nose to the pavement, and began tugging with all his power on the leash. "He pulled me along," Dennis said, "all over the place. We trotted down the slope, along the fence, back up, with him sniffing the ground everywhere." Sam even led Dennis through the chain link fence opening, down to Bear Street, and to the motel. "He wanted to go to the motel, and to a nearby storage facility. We had to give up because it was getting dark."

Wondering if Sam had really been on the trail of something important, Dennis returned in the light of day and let the dog lead him again. "He picked up where he had left off." But as determined as Dennis and his loyal dog Sam were, they only managed to exhaust themselves.

Ten days of turmoil, worry, and crumbling optimism passed before Ione and Dennis finally spoke again to news media reporters. Because they knew and truly liked Jonathan Volzke, they invited him into the home. While sitting on their living room couch, Dennis acknowledged that they still clung to hope that Denise was alive. A photographer snapped pictures of them as Dennis said, "I guess we're probably praying for that now, that somebody is holding her somewhere." He paused, maintained composure, and continued "That probably is the lesser of two evils."

With his arm around Ione's shoulders, Dennis said, "You jump three feet every time the phone rings, at first. We've gotten used to that. Now it's support calls, and you want to hear those. But the nightmare is still there; we haven't woken up from the nightmare. It's there all the time."

Their hope that someone, perhaps a witness, would come forward, and their faith in the Almighty, he said, had helped sustain them. "We're just looking for the one person that might have seen something. I have faith in God. God has the power to bring her back." Grateful for the support offered by friends, acquaintances, and even strangers, Dennis wanted to publicly thank them. "It's an unbelievable thing. We have thousands and thousands of people all over the United States praying for us. That's the only thing that keeps us going. We've got an organization that just won't quit."

Hoping that if Denise had been abducted, the person holding her captive would hear about all the support, Dennis said, "If someone is holding her and she is alive, I want that somebody to feel the pressure. We're not going to give up on this thing. I want them to know that no matter what, this thing will keep on going."

* * *

Sgt. Ron Smith certainly had no inclination to ease the pressure. On the night of June 16, at 2 A.M., he stationed two officers on the site where the Honda had been found. They noted the license plates of over 100 passing motorists. Smith arranged for each driver to be contacted, hoping one of them drove regularly by the spot, and had seen something thirteen nights earlier.

That week, the popular television show, *America's Most Wanted*, also profiled the case. John Walsh, who had lost his young son, Adam, to a murderous abductor in the early 1980s, made a personal appeal for the public's help to find Denise Huber. The show generated over two dozen calls from viewers who thought they might have seen her, or knew a possible suspect. None of the tips panned out.

Chapter 5

Unsolved crimes are to police detectives what elusive cures for cancer or AIDS are to medical scientists. Dedicated investigators push themselves to the limit, and sometimes well beyond it, in the search for answers. Considering the staggering volume of violent crimes in urban areas, it's amazing how many are eventually solved by hardworking law enforcement agencies. Of course, investigators ideally want solutions for every case they work, but that is impossible. People vanish and are never heard from again. Families and loved ones of the missing victims spend the rest of their lives hoping, praying, and never finding the answers.

Just prior to the July 4th holiday, a group of people assembled in front of the apartment building on Bear Street, at the bottom of the slope where the Honda had been found. Dennis and Ione watched as a few of the men climbed to the roof of the apartment. Rob Calvert and Jason Snyder climbed with them. At the top, they unfurled a huge canvas banner, thirty feet long, six feet high.

Printed on the banner was a portrait of the missing woman and the words, "HAVE YOU SEEN DENISE HUBER . . . Car Found Here 6-31-91, 55&73 FWY." The police telephone number appeared below her name.

The men stretched the heavy banner tight and secured it with ropes. Motorists on the 73 freeway couldn't miss the clearly visible display. It would be seen by millions of passersby. The news media gave extensive coverage to it, throughout southern California. If only one person who had some knowledge of the case caught sight of the graphic plea, and would come forward, they could conceivably provide an essential link in the chain leading to Denise or her abductor. The portrait and message touched the hearts of millions. But in the laws of physics, and in human behavior, every action causes certain reactions, some of which may not help achieve the desired effect. Publicity in the Huber case would be a double-edged sword, stained with avarice and greed.

At that stage in the case, the parents and the investigators agreed on taking certain risks to solve the perplexing riddle. Denise had been missing for a full month.

Homicide Detective Lynda Giesler had the distinction of being the first woman in the country to carry the title of homicide detective. She began her distinguished career in law enforcement with the Costa Mesa Police Department in 1963, when the glass ceiling for women was low, thick, and virtually unbreakable. Women were consigned in police departments to desk jobs or superficial investigative duties in juvenile divisions. Giesler would not only find a crack in the ceiling, but would pry it wide open for thousands of women to climb through.

A true native Californian, Lynda's parents transplanted her from Los Angeles to Oregon by the time she had reached her third birthday, first to Medford, then to the forested, wet country of Eugene. She finished high school there, and fervently planned to follow the footsteps of an older brother to college. "To me," she said, "he lived a very impressive lifestyle in college. I never even considered doing anything else. Until the day came to enroll. I was seized with panic! I couldn't do it and I didn't know why. By that time, my brother was in the U.S. Marine Corps in Hawaii. So I decided to take a short trip over there to visit him and think things over. The trip lasted eight months! I found enough work there to support myself and to enjoy the islands."

When Giesler did return to the mainland, and to her parent's home, her father worked hard to convince her to finish her education. He offered to support her if she would enroll at the University of Oregon. Or she could find a job and pay for her room and board. Another alternative would be to move to southern California where she could stay with an aunt and uncle, and attend junior college (now called community college). At that time, Oregon had no free junior colleges, just private ones that Lynda thought too expensive.

"Well," she recalled with a mischievous twinkle, "being nearly nineteen, the thought of living with my parents, following all the rules, didn't really look that appealing. So I moved to Balboa Island, near Newport Beach, and lived with my aunt and uncle for a year, attending Orange Coast College." With the urge for greater independence pulling her, she and several female pals rented a separate house on the island.

One of the college classes Lynda took offered credit for participating in a "work experience program," (now called "internship" by industries which utilize the practice). She would attend class several hours each week, and then report to the Costa Mesa Police Department for her "work experience." A sergeant assigned her to toil in the juvenile crimes division with an experienced officer named Doris Morris. Giesler would one day acknowledge that Doris had a life-altering influence on her.

Another outdated policy in effect at that time prohibited employees, in any department of the city, from being married to each other. When Doris fell in love with a lieutenant and they exchanged wedding vows, she couldn't stay, so she took an early retirement. In the interim, Doris coaxed, wheedled, and pushed Lynda Giesler to apply for permanent employment with the CMPD.

"I was young, twenty-one, and feisty, and not ready to settle down," Lynda recalled. "I still had that youthful mindset." She also had dreams of returning to the north country, where there were really four seasons in a year, with rain, fall colors, and flowers in springtime. She and a roommate even considered moving to San Francisco to complete their educations. So when Doris persuaded Lynda to fill out an application, she conveniently "lost" it. Undeterred, Doris stood over Lynda while she filled out another one.

A long, remarkable career took root.

As did the few other female police officers, Giesler worked

juvenile, forgery, thefts, burglaries, and sex crimes. In 1972, a sergeant casually mentioned that one of the homicide sleuths needed some help, and sent her over to see if she was able to cope with the real stuff. "There was nothing official about the move. Just an assignment to help another detective."

Lynda Giesler more than coped. She learned the walk and she learned the talk in a profession that had been male-dominated forever. She demonstrated mental and physical tenacity that gained respect from even the toughest, grizzled, cigar-smoking gumshoes who'd been chasing killers for years. From the early seventies Giesler eventually worked nearly eighty homicides, with a rate of successful conclusions that competed favorably with any city's. But, Lynda would say, while it feels great to solve a difficult case, the ones that truly lodge in her mind, forever, are the unsolved cases.

"I have always had a dread, almost a fear, of not finding the solution to the crimes I work on. Especially those in which there is an innocent victim. There is constantly a mental process, something like Monday morning quarterbacking. Did I overlook something, some key element, that might lead to the perp? The pressure is always there."

Off duty, Giesler found relief and fulfillment with her dogs. Like a young woman named Denise, Lynda developed an abiding fondness for the intelligent creatures who are able to give unconditional love and loyalty in return for a home, regular meals, and a few pats on the head now and then. Giesler made a hobby of dog obedience training, and would proudly point to her best pals, terrier mix Tasha and shepherd-Lab mix, Shada. Both had been abandoned when Lynda found them and gave the two grateful dogs a permanent home.

When a Newport Beach officer telephoned the CMPD detective bureau on Monday, June 3, 1991, Detective Jack "Arch" Archer happened to be sitting next to the sergeant who answered the call.

"We got a report of a missing person, a woman whose car was

found on the freeway, that belongs in your turf. Want us to handle it, or do you want to take it?"

The sergeant looked at Archer, who said, "We'll take it."

Lynda Giesler came to work on Tuesday morning and listened as her partner, Archer, told her the scant details. Together, they drove to Vista Grande in Newport Beach to interview the parents. After introductions, Ione Huber ushered them into the comfortable condominium, and invited them to sit around the dining room table. The investigators asked all the necessary questions and requested a complete description plus a photo of Denise. They required detailed personal information: Who were her friends? What she was wearing? Did she have any particular problems? Had anyone been bothering her or stalking her? Giesler's background in juvenile and sex crimes helped her to formulate exactly what she needed to know. She also recognized that the missing woman was twenty-three years old, and the probability that someone that age might not tell mom and dad everything going on in her life.

With Dennis Huber leading, they took a tour of the home's interior. Denise's bedroom was downstairs, and separate, almost like her own apartment in its privacy. She could come and go, using a nearly private entrance, without disturbing the rest of the household, most of which occupied the second floor. The neatly maintained room, with the bed unruffled, seemed hauntingly empty and quiet. The two detectives knew full well the anguish that smothered Ione and Dennis Huber, and realized that words of sympathy, though necessary, offered little consolation.

Using a list of names the Hubers provided, Giesler and Archer started the long routine of tracking down all of Denise's friends. They interviewed Rob Calvert, Tammy Brown, Jason Snyder, and a host of other acquaintances. Through these contacts, they developed even longer lists of people who might be able to provide insight into Denise Huber, her routines, patterns of behavior, any problems she might have, and who might dislike her. The latter list had zero entries.

Even though the close circle of Denise's buddies seemed sincere in their stories, and had no ostensible reasons to want her harmed, seasoned investigators know the importance of keeping an open mind. You don't prematurely rule out anything. "The question that haunts a detective the most," said Giesler, "is, 'What did I miss?' Each of us wonders if someone we interviewed has successfully deceived us."

As the mystery of Denise Huber deepened and spread through the southland, with extensive media coverage, the pressure on Giesler, Archer, and other detectives assigned to lend a hand, became intense. "Our bosses wanted answers. The public wanted answers. And of course, most important of all, the parents wanted answers . . . We had frequent contact with Dennis and Ione Huber. And I certainly understood. They needed to know what happened to their daughter."

With each passing week, Lynda's immediate boss, Sgt. Ron Smith, assigned more help to the team working on the Huber case. He had met the family, too, and truly wanted to help them. Chief of Police David Snowden gave them every resource he could spare.

"We got hundreds of calls," said Giesler. "People reporting that they had seen a woman who resembled Denise. And the psychics. Some were very well-intentioned, and some were out to lunch. Real pain in the butt stuff. But we had to trace down any plausible lead."

Weeks and months slipped by with no strong leads. A Hispanic woman cost the cops precious time with her story. She claimed she knew the man who had kidnapped Denise Huber, and that he was associated with a Mexican gang. They were holding the captive in Tijuana. But when asked to give specific details, the woman retreated into tight-lipped silence. Giesler and Archer recruited plainclothes cops to follow her, put stakeouts in the neighborhood where she lived, and even arranged for an acquaintance of hers to wear a wire during their conversations. The detectives transported her to Tijuana to see if she could guide them to the alleged hideout. "It all turned out to be a big hoax," Giesler lamented. "All she wanted was a free trip to Mexico."

Another witness came forward with what might have been a good lead. He'd been watching the news one night, he claimed, when his adult son said, "Hey, I saw that car on the freeway that night." After the father contacted police, the body-builder son clammed up, and began a cat and mouse game with the detectives. When Giesler and Archer finally pinned him down for an interview, he insisted it be at his home, with his mother present. Reluctantly, the two cops agreed. But the exchange resulted only in a string of waffling "I don't know" and "I don't remember" answers. At last, they asked him if he would be willing to undergo hypnosis, even though the results would probably not be admissible in court. He refused at first, but finally agreed to do it. Once again, the results proved negligible. Giesler felt suspicious of the man's evasive lack of cooperation, and had him staked out for several days. He seemed to enjoy exposing his followers, as if the whole thing was a contest of wits. Once more, a great deal of valuable time drained away.

Another Hispanic resident commented to strangers that he had inside knowledge of the case. It took weeks for the officers to track him down, and make telephone contact with him. In his agreement to meet with Giesler and Archer, he set specific conditions. It had to be in a public place with lots of people around. He picked a large pizza restaurant that is similar to a small theme park with games for children. He wouldn't even give Lynda Giesler a description of himself, insisting that she describe herself, and he would find her in the crowd.

With her guts sizzling over the man's arrogance, and growling because she was hungry, she drove alone to the pizza place. Several undercover officers had already arrived and blended into the crowd, as a backup for Giesler. The informant found her, and Giesler was startled to see that he'd brought his wife and several children. He told her a convoluted story of seeing the stalled Honda on the freeway that night. His sighting placed the car about 200 yards from the actual location, but Giesler felt some sense of encouragement that he seemed to be at least in the general vicinity. Of course, he could have learned the location from news reports.

According to the witness, he and his wife had argued that

night, and he'd stormed out. He saw the Honda on the freeway shoulder, and observed two guys fighting with a woman in the dirt. One of them shoved her into a truck. The witness said he circled around and drove slowly by again to take a closer look. One of the men pulled a gun and shot a hole in the witness's passenger window, so he'd hurried away from the scene.

Lynda Giesler sat, taking notes, her stomach gurgling with hunger. The witness and his family munched on pizza. That wasn't so bad, but when she looked over at dark tables along the wall, she saw her plainclothes backups also chewing on pizza. She didn't have time to order any, and no one offered her a bite.

After allowing the man to take his family home, Giesler, still hungry, took him for a drive along the freeway. Even though the summer sun remained above the horizon, she had her lights on so her covert partners could follow her taillights. She hoped that her passenger wouldn't notice. He pointed to the spot where he allegedly saw the struggle.

On the freeway shoulder, he allowed Giesler to exam the cab of his truck, where he pointed to a few shards of glass on the floor, which he claimed came from the gunshot-shattered window. He said he had replaced the glass a few days earlier.

After that evening, the witness apparently decided it was not in his best interests to cooperate any further. He withdrew and evaded all requests for additional information. He even ignored a written plea from Ione Huber to please tell the police everything he knew. His only answer, from then on, was, "I don't want to get involved."

Ultimately, Lynda Giesler figured the man had been after the reward money, and really hadn't seen anything at all that night.

One of the best breaks had been the *Orange County Register* delivery woman, Cynthia Brown's placing of the Honda on the freeway at "0225 hours," or 2:25 A.M., which helped the investigators avoid following false leads up dead-end trails. Her information helped them eliminate alternative scenarios in which Denise had been abducted elsewhere and the car abandoned without her. The marks made on the pavement by the shredded rear tire also supported the theory that she had been driving from Rob Calvert's house, and had been stranded by a blowout.

As theories and leads developed, only to evaporate like morning mist in Newport Beach, Lynda Giesler refused to capitulate. She worried and fretted over that single detail somewhere that she might have overlooked, that single strand of evidence which might lead to a solution. She lost count of the times she parked her unmarked police car, or her personal car, on the freeway shoulder where the Honda had sat, and tried to piece together what she knew of the case. Sometimes she'd sit there in the daytime and sometimes late at night, searching her mind for the elusive clue. She would not accept the idea of an unsolved crime.

As 1991 slipped into history, Det. Jack Archer accepted a reassignment to the narcotics division, and Lynda Giesler became the lead detective or, in CMPD vernacular, the "primary" detective. A youthful looking, extremely bright, and energetic officer, Detective Frank Rudisill became her partner.

As much as they hoped to find Denise Huber alive, both Rudisill and Giesler began to wonder if she had, indeed, survived. "You begin to fear," said Giesler, "that you will get a call from someplace where a pile of bones has been discovered, with no clue to how the victim died. If the bones can be matched to the missing person, you face the frustration of never learning what happened."

The private enterprise Dennis Huber had planned to start remained on the back burner while that first agonizing summer brought nothing but pain and disappointment. Concentration on business matters was impossible. Everywhere he went, he looked for Denise, her absence haunting him incessantly. He glanced in every passing car, checked faces in supermarkets and in malls, even watched crowd scenes on television on the chance he might see her face. All of his energy focused on trying to find her. As September approached, Ione Huber considered the possibility of returning to her job as a substitute teacher, but she too realized the futility of trying to manage a room full of children while her thoughts remained on her daughter. Ione's heart would be elsewhere, so it wouldn't be fair to the young students.

Savings accounts and investments sustained the couple financially, but they both knew that wouldn't last forever.

With each passing day, the Hubers tried to maintain faith and hope. They talked frequently with detectives of the Costa Mesa Police Department, hungry for the slightest tidbit of good news or to learn that the investigators had turned up a new clue. Sgt. Ron Smith would have liked nothing better than to provide the hurting family with some encouraging news, but he couldn't give them what simply did not exist. He allotted as much of his investigative resources as possible to the Huber case, but also had other crimes to handle. Frustration shrouded everyone connected to the search.

Growing more desperate for any new facts that might help find Denise, Dennis and Ione waited. Inevitably, they began receiving calls from strangers who wanted to help. Some were good-hearted people who sincerely offered to join in the search, some apparently wanted to exploit the opportunity to be in the spotlight, and some were simply cranks. Several psychics called and claimed to have extrasensory information about Denise and where she was.

Looking back, Dennis said, "I don't believe in psychics. None of them are right, they just seem to offer wild guesses that might appear close to the facts. We had them calling to offer us help. We didn't want to deal with them."

Ione observed, "A lot of psychics try to help the police. I've seen television shows where they seem to have some insight into body locations."

Trying to remain open-minded to any possible opportunity to find Denise, the couple finally relented and allowed a well-known psychic to meet them in their home. The woman came with a reputation of being one of the best in the country. As she began her probe into the mysterious depths of her mind, the woman began speaking of a black dog close to Denise. Sam, the Lab, was not in the room. Skeptical, Dennis wondered if the mystic had learned from some other source about the loyal pet. Within a few moments, the psychic "saw" more dogs. In recalling it, Ione said, "She described Fifi, our white poodle, and Coco, a brown mixed breed we had owned. Both of those pets were deceased. Finally, the woman described a curly, blond Spaniel which could only have been Shandy, Pat and Gillian Fay's dog, which we had taken care of during their trip to England."

If the Hubers allowed the psychic's canine capers to excite them, the sensation disappeared within moments. Dennis recalled, "It seemed to be hopeful at first, but then she trailed off into a lot of stuff that didn't make any sense at all." Before the woman left, Sam ambled in and gave her a cold stare along with a rumbling growl. "Sam is a very mild-mannered dog," Dennis said, "but he didn't like her."

Because they really didn't expect any positive results, the Hubers hadn't allowed themselves to become enthused over the experiment. The failure simply reinforced in their minds the importance of sticking with more practical methods. They began to consider the possibility of hiring a private investigator to augment the police search. "We just felt that we needed to do everything we could for her. You have to go for your own peace of mind. We talked about this over and over. It's so horrible. It's terrible."

Perhaps a private investigator could help, but there was one major roadblock. The Hubers did not have an unlimited supply of money, and a P.I.'s services were not inexpensive.

As it would time and time again, the generosity of friends and acquaintances helped shoulder the burden. Denise had been working part time at The Cannery Restaurant in Newport Beach. In one of the channels of Newport Harbor, on a dead-end waterway shaped like a bent finger, the restaurant occupies a view site near the fingertip. It had actually been a fish cannery during the mid-century heyday of the Pacific fishing industry, and had been restored with many of the rusty old boilers, conveyors, and chutes still intact as part of the restaurant decor. A well-dressed, articulate, gregarious gentleman named Bill Hamilton owns and manages the popular eatery. Hamilton makes it a practice to know his employees, and personally liked the young part-time waitress named Denise.

When Bill Hamilton learned of her disappearance, he felt a deep sense of compassion for the Huber family. Denise was a terrific, hard-working girl, moral, honest, and personable. No one deserved such a rotten break. Hamilton wanted to help.

Following a contact with Mr. and Mrs. Huber, in which he heard of their desire to retain a private investigator, Hamilton had an idea. As part of the restaurant, he operates a charter yacht which is moored near the dockside tables which offer a magnificent view for diners. Named *Isla Mujeres* (Island of Women), the sleek white yacht is fifty-eight feet long, with two deck levels, the lower one enclosed by expansive picture windows, and an awning-covered upper deck, for up to seventy passengers who want the full ambience of wind and sea. It is kept busy with at least three harbor cruises on weekend days, and longer charters during the week.

In a gesture of remarkable generosity, Bill Hamilton donated the funds generated by the yacht, twice, to help offset investigative expenses incurred by the Hubers. The grateful parents could not find adequate words of gratitude, but would always include Hamilton in their prayers.

Part of the money paid bills for printing more fliers and bumper stickers, postage, and telephone bills. Now, they could also hire a private eye.

On television, in books, and in movies, private investigators have superlative, almost mystic, powers to dig out the facts of any case, often making the police look foolish by comparison. While many P.I.s in real life may be effective, they seldom perform to the level of their fictional counterparts.

Not long after retaining a licensed private investigator, the sleuth reported back to them that he believed Denise was not a victim of "random circumstances." She was abducted, he said, and possibly killed, somewhere other than the freeway site of the abandoned Honda. He claimed he'd interviewed several people who had passed the freeway site between 2:15 A.M. and 5:30 A.M., and had not seen the Honda parked there. "If it happens to be the wrong scene of the crime, they [the police] will never solve it," he reported, adding that he was "eighty percent" sure that Denise was dead. All fingerprints had been wiped from the car, and he felt pretty sure the flat tire had been staged to look as if it had blown out. In addition, he said, Denise had left El Paso Cantina that night in the company of another man for a short time. (Rob Calvert would confirm this, but said it was a guy they both knew, and she stepped out to the parking lot with him for only a few moments.) Finally, the sleuth said, some of Denise's friends had told him she always drove home from Huntington Beach via Pacific Coast Highway, not the freeway.

To the Hubers, the report appeared unsupported by any hard evidence. Trying to cope with another disappointment, Dennis later said, "The private investigators kept coming up with theories, but found nothing to substantiate them. They interrogated the kids Denise knew, and hinted they were somehow involved."

At Costa Mesa PD headquarters, Sergeant Smith commented patiently on the scenarios suggested by the independent Sherlocks. "We welcome any credible help we can get. Hopefully, they, or we, will turn up something new. The parents are such nice, decent people that you hate to see them suffer so much." Pressed to comment on the reliability of the private eye reports, Smith diplomatically stated, "My approach is not to go chase theories. I'd rather concentrate on facts and keep an open mind to all possibilities."

A young man in Huntington Beach wasn't especially impressed with the gumshoe detectives either. Rob Calvert would later say, "I wasn't happy with them at all. I thought they were only interested in money and publicity. For all I knew, they would point the finger at me without any evidence. From what I heard, they were completely wrong in most of their assumptions. One of them seemed like a real crackpot operation."

Jeff Huber had his own opinions of the private eyes. He thought they were more interested in making a buck than finding his sister. Agreeing with his father, he said that in his opinion, they would either manufacture improbable theories, or simply feed back what they thought the parents wanted to hear.

During the first few hours of the crisis, Jeff had wondered if his sister was "pulling a gag or something." But he quickly realized that idea wasn't very probable. "Nah. No way," he said, and faced the hard fact that the situation was serious. His early hope that it had been a gag changed to despair. "I resolved in my own mind that she was gone and I would never see her again. I never got my hopes up. If she did turn up safe, then it would be the happiest bonus that could happen. But I didn't expect it."

Occupying himself with trying to keep his music career alive, and starting a new band, Jeff still thought frequently of his missing sister. "There were always reminders. I drove by that banner quite often. It was constantly in the back of my mind. I knew she had no enemies, so I couldn't even form any theories or suspicions on who might have kidnapped her."

In his spare time, Jeff joined groups of friends to pass out fliers, and spent time with his parents, watching them age visibly in the months since Denise vanished.

National attention had been given to the case by *America's Most Wanted*. In the fall of 1991, another well-known television show, *Inside Edition*, contacted the family to run a segment about the mystery of Denise Huber. When it aired, viewers watched Ione and Dennis Huber make an impassioned, tearful plea for the abductor of their daughter to please, please, let them know if Denise was dead or alive. They begged for any information. Across the entire country, television audiences could feel the unendurable agony being suffered by these heartbroken parents.

In late October, Costa Mesa PD Chief Dave Snowden, who had become personally acquainted with the Hubers, decided to organize another massive search for her. He recruited a team of officers and volunteers, some on horseback, to comb every inch of the grassy slopes and waterfront along Upper Newport Bay and the underbrush of Bonita Canyon, all within a short distance of the Huber home. Perhaps someone had picked her up from the freeway, given her a ride towards home, and assaulted her before arriving at the house. If she had been killed, the body might have been hidden in the rugged terrain of the area. Or, if she had been assaulted and transported elsewhere, some clue might have been dropped in the brush, sand, or mud. Of course, chances of finding anything were slim, but Snowden wanted to at least give it a try. If nothing else, it would eliminate the area as a focus of the investigation.

So, on a Saturday morning, the assembly of searchers gathered, including Orange County's Search and Rescue Team, and spread out over hundreds of acres.

It turned out to be another fruitless effort. Dennis Huber told reporters that he was grateful for the turnout of people who wanted to help, and for the diligent police work. He was actually relieved, he admitted, when the search failed to produce a body. But, of course, that still left him and his family in a state of limbo, wondering what had happened to Denise. "We don't know whether to mourn her or what. The lack of evidence give us no straws to grasp at, but a lot of people are praying. That is the only thing that gets us through."

Chief Snowden, also disappointed, said, "My investigators are very frustrated by the lack of concrete leads. The family hasn't given up hope and we haven't either."

One of the volunteers hoped the massive effort had at least helped the Hubers cope with their pain. She said, "I have noticed that they have relaxed a little this week, knowing that people are helping them. When you lose a daughter, you can't give up hope until every possibility is exhausted."

Chapter 6

Agony, for the Hubers, refused to dull its sharp edge as 1991 ground to a miserable end. Denise's birthday, November 22, a day when there should have been merrymaking while she blew out twenty-four candles, passed empty, silent, heavy. A month later, Christmas carols on radio, television, and in stores brightly decorated for the Yule season, sounded hollow and melancholy. "Joy to the World" had little meaning to Ione and Dennis as they managed a few stabs at shopping for gifts, but found little pleasure in it.

For Jeff Huber, his music provided some escape from the pain. He focused his mind and daily work routine on making his band successful; developing new arrangements, practicing long hours, searching for new gigs. He missed Denise, thought of her, and continued to join his parents and groups of volunteers to distribute fliers, but he could not allow the crisis to stall his life. He spent his spare time with a young woman who shared his love for music, and married her in early 1992.

Dennis and Ione, too, gradually accepted the hard fact that they could not be completely consumed by the loss of Denise. A mortgage banking company offered him a job, and he accepted.

They would not, however, capitulate to the evil thing that had happened. At every opportunity, they passed out bumper stickers, distributed fliers, and mailed appeals to help find their beloved daughter. It helped the time pass and gave them some degree of satisfaction in believing they were doing something productive.

The cloud of discomfort hovering over Rob Calvert, the man who had accompanied Denise to the Morrissey concert, would not relent. In his view, people seemed to look at him out of the corners of their eyes as if they suspected him. An unexplainable feeling of guilt clouded his emotions. He asked himself repeatedly, if there was something he could have done to prevent her loss. When detective Lynda Giesler requested that he come in for a lie detector test, Calvert at first welcomed the opportunity to clear the air. But as the time grew closer, he had second thoughts. "What if I go in there, and for some reason fail the darn thing?" He knew very little about the technology of the polygraph, and worried about its accuracy. Good Lord, could they try to pin her disappearance on him if the graphs and needles didn't reflect his innocence?

Calvert drove to the Costa Mesa PD office alone, becoming more nervous with each mile. With his preconceived notions of lie detectors, he had the impression that it might be a "pass or fail" test. But he convinced himself it was the right thing to do. Detective Lynda Giesler escorted him in, and with the help of the polygrapher, explained the procedure. Rigged with attached electrodes, Calvert answered a set of control questions, then specific questions about his knowledge of Denise Huber. He couldn't avoid feeling nervous, but hoped the jumping graph pens weren't indicating untruthfulness.

He needn't have worried. The polygraph results left no doubt of Calvert's complete innocence in the matter.

Near the end of a chilly day in February 1992, a pedestrian shuffling along the windy I-10 freeway in the middle of the Mojave Desert at Indio, California, stumbled on some human bones seven miles east of Dillon Road. Over a hundred miles from Newport Beach, past Palm Springs, through the Coachella Valley, the windswept town is called the date capital of the world, referring to the fruit from palm trees. It's not far from the rugged desert terrain where General George S. Patton trained his army tank divisions in preparation for WWII action in the barren wastelands of North Africa.

For some insiders, the grisly discovery raised the possibility that Denise Huber's remains had been found. A few months earlier, one of the mystery callers had said, "You will find her bones in Riverside." Indio is in Riverside County.

Local police carefully scooped up the partial skeleton, which appeared to be human, and eventually sent them to forensic anthropologist Judy Suchey at California State University, Fullerton. She measured, examined, and tested them with meticulous care, and announced they belonged to a woman who stood between five-four and five-eight, who was probably in her late teens or her early twenties. The victim had been dead from six to eighteen months before the grim discovery.

Frank Rudisill, now the partner of Lynda Giesler at CMPD, learned of the discovery. He arranged for more tests, and contacted Dennis and Ione Huber with a suggestion they talk to Judy Suchey.

Dennis later spoke of the meeting. "We had a weird deal. They found a thigh bone, some ribs, hipbones, and part of a shoulder. A Fullerton anthropologist had to work on it. A motorcycle had run over the remains, and broke one of the bones."

Said Ione, "Denise really had long legs just like I do. I was going to a chiropractor for some treatment, so I asked him to X-ray my legs for comparison purposes. When we went into the anthropologist's office we saw the bones that had been found. We were thinking, *This could be our daughter!* There were many boxes of bones there that had never been identified."

When Rudisill spoke to the press, he commented, "It's worth looking at. But we do not believe they are Denise Huber's remains."

He turned out to be correct. The pitiful pile of bones would be filed away in a box, perhaps never to be identified.

Dennis Huber, his hopes again splintered, had mixed emotions. With each such find, he and Ione experienced ambivalent feelings. They wanted answers, but on the other hand, felt relief when new evidence failed to conclusively prove that Denise was dead. That way, they could still hang onto the thinning strands of hope. But each bump in the long trail did its damage. Dennis said, "I think it's worse than before. It's like a cloud. It's a door that's open, and you've got to close it."

On June 3, the first anniversary of Denise's disappearance, friends and well-wishers, including *Orange County Register* reporter Jonathon Volzke, gathered at the Huber home on Vista Grande. Volzke joined a cadre of supporters who traveled with Dennis and Ione to the freeway site, at which news media reporters gathered, along with a phalanx of video cameras. Standing at the bottom of the slope, with fresh tears in her eyes, Ione made an emotional appeal to the perpetrator of the crime against Denise: "We're pleading with you to have some compassion and break your silence. Look at us right now. We're not out for revenge. We're just looking for some answers. We need to find out, even if it's the worst possible news. By keeping silent, you're compounding our suffering."

Anyone who heard her words, live or later on television news, had to feel compassion and wish that if Denise had been abducted, any individual involved would at least contact the grieving parents and let them know if their daughter was dead or alive.

Sgt. Ron Smith joined the gathering, along with his boss, Police Chief Dave Snowden, who spoke next. "This is a very puzzling case for us," he said. "But the investigation is still very much alive. I'd like to make a plea that anybody who rolled by Denise's car that morning call us. . . . Let us determine whether or not what you saw is significant."

Dennis Huber added, "The number one thing we can do now is keep on with the fliers, keep on with the publicity. Somebody out there knows something."

Ten days later, new hopes vaulted skyward when a private investigator announced what he had unearthed. He produced a drawing of a dark-haired man, about five-eight, olive skin, dark eyes, weighing about 155 pounds. The sleuth had even gathered details about where the sought-after man lived—right there in Costa Mesa. The description would have fit many Hispanic residents of Orange County, so the P.I. made it clear that the individual spoke perfect English.

No, the drawing did not represent a suspect in the abduction of Denise Huber. But, the P.I. said, the man had information which might lead to a suspect. In a report delivered to the Hubers, and examined by the Costa Mesa police, the P.I. told a complex story.

Across Fair Street from the CMPD is the Orange County fairgrounds, at which a giant weekly swap meet is held. It is a massive affair, drawing hundreds of vendors and thousands of shoppers. Traffic backs up on the 55 freeway, almost to the point where Denise Huber's Honda was found.

A female vendor at the swap meet, ferreted out by the P.I., said that she kept one of the fliers picturing Denise taped to a post at the space where she sells automobile rims and tires. On the last weekend in May, the dark-skinned man had spotted the flier, and asked, "Is that kid still missing?"

The vendor answered, and conversed briefly with the dark stranger, who said that he had been driving along the freeway a year ago, and had seen that Honda parked on the shoulder. Not only that, he had seen Denise Huber standing behind the car, talking to two men!

Gripped by the incredible account, and hoping that she might have found someone who held a key to the puzzle, the vendor asked for more details. She listened to the stranger describe one of the men with Denise as tall, blonde, and "beachy," and added, "I will never forget that man's face."

"Did you tell this to the police?"

"No. I don't like the police."

In the brief conversation, he told the vendor that he lived in Costa Mesa, but evaded answering any more questions, or volunteering details such as his address or phone number. Volunteering nothing more, he melted into the crowded throngs of shoppers.

* * *

When the P.I. reported his find to the Hubers, they excitedly called Sergeant Smith at the CMPD. To Smith, who wondered about the veracity of the incident, such a man might be in trouble with the law himself, which might account for his reluctance to come forward with information about Huber. Dutifully, the sergeant issued a statement assuring the stranger that if he would deliver his story into the proper hands, he needn't fear the police. "Whatever problems he has, we can work with him," Smith announced. And of course, the provider of valid information might be eligible to collect the $10,000 reward.

If such a man existed, he never surfaced again.

Once more, hopes melted like Mt. Baldy snow in hot Santa Ana winds.

Nancy Streza talked later about the private investigators. "I really disliked one of them. He came up with some story theorizing that Denise had not been abducted at all, and kept hinting that her friends were involved in her disappearance. The guy was arrogant, didn't listen. Put together another absurd concoction about her being grabbed by an Asian slave trade gang, like some Tom Clancy novel or something. He spent hours in disguise, charging for it all the while, trying to meet with some Japanese high rollers in a bar somewhere. Worst of all, he told reporters that Denise was obviously drunk that night." After that, the group had no more use for the private investigator.

Dissatisfied with outside help, Streza organized her own task force, mostly from the church group, to meet frequently at the Huber home and brainstorm ideas. They counted cars passing the freeway site of the Honda, day and night; checked airline flights in and out close to the date Denise vanished, and conducted independent searches. Nancy found a Morrissey fan through the Internet, and persuaded her to help pass out fliers at later concerts. Bumper stickers and fliers became the main weapon for Nancy's group of volunteers as they mailed bundles to churches across the country. Eventually, more than 100,000 would be distributed. The fliers grew geometrically as recipients reproduced them and posted the plea for help anywhere they might be seen. The cities of Costa Mesa and Newport Beach cooperated by putting bumper stickers on every official vehicle.

An explosion of riots in Los Angeles drew Sgt. Ron Smith away from the Huber case in April 1992. A few months earlier, a motorist named Rodney King tried to evade arrest by speeding away from pursuing LAPD officers. At the end of the pursuit, the blue-clad cops circled King and beat him mercilessly, while a witness videotaped the whole incident. At a subsequent trial, a jury exonerated the officers, and all hell broke loose in south central and west Los Angeles. Roaming gangs of looters set fire to whole blocks of buildings, and fights broke out on the streets.

Police agencies from L.A. and Orange Counties rallied in an attempt to curtail the violence. Sergeant Smith led a SWAT team into the maelstrom. In mid April, while in the combat zone, he learned that his promotion to lieutenant had been approved.

Upon his return to Costa Mesa, Lieutenant Ron Smith took over a backlog of administrative duties. Sgt. Tom Boylan would now lead the detectives charged with finding Denise Huber.

In those tense days, dark clouds of depression and pessimism loomed over the Huber family, but one bright ray of sunshine broke through on September 9, 1992. Jeff's wife produced an addition to the Huber clan, a beautiful baby girl. They named her Ashley Denise in memory of her missing aunt.

The child helped lighten the holidays that year, giving the doting grandparents a better reason to shop and mingle among crowds in the malls, and making the Christmas songs more meaningful. But the big emptiness in their souls remained.

Probably exacerbated by stress and worry, Ione Huber discovered a lump that would turn out to be breast cancer. She found it early enough to prevent a life-threatening crisis, but it was another blow she didn't need. The fates seemed to be pushing her to the absolute limit.

On the Sunday after Valentine's Day in 1993, just prior to Ione's fiftieth birthday, her family and friends tried to cheer Ione up with a little party. She smiled at each and every loyal supporter, and told them of her single most important birthday wish.

"To have Denise back home. That would do for all the birthdays for the rest of my life. That would be enough."

Serving lasagna, followed by an artfully decorated cake, the faithful crowd did their best to introduce some humor and light into the day. But none of the well-wishers, including Police Chief Dave Snowden, could ignore the empty void created by the absence of Denise. So the group busied themselves by stuffing 4,000 envelopes to be sent to police chiefs in every state. The contents, signed by Snowden, requested a special effort to keep Denise Huber's name alive by renewing the quest for information that might lead to finding her.

Recognizing that chances were growing increasingly poor to turn up anything new, Dennis commented, "The odds are against us heavily. But it's a labor of love. These people knew Denise and loved her. It's an effort to try to find her. We won't give up the effort. It's our Valentine's gift to her."

Chief Snowden acknowledged the paucity of any new leads and expressed hope that the group's efforts might lead to something positive. "If this mailing jogs someone's memory and results in a lead, it will certainly be worth all the time and energy. We will not give up hope that Denise is somewhere, alive and well, until we have evidence to the contrary."

As the gathering ended, and departing individuals waved their goodnights, Dennis spoke to a reporter. "If whoever did this would leave a clue of some sort. If they would just leave a clue, an anonymous message on the phone, just anything. They could not torture us any more than they have been doing. Please have mercy on us. Please, if you have any compassion at all, leave a clue."

Another television show, *Hard Copy*, aired a segment on the mystery of Denise Huber in April 1993. In it, her weary, heart-worn father made another plea to the abductor. "Not knowing is the most horrible thing. You'd be better off to kill us than let us go on not knowing."

Viewers heard and responded again. Nearly sixty telephone tips poured into the investigators, and each one consumed necessary investigative resources to check out. One caller reported that he had seen a truck that night, parked on the freeway shoulder a short distance from Denise's Honda. The police were unable to verify the report, or track down any such truck. Another caller said she knew someone in Mexico who could provide vital information, but it was just one more dead end.

It became increasingly difficult for the Hubers to watch television news reports or to read newspapers. Seldom did stories announce happy endings to searches for missing persons. Instead, most ended in tragedy. On the exact day of the second anniversary of Denise Huber's vanishing, a story in the *Orange County Register* described a mother's testimony in the penalty phase of a local murder trial. Her nine-year-old daughter had vanished, but was eventually found dead in a trash can in Griffith Park, not far from the stadium where the Los Angeles Dodgers play baseball.

The defendant, Richard DeHoyos, had brutally raped and killed the child. He would be convicted, found sane, and sentenced to death. But the taxpayers, and the victim's family, would be required to go through the whole thing again when a judge overturned the findings on a technicality. Fortunately, the second jury sent DeHoyos to death row once more.

For the Hubers, such news provided no consolation.

On that second anniversary, reporter Jonathon Volzke once again joined the Huber family and friends on Vista Grande in Newport Beach, for what Volzke would describe as a "pizza and prayer" gathering. He noted that the anniversary was endured, because of course it was not an event to celebrate.

Dennis Huber said, "Things are not a whole lot better. I'm probably functioning a little better, but my feelings go all over the place, from sad to mad . . . wanting to do something and not being able to."

Agreeing with her husband, Ione added, "I guess at this point I probably believe she is not alive. But I want to believe there'll be a miracle of some sort."

* * *

Volzke interviewed Lynda Giesler who told him, "It's still an open investigation. Periodically, I get information to look into this, look into that, an unidentified body is found here or there. I follow up on all of it. There's always hope."

Literally millions of motorists passing the site where Denise had vanished had seen the sixty-foot banner asking for help in locating her. Perhaps more would see it if the vantage point changed. Volunteers removed the huge sheet of canvas from the side of the apartment building where it had been hanging. The generous owner of a nearby lumberyard gave them permission to display it on his building.

Just between themselves, Dennis and Ione had started to discuss the possibility of escaping the scene of so much pain. Everywhere they looked, they saw reminders of Denise and felt the aching vacuum of her absence. The Dakotas. Maybe, just maybe, the peaceful country of their roots could nourish the grieving parents back to something resembling normality. Maybe the peaceful life, clean air, and quiet farmland would allow them to begin again, find renewal, and diminish the constant agony. Home.

By June 1994, the idea was to go back to mid-America, the plains and rolling grasslands, where four seasons really mean something, where people know each other and crime is a rarity, where residents don't have to lock their doors or fear a cruel night-stalking predator. The Hubers might be able to really start the healing process. Three long years had crawled by, with no clues at all to nourish their fading hope. While the thought of leaving Jeff and little Ashley Denise bothered them, they knew they had to make a drastic change in their lifestyle if they had any chance at all of surviving the nightmare. They could certainly keep up family contacts and exchange visits as often as possible. And, of course, they would put subtle pressure on Jeff and his new family to also relocate to God's country.

Dennis had found a new business opportunity, selling computer software designed for the mortgage banking industry. Ione thought she might make a go of selling real estate. It might break the pattern, end the doldrums, create a fresh new start. Dennis put it in words: "There's not much more we can do here. We've done everything we can think of. I have to get to the point where I can accept things the way they are, that they may never change."

Yet another telephone caller presented a dismal forecast. Nancy Streza, the faithful supporter from Aliso Creek Presbyterian church, heard about it from a pastor who had received one of the fliers, along with a letter. He said, "I want you to talk to a man who says he knows something." When Nancy heard the man's story, it chilled her.

The caller, who belonged to a different church, said he'd often passed the banner in Costa Mesa which portrayed Denise. He had frequently prayed, he said, and God had given him a message. "You will find Denise Huber in the hills above Phoenix."

That was it. No more details. But the entire support group in which Streza worked so hard to help the Hubers rallied. They sent more letters to all pastors in the Phoenix area, requesting that they pray for Denise and ask for her deliverance.

According to Nancy Streza, when Dennis Huber heard of the epiphany, he was ready to get in his car and launch a new search. But details were too scanty. Streza did take a trip through the Arizona desert, to Phoenix. "I wanted to find her," Streza said. "And I felt chills, creepy feelings." She wondered if a Satan worshipper could have taken Denise to the region, and sacrificed her in some demonic ceremony.

By spring, 1994, the time nature sets for renewal, the Hubers took a trip to Mandan, North Dakota, across the river from Bismarck. Searching with new excitement for a place to escape the haunting pain of California, they found a house for sale, made the decision to move, and bought it. Back in Newport Beach, they sold the condominium on Vista Grande, and started packing for the move.

Ione, with a new sparkle to her voice, told reporters, "We're just looking forward to a whole new start, a fresh start." Pausing a moment to examine some photos of Denise, she continued, "I'd like to have it resolved by the time we leave, but after three years, that's probably asking too much. It will never be the same, but you have to create a new normal. It will never be the way it was. Looking forward to the move has been good for us. It's given us something to focus on that is new and different."

The third anniversary of the blackest day in the lives of the Hubers passed solemnly. In their minds, they hadn't given up on finding Denise, but could now focus on the pending relocation. At least, the setting of their tragedy would be behind them. Even though delays in the home sale transaction had caused a one-month delay, the couple planned to complete the move before the end of July.

PART III
DISCOVERY

Chapter 7

Elaine Canalia and Jack Court first met the bearded painting contractor in May, 1994, then ran into him several times again at a swap meet in Prescott Valley, Arizona. They often made the ninety-mile trip north from their Phoenix paint manufacturing warehouse to buy and sell products at the open air market near Prescott.

A slim, attractive, forty-something woman, with shoulder-length blond hair and pleasing features, Canalia had been in business with Jack Court for four years. They had met while employed at the same firm in 1988, and soon discovered a host of interests in common. In 1990, they decided to give up their jobs and take the big risk of launching a business partnership. It worked, and with financial success, their entrepreneurial teamwork developed into a more serious relationship. Elaine had fallen in love with the amiable, late-fifties, soft-spoken Jack, who returned the devotion. Their friends thought they made a perfect couple. Together, Court and Canalia made business and pleasure a perfect mix. They mutually developed a deep interest in the Pacific Islands, and wondered what it would be like to live there one day.

From their allotted space at the swap meet, between Prescott and the small town of Dewey, Elaine and Jack marketed their paint and established contacts for future sales. One spring afternoon, while strolling between rows occupied by other vendors, Elaine spotted stacked cans of paint for sale. She commented to the bearded man behind the stacks, "Oh, I see we have a competitor."

The "competitor" laughed and explained that he had been a painting contractor in California and had moved to Arizona to start anew. Business hadn't been as good as he'd hoped, so he wanted to sell his surplus supplies. They exchanged pleasantries, after which she left. During the next few weekends, Canalia and Court met the gaunt, bearded man several times. She would recall, "He was personable, seemed quite intelligent, and his speech was articulate." Regarding his personal appearance, she thought he wasn't ugly, just average. "I really wasn't very interested in his physical looks. Just his paint."

On a hot Saturday, July 9, at the swap meet, the couple encountered the bearded contractor again and chatted for several minutes with him. He stood behind a van he used to transport his wares, and told them that he also owned a pickup truck. During the conversation, he mentioned that he had an abundant supply of colorant stored at his home near Dewey. Court and Canalia expressed interest in buying the colorant, so the contractor asked them to follow him to his house.

Driving behind the white van, Court steered his pickup through the sweeping curve on State Highway 69 and turned into the exclusive tract of top-dollar homes just outside Dewey. En route, Court's ten-year-old grandson who had made the trip with them that day announced that he had to go to the bathroom.

After winding through the new development of luxury custom residences, along the greens of an expansive golf course, they slowed at a corner lot. Smooth river stones artfully decorated the yard in front of a split level L-shaped house with a curved driveway leading to a two-car garage. The contractor led them around the corner to a side concrete driveway, or parking pad, perhaps twenty feet deep, ending at a wooden fence. They parked in front of a truck which had been backed into the pad, and was partially covered by a canvas tarpaulin. A variety of unlabeled cans, presumably paint, surrounded the yellow truck, which bore the Ryder rental company logo. It had obviously been sitting there for some time, next to a white pickup.

Canalia felt hairs on the back of her neck rise. Why would this guy keep a rental truck parked close to his house, maybe for several months? Jack, too, wondered why the man would have the Ryder truck, when he also had a van and a pickup truck.

Canalia, Court, and the grandson followed the gaunt painter into his backyard, enclosed by a six-foot wooden fence, and saw hundreds of paint cans of various sizes covering the entire grounds, stacked everywhere among ladders and dismantled scaffolding. With the help of the contractor, they began loading cases of paint colorant into the back of their pickup. Court's grandson reminded him that he needed a restroom. They asked the contractor if the boy could use the facilities in the house, but the bearded man instantly shook his head, saying that would be impossible because the water had been turned off. No water, no toilet. To Canalia, the contractor's attitude seemed abrupt and unconvincing. She became even more concerned at his brusqueness when the child began playing with a cap gun that made popping noises. The bearded painter snapped, "Don't do that. This is a quiet neighborhood and we want to keep it that way."

Later, Canalia couldn't remember how the lad had solved the problem of needing a restroom. "He either waited, or he found a place behind all that stuff piled in the yard," she said.

Upon completion of the loading and the business transaction, Canalia, Court, and boy said goodbye, climbed into their pickup, and started to back out of the parking pad. Still experiencing a strange feeling about the Ryder truck, they glanced at each other. They'd both noticed the license plate from Massachusetts. Jack whispered, "I'll bet the doggone thing is stolen." Having been recent victims of theft, Canalia and Court felt they should take counsel of their intuitions. They realized that the contractor still stood outside, watching them leave. With the truck still in her sight, Elaine grabbed a scrap of paper, bent over so the painter couldn't see her actions, and jotted down the license number, along with the rental company's serial number printed above the cab of the dusty Ryder truck.

Back at their own warehouse in Phoenix, Canalia tossed the slip of paper onto a desk, and pushed it to the back of her mind.

She paid no heed to it until three days later, July 12, when a law enforcement friend visited their warehouse to purchase some paint. They had known Det. Steve Gregory of the Phoenix P.D. for several years and exchanged the usual banter with him. Canalia mentioned the strange Ryder truck she'd seen in the Prescott Country Club tract, and gave him the license number along with the Ryder serial number.

Curious about the odd circumstances, Gregory figured he'd better find out if the guy had perhaps bought the truck, or if it might show up on a hot list of missing vehicles. He telephoned the Ryder Company. They responded that they had no report of that particular vehicle being stolen. With the natural suspicion of an experienced cop, Gregory asked the representative to double check and said he would wait for a return call.

Within the hour, Gregory heard from the security department of the Ryder company. The truck had been missing six months, since January, from Orange County, California. But through some oversight, no one had ever contacted the police. The next morning, the rental company corrected the problem by making a report to the Orange County Sheriff's Department, and relaying that information to Detective Gregory. He also asked for the vehicle identification number (VIN) and made note of it.

Gregory called the Yavapai County Sheriffs Office to pass on the tip about the stolen twenty-four-foot GMC Ryder rental truck bearing Massachusetts license plate number 486595. On Wednesday morning, July 13, a little past 8:30, Deputy Joe DiGiacomo received a dispatch to check on the vehicle Canalia and Court had seen parked in the upscale residential tract. The Phoenix detective had courteously provided directions to find the home. As an aid to locating the right house, the information even included an estimate of its sales value, approximately $300,000.

DiGiacomo cruised the neighborhood for a short time, and close to a house on Cochise Drive, spotted the partially obscured truck with RYDER printed in bold letters on the panel over the cab. He observed that the residence faced west and the truck was backed into a side driveway.

On foot, DiGiacomo approached the vehicle and brought out his notes to compare the license number. Something was wrong.

The truck he found had plates from Maine, not Massachusetts, and bore the numbers 488708. It seemed strange to the officer that two Ryder trucks might be in the same tract, but since this one had different plates, he had no choice but to leave and request more information. Because the disparity didn't make sense to Deputy DiGiacomo, he decided to contact the Phoenix detective.

Coincidentally, Detective Gregory had dropped into the warehouse belonging to Jack Court and Elaine Canalia, to pick up the paint he had ordered, when his beeper went off at 9:48 that morning. After conversing with Deputy DiGiacomo, Gregory asked Canalia to verify the location of the truck she had seen. It corresponded perfectly with the site DiGiacomo had visited. Something seemed really out of whack. Gregory had confirmed that the truck was stolen and that Ryder wanted to press charges. Maybe someone had switched the plates overnight. He asked DiGiacomo to take a second look.

To play it safe, DiGiacomo took a backup officer with him, and returned at noon to the location where the truck sat. This time, he checked the VIN number. Bingo! It was the right truck. Something else nagged the back of the officer's mind. Buckets, five-gallon cans, and one-gallon cans, many of them unlabeled, littered the driveway, all around the truck, and in the yard on the other side of the fence. DiGiacomo had no way of knowing what they contained. Furthermore, a thick electrical extension cord snaked from under the locked back door of the truck, and looped over a fence to a large home on the north side. The scene had all the makings of a clandestine drug lab.

Attempts to raise anyone in the house produced only silence from inside. DiGiacomo contacted the Prescott Area Narcotics Team (PANT).

The narcs arrived at 1:15 P.M., listened as DiGiacomo briefed them, and conducted an examination of the various containers. They found no trace of chemicals used in drug labs, but the extension cord coming out of the truck's rear doors made them wonder if illegal materials could be inside. A secure lock kept them from opening it for an inspection. They noted that the vehicle apparently hadn't been moved for several months. The long orange extension cord looped over the wooden fence, across the backyard to the adjacent property. The detectives would wait for a search warrant before asking the residents of the neighboring home why they apparently were supplying electric power to the truck.

Examining an older model white Dodge pickup truck parked beside the Ryder vehicle, the investigators found nothing unusual or suspicious. They wrote down its license number, and called in for a make on the owner's name.

Deputy DiGiacomo summoned a local locksmith, who showed up within a few minutes and easily unlocked the Ryder truck's back door.

In the shadowed interior, more cans of paint stood stacked in the spacious cargo section. Close to the rear of the truck bed, the officers could see a large off-white rectangular appliance which appeared to be a chest-type freezer. They found a switch in the "on" position, with the appliance running to keep the contents frozen. It, too, was locked, and a dozen wide strips of heavy masking tape had been placed at intervals to seal the lid. The locksmith went to work again.

Detective Mike Garcia, a member of the PANT team, wearing a white apron, placed a gauze mask over his mouth and nose, donned rubber gloves, and ripped through each strip of the masking tape. When he raised the lid, a foul odor assaulted the assembled cops' noses. Garcia, controlling an urge to heave, said he thought it smelled like decaying flesh. As he and two other investigators peered into the interior, they could see frost on the inside walls, and a large object completely covered with black plastic garbage bags resting at the bottom.

Garcia tentatively reached in, and felt along the top section of plastic. His face grim, he withdrew his hand and said, "It feels like a human arm!" He added that it seemed to be frozen solid. The PANT officers, realizing they very likely had found the makings of a homicide, carefully closed the freezer lid and halted their portion of the investigation to summon the homicide team.

* * *

A young, clear-eyed lieutenant, Scott Mascher had climbed the sheriffs department ranks faster than mountain sheep ascend craggy mesas of the Juniper Mountains above Prescott. Standing five-nine, a solid 165 pounds, with eyes the color of Arizona sky, light brown hair with matching full mustache, and an outdoorsman's tan, Mascher hailed originally from Wilkes-Barre, Pennsylvania, but had been transplanted to Arizona as a young child. He adapted to the rugged desert like a young cougar. Nothing pleased him more than to explore sheer red cliffs, wide basins, and flat mesas all the way from the lower Sonora desert to the sandstone and granite buttes of the high country. As he grew up, he became intimately familiar with wash trails winding among prickly pear cactus, stately saguaros, scrub oaks, junipers, up to the towering ponderosa pines. After his high school years in Phoenix, Mascher attended Yavapai Community College. While still taking classes, in 1984, he joined a volunteer sheriff's reserve group, and accepted a full-time job the next year in Sedona, the red-rock surrounded artist/tourist town where New Age thinkers find magic. A stint as an undercover narc followed, in which he worked everywhere in the 8,000-square mile county. Promoted to sergeant, then detective sergeant in the major crimes unit, he worked the dozen or so homicides committed each year in Yavapai County. By 1993, Mascher accepted a remarkably rapid promotion to lieutenant.

In his spare time, Mascher still exercises his devotion to the wide open spaces by guiding elk hunters through the mountains, and as a licensed boatman-river raft guide down the rapids of the mighty Colorado in Grand Canyon. He and a buddy, Garry Saravo, who investigates crimes for the county attorney's office, experienced near disaster in 1983 during a surging flood in the canyon. Water rose above the dam at Lake Powell, causing the river to become a torrent. On an inflated raft, Mascher and Saravo, at the lower end of the lake, felt the massive crescendo of water grab them. Said Mascher, "It flushed us out sixty miles in one day!" At one point, the pounding waves flipped the boat over. "We got it upright, and used canoe paddles to get down river to Lake Mead." Mascher grins, and says, "I've been addicted to that life ever since."

* * *

Also addicted to police work, in which Mascher proudly points to a ninety-nine percent rate of solved murders ("We know the perp in the other one, and we're still gathering evidence to nail him"), the energetic lieutenant would lead the investigation into the mysterious frozen contents of the Ryder truck.

Mascher arrived at the Cochise Street address a few minutes before four that afternoon, along with one of his detectives, Lonnie E. Brown. DiGiacomo briefed them. They once again tried to raise someone in the house, but got no response.

With his fellow investigators wearing protective aprons, masks, and gloves, Mascher operated a video camera to record the opening of the freezer, while he spoke into the microphone. "So, at this point, let us open up the freezer, and, uh, see what's inside." Lonnie Brown, also wearing a "moon suit," used a knife to carefully slice through the rigid top layers of black plastic and peel them back one by one. As he lifted the third layer, both men could see a nude human shoulder and an arm. Gradually, Brown exposed more icy, whitish flesh. A pair of frozen hands came into view, in the middle of the body's back. Silver colored steel handcuffs bound them together at the wrists. It caught the detective's attention that the fingers were well manicured, with long nails cut square at the ends. Brown observed, "The body was in somewhat of a fetal position with the back towards the front of the freezer and the head towards the left rear corner." The detectives wondered why the corpse had been curled into such a tight position, since the freezer's large interior would easily have allowed fuller extension of the body.

The video camera continued to run. Mascher observed the ghoulish scene and later described what he saw. "The freezer was still running and it was ice cold inside the chest. When you look down into the freezer, there was a lot of apparently frozen blood, body fluids, and ice crystals."

Each of the investigators' grimacing facial expressions reflected the horror they gazed on. As Brown peeled yet more of the frozen plastic away, he revealed the frost-covered back of the dead victim inside the freezer. They couldn't even yet determine the body's gender, but could see that the head, bent at the neck toward the knees, was covered by smaller white plastic bags. Brown wondered if the head had been severed, then covered by the different bags. He said, "In my opinion, the victim was not killed at this scene, inside of the chest freezer." He based the judgement on his observation of frozen blood and fluids at the bottom of the freezer, with no evidence of blood splatter on the sides or top of the appliance. He also noted that some decomposition had occurred, leading him to believe that the body had not been frozen until at least a few hours, maybe longer, after death.

Noting the make of the freezer, Mascher jotted down that it was a Signature 2000 with a capacity of twenty-three cubic feet, deep freeze chest-type model. He would later learn that it was manufactured in March 1991 by Montgomery Ward.

Because any further handling of the frozen-body might disturb potential evidence, Mascher directed Brown to discontinue the tragic unveiling, then called the Yavapai County Medical Examiner. After a brief telephone conversation, the M.E. suggested that the freezer be closed, with the corpse still inside, and transported to a fully equipped lab. That way, the body could be extracted using more scientific procedures to retain whatever forensic evidence might be available.

The best way, Mascher decided, was to have the entire truck, containing the charnel freezer, towed to the Arizona state crime lab in Phoenix, and let the Maricopa County Medical Examiner's Office send a forensic doctor to examine the human remains. With extreme care, they might be able to lift fingerprints. The prints would be needed, because nothing else in the truck or freezer provided any inkling of who the frozen body might be.

One of the detectives, canvassing neighbors in Prescott Country Club, found two different residents who said they had first seen the Ryder truck about six months earlier, in January 1994. It had been parked at the same spot for about two months.

Meanwhile, the Arizona Department of Motor Vehicles responded to the request officers had made to determine who owned the white Dodge pickup parked next to the Ryder truck.

It belonged to a man named John Joseph Famalaro.

On that same day, July 13, John Famalaro, accompanied by his mother in a red Jeep Cherokee, slowed near the house where he lived on Cochise Street. As soon as he braked to a stop in front of the home, at 5:30 P.M., Deputy Chris Sorensen placed him under arrest for felony theft of a Ryder rental truck. He received a free trip in the back of the deputy's cruiser to the Yavapai County Sheriff's Office detention center.

Det. Lonnie Brown spoke to the startled mother, and gave her a ride around the corner to her home, on a lot that connected to the property where the body had been discovered. In a short conversation between the detective and Mrs. Famalaro, she told him that she thought her son had been in possession of the Ryder truck about two months and that she assumed he used it in connection with his house painting business. The neighbors had complained of his storing so many cans in the yard, she said, and she thought he planned to utilize the truck to move them. She and her husband had leased the red Jeep for John to use in his new venture, a real estate business in Sedona. Mrs. Famalaro denied any knowledge of her son purchasing the deep freezer. She also told the detective that she didn't think her boy had any close friends, and that he was a workaholic who hadn't had any fun in months. All he had been doing, other than working, was visiting his gravely ill father at the Veterans' Administration hospital in Prescott.

Protocol in Yavapai County calls for the chief investigator of the county attorney's office to assist the sheriff's personnel in homicide investigations. Roger Williamson filled that requirement with gusto. Normally light complected, slim at five-nine, 175 pounds, the mustachioed Williamson's tan face reflected his love for the outdoors and Arizona's constant sun. Williamson received notification within minutes after Scott Mascher's team found the frozen body.

On the evening of July 13, he spoke to Deputy Sorensen, who

had transported and booked John Famalaro. The deputy mentioned that he'd been to the Cochise Drive house where he saw
a set of three keys on a ring belonging to the suspect. Famalaro
had told Sorensen that the keys would fit a white van parked in
the lot of a Safeway market in Prescott Valley.

When Lt. Scott Mascher traced the orange extension cord to
an outlet of the adjacent home, he ordered both houses to be
secured with yellow crime scene tape until they could be legally
searched. After the arrest of John Famalaro, Mascher and Investigator Williamson spoke briefly to the shocked mother, who
owned and occupied the neighboring home. Mascher informed
her that she would be provided a motel room for the night.
Officers took up positions to guard the houses until search warrants arrived.

As soon as he left Mrs. Famalaro, Mascher hurried to headquarters hoping to interview John Famalaro. It turned out to be
an exceedingly short session. In a cube-shaped room, the suspect
sat in a corner with his legs under a table. After he'd heard the
Miranda warning a second time, he told Mascher that he preferred not to say anything without the presence of his lawyer,
then crossed his arms on the table and dejectedly dropped his
head on them.

The only thing that Famalaro had said to anyone was a mention of his van at the Safeway market. With Williamson early the
following morning, July 14, Mascher found the 1993 Chevrolet
van, which had no license plates. At that hour, it was the only
one in the parking lot. They examined the exterior and found
a small hole on the left side of the vehicle. It appeared that a
bullet had been fired, inside the rear compartment, and had
pierced the metallic skin. They called for a tow truck which transported the vehicle to the county impound lot for further investigation.

Wondering why the extension cord had been strung all the
way to the home of Famalaro's parents, Scott Mascher checked
with the Arizona Public Service Company in Prescott. A representative informed him that electrical service for the Cochise

Drive house had been discontinued on July 11 for one day only. Power had originally been placed in service several years earlier for the occupant of that residence, Marvin Kraft, who had terminated it two days ago. It had been reconnected on July 12 by John Famalaro and his mother, in his father's name.

Marvin Kraft, detectives discovered, had been married to John Famalaro's sister, Francine.

Back in Prescott Country Club, Mascher and Williamson met Mrs. Famalaro again, in front of her home. She insisted that they not tape the conversation. Explaining why the extension cord ran to her house, she said that when her son's power had been cut off, he had plugged the extension cord into an outside outlet at her house to keep his refrigerator running. He had also brought over some food for her to keep until restoration of power the next day.

The truck, she repeated, had been parked at her son's place for approximately two months. To Mascher's questions about John's background, she said that her son had never been married and that girls "have just broke his heart." To her knowledge, John didn't have any friends and had been living alone at the house on Cochise Drive. No, she said, she didn't know anything about the Ryder truck, was shocked to hear of the body inside, and knew nothing about the freezer. Mascher learned of two more white vans Famalaro possessed when Mrs. Famalaro told him that John kept them parked in her driveway. The investigator wondered what the guy needed so many vehicles for.

Mrs. Famalaro would later say about the freezer, "I didn't know what he had in there. I thought he was moving paint." About her son, she added, "I really can't tell you much about him. I just don't know. I think he's a good boy. I don't know what to make of all this. Pray for him. Please pray for him. Our hearts are breaking over this. We are the kind of people who keep to ourselves. We're conservative, Christian people."

County records showed that the house on Cochise Drive had been sold to Marvin Kraft several years earlier. Roger Williamson traced him down to a residence in Prescott and telephoned him.

Kraft told of a divorce from Francine Famalaro and of John later moving into the home with him. John had attempted to buy the house, but recent litigation regarding ownership complicated the transaction, so Kraft refused to discuss it with Williamson. He claimed he hadn't seen John Famalaro since May, at a birthday party.

Williamson asked Kraft if he knew anything about Famalaro's association with women, but learned very little. Kraft said he had just recently learned of the Ryder truck being parked in the driveway when he passed by the house in early July. Famalaro had moved into the place two years ago, he said, from somewhere in Orange County, California. Kraft had helped him with the move. John seemed to have lots of cars, Kraft said, including a new red Jeep Cherokee, two white milk-type trucks, a large white cargo van, and a white Dodge pickup, most of which he usually kept parked at the house or nearby at his parents' home.

Famalaro, Kraft said, had been a painting contractor, but recently tried to go into real estate sales. Williamson asked Kraft when he had moved out of the Cochise Drive house, and heard him say that he'd left in January 1993. No, he hadn't left any of his possessions there.

As the scorching July sun reached its zenith on that Thursday, and began the long drop toward the horizon, Scott Mascher and Roger Williamson continued the search for information. At 3:30, they joined the team of homicide detectives with search warrants in hand to enter the house where John Famalaro had been living. The warrant included permission to examine the red Jeep Cherokee, so Williamson walked over to Mrs. Famalaro's home, informed her that he needed to get into the Jeep, and opened the car's door. Inside, he found the key ring he'd hoped to see. It contained a key to the Cochise house, forestalling the need to break down a door.

Inside the house, Mascher made certain video and still cameras recorded everything in the interior before the searchers moved or disturbed anything. The officers divided themselves into two teams to search the split level home. First, each group conducted a preliminary walk-through, cursorily looking for bloodstains. The clutter of boxes, paint cans, and piles of newspapers and magazines, raised all of their eyebrows. One room, though, had been set up as an office, containing three walls of bookcases, all filled with hundreds of volumes, neatly arranged by subject. Other rooms contained even more shelves and books.

Sparse furnishing in the interior occupied the few spaces between stacks of boxes. As Mascher and his searchers scoured through each room, they found several items that caught their interest:

1) A cardboard box, with the word CHRISTMAS printed on it, containing another smaller box. Inside the second container, a "nailbar" with possible bloodstains, an empty handcuff box, duct tape, and a cloth with bloodstains.

2) A pair of handcuffs similar to the cuffs on the victim's wrists, and handcuff keys.

3) Several identification documents, all with women's names.

4) A second cardboard box marked CHRISTMAS, containing a bloodstained knapsack and a claw hammer appearing to be spotted with dried blood. A bloodstained black plastic bag contained items imprinted with the name Denise Huber.

Mascher and his team descended stairs into a bonus room, thirteen by forty-five feet, one wall of which abutted a slope in the ground. Someone had chiseled a hole in the cinder block wall and dug an excavation into the rocky earth. The cavern measured six feet below the foundation of the house. Hundreds of one gallon paint cans had been stacked into the dirt chamber, which the investigators soon began calling "the dungeon."

In other rooms, they found several guns. Mascher noted that the cause of death of the body in the freezer had not yet been determined, so took special interest in the firearms. Videotapes turned up in the search, many featuring the blonde actress

Suzanne Somers, others focusing on Charles Manson and Jeffrey Dahmer.

Questions raised by the findings, and the circumstances, led Mascher to request additional warrants for more precise searches, especially in the excavated dirt room. They found nothing of any particular interest in the home of John Famalaro's parents. Both searches ended at 1:25 A.M. Friday, July 15.

In addition to the name Denise Huber, searchers found items involving ten more female names, along with a variety of credit cards, birth certificates, driver's licenses, and personal property that might typically be in the possession of young women. Scott Mascher and his detectives began to give serious thought to the possibility that they had stumbled onto the trail of a serial killer.

Back at headquarters, Mascher typed the names into a computer. Within moments, he received feedback on the name Denise Huber as a missing person, related to a report issued by the Costa Mesa, California, police three years earlier, in 1991.

Midway through Thursday morning, Mascher called the Costa Mesa PD and spoke to Sgt. Tom Boylan, who was in charge of the detail of officers still assigned to the Huber case. "I advised him that personal belongings of Denise Huber were located in a residence during a search on a homicide investigation." A surprised and excited Boylan filled Mascher in on the details of how Denise vanished in June 1991, the ensuing intensive search, and that she hadn't been heard from since. Mascher entered in his report, "I told Boylan that our victim was found frozen in a chest freezer and has not been identified as of yet, and that a gender has not been determined due to the frozen position of the body. An autopsy will be conducted upon the thawing of the body, tentatively scheduled for Friday, July 16. Sergeant Boylan gave me a clothing description of Denise Huber on the night of her disappearance. She was wearing a black short dress, blouse, black jacket, and pump shoes."

Agreeing to call Boylan back as soon as he had more detailed information, Mascher hurried to the evidence room with Roger Williamson. The lieutenant instructed an officer to don protective gear, avoiding possible contamination of the evidence taken from the Famalaro house, then to place a white sheet on the floor. The officer complied, and emptied contents of the two cardboard boxes marked "Christmas" which would become well known as boxes 212 and 213. He placed each of the items on the sheet. Mascher and Williamson surveyed the evidence, and listed:

   a California driver's license in the name of Denise Huber
   numerous credit cards in her name
   a checkbook in her name
   a "Hawaii" key ring with Honda keys
   a black dress, black blouse, black 9West pumps, all specked
      with what appeared to be bloodstains
   a tool known as a roofer's nail puller, spotted with dried
      blood
   a claw hammer, also apparently bloodstained

   Scott Mascher now felt certain he knew the name of the victim in the freezer. He telephoned the Costa Mesa PD again, expecting to speak to Sergeant Boylan, but learned that a lieutenant had been placed in charge of the Huber case.

   In Costa Mesa, Tom Boylan had been doing everything possible to keep the search alive for Denise Huber, plus working scores of other investigations concurrently. That July 1994, he had invested in a long-planned vacation to the Caribbean, with unrefundable deposits already spent. In order to stay with the Huber case, he volunteered to sacrifice the money and cancel his trip, but Chief Snowden wouldn't allow it. He told Boylan to enjoy his vacation, and assigned Lt. Ron Smith to pick up where he'd left off back in 1992, before the promotion. Smith gladly assumed the reins of control again.
   Boylan advised Smith to be expecting a phone call from Arizona.

Chapter 8

In Costa Mesa, Lt. Ron Smith answered the telephone call from Lt. Scott Mascher in Arizona. He listened to Mascher's news, and at first wondered if the fellow officer, for whom Smith would soon develop great respect, was pulling a practical joke; like some New York cop calling a fellow detective and announcing they'd found the remains of Jimmy Hoffa. Police officers everywhere use dark humor to buffer the grim facts of underworld stress.

The caller's earnest tone, though, made it clear that Mascher couldn't be more serious. Smith's pulse rate nearly doubled.

Mascher pointed out that body identification had not yet been positively confirmed, and couldn't be until the autopsy on Friday. Even then, it would depend on the ability to lift usable fingerprints or to compare dental records. But, the Arizona investigator said, he felt confident that they had found the frozen body of Denise Huber. Mascher detailed the list of items his team had located in the house after they'd made the gruesome freezer discovery. They had Huber's driver's license, credit cards in her name, a dolphin-shaped ring, a black dress, shoes, and a purse that matched descriptions on the missing person report. The driver's license and credit cards had been found still inside her wallet.

Equally important, Mascher said, he had a suspect in custody. The guy might even be a serial killer. Mascher invited Smith and his detectives to attend the autopsy and afterwards to meet and exchange ideas on the investigation. The autopsy, he said, would be performed on July 16 at noon in Phoenix. Mascher's generous offer was the first step of cooperation in the multiagency investigation that would eventually be noted as one of the most effective cooperative efforts in the annals of police work. It should be used as a model for such efforts.

It took Ron Smith about two milliseconds to accept the invitation. Of course, he would have to clear it with his superiors before traveling to another state, into another jurisdiction, for the purpose of investigating a body discovery. The victim might not even be the one for which he had been intensively searching for three years. If it did turn out to be Denise Huber, Smith had no evidence to prove that she had been murdered, and if she was a homicide victim, he had no proof that it happened in Costa Mesa, Orange County, or even in California.

Under ordinary circumstances, officials might scoff at the request to travel to another state with such flimsy reasoning. But Smith knew full well that no one regarded the Denise Huber case as routine or ordinary. He had no qualms at all about walking into the office of Chief David Snowden to discuss an invitation to Arizona.

After a short conference, Snowden agreed that Smith should not only go to Phoenix, but should take Lynda Giesler and Frank Rudisill with him. Both detectives had worked their hearts out on the frustrating case and should continue to its final resolution. To be certain that no one stepped on jurisdictional toes, Snowden and Smith thought it would be a good idea to confer with the county's top cop and the head legal office. They set up a meeting with Orange County Sheriff Brad Gates and with the district attorney, Mike Capizzi. Capizzi had developed a solid reputation of being one of the toughest prosecutors in the nation, abetted by his "no plea bargain" policy for suspects accused of felonies.

Both officials fully supported the trip for Smith, Giesler, and Rudisill, as did their counterparts in Yavapai County, Arizona, Sheriff Buck Buchanan, and County Attorney Chick Hastings.

Detective Lynda Giesler's pager beeped within minutes after Smith received the approvals. Expecting a routine call, she glanced at the readout and saw Sergeant Boylan's number, plus the private symbol which meant to respond as soon as possible. Because she was only a few blocks from headquarters on Fair Drive, she drove in and arrived sooner than she could have made a return call.

When she found Boylan, his face was "as white as a sheet of typing paper." He strained to keep from shouting. "You're not going to believe what just happened!" The unflappable Giesler, her expression calm as usual, waited. Few announcements surprised her anymore. Boylan continued. "Denise Huber's body has been found. The identification is based only on her purse and her personal documents inside it. They're going to try to verify it's her at the autopsy." The sergeant explained that the body had been kept frozen all those years.

Despite herself, Giesler's heart began to pound, too. Three years. Most people had given up on ever finding Huber. Now this. Incredible! Giesler wanted to know more, so she called Lt. Scott Mascher. She heard the description of identification cards and jewelry. Giesler knew it was Denise when Mascher told her of a ring with a dolphin figure on it. She thanked the Arizona officer, and swallowed hard to keep the tears back.

A long time ago, Lynda Giesler had promised the Hubers that if she ever heard anything, they would be the first to know. Keeping promises ranked at the top on Giesler's list of important priorities. Putting on her impassive cop's mask, and clearing her throat to achieve the vocal objectivity necessary to her job, Giesler punched in the Huber's telephone number. Ione answered. Lynda said, "Hello, Ione. A couple of things came up on the case that I'd like to talk to you about. Will you be at home for a while?"

"I will be," Ione Huber responded, "but Dennis is out on business and won't be home until this evening." Giesler said she would be over in a few minutes.

Emotionally, it was a tough decision for Giesler. Should she tell Ione without Dennis being there, that their daughter's body had been found? Or should she wait until they were together? By waiting, she would run the risk of the information leaking to Ione, at home alone, from an overzealous reporter, maybe from

Arizona or some local news agency. Giesler would wade through hell before she would allow that to happen. She had promised.

Accompanied by Frank Rudisill and Tom Boylan, Lynda Giesler knocked on the door at Vista Grande. Ione answered and invited them in. Her facial expression told Giesler that Ione realized this was no routine visit. The officers could see boxes stacked around the house, and knew the Hubers had been preparing to move to North Dakota.

As gently as she could, Giesler told Ione of the discovery, and that the identification had not yet been confirmed. She apologized, saying, "I'm so sorry Dennis could not be here."

Years later, in recalling the visit, Lynda would compliment the strength she saw in Ione Huber. "She didn't fall apart. And she courteously declined our offer to stay with her. Ione is a strong woman, and I admired her ability to cope with the sad news."

Ione Huber would recall that when she saw the three detectives coming up the walk, she knew they had something important to tell her. "I cried. I just cried." Probing her own memory, she said, "You think you're going to be prepared, but I wasn't. I was in shock. I had pretty much accepted the idea that Denise was no longer alive because I knew that if she had any way of getting in touch with us, she would have. This is hard. This is very hard."

Dennis would learn of the discovery later that day, and talk to Lynda Giesler by telephone. The news wasn't what he had hoped for, but at least it would answer some of their questions, and end the constant searching in crowds, on the freeways, looking for Denise everywhere they went. He could at last stop feeling a rush of adrenalin every time he saw a tall woman with long brown hair. "We always wondered where she was, what she was going through. It was always on our minds." He would still need many answers, but finally, after three long years, he might be able to get some peaceful sleep. But first, they had some important calls to make. The detectives had asked the Hubers not to speak to the news media yet, but agreed that it would be okay to tell their loved ones.

In Sunset Beach, Gillian and Pat Fay, the Hubers' loyal friends with whom they and Denise had traveled to Hawaii, came home on Friday night from a dinner engagement. They saw the flasher on their answering machine, and played the tape. The voice of Dennis Huber, sounding unusually flat, said, "Hi. When you get in, give me a call."

Gillian frowned, and in her English lilt said to her husband, "Wonder what's wrong with Dennis?" She'd had an ongoing relationship with Huber that involved a great deal of teasing with good-natured insults. His message sounded serious, so with tongue slightly in cheek, she said to Pat, "You call him."

Pat Fay made the connection, and heard Dennis Huber's tense voice say, "Keep it quiet now, but I think they have found Denise."

Gillian, standing close, heard her husband repeat, ". . . found Denise?" She would later describe her reaction as "I flew" to the other phone. "Please tell me she's alive."

"No."

Gillian screamed.

Jeff Huber had been in Costa Mesa on that Friday. When he arrived home, he heard the phone ringing. He picked it up, and his mother said, "You need to come over. We found out some stuff today." It took him a short time to drive to Newport Beach, where his mother and father told him of the discovery.

Years later, he would recall his reaction. "From the beginning I had resolved that Denise was gone forever. I had accepted that I would never see her again. If I did, it would be one of life's bonuses. But I never really had my hopes up. So when I heard the news, it came as no real shock that she was dead. But the details, about the freezer and all, were absolutely stunning."

* * *

During the horrible three years, the Presbyterian church group had been so supportive, in every possible way. Ione felt it would be disloyal not to notify the Reverend Walt Shepard, pastor of the Aliso Creek church. Then, she would call Nancy Streza, who had been a close friend since the time Streza was Denise's Sunday school teacher, and had been an organizer of financial, logistical, and emotional support during the long crisis. Ione managed both calls with one try. Streza happened to be at the church, answering the phone. She heard the incredible news, and controlled the urge to cry. She offered to be at the Huber's side, and agreed not to speak to reporters until the police made an official announcement.

From John Wayne Airport in Orange County, Lynda Giesler, Ron Smith, and Frank Rudisill took a short forty-five minute hop to Sky Harbor Airport in Phoenix. From there, they went directly to the Maricopa County Medical Examiner's Office and met with evidence technician Mike Winney. A civilian employee of the Yavapai County Sheriff's Office, Winney had been the identification and property supervisor there for eight years, responsible for all fingerprint operations. His duty in Phoenix would be to determine the feasibility of obtaining prints from the frozen body and take them, if possible. Giesler gave him a certified copy of Huber's driver's license, including the right thumbprint.

Winney and the three Costa Mesa officers assembled in the autopsy lab and met Dr. Ann Bucholtz. The slim, brown-haired woman with pleasant features had performed more than a thousand autopsies, and would conduct the examination of the thawed corpse transported from Prescott with the objective of discovering what had been the cause of death. She had already taken the important step of being present when the freezer arrived in Phoenix to observe the body before it was lifted from the icy interior.

Discussing what she had seen in the freezer, Dr. Buchholtz said, "The body was actually frozen so solid that it was stuck to the bottom of the freezer where there was a layer of liquid. Enshrouding the exterior portions of the body was this black . . . heavy plastic material which was also stuck down in the fluid."

Pathologists seldom face the unusual conditions Dr. Buchholtz encountered when she saw the contents of the freezer. She couldn't know exactly what she faced until extraction and thawing of the body, thus removing the black plastic shrouds. Curled in a tight, tucked fetal position, with the knees drawn snugly up to the chest, the arms behind the back with wrists locked in handcuffs, and the head forced down and forward so it stretched almost to a position between the knees, the body was positioned in the freezer's bottom. When officers had peeled back the layers of frozen plastic, they had exposed the back, hands, and wrists. The head, encased in white plastic bags, had been forced down toward the chest with heavy force that injured the neck muscles. But Buchholtz could see none of that when she first peered into the ghoulish frozen chamber.

After the body, still encased in frozen black plastic, had been lifted from the freezer, and transported to her lab, Dr. Buchholtz started the first steps of the examination procedure. First, with some help, she had to begin the process of thawing and removing the black plastic. Using hair dryers, they blew warm air on the plastic and gradually peeled it away, exposing the back, arms, and hands. Little by little, Dr. Buchholtz began the examination. She had already seen enough to realize the victim was female.

"We evaluated the hands. They were handcuffed to the back of the body, and the cuffs had to be removed. They were taken off with bolt cutters because they were so tight . . . tight enough that I could not pass my fingers underneath." Following removal of the manacles, the doctor scrutinized the hands and inspected underneath the fingernails to see if the victim had possibly scraped flesh from her abductor.

The next step would be to determine if a sexual assault had taken place. This required the taking of fluid samples from body orifices. "The problem was, the body was still frozen relatively solid. It is difficult to deal with that kind of evidentiary collection." The body's position made it easier to start with the anal area, and the doctor was able to scrape some icy samples into a sterile jar. Gradually, with more thawing, she succeeded in extracting vaginal samples, too.

Because the head was bent so far forward, and encased in white plastic bags, Dr. Bucholtz hadn't yet examined it. Again using hair dryers, she and her helpers managed to loosen the bags. "We got enough flex to see the face. There were plastic bags adhering to the hair and the upper torso. At that point we saw a piece of gray tape fastened over the upper lip area and extending to the upper eyelid area." When the mouth became visible, the doctor observed that it was in an unusual round configuration, in the shape of the letter "O." It would become apparent that the victim's mouth had been stuffed with rags, and taped over. The eyes, too, had been covered with tape, which had slipped down as the flesh decomposed.

Through the entire process, Buchholtz listed an inventory of jewelry she noted on the body. "There was one dislodged earring adhering to the hair, a yellow metal necklace containing a hollow heart pendant with a single clear stone. On the right ring finger was a yellow metal ring containing a single light green stone. On the left little finger was a corroded metal ring that had a dolphin shape on it. In the left ear was a loop earring containing a pearlescent triangular pendant. Also in the left ear was a clasped hoop earring. The right ear, though pierced, had no earring."

The head had been savagely damaged. Injuries included, "a large gaping laceration or tear over the scalp above the left eye and extending to the left hairline." The wound exposed the fractured skull, as did a second gaping wound on the forehead, and a third one on the left side of the scalp. Additional injuries appeared on the scalp, revealing more bone fractures and leaking of gray matter from the brain. Buchholtz would estimate the number of times something struck the skull to shatter it so completely as "a minimum number of fourteen [direct] blows and seventeen glancing blows." Someone had used a weapon, or weapons, to strike the head of the victim at least thirty-one times.

One of the skull injuries appeared to be oval or round, while others had a different configuration.

* * *

With the Costa Mesa trio observing, technician Mike Winney opened his fingerprint kit. He used a small roller, inked it, and covered the victim's fingertips with the black ink. He then applied them to a white cardboard strip to obtain impressions of all eight fingers and both thumbs. He told the Costa Mesa team that it was lucky he'd been able to take the prints at that time. If he'd waited just one more day, the skin slippage as the result of flesh decomposition would have made the process impossible, and he would not have been able to get a positive I.D. from the prints.

Dr. Bucholtz completed the autopsy by examining the internal organs. She found nothing unusual about any of them.

Later, Winney compared the right thumbprint to the one on Denise Huber's driver's license. It matched perfectly.

The mystery of a woman missing for three years had been solved. The body found frozen solid, curled into a tuck position, handcuffed, nude, with a shattered skull, was positively identified as Denise Anette Huber.

Such extensive damage had been inflicted to the skull, it would require an additional step by Dr. Bucholtz to complete the forensic examination. It fell to Lynda Giesler to contact the victim's parents and notify them of the unusual requirement. She dreaded making the call to Dennis and Ione Huber to describe the necessary procedure; the pathologist needed to remove the damaged head from the body to reconstruct the skull.

Giesler gritted her teeth, and keyed in the telephone number she knew by heart. With all the courage and tact she could muster, she told Dennis Huber of the proposed task. Giesler would later sincerely commend Dennis for his calm composure and for trusting her to make the tough decision. He asked only two questions. "Is this the best thing to do, Lynda?"

"Yes, Dennis, it is. It is necessary if we are to get evidence that might help convict her killer."

After a few moments of silence, and with his voice cracking, Dennis asked, "Is she viewable?"

"No!" Giesler firmly responded. "Do *not* do that."

Dennis and Ione Huber would never see the body of their beloved daughter.

The complex reconstruction of the shattered skull requested by Dr. Bucholtz required the assistance of two expert forensic anthropologists. Dr. Laura Fulginiti and Dr. Walter Birkby worked long hours placing jagged particles in order. Slowly, they fitted together each one, and glued them into place. Even then, gaps between the bone fragments told the story of unimaginable violence.

Following the reconstruction, Dr. Bucholtz said that the number of blows inflicted might have been even more than the maximum thirty-one she had earlier estimated. "There is really no way for me to know the maximum number. Each injury, whether they are from full, directed, or glancing blows, may result in a fracture, or may not cause one. There may be fractures on top of fractures if the blow is repetitively directed to the same area." She concluded that tiny shreds of plastic had been imbedded in the broken skull, suggesting that the perpetrator had inflicted many of the blows after the head had been covered with white plastic bags.

The cause of death, Dr. Bucholtz concluded, was blunt force trauma to the head.

Among the items found in John Famalaro's house, in two boxes marked "Christmas," investigators had discovered white plastic bags, a bloodstained roofer's nail puller, which is a flat metal bar about fourteen inches long, bent to a C shape on one end, and a wood-handled claw hammer apparently spotted with dried blood.

In Dr. Bucholtz's examination of the victim's skull, she concluded the roundish one was consistent with the hammerhead, and the others were consistent with the shape of the nail puller.

That evening, Lynda Giesler and Frank Rudisill drove behind Mike Winney and Ron Smith to Prescott. They caucused with the Yavapai County officials, including the sheriff, county attorney, and all detectives involved, to bring the Costa Mesa team up to date and to work out a plan of cooperative investigation. Giesler agreed to join forces with the county attorney investigator to interview Famalaro's relatives. Frank Rudisill would assist officers executing search warrants. Ron Smith would act as liaison with Scott Mascher, interface with news reporters, and keep in contact with the home office in Costa Mesa.

Something else happened at that meeting. Actually it had been gradually happening from the instant the three Costa Mesa cops stepped off the plane at Phoenix. Lynda Giesler later explained. "During the trip over there, we wondered what we were getting into. Were we going to be dealing with a bunch of cowboy cops, hicks from the Yavapai County desert? The sheriff's name was 'Buck' Buchanan. We were sophisticated big city urban detectives. Well, we were in for a shock. We soon discovered these people were efficient, intelligent, excellent investigators. And personable to boot. Scott Mascher is one of the best. Sometimes, when one agency works with another, you can run into professional jealousies, politics, different procedures. Not only were these officers smart and effective, they were sophisticated professionals. We were proud to be working alongside them. Believe me, I was very impressed."

The combined teams faced some vexing problems.

Denise Huber's body had been found in close proximity to the home of John Joseph Famalaro, and her personal possessions had been found in boxes stored there. Had he killed her? Or had someone else committed the heinous murder and enlisted Famalaro's help to store the grisly remains for three years?

Any number of scenarios reeled through the investigators' minds. They had located her abused body. Now, they faced a mountain of work to discover exactly who had murdered her.

Another team had also flown from Orange County.

A few days after the Costa Mesa PD trio landed, a contingent from the Orange County District Attorney's Office arrived. At first, they encountered a cool welcome in comparison to what the police officers had experienced.

Christopher Evans, one of the top prosecutors in D.A. Michael Capizzi's stable of lawyers, supervised the homicide unit. The publicity generated about the young woman being found in a freezer, and her background, revived personal memories in Evans' mind. He recalled his frequent visits to dine at the Old Spaghetti Factory a few years earlier and was convinced that Denise Huber had served him, probably several times.

When the news broke about the discovery in Arizona, Capizzi took immediate interest. He conferred with Costa Mesa Police Chief Dave Snowden, then summoned Chris Evans. Clearly, the jurisdiction for a possible trial hadn't yet been determined. But if it turned out that the homicide had taken place in Orange County, Capizzi and Evans both wanted plenty of first-hand advance preparation.

After Evans and his boss had examined the brief facts available, the young prosecutor asked Capizzi, "Mike, will you authorize me, along with a pathologist, a criminalist, and one of our investigators to fly to Arizona and look into this? Dave Snowden sent three of his people, and we should certainly be in liaison with them. We need to know what they find in the autopsy, and in searches of the suspect's house and vehicles."

Capizzi had never been indecisive or weak. The citizens of Orange County stood firmly behind the D.A.'s tough-on-crime policy of not allowing plea bargains in felony cases. If he ruffled a few political feathers, his constituents applauded even louder. The criminal justice system needed someone who would stand his ground.

In his unequivocal method of expression, Capizzi said, "Yeah. Go now. You've got the authority to use whatever resources you need."

But when Evans arrived in Phoenix, accompanied by Dr. Richard Fukumoto from the coroner's office, criminalist Dan Gammie, and D.A. Investigator Don Null, they encountered a puzzling obstruction. After they waited over four hours, they found the door closed to the medical examiner's facilities. The organization's chief officer stated that his county had jurisdiction. He said, "They came down from California and were a little offended. I guess I didn't let them get what they wanted."

Still perplexed, Evans sent Dr. Fukumoto and Dan Gammie back home, figuring he could gain access to pathology and autopsy reports later. He and **Don Null** drove up to Prescott, where Sheriff Buck Buchanan, **Lieutenant** Scott Mascher, and the county attorney welcomed **them** aboard.

While Don Null rolled up his sleeves and helped with the search on Cochise Drive, Chris Evans observed, researched legal issues, and conferred with the Yavapai County Attorney to plan legal strategy. In the evenings, when Evans and Null wearily returned to their hotel, they were both astonished at the army of news reporters surrounding the place, looking for any tidbit of new information.

It would be a few days before a stunning development would satisfy reporter's appetites.

Shortly after the arrest of John Famalaro in Arizona, and the ensuing publicity, a career counseling firm in Prescott contacted the police, and sent a copy of a résumé they had prepared for Famalaro four months earlier. In the information he provided to the resume maker, Famalaro described the businesses he had operated:

RÉSUMÉ: JOHN JOSEPH FAMALARO
WORK EXPERIENCE

PRE-1980
At age 13, established a successful landscaping business, where I effectively managed other young people in this endeavor. Developed a strong work ethic beginning at age seven, where I worked within the neighborhood doing odd jobs. As a teenager, worked in retail men's clothing, telemarketing products, and home improvement area.

Worked one year with the Los Angeles Sheriff's Dept. as a Reserve Deputy

PERTINENT WORK HISTORY

Villa Associates, Santa Ana, CA.   *1979-1980*
Licensed Real Estate Agent. Accomplished a fast start and acquired an excellent number of listings, with a goal to fund further education.

The Maintenance Doctor, Orange County, CA.   *1980-1992*
A highly successful painting and decorating company which grew to more than $5 million dollars gross sales/yr. Managed all phases of the business including sixty employees and ten subcontractors.

Consultant, Orange County, CA.   *1989-1992*
Acted as a consultant to other contractors; successfully increased organization and productivity of in-field operations. Received excellent results in the growth of client businesses by emphasizing creative marketing techniques and higher customer service standards.

Masterpiece Restoration, Prescott, AZ.   *1992-present*
A property restoration business. Growth has been rapid and profits brisk. Due to changing personal goals and family responsibilities, I have purposely limited the current size and growth of the organization.

According to the stated purpose of the resume, John Famalaro had a goal of becoming involved in the real estate business. He described himself as a skilled marketer, with effective interpersonal skills, extensive personnel management experience, and excellent skills in running business functions. Listing educational accomplishments, he claimed to be an honor student at St. Michael's Seminary in El Toro, California, and holder of a master's degree from University of Bridgeport in L.A., with a 4.0 grade point average in his major. At the Cleveland Chiropractic College, L.A, he said, he had earned a bachelor of science degree in human biology, with another GPA of 4.0 in his major, and was a doctor of chiropractic, in which he had earned another string of perfect grades.

Personal activities Famalaro listed on his resume included being a member of the National Rifle Association as an active pistol marksman, and a black belt holder/instructor in Kung Fu San Soo and Kenpo Karate.

The veracity of Famalaro's self-appraisal would be questioned by some of his customers, and later, by police investigators.

PART IV
DARK RELATIONS

Chapter 9

In stark contrast to the cohesive love binding the Huber family together, such warmth seemed to escape the family of a young boy living in the center of Orange County. In 1955, the year Disneyland came into existence and focused a national spotlight of wholesome entertainment on the region, living conditions on peaceful Victoria Drive in Santa Ana should have been ideal. Lined on both sides with ancient, twisted cedar trees shading expansive yards, the wide street had attracted wealthy urbanites during and after WWII. They erected lavish multi-story homes decorated with ostentatious columns and crafted stone facades in Tudor, Georgian, and ranch styles, all reflecting posh affluence. Prosperous owners lived in comfortable safety insulated from the ghettos and barrios in poorer sections of Orange County or neighboring L.A. County. The civic center, which included the Santa Ana Police Department, government buildings, and the courthouse, could be reached in a five-minute walk from Victoria Avenue. Main Street shopping, with all the major department stores, also lay within a brief stroll. Few would deny that the neighborhood could be regarded as a slice of upper middle-class America.

Inside the walls of the Famalaro home, though, a frigid tension languished, at least from the viewpoints of the three children.

Six-year-old Francine Famalaro saw the need to act as a substitute mother for her frail three-year-old brother, John. Their mother, Anna Mae Famalaro, had reportedly suffered a difficult

pregnancy with John, forcing her to take to her bed for long periods of time. As Mrs. Famalaro reverted to the habit again, it
gradually became apparent to Francine that the relationship between John and their mother fell far short of any normal symbio-
sis. Years later, Francine would recall, "There wasn't a lot of
bonding" between the child and his mom. So, with the help of
her maternal grandmother, Francine did her best to provide the
nurturing that John craved. Her fosterage grew in importance
considering the smallest child's frequent symptoms of illness. "He
was sick a lot. I don't remember the nature of the illnesses . . .
Just a lot of colds. He was the one who got the chicken pox first
and the measles first, and that kind of thing. He was sort of weak
at that age."

John's brother, George, five years older than his male sibling,
agreed with that diagnosis. "He was ill with something all the
time. He had a hard time. Things were slower coming to him.
Seems like there were headaches. He had kind of twitch stuff.
The thing that scared me the most was . . . bleeding colitis, a lot
of colon stuff."

All three of the Famalaro children were born on Long Island
in New York, George in 1952, Francine in 1954, and John in
1957. During John's infancy, the parents made a decision to relocate to one of the fastest growing counties in the United States
where their father, Angelo Famalaro, would embark on a thirty-
year career as a storm window and aluminum siding dealer. In
1962, they built a six-bedroom home with three and a half baths
on Victoria Drive and immediately outraged conservative neighbors by painting it a pumpkin orange.

With other investments contributing to their income, the
Famalaros flourished. Economic stress which often rips families
apart did not exist for them. If seeds of disfunction sprouted
and grew in the family, the reasons might have been diagnosed
in those early years by a counselor, but no one thought of seeking
professional help. Only the children, it seemed, recognized the
problems.

In Francine's view, her older brother, George, not only attracted most of their mother's attention, but he appeared to be
apathetic toward his brother and sister. At first, Francine hoped

for aid from George in shielding their kid brother from tormen-
tors, but he demonstrated little desire to act as John's protector.
Instead, as she saw it, George selfishly basked in favoritism given
by their mother. Francine remembered: "He generated a lot of
interest from my mother and received a lot of attention because
he was in piano recitals and a debate team. He had a very outgoing personality [which] really paralleled my mother's personality." The mother appeared to be vicariously living her personal
goals through the life of her older son. She incessantly praised
him for good grades in school, and encouraged him to partici-
pate in extracurricular activities.

George saw it differently. "John got the wrath of my mom . . .
she didn't feel like she knew what to do with me, so she would
hammer on John, take it out on John. I knew he didn't feel the
love from Dad that he would want. I really feel bad about John
in the way things were in that household. It was very tough for
him. Since there were no children after him, he was on that
conveyor belt the longest. He was in the incubator the longest,
taking all of what he took from Mom. . . ."

Recognizing the void in John's life, Francine's maternal defense of her little brother became even stronger. "As we grew
older, I pretty much protected him from the family dynamics
that were in the home at that time. Then, when we started school
together at St. Joseph's, I was sort of the guardian. He was weak,
and people would pick on him. It became my role to take care
of him." Her own personal relationship with their mother fell
somewhere in between that of the two boys. "I really just stayed
away from her. I didn't want the attention. I figured out early
on that the less attention, the more tranquility I would have in
my childhood. So I leaned more towards staying in my room
doing my homework. I didn't ask for a lot of attention, and I
didn't want it."

In John's early school years, he began to demonstrate certain
odd behavioral characteristics. He often found himself in trouble
with the nuns. And at home, for some reason, he began locking
his brother George out of the house. According to Francine,
their mother did little to correct her youngest son. "She would
be angry but would just put him in his room so she didn't have

to deal with it." Sometimes, she would simply delegate his care to Francine, ordering her to take the child outside; "Take him for a walk, go ride the Big Wheels, something, get him out of there."

Mrs. Famalaro, in assessing her youngest son's childhood, recalled that he was hyper, but thought he was reared under normal circumstances and seemed like a happy child with playmates in a nice neighborhood. "John was part of our little pack. There were two girls up the street who were their friends, and a little boy who was George and John's friend. My husband and I would take them everywhere. We would go to Knott's Berry Farm, or to Disneyland, or to a particular movie that would be all right." Her children, she said, "would go out in the street and do their thing. And they brought these kids home, and that was fine."

Regarding John, Francine, and George visiting other playmates on the block, Mrs. Famalaro said, "There weren't that many children on Victoria Drive."

Some aid in John's nurturing came from their maternal grandmother. Francine later recalled, "Nana also had an apartment when my grandfather was dying in a nursing home. She maintained it close to him so she could visit on a daily basis. I believe he died in 1966. Prior to that, she did live with us on and off, and once Grandpa died, she lived with us full time." Francine welcomed the help from her grandmother. "She was a great lady, very strong. She had been through a lot, raised five brothers . . . [but] she was a cold woman. She displayed affection in other ways, meeting your physical needs, but not at all an affectionate person." The grandmother did, however, show a certain fondness for the youngest child, John.

On weekends, instead of gathering with a group of other children, John would make a beeline to his grandmother's apartment and "hang out" with her. "He would watch TV, make Jello, walk in the park with her, and those kinds of things," said Francine. When he came home on Sunday nights, he seemed sad. "He was always . . . hyperactive, very active, never stopped in motion. But when he was sad or down, he would just really retreat to his room. It would be over by Monday. He would get up and go to school. It would be okay by then. But he really looked forward to the weekends with Nana. I spent some of those weekends there with him."

Even Mrs. Famalaro generally agreed that John enjoyed a particularly close relationship with her mother, saying, "She singled out John because he was the baby, and my father called him, 'Honey Boy.' My mother couldn't get enough, to be around him enough. So I relinquished a lot of my powers to my mother on John."

The bonding between John and his grandmother, as George saw it, was strong. "It wasn't your normal grandmother/grandson relationship. It was—there was more intertwining. And I think that John looked to Grandma for what he wasn't getting from his mom. There was an attempt to get affection and tenderness from Grandma that wasn't there from Mom. It was kind of weird, but I think they worked out a balance to where he got something he needed from her and she got something she needed from him."

The children's father, according to Francine, "was a great man. But my mother was the dominant force in the home, and my father tolerated it to keep the peace. I learned survival skills from him." In full view of the children, she recalled, Mrs. Famalaro would verbally abuse her husband. Somehow his patient tolerance, although not entirely understood by the three children, drew their sympathy and affection, if clouded by a mix of resentment "One night," Francine said, "I remember my older brother and I sitting up in Father's den and asking, 'Why? Why do you take this?' And he went into this whole Italian-Catholic thing that this is what you do."

George Famalaro's memories, for the most part, coincided with those of Francine, seeing their father as rather ineffectual. "He was the mediator, the peace-keeper, trying to love his children as best he could, but walking the line in pleasing Mom. Because if he didn't, then there was hell to pay in the house. He was passive and withdrawn, and didn't stick up for us."

Their mother, George said, tried to control everything, including an attempt to regulate what was taught in the parochial school the siblings attended. "My mom found herself being very active in what the curriculum was going to be, especially about morals, discipline, that kind of thing. Just going in and basically telling the nuns and priests how to do their job. You would see her show up, and she would have side talks with the nuns and priests. You know, other moms weren't coming and showing that kind of interest. It seemed fine at the time."

Mrs. Famalaro, he said, exerted a smothering influence to prevent the kids from participating in ordinary activities. "Don't venture out. Don't talk family business. Don't talk politics. Don't talk religion. Stay to ourselves. 'It is us against them' kind of situation." Other children in the neighborhood, George said, ". . . would have sleep-overs. We wouldn't. They could invite people to their house. We couldn't. We were definitely different."

Even while the family traveled in a car, their mother kept a tight rein on the three youngsters. Francine recalled the rule against whispering. "She would align herself in the back seat between two of us, and one child always sat in the front passenger seat. She would sit between the two in the backseat so we couldn't have a conversation." Whispering among the siblings, Francine said, was strictly prohibited.

To prevent painting an entirely dark picture of her home life as a child, Francine pointed out that there were some good times. "There were peaks and valleys. On some days, when she was up, we would have a wonderful day at Disneyland, and everyone was happy. It was like a normal, happy family. But the valleys . . . she had a very short fuse, I guess, if I had to describe it. Her tolerance was very low for anything she didn't agree with or think was the right thing to do."

The anger expressed by the children's mother took forms often more hurtful than a simple spanking. Francine wrestled with a description. "She would have an outburst or just psychologically cut [us] off I don't know how to describe that. Just a very cold effect like we didn't exist. You got the cold shoulder and that could go on for days. She wouldn't look at us, wouldn't talk to us for days." Often, Francine said, when her mother did choose to speak, she would transform the incident into a religious transgression. "She would make it a much more serious offense than it was in reality. So it became a more frightful thing."

One of the reasons the children couldn't have guests in the home, they recalled, stemmed from the embarrassingly messy interior. According to Francine, their mother had a remarkable habit of saving every piece of paper that came into the house, newspapers, periodicals, magazines, amassing huge stacks in every room. The laundry, Francine said, stood in piles four feet high. Boxes of unpacked junk brought from New York filled the garage. The mother seemed reluctant to dispose of trash. "She went through it piece by piece so she would know what the three of us were throwing away."

Certain rooms in the house were off limits to the children. "My folks had a master bedroom suite. We couldn't go in there because she had . . . all these piles of stuff. You could barely navigate through the room. There were other areas. We didn't go in the living room. We didn't sit on certain pieces of furniture."

While the disorderly stacks of newspapers and boxes kept the house in disarray, Mrs. Famalaro insisted on very orderly procedures for her children, according to Francine. No deviation could be allowed in the dining room seating order. For watching television in the family room, "We each had these stools, and she was in charge of the order. I was always in the middle, between the two boys, because I was the least rambunctious." Whenever the opportunity presented itself, Francine escaped the dining experience at home by eating at her grandmother's house.

Francine also suspected that her mother secretly developed a fondness for alcohol. "She would try to hide it from the kids. The big joke with John, George, and I was, she was going to have her 'juice.' Later, I found out that it wasn't juice. At some point, my dad came out of his weak state and just pretty much leveled with her to stop it now. And she did for a long time."

The tension and stress Francine felt became even worse as a result of George's treatment of their little brother. "George was tough. He didn't treat John very well. A lot of ridicule, making fun. He did the same with me, but not to the extent that he did with John because of age differences. George made fun of John's inability to do sports and everything from the size of his head to . . . little things. John was real uncoordinated, those kinds of things."

George did not entirely agree with the criticism. He might have teased his little brother, he said, but he wasn't deliberately cruel to the kid. "I certainly never beat him or anything like that."

The older brother's attitude caused Francine to draw even closer to John. She would never forget how sorry she felt for the little boy when he fell ill in 1960. "It touched me probably more than anything else. He was very sick, throwing up, and diarrhea. He was just very, very sick and he was laying in bed screaming for my mother. And she refused to go to him and wouldn't let me go help him." Francine hung her head as she recalled the incident, hiding the tears in her eyes.

The nearest thing to professional help ever obtained for John came when his mother began sending him to a tutor in an adjacent town. Once a week, Francine recalled, "We would go to Orange. I remember sitting in the car and waiting for him. Mrs. Klink was a school tutor [hired] to help him with his studies since he wasn't able to focus with that many kids in the classroom. We thought the one-on-one would help, and he really did bond with her. She was a very sweet, nurturing woman, and that seemed to help him."

John was very nervous and active, Francine said. He couldn't sit still, was always in constant motion. "You know, if I knew then what I know today, I would probably say he had attention deficit disorder. He was just constantly moving. He had to be entertained on a continual basis or he would run amok. There would be some kind of trouble that would ensue if you couldn't keep him in an organized activity."

Knitting her eyebrows as she looked back in time, Francine observed another oddity about the child. "He had a neck and head twitch that seemed to be exacerbated by some kind of stress or fretting over something. Sometimes he dreaded going to school, so like on a Monday morning, he would have that kind of a twitch." She commented that her mother had a similar twitch. "John's . . . started at the torso up through the neck area and head. Hers was strictly a facial twitch, and it wasn't continual.

It was just when she was escalating into one of her nervous deals."

Yet another trait about John seemed peculiar to Francine; an almost ritualistic compulsion. "If we were playing a game or I was sitting at the table helping him with his homework, and I would reach over and touch his hand, he would make me touch his other hand. It would be ever more so in ball games. If someone brushed his shoulder, he would have to have his other shoulder touched, so it would be even."

A female classmate of John Famalaro's, in St. Joseph's Elementary School, couldn't recall seeing him associating very much with other children on the wide, well-manicured lawns of Victoria Drive. "I don't remember him being outside playing. There were quite a few children in the neighborhood who got together and played, but I don't really remember him playing outside with us." When she did see the fragile child, she noted that, "He appeared to be a loner, a lot by himself."

Mrs. Famalaro, though, caught the attention of the eight-year-old girl in a different way. She later recalled, "I was walking my dog down the street and the dog lifted his leg and urinated on the sidewalk. Mrs. Famalaro came out of the home and scolded me. She told me to clean that up. So I had to go home and get a bucket and broom and come down to clean the sidewalk."

Another young girl who attended St. Joseph's School with John Famalaro also recalled that the boy sometimes seemed isolated and friendless. Her main recollection, though, related to seeing him with his family in church. They were very "focused," she said. "I know that I got in a lot of trouble during mass and as classmates we all tried to find each other. But the Famalaros remained together and very focused. John's head was straight ahead, never moved left or right."

Recollections of elementary school classmates dim with time, especially of colorless children. Few of John Famalaro's fellow students could find him in their memories, and those who did had only sketchy comments to offer. A classmate at Santiago Elementary School in Santa Ana described him. "I would say John was quiet. He was thin, kind of, I think the word I would use is awkward. You know, you had different kids that you would recognize as outgoing and some that were quieter and John was to himself." Recalling that some of the tougher kids often teased the meek ones, the classmate said, "John was teased. I don't know the extent as compared to anyone else, but I remember instances of John being teased." A smile flickered across the man's face as he searched his memory for an example and found one. "You know, there were nicknames. John was called 'Femalaro' you know, with an 'e,' because he was meeker than others. Even I had a nickname. I was called 'the earboy,' " he laughed.

Somehow, John's hyperactive streaks escaped serious notice by Mrs. Famalaro. She later recalled, "There was a friend of mine who, when she saw how hyper John was, suggested that we have someone look at him. Her husband was a doctor and she thought John was manic." The neighborly advice went unheeded. "I guess it went right through my head. I'm sorry to say, I just didn't think. I was so busy, you know, chasing George around and doing the work and just trying to raise three kids that probably, like Scarlett O'Hara, I would have taken care of it tomorrow. And I guess I never did, obviously."

There seemed to be general agreement that Mrs. Famalaro's favorite was George. Her comments about him give that impression. "George played the piano really well . . . in high school. He would win all the talent shows and so forth. I was very proud of him. I got very captivated with my children. As I look back, I was overly absorbed with them . . . They would go to church every Sunday, and they would pray. That evening, we would have a little play. Of course, George was the ring leader. He would come out and do his little acts, you know, and lead this little group that we had. They would follow George. He was the leader. It was a nice family at that time."

During Lent, she said, they went to church every day. "I felt I had to reward them. I would take them into Buffum's and get them a little treat. How wonderful they were, you know."

* * *

Neighbors observed that the Famalaros always kept the drapes closed in their home. Mrs. Famalaro expressed what she regarded as a logical reason. "Well, I kept the drapes in the family room closed because that's where the kids were playing all the time, and there was a lady in the backyard, and she would be behind her drape and peek into our house . . ." To clarify, she explained that the woman lived in a house abutting the rear of the Famalaro property and had a view from the upstairs window of an add-on room. "They built an upstairs . . . with a picture window that made us like a TV screen. They would be there looking at us."

In her rationale, Mrs. Famalaro didn't mention that she had reported the neighbors when the construction started, resulting in a six-month delay in the work to obtain building permits. Frazzled relations between the two families ensued when the Famalaros planted trees to block the view and the neighbors allegedly put salt at the base of the trees to kill them. Mrs. Famalaro complained to city officials again when the neighbors built a playhouse in their yard. The woman accused of spying from her upstairs window would later comment on Mrs. Famalaro's behavior regarding the completed playhouse. "She would water the trees and the water would go up in the air and come down on the children."

It has been said that more people have been killed in the name of religion than for any other reason. Certainly, religion has always been a matter of controversy and struggle. Some critics suggest that certain religious organizations keep their followers in poverty while the church hoards the wealth. Theologians ponder the tendency of humans to follow the creed of their chosen deity and adamantly hold that their faith is the only valid one, condemning all others as heretics or hellbound lost souls. Few compromises are made when it comes to strong religious beliefs.

For most believers, though, religious faith provides serenity, comfort in times of stress, and a path by which to guide one's life.

Religion played strong and diverse roles in the lives of two families, the Hubers and the Famalaros.

It especially affected the three children of Mrs. Famalaro, who professed extreme devotion to the Catholic Church. Francine tried to define how her mother used religion. "As a family, we always went to church on Sunday, which was great. Two of us went through eight years of St. Joseph's Catholic School in Santa Ana and that was a good experience. It was a good education." Francine's face tensed as she described her mother's application of religion in the family. "The way it got taken to extreme was again relating everything to religion, and you can't do anything wrong or you go to hell. And, you know, I have got to save your souls, that type of verbiage. It seemed a little odd to me at the time . . . [our mother] used religion more as a punishment rather than a Christian way of life."

Much later, Francine would make a startling observation about her mother's use of religion. "I now know that what she is is not religious. She was an eccentric religious person. I wouldn't call what she was being was really religious. She viewed herself that way. In other words, she talked it." The talk, in Francine's view, seemed empty and used only to advance selfish goals.

According to George, his mother held powerful religious beliefs, and did everything possible to inculcate her children with the same faith. Religion, he'd reportedly been told, provided a pathway to heaven, and ". . . a way to keep from going to hell. The Catholic Church was the only thing going. There was nothing else. As it got more and more to the right, conservative, it had to be Latin. It had to be a certain way. The Pope didn't know what he was doing any more. We started to know it was not a normal situation."

An incident at school caused George to question the compassion of priests and nuns. "I think it was in the seventh grade, I tried to hold a girl's hand. I was brought up in front of the whole student body assembly, in front of everybody. So was the girl. We were just humiliated by the priests and nuns."

George had hinted to his mother that he might become a priest, largely to please her. His sister recalled it. "He went to Our Lady Queen of Angels prep school in Los Angeles."

During his second year there, Mrs. Famalaro received a shock one day when she walked in his bedroom and allegedly found him masturbating. In his version of the story, George didn't mention being caught indulging in autoeroticism. "I went off to a seminary. I lasted two years, and damned near had a nervous breakdown. Had to get out." At age fifteen, he bailed out of the training for priesthood.

His decision and his sexual behavior severely disappointed his mother and caused her apparent favoritism to suffer a major setback. Mrs. Famalaro recalled that George came home one day, and announced he no longer wanted any part of the school. "And, of course, I was disappointed." After she had caught him indulging in sexual experimentation, she wondered what he was getting out of the Catholic school. "We realized he wanted out. So we let him out. He went to Santa Ana High School, and became the toast of the town." After that, she said, he became a "chronic liar."

Soon afterwards, upon his return to Santa Ana High School, George recognized in his mother a distinct change in her attitude towards him. "She pulled back emotionally and never was the same with me. I didn't do things the way she wanted me to . . . I bucked the system to try to have my own life, my own thoughts. She got kind of worn out after that . . . When I got to puberty, I got ostracized as the black sheep for not becoming a priest." The mother's apathy apparently extended to John as well. George theorized that Mrs. Famalaro could no longer summon the will and emotional strength to give much attention to young John, and that his father had also withdrawn from any bonding attachments. "I don't think there was a lot left to give to John."

The situation disillusioned George. "I think from my selfish standpoint at the time, when I felt that I was kind of . . . had this picture of myself paving the way for Francine and John, and I was going to stand up to tyrants. Look, we wanted to have friends, we wanted to choose our religion. When Mom would get mad at me and take it out on the family and turn them against me, I felt a little betrayed. They wouldn't see that I am trying to do this for all of us. I felt they kind of sold me down the river to just have a peaceful life."

Perhaps, George thought, his mother still wanted to have a son enter the priesthood, so she redirected the desire toward young John. The boy spent time in three Catholic schools, St. Joseph's, St. Michael's and St. Thomas Aquinas. He would never be a priest.

In John Famalaro's early years of parochial school, he conflicted with the nuns who ruled over the classrooms. According to Francine, "He was in trouble a lot in grammar school at St. Joseph's, in the very younger grades. Got sent home a lot. Parent-teacher conferences a lot. Phone calls from school. He didn't do awful things, but he just had an inability to sit still and focus on what was happening in the classroom at that time and disrupted the other kids. Therefore his grades were not good." In her attempt to help him past this stage, Francine set up a card table in his bedroom at home. "Every night we would sit and do his homework."

Interpersonal relationships at school also gave the youngster considerable trouble. According to John's sister, people made fun of him. She speculated that some of the teachers may have resented the child's inability to focus in the classroom. Other kids picked on him during the bus ride home. She tried to protect him as much as possible. "That's why I started riding the bus with him." She noted that John didn't seem to have any friends. "He was the weakling. He was the odd man out. He couldn't take care of himself. I threw people off buses for making fun of him. I was the violent one, I guess, because they were picking on him."

The abuse John experienced at the hands of other children rang a bell in George's mind, too. "My memory is him getting beaten up because he had a very, very, small frame. He was thin, very frail, kind of bent over. Francine and I, a couple of times on buses on the way home, needed to protect him."

No one could believe it when officials at St. Joseph's School expelled John from the fourth grade. Mrs. Famalaro said, "He got kicked out. It broke my heart, because I had tried so hard to make St. Joseph's work. George and Francine had gone through and everything was swell. George was a great speaker, and he did all these wonderful things. I was so shocked. I think it was Mrs. Gleason who threw him out. I didn't go to ask, 'What did he do?' I just felt if she threw him out, he must have done something, and we went on from there."

She had helped John in many ways, the mother said. "Oh, I read books with him. I think I am known as the book-reading mom, and they became great readers. Every one of them. We read constantly." She couldn't recall him having any trouble. "He was very interested and he would try." But sometimes, she recognized a certain moodiness in her youngest boy, unlike her first son, George. "George is very gregarious, outgoing. He can always tell everybody how to do everything. And Francine was quiet and reserved. She seemed to fit in with the two of them all right."

It still rankled the mother that George had dropped out of Catholic school and given up his preparatory training to become a priest. John did not have priesthood goals, but his mother encouraged his attendance at the parochial boarding school. "He went to St. Michael's and, in my opinion, I think he did very well there. He looked so nice. We would take him back up to school every Sunday night, and he seemed truly interested. And I think he was put on the academic decathlon one year."

During the period he attended the boarding school, Mrs. Famalaro observed something she hadn't noticed before in John. "You must remember, all we saw him was on the weekends. It seemed to me he was very interested about a lot of things . . . he seemed very intelligent. But I saw a thread going through there, very nervous, very sulky. Those things worried me." Comparing herself again to Scarlett O'Hara, Mrs. Famalaro in retrospect, said "I will take care of that tomorrow. You know. I guess poor John got caught up in all this and never got any help."

The troubles John experienced at St. Joseph's were left behind when he transferred to St. Michael's. Perhaps the opportunity to be housed with other boys five days each week in the boarding school had some influence. Francine observed, "My understanding was when he changed schools he improved all around as far as his grades and his initiative to try to do better and excel rather than cruise through."

George took a different view of why little brother John was sent to St. Michael's and that some expectations might go unrealized. "I think that our mother had hopes that John would pick up where I left off, hoping that he was finally going to do the right thing by becoming a priest. I think that would have bonded them more."

The pressures and problems did not prevent John from developing goals, though, while attending St. Michael's. Disappointment apparent in her voice inflections, his mother said, "He had about twenty goals. He was going to be a chiropractor. He was going to be a journalist. He was going to be a mortician. I think I put that one in his head. I said, 'George will treat the patient, and you bury them.' Big joke . . . big joke. Chiropractor. Journalist. He really meant well."

Chapter 10

If their mother's religion imploded on the children, they struggled even harder with her unconventional behavior in other matters. Mrs. Famalaro, according to her oldest son, washed her hands continually, scrubbing them for ten or fifteen minutes at a time. Her habits in doing laundry also tended to be rather unusual. "We had a new washer and dryer. But I don't think I ever saw it used. Everything was washed by hand, one article at a time, and carried out to line dry . . . come back in, wash a sock, carry it out, come back in, wash a shirt, carry it out. It wouldn't have been clean enough in the washer and dryer."

The three children tried to understand. But their mother's odd washing habits seemed no more comprehensible to them than her continual warnings about the world catastrophe they faced. George, his face glum, told of her verbal doomsaying. "Oh, the Russians were coming. Most of us were going to wind up in hell if we had any views other than her views. It was a very fearful perspective." Her way of expressing these admonitions, he said, was "hysterically manic. You could feel the energy coming at you. You had to do things her way as a kid, or you weren't going to make it."

Of course, his mother could show a loving side, under the right conditions. "When you were the exact clone of what you were supposed to be for her ideal, she was very loving." But if the children failed to conform, "You would feel the pull back and the abandonment. Total isolation. She would go to bed at two or three in the afternoon and leave us to fend for ourselves, ignore us, brush us off."

To deal with his mother's strange ways, George said, he tried hard to meet her expectations, tried to be "the good son." It generally worked. "I got all kinds of rewards and cookies and benefits. Lots of love." But it didn't last. His mother eventually withdrew the affection. "It felt awful. You know, it is tough to describe when you are shielded from the outside world, and all you have is looking to your mom. And your father is kind of quiet and passive. And when that [love] got yanked, it was just . . . it was huge. I didn't know what to do."

The elder son observed how his young sister and brother reacted. "Francine withdrew and went quiet, inward. She did the best she could, but became withdrawn. John seemed to go the other way and try to do what I did, which was to perform to please. He tried to make our mother happy. He saw that my methods didn't work, and he saw that Francine's methods didn't work, so I am sure he was struggling to find his own way."

To mention anything related to sex in the presence of their mother could bring down the wrath of doom. She absolutely forbid any such utterance in the Famalaro household. With a grim expression, George described it. "It was never talked about or brought up in our home . . . anything remotely related to sex. If you did it, you are in deep trouble, both in the family and spiritually later in life. She used the church as a club to be the enforcement mechanism." The suppression of sexual content also extended to entertainment. On television, the children could only watch cartoons and "Disney stuff." George recalled that his mother planted herself right next to them to assure they viewed nothing immoral or tinged with sex. If any allusion to the forbidden subject slipped into their television viewing, Mrs. Famalaro reacted instantly. "She would get real uncomfortable and squirmy." The depiction on the screen of any affection beyond holding hands, George said, would cause the mother to quickly shield their eyes or demand they tuck their heads down.

When Mrs. Famalaro took her children to movies, she carefully selected only the most innocuous family fare. Even in the dark theater, George said, she would react if she thought the

scene contained any provocative material. The children understood that when she jabbed them with a sharp elbow, it meant
for them to close their eyes or look at the floor, and to avoid
listening to the words being spoken by the actors.

Cleanliness was next to godliness, Mrs. Famalaro taught her
children. To be certain they understood, she personally saw to
their cleanliness, but with a strange twist. Even with her preach-
ing about the necessity of clean bodies, according to George and
Francine, she allowed them to bathe only once each week, on
Sundays. And she personally administered the baths.

Clearly uncomfortable with the subject, George explained the
process. "One by one, on Sunday nights, [we] would be taken
into the bathroom, and given baths." The ritual continued even
as the children approached puberty. "She would put us in the
tub and scrub us to make sure we were clean enough." Her
personal scrubbing of the boys, according to George, included
close attention to their genitals. Asked if he noticed anything
about his mother when she performed those ablutions, George
spoke with hesitation. "She . . . got different. It was more like . . .
an unconscious thing." His mother, he said, seemed to rationalize that the genitals were a very sensitive area and she wanted
to make sure that it was cleaned right. "Maybe I was starting to
get self-conscious, so it seemed like it was more than what was
needed or necessary. Her breathing changed. It was kind of escalated. Looking back now, it just felt like an energy surge of
some kind."

Normal sexual urges of children were not allowed to exist in
the Famalaro household, said George. Francine also later discussed the issue of masturbation, when she learned that most
young boys experiment with it. She said that her mother never
explained anything about sex to her. In retrospect, Francine recognized that Mrs. Famalaro may have been trying to prevent her
sons from indulging in autoeroticism. "I didn't relate it to that
at the time. I didn't know what it was. But I know she hovered
outside their bedroom doors at night, listening, because I could
see her from my room, at George's door. And she would be real
quiet, and all of a sudden barge into the room, you know. Scared
the hell out of him. Later, I sort of figured out that was probably

what she was trying to do, [be a] detective." In her childish ignorance of sexuality, Francine said she wondered what her brother was doing to attract that kind of attention from her mother. "I thought maybe he was playing cards in there. I didn't know what he was doing."

The forbidden issue of sex would become even worse as the children grew older.

In the sixties and seventies, most schools provided very skimpy sex education, if any. Mrs. Famalaro later described her personal attempts to deal with such matters as sex education. "Well, that was something that bothered me then. The free love thing really got to me. I cannot handle free love . . . At that time I would try to keep them immune from getting into that." She expressed sarcasm at some of the contemporary nineties methods. "Go pass out a condom and, here, have a good time. I couldn't get into that culture. And so I would take them here or take them there, and try to reward them in other ways."

The mother especially resented George's relationships with teenage girls. "He would get a girlfriend, and another girlfriend, and another girlfriend, and call them equally, he loves them all. I couldn't handle that. To me, this was sneaky stuff. So we began to have our fights over that."

Extremely concerned about George's dalliances with girls, Mrs. Famalaro decided to spy on him one night. "I had some little advance thing that I overheard on the phone. I thought, 'Okay, George, I am going to catch you red-handed.' I hid in the back of his car. I mean, that was real scary." During her covert operation, the mother neither saw nor heard anything salacious, sexual, or "red-handed" with which to confront her amorous son.

But such incidents seemed to turn Mrs. Famalaro away from George, who had occupied much of her attention. Disillusionment took over in the home. She recalled it, bitterness in her voice, describing the situation as a chaotic environment. She seemed to regret the effect on both of her younger children. "It was a sad thing. Francine and John got together to put on an anniversary [dinner]—I don't remember what anniversary it was. But they baked a ham and they did all these things for my husband and me. And I was like the woman who goes looking for the lost sheep . . . looking for George. Where is George? Francine and John said they were never going to do anything again for us because all I cared about was George. It wasn't true. But it got on their nerves. If you heard your mother arguing constantly with George to try to walk the straight and narrow . . . I know it got on Francine and John's nerves very much. The two of them paid a high price for my having George in that house."

George, in addition to receiving piano lessons, also became a student of martial arts, Mrs. Famalaro recalled with some anger. "He was a karate expert at age fifteen. Once, he threw a karate chop at me." When asked if he had hit her, she choked back her cynicism, and chuckled. "No, I ducked real well."

John also took karate lessons, but his mother recalled that he was gentle, non-violent, and not as selfish as his brother. "He was always engaged in doing something for someone else. For instance, at Christmas time, when he was in his second year of high school, he went over to Montgomery Ward at Honor Plaza. With all the little money he made on his various jobs, he would buy presents for everybody. And he never really seemed to care if he received any presents."

Recalling that she tried to inculcate her children with not only high morals and a sense of personal responsibility, Mrs. Famalaro said she wanted them to learn the proper work ethic, too. "I thought if they had little jobs it would make them responsible and they could save money and do various things. So John started out as a little gardener up the street. He was around thirteen." The boy performed gardening chores for a neighbor for a few months. "Then he developed on to a busboy, and then a very first-class waiter."

Her voice brightening to a proud chirp, Mrs. Famalaro recalled an incident during John's tenure as a waiter that involved a famous comedian. "Tim Conway came in one night where John was working and John, with his little sense of humor, did that little walk up to him. Tim Conway thought that was pretty cute. Just a little thing I remember."

Encouraging her children to take jobs had a double edge, Mrs. Famalaro said, sounding a note of irritation. One of her main goals in rearing her offspring was to keep them away from sinful desire. "While I'm getting them away from the temptations of school, I forgot there's people on the job, too, and there's different temptations that may be even bigger ones. I've committed a lot of sins in all that, all with good intentions. It backfired on me. Their little jobs backfired . . . in the sense that they probably became more worldly than with the little junky things these other kids were doing."

Her retrospective analysis seemed to bring Mrs. Famalaro to the realization that in hindsight, it's easier to see how to avoid mistakes. "You see, isn't it wonderful how smart you get later."

Of John's multifaceted personality characteristics, no one seemed to notice another trait he had inherited from his mother—an urge to save books, newspapers, news clips, and printed material about subjects that caught his interest, never disposing of anything.

Curiosity about sex grew in George Famalaro's mind as he reached puberty, in spite of his mother's efforts to protect him from exposure to anything she regarded as prurient or lurid. Scientists in the field have suggested that a repressive environment may very well increase the curiosity of children. In George's case, he found a channel of expression by digging through neighbors' trash and retrieving discarded *Playboy* magazines. Needing a place of solitude to examine the magazine's contents, George entered an abandoned house on Broadway, a few blocks from his home on Victoria Drive and hid his purloined treasures in a closet. When he could sneak away from his family, he would hurry to the empty house, sit on the floor, and turn the pages slowly while examining the photographs of nude women.

Later asked at what age his sexual interests became known to him, he replied, "Seventh or eighth grade. I wouldn't say sexual, just attracted to girls and would want to hold their hands or kiss them, or. . . ." His voice faded and stopped. After some more thought, considering his mother's attempts to shield him, he added, "Because of the energy and the stigma placed on it, it became larger than life. It's kind of hard to describe . . . like don't think of a pink elephant." Of course, anyone who is told not to think of a pink elephant immediately forms a mental image of one, to the exclusion of most other thoughts.

It is human nature to seek the forbidden. George expressed it as, "When that is hammered on you on a daily basis, that issue becomes larger." The forbidden becomes irresistible.

Accusations would one day be made that George took his little brother and his sister to the abandoned house, showed them his treasure trove of explicit magazines, and allegedly attempted to lure them into masturbation. He denied it, but eventually acknowledged that they did go to the house with him.

Following high school, George resolved to escape the unhappiness of the Famalaro household. He left Southern California to attend Palmer Chiropractic College in Davenport, Iowa. At last separated from his family, and the associated internal conflict always boiling below the surface at home, George Famalaro could concentrate on his studies.

The campus environment, for George, felt cleansing like a breath of cornbelt-country fresh air. At age nineteen, he could lift away the smothering blanket of sexual repression that had inhibited his ability to find female companionship, and openly look at college co-eds without guilt. One fall morning, a bright, wispy classmate with brick-colored hair caught his attention more than others. Nothing like the voluptuous women portrayed in his secret cache of *Playboy* magazines, Velma Finch wore conservative clothes over her slim frame, and cropped her hair in a pageboy style.

After the first tentative conversations with Velma, George felt powerfully attracted to her. They were the same age and shared common intellectual levels. She listened to him as no one had before, and offered riveting companionship. He told her all about his little brother, sister, and his easy-going father. And he told her about his mother. She would soon learn, firsthand, about Mrs. Famalaro, first through phone calls and subsequently through dramatic personal contact.

With a hint of bitterness in her voice, Velma later described the encounters. "George's mother would call me at odd hours of the night, angrily not wanting me to have a relationship with her son, calling me his paramour, that type of thing."

The mother's wrath, though, failed to disrupt the budding lovers' relationship. Velma fell in love with George, and he apparently returned her affection. Mrs. Famalaro, unwilling to be defied, found a bigger sledgehammer in her attempt to drive a wedge between the couple. According to Velma Finch, the irate mother threatened to stop financing George's education if he refused to end his affair with "that woman." Love, it has been said, conquers all. Velma, rather than lose her beloved George, chose to give up her education. "I dropped out of school to help put him through because his mother threatened to stop funding his college career because of me." They agreed to be married in 1974 following his graduation.

Still unwilling to accept defeat, Mrs. Famalaro made one more gambit. According to Finch, she persuaded George that he would be more successful if he would set up his chiropractic practice in Southern California. That would mean, of course, that he would be required to pass the board exams there. His mother offered her personal support if he would return home to study for the boards, while Velma temporarily waited in Iowa.

Not entirely happy with the arrangement, and worried that the separation might damage the relationship, Velma finally agreed to the plan.

At the graduation ceremony she finally met Mrs. Famalaro, who brought her younger son, John, to Davenport to watch George accept his diploma. The meeting did nothing to ease Velma's fears. She felt miserable when he returned to his mother's home.

Disillusioned and lonely, Velma met someone else that summer. The new relationship blossomed, so she notified George that she wanted to end their engagement.

Having been totally immersed in passing his boards and setting up practice with a partner, George hadn't paid as much attention to his fiancé in Iowa as he should have. Not wanting to lose her, he sent flowers and cards begging her to reconsider.

* * *

At the same time George Famalaro studied at Palmer Chiropractic College in Davenport, Iowa, his sister made plans for leaving home to also attend college. Sick of her mother's eccentricities, Francine wanted out. She could no longer stomach the threats of going to hell for the slightest infractions of behavior, the constant control of every move and thought, or the turmoil of never knowing what would happen next. "One day when I got home from school, there was a for-sale sign in front of our house. I didn't know we were moving. But when I asked for an explanation, she told me we were getting out of this society and heading to the hills because the Russians were coming! So that night, I went to bed with mental pictures of these big boots tromping down the street, the red army kind of deal. Those kinds of extremes. We are going to get out of the United States . . . before this happens. [Mother] even saved food so that when the world ended, she wanted to make sure we had some food for enough time to sustain ourselves when somebody bombed us. And she saved silver coins. She thought that once we went to a one-world money system, that we would need those coins to barter for food when there was no longer a society to be able to function in and buy commodities."

Impatiently, Francine waited. When she reached college age, she decided to join her brother George at the chiropractic school in Davenport. He had already been there two years, and she envied his independence. At last, she thought, she would be free of the suffocating constraints continually imposed by her mother. All through high school, Mrs. Famalaro directed every move, denied Francine the chance to make any personal decisions, and had even selected every item of clothing the young woman wore. A neighbor would recall that the Famalaro girl "stood out. She was very tall and always wore very long skirts."

Now, Francine would be able to pick out her own dresses, jeans, and shoes, like any teenager. If she chose to whisper, or to shout, it wouldn't be a violation of mother's rules. She might even find out what it was like to go on a date.

Dating, for the young woman, had been out of the question. Her mother made that clear with the suggestion that dating boys would make Francine an "impure" person, "even if noth-

ing happened." George, on the other hand, had been allowed
to take girls out while he was in high school, which didn't seem
fair to Francine, even though she recognized that stringent re-
strictions were imposed on her brother regarding his relations
with girls. Mrs. Famalaro had always insisted on knowing who
George would be with, where they were going, and what he
planned to do. She monitored George's telephone conversations with his girlfriends and even followed him. With some
bitterness, Francine recalled, "It turned into a new obsession.
Her whole focus shifted to him, who he was seeing, and she
never liked whoever that was."

Relocation to another state would not only allow Francine to
date whom she pleased, but would open a whole new world of
previously prohibited opportunities.

Certainly, Francine realized, her mother would resist allowing
her to move to Iowa to attend college. That would mean relin-
quishing the all-important control. Every aspect of all three of
the siblings' lives had come under their mother's scrutiny. Mrs.
Famalaro would search their bedrooms, examine the contents
of their desks, and read anything they had written. If she found
anything that could be interpreted as immoral, or a violation of
her rules, she would administer punishment. According to
Francine, some infractions earned a whipping with a belt. The
boys, she recalled, were the recipients of most spankings.

None of the three children could have any privacy. When they
used the phone, Francine said, Mrs. Famalaro would listen on
an extension.

By moving away, Francine figured, she could shrug off the
bonds, and even take a bath more frequently than Sunday nights.
She would never forget the strange weekly ritual of being bathed
by her mother. Francine couldn't recall when her mother had
allowed her to start bathing alone, but she knew that she was
"large in the bathtub" when it finally happened.

Eagerly anticipating the new freedom and independence,
Francine packed her clothes for the move to Iowa. She nearly

fainted when Mrs. Famalaro announced her intention to accompany her daughter to Iowa and live with her!

Since the only remaining child, John, was attending St. Michael's parochial boarding school, Mrs. Famalaro had no motherly duties to perform at home. She seemed certain that Francine not only needed her, but would welcome the opportunity to have her mother as a roommate at college.

Crushed, Francine could find no way out of the arrangement. They traveled to Iowa and found lodging together. Recalling the predicament, Francine said, "When I got to college, I actually wanted to go to a party or two. I never did anything in high school. I didn't date. So once I got to college, I really thought it might be time to get a social life. That's when our conflicts started."

It lasted only a few months. Asked years later if her mother had left her, Francine quickly interrupted with "I left her!" Unable to cope with the choking tethers strapped on by Mrs. Famalaro, Francine worked up the courage to rebel. Her mother angrily returned to Santa Ana. Painfully looking into her past, Francine later said, "She totally cut me off because I told her it would be a more normal event in life if I could go to college by myself, and she could go take care of John and my father."

Contact with her family, however, had not been completely severed. Even though communication with Mrs. Famalaro halted, Francine stayed in touch with her father and younger brother. "Dad would write me letters and occasionally stick twenty dollars in an envelope to help me." Sporadically, she heard from John, too. Until George returned to California, Francine also saw him periodically.

Without financial support, Francine found it difficult to continue in college. She began dating a young man, fell in love, and married him. Mrs. Famalaro did not attend the wedding. Later, when Francine underwent major surgery, the mother didn't even bother to make a telephone call. Eventually, Francine obtained a degree in nursing. Not until 1980 did she, and her children, return to California.

By that time, her chiropractor brother, George, was in extremely serious trouble.

* * *

With Francine living in Iowa, and George deeply involved in his fledgling chiropractor business, Mrs. Famalaro could focus most of her attention on John. High school graduation often provides proud parents with the opportunity to lavish gifts on their maturing teenagers, to reward scholastic achievement, to encourage them to attend college, or to make them the envy of their peers. Mrs. Famalaro chose to give her son John a trip to Europe. Of course, she would go with him. Just the two of them, mother and son, doing the grand tour.

In the summer of 1975, she and John spent two months seeing the sights. She recalled, "He knew all the ropes, where to take me, what to do." One incident she remembered frightened her. "We nearly got ripped off, I think in Venice, by a couple of Italian ruffians. We had our luggage on top of the vehicle, and John and I seemed to read each other's minds. We looked at each other and these guys were going to take us. We got off where we weren't scheduled to get off. We had a good rapport. John and I were okay." She acknowledged, though, that she and her son had a few differences of opinion. "Oh, I guess during the trip we had some arguments like any two people would."

Following their return to Santa Ana, John enrolled in college at St. Thomas Aquinas, in the colorful Old West town of Calabasas where the Hubers had joined a Presbyterian church group and met lifelong friends Dick and Nancy Streza.

At the school, John met a young woman named Helen Lyons, and promptly fell in love. Mrs. Famalaro commented: "May I tell you a little thing? I think once again I made a mistake. I always meant well. When John went to St. Thomas Aquinas—because of the girl factor at St. Michaels, not being any girls, I said, 'John, I hope that when you go—,' these words are going to come back and bite me really hard, I said, '—I hope that when you go to St. Thomas that you meet a nice Catholic girl.' I sound like a Jewish mother. Well, John did that. And John had not only met a really nice Catholic girl, he became obsessed with her. Obsessed!"

George regretted leaving Velma Finch behind at Palmer College in Iowa, and continued to plead with her to resume their relationship. Velma, emotionally confused, still felt the embers of love for him. Torn between two lovers, and wondering if the new romance was only the result of being on the rebound, she agreed to make a trip to Santa Ana. Velma hoped that the reunion with George would help her make the right decision.

As she recalled it, "George made arrangements at a motel on 17th Street, not far from his home." In a commercial section of Santa Ana, the motel sat close to the noisy I-5 freeway, with fast food restaurants and a few bars within walking distance. Travelers seeking romantic solitude probably would look elsewhere. There were several nicer inns within walking distance of the Famalaro home on Victoria Drive, but they might have been too close for comfort, considering Mrs. Famalaro's opinion of her son's girlfriend.

Velma stayed two weeks at the motel, during which she still experienced mixed emotions, but felt the old passion for George once again. One evening near the end of her stay, they double-dated for dinner with George's new partner and his wife. It would be an evening permanently and indelibly etched in Velma's memory. "After dinner, George and I went back to the motel. I think we had a few drinks. And then George left. About a half hour later, there was a knock on the door."

Velma asked who was there. A female voice identified herself as the wife of George's chiropractic partner, with whom Velma had shared dinner that same evening. The voice, sounding distressed, said, "Quick, quick, let me in. Someone is after me."

Confusion and fear gripped Velma, who had already gone to bed, wearing only a thin nightgown. "I was suspicious. I really just—I didn't know what to do." The voice didn't sound like the woman she'd met earlier, so Velma answered, "Can you show me some identification?"

The voice screeched, "For God's sake, let me in quick. Someone is after me." Unable to turn away another woman in trouble, Velma opened the door a crack, and instantly fell back as the woman outside slammed against the door, pushed it wide open, and barged into the room.

It was George's mother!

"She entered the room. She had a coat on and she had—it was February, and she had her hands in the coat pocket. She was flapping the coat pocket, and she proceeded to look around the room."

The older woman, who professed such deep religion and conservatism, launched into a verbal tirade that stunned Velma Finch. According to Finch, Mrs. Famalaro yelled, "You love to fuck my son. You love to suck my son."

"The more she got into this, the more agitated she became. I looked up at her once, and she slapped me across the face. Then I sat on the bed, and she proceeded to tell me that I was going to die that night; that she had a long life, and she didn't care whether she lived or not. But that I was not going to have her son. And she said that I shouldn't leave the room, because if I left, she had already paid someone across the street to shoot me. Next, I don't remember her words, but she said something to do with the Virgin Mary. And she got off on to a religious tangent. She went from sex to religion. Then, I finally just thought, 'I guess I am going to die tonight.' "

As panic raced through her, Velma wondered what she needed to do to survive. She cried, "What do you want me to do? I will catch a plane. I'll leave tonight. I'll never see your son again. I will go away. I will go back to Iowa."

As Velma recalled the incredible encounter, she trembled. "Her response was—I remember it well because it sounded like a dime novel." According to Velma, Mrs. Famalaro said, "No. It is too late for you. You are going out tonight, sister. There is nothing you can do at this point. You are going to die tonight."

In the grip of mortal fear, Velma thought, *Oh my God. Here I am, twenty-three years old, and in a motel. No one is going to know. They are going to find this body, and she is probably going to take my identification, and that will be it.* "I sat there kind of like a rabbit for a while. And then I couldn't take it any more. And I said,

'How are you going to do this?' She lunged at me and got on top of me on the bed and began to choke me."

For a few moments, Velma said, she lay there, unable to breathe. "The room started getting a little fuzzy. And then something snapped in me, thank God. I doubled up my knees and was able to push her off me temporarily. I ran towards the door. She grabbed my nightgown, but at this point I didn't care if she tore it off. I ran out the door and she did lose her grip on my nightgown. And I ran down the stairs, into the motel lobby office.

"There was a family that ran the motel and they were watching some black and white movie on television. I ran into the living room and yelled, 'My God, my God, someone is trying to kill me! Someone is trying to kill me! Call the police.' "

As Velma recalled it, Mrs. Famalaro had apparently attempted some early subterfuge with the motel managers. Standing before them, clad only in her nightgown, Velma heard the man say, "No. No. Your mother is here, and she wanted to know what room you were in. Your mother was here to visit you."

Nearly hysterical, Velma choked out her reply to the manager. "No. My God, that is not my mother. She is trying to kill me." At last, the man understood, and called for emergency help. The police arrived within minutes. Velma also called for George, who rushed over with his father. Mrs. Famalaro, remarkably, remained just outside the motel office door, pacing back and forth.

"When the police arrived, they asked me what had happened. I told them. They looked at my neck and said, 'Well, you don't have any scratch marks.' " Feeling that everyone must be against her, Velma asked, 'Well, you know, what was I supposed to do? Wait until she killed me?'

The uniformed officer asked the trembling young woman if she wanted to press charges. "I looked at George, and he nodded his head. So I said, 'Yes, I do.' "

Extending her stay in Santa Ana to put the wheels of justice in motion, Velma waited. But, she recalled, George approached her about a week later, and requested, for his father's sake, that Velma drop the charges. He pointed out that in court, it would be just Velma's word against the denials of Mrs. Famalaro. And the messy business would drag down the family name. She said that George implored her, as a favor to his father, to not carry it any further.

Confused and hurt, Velma Finch agreed not to pursue any legal recourse.

Her acquiescence apparently pleased George. They resumed their relationship and talked again about marriage. But troubling signs in George's behavior caused Velma to gradually wonder if she had made the right decision. She convinced him that they should see a professional counselor. In nearby Garden Grove, they met with a doctor who administered a battery of psychological tests. The results helped her make a final decision. The relationship ended in 1976.

George, Velma would later say, was not a truthful person. She described him as "sociopathic," which she defined as "very smooth, very charming, but without a great sense of right and wrong. No true conscience." He was a person with two sides, she said. "His attitude toward life was that people wanted to be taken and that women were generally stupid."

Eventually, Velma married someone else, but would suffer distress for many years over the nightmare in Santa Ana, and the terror she felt from the attack by Mrs. Famalaro. "It has never gone away. I have had a non-published number for years. Only in the last few years have I had a telephone number that is listed, but it is in my married name. And to this day, I would fear for my life around that woman."

Chapter 11

By mid-1978, George Famalaro had recovered from his broken romance with Velma Finch and replaced her with a new girl-friend, whom he subsequently married. She worked for him at his successful chiropractic business in El Toro, about ten miles from the site where Denise Huber's Honda would be abandoned thirteen years later.

George's mother, incensed at her perception of burgeoning smut and pornography in the community, struggled to curtail the alarming growth. She organized pickets against abortion and led a campaign to shut down a movie theater specializing in sex films. Serving on a civil service personnel board and participating in several private organizations, including the Republican Women's Club of Santa Ana and the Freedom Foundation of Valley Forge, she crusaded against moral corruption. An admirer said, "She's a very wonderful woman. She did a lot of good community work." Bolstered by the accolade and encouraged by an acquaintance, she eventually tossed her hat into the political ring as a candidate for a seat on the Santa Ana City Council.

As a chiropractor, George treated patients of various ages, both sexes. One of them, a youngster, Artie George, had been experiencing migraine headaches for two years, and first came to Dr. Famalaro's office about a week before his tenth birthday, in late October 1979. The child's mother brought him to the chiropractor for the first visit, and the two waited among other patients for about half an hour. During the session in the treatment room, the boy was alone with the doctor.

That day, the child said nothing about his treatment. But after several more visits, Artie's odd reactions to his sessions with the doctor caught his mother's attention. She later reported that the lad started behaving strangely when she took him to the chiropractor. He'd beg not to return, crying, "I don't want to come back here anymore."

Finally, Artie confided in his older brother that the doctor had asked the boy to remove his clothes during the visits, and had touched his private parts.

Stunned and sickened by his kid brother's report, the older brother instructed Artie to "tell Mom and Dad." On January 14, 1980 the boy revealed to his mother what had been happening. She telephoned the Orange County Department of Social Services, who in turn contacted the sheriffs department. Investigator Fred Geller spoke with Artie's mother, who said that she understood the sexual contacts had happened during about one-half of the visits to Dr. Famalaro. The boy, she said, had never even heard of oral copulation before his contacts with the chiropractor.

On the day before Valentine's Day, in 1980, Detective Geller, accompanied by another investigator, entered Dr. Famalaro's office in El Toro. They asked him to voluntarily come to the Orange County Sheriff's Office. He complied. When he arrived there, the officers placed him under arrest. He invoked his Miranda rights, refusing to speak to them, and demanded the presence of his attorney.

An article in the *Los Angeles Times* about the arrest of the El Toro chiropractor, Dr. George Famalaro, caught the attention of young Dolly Williams, age sixteen. She reported that she had also been a victim of the doctor. Disgusted at the report of his accosting a young boy, she decided to tell the police about her treatment at the hands of Famalaro.

Three months later, George Famalaro sat through a grand jury hearing to determine if he should face trial for sexual contacts with two minor patients. His attorney managed to bring out some conflicts in the statements of the alleged victims, and a few circumstances that the lawyer hoped might mitigate the charges. Nonetheless, after they'd weighed the evidence, the grand jury returned an indictment against George Famalaro, charging him with sexual crimes against both young victims. In the early part of that summer, Famalaro underwent a trial in the Orange County Superior Court. On July 9, 1980, the jury found him guilty of the charges. But he would not face hard time in a state prison. After testimony by several psychiatrists about Famalaro's mental status, he was confined in Patton State Hospital, with a maximum release date of November 11, 1989.

George Famalaro would spend two and one-half years in the hospital before being released on probation.

Notoriety stemming from publicity about George's conviction for sexual molestation reportedly ended the political career of his mother.

John Famalaro visited his brother periodically during the confinement, but labored to form his own destiny. Neither George, their father, nor any other man set persuasive patterns for him to follow. Conversely, women had already played extremely influential roles in the life of John, and would continue to do so. His mother, sister, and grandmother had already exerted immeasurable impact on his early life. Their influence would endure, complemented by a host of casual acquaintances and romances that would lift him to euphoric heights and drop him to abysmal depths.

To Francine, John made remarkable changes during his stay at St. Michael's, under the influence of priests and nuns. She would later say that when he completed high school, and went to work at a restaurant near Disneyland, his social skills improved even more.

A flaxen-haired waitress at the restaurant held him in high regard. In looking back to the mid-1970s, she recalled becoming acquainted with John while he still attended college and worked five nights a week as a busboy. "He was a young man full of humor, full of fun, and he worked hard. I always knew him to be funny and lively, and yeah, he was hyper. He did his job well and was very helpful to everybody. We, the other waitresses and busboys, all liked him. He was always busy planning his life, thinking about the future and thinking about studies, about finances, and how he was going to work out his future."

The waitress grew fond of the genial young man and they developed a kinship. "He asked me if he could stay at my house while he was in the process of moving to Glendale," she said, noting that he planned to attend chiropractic college in the city thirty miles north of Santa Ana.

John's maternal grandmother, the waitress recalled, held a big place in John's heart. "They were very close. John being the baby in the family, I guess, he loved his grandma." Shortly after Famalaro moved out of his parents' home in Santa Ana, the waitress said, "He moved in with me, and his grandmother called. Then he asked me if I would help him bring his grandma out and find her a place to live. He didn't have a place to bring her yet, and he wanted to rent an apartment where she could live with him. So we went in my little VW one afternoon to his former home and we picked his grandmother up."

Inside the home, the helpful woman made some observations: "It was strange. Very strange. There was one room that had no furniture in it. It was a beautiful house and there was a pileup of things covered with white sheets. I wondered what was under them. John opened some closets and I saw a lot of paper towels stacked up to the top. And there were Bible scriptures on the refrigerator and the kitchen wall."

The grandmother had already packed, and was waiting for them. "We left very quickly and went to my house. We gave his grandmother the spare bedroom and John slept on the couch for about a week. Then my ex-husband rented her a room for a short time, then I think John and his grandmother moved to Glendale together."

George Famalaro would later comment that the grandmother going to live with John was kept from Mrs. Famalaro. She wouldn't have accepted the arrangement at all. "No, no, no," he said, "That was a definite undercover operation."

* * *

During the period of time John and the waitress were friends, she renewed her interest in Christianity and often discussed the subject with him. "He had quite a bit of knowledge about Christian writings and the belief itself. So he gave me good advice about reading certain books. We went to a seminar together, which was his idea, and had a lot of fun doing that. He was a believer, a very deep believer, but I think he was very preoccupied with his schooling and his future, that it was not predominant. His mind was always like ten feet ahead of him. I think he had so many plans for his future that he was totally busy. He never took time to sit down and watch TV. He was always busy with schooling, work, and planning his future."

Another aspect of John's makeup impressed her, his generosity. After he'd been working at the restaurant a couple of years, he bought his father a Cadillac. John's sister Francine, recalled the remarkable gift. "He bought my dad a Cadillac. Dad had always wanted one, and John just felt like it would be a real treat for Dad's last driving years, to be able to have that and feel important."

One day, John showed up with a girl he wanted the waitress to meet. He introduced Helen Lyons as his girlfriend. "They had been to the beach or somewhere for an outing. She was a real natural kind of looking girl, and real sweet." They had met while attending classes at St. Thomas Aquinas college in Calabasas.

According to George, John was bitten hard by the love bug with Helen Lyons. "They were very close. They seemed really into each other. I know John was very much in love with her, talked about her all the time in very favorable terms. Really was close to her."

The love affair would be a turning point in the life of John Famalaro.

Still trying to decide what to do with his life in the early eighties, John made a decision to follow in his brother's footsteps and become a chiropractor, but not at the same school. While still enrolled at St. Thomas Aquinas, and spending as much time as possible with Helen, he enrolled in 1980 at Cleveland Chiropractic College in Los Angeles, between downtown and Hollywood. Also working part time to support himself, he took the necessary classes in 1980 and 1981.

Several of Famalaro's classmates, who rode buses to the school and arrived an hour before the first session, often gathered at about 6 A.M. across the street from the school at a coffee and donut shop. On the morning of August 13, 1981, John joined two of the students he recognized to make the short walk for coffee. En route, they passed two scruffy-looking men who seemed to be in a dispute over a bicycle. They stepped around the arguing pair, entered the cafe, and seated themselves over coffee to discuss last night's homework. One of the street thugs, tattered, unshaven, and apparently under the influence of booze or drugs, swaggered into the coffee shop, mumbled something, and began waving a knife. As Famalaro's two classmates leaped for shelter, he stood, confronted the hoodlum, and pulled a canister of mace from his pocket. The spray had no effect. Simultaneously, the cafe owner rushed from behind the counter, wielding a broomstick. Famalaro took it from him and used it as a lance to force the thug outside. Still not satisfied, Famalaro followed him and pushed him over the bike that had been the object of the earlier dispute.

A few minutes later, as the trio of students walked outside, they spotted the assailant again across the street, still behaving in a belligerent manner. They watched as he approached a woman standing at a bus stop, put his arm around her neck in a choke hold, and held the knife to her ribs. John Famalaro dropped the donuts he was carrying, and dashed in a straight line toward the attacker. As the woman screamed hysterically, Famalaro, a few feet from the struggling pair, dove through the air, grabbed the assailant's arm, wrestled the knife away, and using what appeared to be martial arts techniques, slammed him to the ground. One of the classmates arrived, and helped Famalaro pin the thug to the ground until police arrived.

The trio of excited students still managed to be on time for the first lesson that morning.

Over the next few months, Famalaro completed the required

curriculum to become a chiropractor. In the early part of 1982, he appeared at the school to take the final licensing examinations. One of the men who had been with him in the cafe the previous August sat close by.

As the exams were about to commence, the companion noticed that John Famalaro excused himself to go to the restroom.

He never returned. He never took the exams. He gave up the idea of being a chiropractor.

In May 1983, John Famalaro chose to give another profession a try. He filled out an application to become a reserve deputy with the Orange County Sheriff's Department. That night, in his bedroom, he wrote about it. "Early this morning, I went to the Orange County Sheriff's orientation and testing regimen to gain entrance to the academy. I was the only one out of the group, applying for uniformed officer, who passed that day. After all was said and done, I think they were more impressed with me than I was with them. It is a long-standing point of common knowledge or rumor that L.A.P.D. is far superior to the L.A. County Sheriff's or Orange County Sheriff's Department. The sheriff's departments always deny it and point to one thing or the other as proof for their argument. But I must say, as an outsider, who doesn't have a vested interest in any of the departments, I am becoming less and less impressed with the Sheriffs' Departments of both counties. In the orientation and testing experiences I have had with both of them, we are talking 'shabby' displays. L.A.P.D. on the other hand impresses me greatly, and has since the first day. They seem to have superior people, superior training, and certainly superior facilities. Their academy is ranked among the top in the world." He added that he'd have to make up his mind pretty quick about which one he would choose to work for.

Within a week, Famalaro paid a visit to the LAPD personnel department and took more tests. "The guy in personnel told me he had never seen anyone get straight one hundred percent before. He was pretty surprised . . . It should be a kick going through the rest of their processing." It would be a kick Famalaro would never experience, for reasons of his own.

He selected, instead, to pursue the Orange County Sheriff's Department. After he passed written and physical examinations, interviews, and a physical agility test, his name appeared on the short list for acceptance. But Famalaro failed to contact the department within a specified time frame, and was dropped as a candidate. It would later be suggested that a broken romance had driven him into such depression that he lost interest in the effort. The influence of a woman once again changed the course of his life.

Apparently, Famalaro's desire to enter the law enforcement field flared up again a few months later. In November 1983, he gained acceptance to the Los Angeles Sheriff's Academy for the six-month training program to become a deputy. As a cadet, he was issued a class A uniform, and probably bought a class B washable uniform to be used in bad weather or other circumstances inappropriate for the dress clothing.

After completing four months of the training, one of his knees swelled up. He went to his brother, George, for examination and treatment. In March, two months short of graduation, Famalaro turned in the issued uniform, kept the ones he bought, and walked away from the academy, giving up his chance to become a full-fledged member of the sheriff's department.

Twice more, Famalaro subsequently stepped forward to make a stab at becoming a police officer. He made another application to the OCSD, and let it time out again. Finally, in 1984, he applied with the Irvine Police Department but once again let the effort die.

A first love sometimes stays in the heart for a lifetime. Even when the relationship disintegrates and fades into the past, the love often remains. Many of the people who associated with John Famalaro thought that his first love, Helen Lyons, changed his life forever.

The couple met while they both attended St. Thomas Aquinas, a four-year Catholic liberal arts college. Located in Calabasas, on the north slope of the Santa Monica mountains, the college was a one-hour drive from the Famalaro home in Santa Ana, so he took an apartment near campus.

Famalaro was drawn to Helen Lyons' wholesome appearance, her long brown hair, her sparse use of makeup, her intelligence, and her serene demeanor. She fit into his life as the perfect counterpoint to his hyper personality. As Mrs. Famalaro observed, John became "obsessed" with Helen.

Lavishing attention on his new love, John took her to restaurants, to the beach for long walks at sunset, to the Queen Mary in Long Beach, and to show her off to his acquaintances. They attended mass together, and spent long hours talking about the Catholic Church and the sacraments. By focusing all of his attention on Helen, Famalaro's grades began to slip. His complete devotion to the woman of his dreams left little time or inclination for study.

As they grew closer, the relationship became a sexual one. Neither of them had much experience or knowledge, and the inevitable happened. Helen found herself pregnant.

The young couple agonized over what to do. John wanted to marry her and start their family, but Helen didn't think they were quite ready for that. She chose to terminate the pregnancy through abortion. The mental torture of losing the child traumatized both of the lovers. They continued expressing their undying love for each other, but deeply felt the damage. Eventually, Helen transferred to a college in Missouri. She returned frequently for visits to relatives in southern California, though, and finally moved back within a tantalizing distance of Famalaro. And she maintained just enough affectionate contact with him to keep his hopes alive.

Almost daily, during her absence, they wrote to each other. Famalaro, who had inherited his mother's proclivity for saving documents, newsclips, books, and nearly anything committed to print, carefully packed each of Helen's letters away for safekeeping. Little by little, he detected that the luster of her love seemed to be fading. Finally, she announced that it would be better if they ended the relationship. Famalaro's world crashed.

He couldn't talk about it to his brother, who by now was incarcerated at Patton State Hospital. He certainly couldn't talk to his mother, who hadn't approved of the affair in the first place. His father couldn't help, and Francine was busy raising her own children. Famalaro had no intimate friends. At last, he sought solace in the church, in the person of a priest, Father Vincent Young.

The short, stout, bearded, and bespectacled priest, with his deep, soothing voice, heard John Famalaro's troubles at a Los Angeles rectory, and sympathized. He listened as the troubled young man described his need to get his life organized, to "get it back together." They discussed the abortion Helen had undergone. "It seemed very painful and traumatic for him," Young would recall.

The two men met and talked several times each week. Over the ensuing months, Father Young thought Famalaro made good progress in shaking off his depression and coming to grips with reality. "He became less self-absorbed and concerned about his grief." As Famalaro's spirits rose, he would bring wine and fruit to the priest to show appreciation for the help, and to symbolize his progress. "He even expressed concern about using too much of my time."

It didn't help Famalaro's state of mind when he heard that Helen had started a relationship with another man. Almost twenty-five years old, Famalaro felt that his life had come to an end. He didn't know how he could stand to keep going. On April 19, 1983, he sat down at a desk, and began making entries in a new journal.

"A tragic loss, but yet hope for a new beginning. Today is the first day of my imposed 'sentence' away from Helen. I have a real need to hold her—to see, touch, hear her voice, and express my intense love. I want to start this journal as a free flowing expression of my feelings for Helen, and life. I remember in the late '70's when she went to school in Missouri, that the daily (and very vigorous) storming in my journal was the second most important thing that kept me going (her phone calls being the first.) I have not kept a regular journal in the years since that time. I feel it would be healthy for me to do so now. It will give me an additional sense of union to Helen in her physical absence. There are so many things I want to say to my love in the next few months, but she will not hear me. At least if I write it down, I will not explode."

Father Young had advised Famalaro, giving him a "prescription" to back away from the problem for a minimum of three months to evaluate it, and to give Helen some time to think about it. Famalaro wrote:

"That's a long time! I know he could have justifiably been a lot harder on us than he was. But this is hard enough for me. I thank God that Father Young has been there to help us so many times. I really intend to use these months wisely for the enrichment of my soul. I want to be able to give Helen a more complete person. I am making a full time job out of praying for my love. Oh Helen, if you only knew how I prayed for you. I know that God is with you and watching over you in a very special way. As long as I have a breath in me, and as long God will hear me, you will be fine, honey."

As Famalaro scribbled in his journal, he wondered if he had lost his mind by writing to Helen as if he were speaking to her. Then, he launched into a rhapsodizing description of spending an evening with her, strolling at sunset along a romantic stretch of beach, gazing at her beauty, and talking to her about how the separation might, in the long run, help them grow, mature, and reunite. Her absence, he hoped, was only temporary. He must keep up his spirits in preparation for their future together.

Each day, for nearly three months, Famalaro entered his ruminations, self pity, worry about Helen, doubts, anger, and recriminations in his journal. He jotted down his thoughts on "all the bad things" that Helen had done. He vacillated, from entering descriptions of her behavior, calling her a creep, irresponsible, and not very truthful, to stating that his love for Helen was carved in granite and forged in steel. "Wake up, Famalaro," he wrote, "Helen has lied to you." He plunged to the depths when he discovered that she had been seeing another man, one with whom she had previously broken up. Especially since the man, in Famalaro's view, was a "flake." It brought pain, he noted, to realize that when Helen faced a choice whether to be with him or the other man, she chose his competitor. Even after Famalaro had asked Helen to marry him, she continued to spend time with the "flake."

Other women Famalaro had previously dated, he wrote, were trying to get back together with him. But out of loyalty to Helen, he refused to see any of them. Why couldn't she be as faithful to him? "This whole thing stinks," he scrawled. "Where's Father Young?"

One Sunday, he put his words into action, had lunch with Father Victor Young, and congratulated the priest on his upcoming trip to Rome to celebrate the Holy Year. That evening, Famalaro drove sixty miles up the coast to Santa Barbara to see a benefit concert held for St. Thomas Aquinas College. He noted that it was a beautiful trip, but that it made him miss Helen even more. He described the "empty" feeling caused by the fact that "all the special things in my life are screaming out to include her." He missed everything from her gleaming smile to her magical ways. "I offer myself to her as an empty vessel, to be filled with love and a lifetime of happiness together." It puzzled him why she couldn't accept his magnanimous gift.

One Monday, he wrote, "The constant uncertainty over such a long period is surely killing me. Stress is fatal. Sometimes I wish it was not such a slow process."

Everything he did, Famalaro said, made him wish for Helen. He watched a "hilarious" movie on pay television called *Stripes* starring Bill Murray and John Candy. He could only think of how much more enjoyable it would have been if she had been with him. Repeatedly, he entered comments lamenting how he could not understand why Helen didn't want him. His words echoed an inflated opinion of himself. "Life is so ironic. I am always getting attacked by beautiful, intelligent, witty, talented, sensuous ladies. I am pursued constantly. If I went with the flow, they would have been successful in marrying me off about seventeen times now . . . The only woman that I have ever truly loved, the woman I adore, the person I long to spend the rest of my life with is the *only* woman who has not fully reciprocated her love. In the meantime the line is getting longer and people will have to start taking numbers." A woman from his past called, he noted, and appeared to be trying to rehabilitate their old relationship. He felt sorry for her. She seemed to love him as much as he loved Helen.

Redirecting his focus, Famalaro wrote in early May of his progress in attaining his educational goals. "As it stands now, I will ultimately have two Bachelor's degrees, probably one in human biology and one in anatomy. A Master's degree in clinical nutrition, and a Ph.D. in clinical nutrition. Not counting, of course, extensive Kung Fu training, going through the police academy, and my real estate certification. My favorite time of all, naturally, is the wonderful time I have spent getting my Doctor of Chiropractic. What fun. I may be over-qualified for most jobs. Well, I could always go back to being a waiter."

Two days after his upbeat, self-aggrandized litany about education, Famalaro again wallowed in depression over Helen. "It bugs the hell out of me that she is always with everyone else and very seldom with me . . . I keep wondering what she is doing, how many guys she is dating, who she's with, what they are doing. I hate it. I'm going to let go of the whole mess."

To celebrate his sister's birthday in May, he took Francine, her husband Marvin, and his grandmother, to Benihana's restaurant in Newport Beach, not far from The Cannery. They celebrated, he said, in grand style, noting that his relatives seemed quite impressed with the place. As he made his journal entries the next night, he said, the tears were rolling down his cheeks.

Mother's Day came, and John Famalaro took the same trio, Grandmother, sister, and brother-in-law, to mass and later to brunch. He made no mention in his journal of his mother.

That same night, he suffered another emotional blow from Helen. While he was out jogging, she dropped by his apartment and left a note informing him that she was going to Texas for a few weeks. "Of course," he wrote, "the first thing that flashes through my mind are all the 'cowboys' that she will be hanging around with. It makes me feel like shit."

With long days in classrooms, Famalaro liked to break them up by attending mass at a nearby church during his lunch period. On Ascension Thursday, May 12, parochial school children packed the church. "It brought back a lot of childhood memories to see them," Famalaro wrote. "The years at St. Joseph's in Santa Ana were good times. All of us in our little uniforms nicely lined up singing the national anthem, or kneeling in church, but always causing kaos (sic). I'm surprised I wasn't murdered as a child by one of my teachers." Perhaps he had forgotten that the good times at St. Joseph ended when he was expelled.

Longing memories of Helen still plagued him. He entered in his journal, "Things about Helen were haunting me all day, including the recent escapade in which she made me feel *so* important by hiding me in the bushes while she visited her brothers. The fact that her whole family was there didn't help things." More and more, anger seemed to be creeping into Famalaro's chronicle.

In late May, he drove to Patton State Hospital. "I went to visit George last week. He is doing very well. He will probably be getting out in a few short months. They have issued him out-patient status. That is what he has been waiting for. His wife is very excited."

* * *

On the last day of May, he scanned some newly developed photos, and wistfully thought how beautiful Helen looked in them. "I miss her so much. An energy and excitement is flowing through my entire body just at the thought of seeing her again. There is nothing more important in the world to me than my love for Helen." He worried that she was selling "our relationship down the river for so many unimportant things." On the evening of June 1, he covered three full pages of his journal with gushy declarations of his deep love for Helen along with prayers for her. He was in for a rude shock.

"Desolation," he printed, instead of wrote, in his book of lamentations on June 2nd.

"That's all I can feel. I am in an utter state of shock. I just found out that Helen is having an affair with her ex-boyfriend the whole time she was in Orange County seeing me. I am sick, mentally and physically ill. How could she do this? This is the ultimate betrayal. She has become my Judas. First, a series of lies, then the 'great escape' (again), and now this. This is the deepest hurt I have ever felt in my life. Even when Helen left me . . . and I hit bottom, as bad as that was, this is infinitely worse. The pain was so terrible when she left me. But at least it was tempered by the rationalization that she needed to get away and deal with her problems and maybe she would be back some day. I never lost hope. But what hope do I have now? This is totally different. This is a complete betrayal. The sickening thing about it is that it took place over such a long period of time. I search in my mind for some way to give her the benefit of the doubt. Some way that would indicate that she didn't mean it, or that it was a mistake, or that was a 'flash in the pan.' I feel like throwing up. I just can't stop crying or heaving. I've never been like this before; never this bad.

"Oh God, please help me. I feel so much agony. My

anxiety level is so high, I need the help of your graces to
see me through. Right now I don't even feel like I'm going
to get through it. I feel like I'm going to die. I want to
die. I want to die!"

Crying on the pages, Famalaro made no more entries in the
journal for five days.

For his twenty-fifth birthday, Famalaro received a welcome
telephone call, on Friday, June 10. "Helen called me today. It
was great to hear her voice. But even with that consolation, it
has been a truly miserable birthday once again . . . Today it was
so difficult to speak, to listen, so difficult to be aware of the
dishonesty flowing through her veins. A dishonesty directed at
me . . . at me."

If he had hoped for a new flood of calls from Helen, Famalaro
was disappointed. By mid-June, his entries bemoaned the fact
that he hadn't heard another word from her. "Why is she so
inconsiderate of my pain?" He stated that she would have to
choose soon because he knew his Creator wouldn't want him to
stay on earth and experience the cruel and perverted suffering.
"Penance is one thing. Murder and suicide is something else."

He was tired, he wrote, of so many things. If he could speak
to her, he would say, "I'm tired of not spending holidays with
you, tired of never being considered a priority, tired of being
physically ill from stress and the uncertainty you have so skillfully
created, tired of this sore abdomen from throwing up every
day . . . But most of all, I'm just tired."

Needing some temporary respite, Famalaro flew to Washington D.C. where he was met by a young woman he had previously
dated. She drove him to Christendom College, the surroundings
of which he thought looked as beautiful as anything he'd ever
seen comparable to some of the places he'd visited in Europe.
The retreat, he wrote, was to help the participants realize the
severity of their past sins, to meditate, and to prepare for "general life confession." Famalaro called it a very difficult experi-

ence, but a very moving one. He believed that his sins had been forgiven. But instead of helping him to forget Helen, the experience intensified his feelings for her. During his "general confession," he wrote, "I cried and I screamed and I wept, and I sobbed. I realized that my pain was coming from my love and need for Helen."

Through all the soul-searching, just when he felt he might be able to release the compulsive attachment to Helen, he received some surprising advice. A priest at the retreat, according to Famalaro's understanding, said, "You and the woman are well suited for each other. You should marry the girl." Famalaro asked if the priest was sure. The reply confirmed it. "You fool, these problems happen with every woman before they get married. They are immature."

Pressing for further reassurance, Famalaro, as he recalled it, asked if his wailing about Helen had perhaps prejudiced the priest to make a hasty recommendation. "No, no," the Father reportedly exclaimed. "You are no longer of the 'second-class' in the three classes of men. You are willing to give Helen up now if God wants it of you. There is *no* reason to give her up."

Famalaro wrote, "To make sure that it coincided with God's will, I felt compelled to question (the priest). Well, excuse me for living. This angered the Father very much. He crumpled up my paper and threw it back at me across the table. He screamed, 'Get out, get out! You are a silly child. You think with your feelings, not with reason. Use your reason! You are immature, you are both immature.' Well, this is where I found out he was really a pussy cat. I roared back. He shut up."

After volleying the subject a few more minutes, Famalaro noted, the priest shouted, "Go now. I have told you to marry her. If you don't want to listen, don't listen. I have other retreatants to see. Goodbye!"

Famalaro rushed out shouting in jubilation. "Hurray! Hurray. The good news. I don't have to give up Helen!"

In his entry of June 28, Famalaro described the sylvan charms of waking up in the middle of a verdant forest, serenaded by the sounds of nature. He told of examining the wonder of insects, small wild animals, and walking in the gladed paths. Suddenly, he said, he was struck with the intuition that the world was coming to an end. "There was a shrill, almost demonic wailing scream only a few feet from me. I quickly fixated on a wild-eyed and obviously angered raccoon." He figured that he had startled the female close to her young, and she was bluffing him. "She would raise her arms to the side and bloat the lateral aspect of her body, trying to make her opponent think she is much bigger than she really is."

Feeling vulnerable to the wild creatures lurking about, Famalaro thought he needed a weapon. He climbed a tree and snapped off a long branch. Using a stone, he skinned the wood of bark and leaves, making a long, clean shaft. "Ah that was more like it. Now I've got those creepy critters on my turf . . . a Kung Fu staff." He joked that next time he came to the country, he must remember to bring a rifle instead of a prayer book. "Unfortunately, bears don't read."

As he emerged from the woods, hurrying to beat an afternoon thundershower, he approached the cluster of church buildings. Stopping in his tracks, he couldn't believe what he saw. Two pickup trucks sat in his path. "God, I can't escape it no matter what I do. I fly from ocean to ocean, disappear into the woods . . . then Helen and her lover still find me! Unbelievable! There's no escaping it."

He did not make it clear whether the entry for that day was the description of a real event, or an hallucination. His next entry describes his ruminations on the plane while flying home. Concerned that the serenity and lessons of the retreat might be only temporary, he resolved to make every effort to hold onto the newfound spirituality.

"Helen called me today," began the entry for June 29. But, he wrote, the conversation hadn't been a very nice one. While he had been engulfed with warm feelings, loving, reconciliatory, she had been very angry about a long letter he'd written to her. "She can't be very happy with herself after the lying and deceit." They spoke again the following day. "She keeps telling me that she loves me and wants to be with me, but she never does it. The one time she did try it, she had to ruin it by continuing to see her lover."

Helen remained angry and told him she planned to stay away another month. "Three months away from each other was already unbearable . . . now she wants to make it four months, without even a second thought or inquiry with Father Young or me."

On the Independence Day weekend, Famalaro wrote, "I can't stop thinking about Helen, about how unanxious she seems to come back here. Even when she does come back, she's coming for a family party, not to see me. Pits. I don't feel like writing much. I do a lot of staring at the wall and a lot of crying. Just can't accomplish anything anymore. I haven't been to school a full day in weeks. I feel terrible. I miss you Helen."

In one last page of his journal, the 104th, he made some mention of taking a physical exam at the sheriff's academy, then about how he had been thinking of Helen incessantly. "I wish she would come home, give me a big hug, and never let go."

The remainder of the journal book contained only blank pages.

Famalaro would soon drop out of St. Thomas Aquinas.

And he would be reunited with Helen. Just when Famalaro seemed stabilized enough to resume working toward other goals, Helen came back into his life.

Father Young would later characterize Famalaro's reaction. "He was euphoric, excited. He had a new life." The priest wondered if resuming the relationship was in Famalaro's best interests, and advised him to be cautious. He spoke to both of them, together and separately. But the love-bitten young man ignored his Catholic counselor.

Within a few months, though, Father Vincent Young was thunderstruck when he heard that Helen was pregnant again! He spoke to Famalaro. According to Young, "John's reaction was very strong. He was confident that he could work it out okay. He wanted to marry her and have a dream family. In preparation for the birth, John learned Lamaze techniques and studied intensely to learn all about child care."

Once more, Helen had second thoughts about bearing a child for John Famalaro and spending the rest of her life with him.

She unilaterally decided to leave him again. This time though, she would go through with the birth, but put the child up for adoption. She vanished from Famalaro's life while still pregnant.

As Father Young remembered it, "John was destroyed. Beside himself with grief. He wanted custody of his baby."

Famalaro searched for his missing love, but to no avail. He spent every cent he could find in the search, and all of his spare hours. He went to court, and obtained an order allowing his access to the child, effective only if the birth took place in California.

"So," recalled Father Young, "it was back to square one to try to get John Famalaro to accept the loss and cope with his problems." He recommended to Famalaro that he let Helen determine the best course of life for the baby. "He was obsessed, though, with finding and taking custody of the child."

The quest to find Helen failed, and so did all efforts to take the child.

He would never forget Helen, but a few months later, he would meet a beautiful, sophisticated, sexual woman and eventually take her to New York for an evening of fun and games on Broadway and Times Square.

Chapter 12

Acquaintances of John Famalaro couldn't understand how he attracted such gorgeous women. Sure, he was a smooth talker and dressed nicely. And maybe physical attractiveness is not such an important issue with women. But John looked for all the world like a tall Toulouse-Lautrec with his weak beard-covered chin, long aquiline nose, and mop of dark brown hair above a high forehead. Instead of the pince-nez glasses used by the stunted artist, Famalaro wore large pilot-style spectacles over his close-set brown eyes. At six-one, 150 pounds, with narrow shoulders, he appeared frail.

Maybe women found him irresistible because they wanted to mother him, or perhaps because he willingly spent a lot of money on them.

And maybe other men's criticisms reflected pure jealousy.

After so many false starts in Famalaro's professional choices, he finally settled into a house painting business. Utilizing his hyper energy, he made it a financial success.

Perhaps the business achievements inspired more confidence in personal relationships. When Famalaro started going with Darlene Miller in 1987, he confounded even more men, who licked their lips while having a second look at his companion. She worked for a chiropractor who introduced her to Famalaro in the spring of 1984. Tall and buxom with long blond hair, high cheek bones, and come-hither hazel eyes, around forty, Miller not only attracted men by her beauty, but also by her sophisticated apparel, wit, and intellect. She dazzled Famalaro. But she was engaged to another man. Gradually, Darlene and John became friends, and it took Famalaro three years to finally convince her to go out with him, only after she and her fiancé broke up. It didn't bother Famalaro at all that she had a daughter in college, and three sons ranging from eleven to eighteen.

Determined to make it a romantic relationship, Famalaro did all the right things. He gave her flowers, took her to the best restaurants, lavished her with gifts, in addition to courting her with intelligent conversation and lively companionship. Even though Darlene found him oddly secretive, she began to feel the stirrings of love for him. He invited her to his Irvine apartment, not far from Newport Beach, and she accepted. Inside, Darlene observed a peculiarity she couldn't quite understand; he kept one of his rooms securely locked at all times. She couldn't know that his mother had done the same thing. If he answered the phone during her visit to his domicile, he would furtively whisper, then take it into his bedroom where he could speak privately. He would never listen to his answering machine messages with Darlene in the room.

Still, she admired him in many ways. He seemed so courteous, pleasant, with a *"joie de vivre* attitude for life." And he was intellectual. "He had an incredible collection of books," she said. "The other thing I noticed was his newspapers. He had newspaper clippings, and I asked him about them. He said there were certain things that he was interested in that he followed, and that he kept files on them." Once, she got a peek inside the secret locked room, and saw that it was filled with file cabinets and shelves. No light filtered in through the heavily draped and covered windows.

Darlene had met few men with so much energy. "I guess the closest analogy would be like a three ring circus. That is probably an overused phrase. It had the flavor of activity going on in so many different realms. There was this high energy and fragmentation of focus. I had a sense there were a lot of things going on in his life." It bothered her though, that he acted reluctant to share with her the nature of his activities. And he didn't seem to have many friends.

Any shortcomings in his makeup, though, were compensated

for by his gallant treatment of Darlene. "If we went somewhere, John treated me like a queen, essentially. He did everything first class. We went to theaters or stadiums and had first row seats, front row center, whatever event we went to. He would sometimes hire a limousine to go to a restaurant. He had flowers sent to me that were huge bouquets, the kind you might see in a hotel. Ostentatious. And he quite often had a lot of cash, hundred dollar bills. You don't see many people with hundred dollar bills."

Darlene also liked the way Famalaro seemed to relate to her eighteen-year-old son. She thought her son looked up to John and regarded him as role model. The youth even turned down a scholarship to remain at home and work for Famalaro in his house painting business.

As any serious suitor might do, John took Darlene to meet his family. She had mixed impressions of them. Especially John's sister, Francine, who didn't seem to match the notions Darlene had formed from John's previous descriptions of her. "I had assumed that she was very professional, very sophisticated in a lot of ways. And I didn't come away with that impression. I felt maybe there was something else going on behind the scenes that I wasn't aware of." Francine, said Miller, seemed almost to be holding her breath. She didn't say a word. "I wondered what was going on. Was it me?"

Invited to another Famalaro family gathering, Darlene noticed that John appeared to be particularly fond of his sister's daughters. "He absolutely adored them. It was mutual." John's mother, though, seemed "distant and not really open to developing a relationship."

Because Darlene loved live stage plays, John decided to give her a special treat for her birthday during the Independence Day weekend in 1987. He flew her to New York, bought tickets to *Les Miserables,* plus two more Broadway hits, and escorted her into a luxury hotel near Times Square. Few women could have resisted the lavish attention and generous gifts.

They shared gourmet dinners, saw two of the musicals, and planned to see a third one on Sunday afternoon. But John had another surprise in store for Darlene.

When they woke together in the hotel room, on Sunday morning, Darlene hoped that John had shaken his depression from the previous evening. She hadn't understood what caused it, but didn't want it to spoil their last full day in New York. His early-morning demeanor relieved her worries. Darlene recalled, "John had been rather depressed the night before. And in the morning he was exceedingly happy, laughing and joking and was kind of play-housing, tickling." She would later say she assumed he was attempting sexual foreplay. "It got too rough, though. It was too much. I remember trying to pull away a little bit. And when that happened, we were moving out of the bed, and part of my nightgown started to slip. He was still tickling, and before I knew it, I was handcuffed to a bar at the window!"

It happened so fast, she said, that she couldn't even remember how he got the cuffs on her, or where they came from. She denied having seen them earlier. "It happened in the blink of an eye."

Confused by the sudden binding of her wrists with cold metal, fastening her to a bar across a large window, Darlene tried to laugh if off. "I was laughing nervously because I was afraid. I was hoping that it was just a joke. A blown out of proportion joke."

If it started out as a playful act, the bizarre incident soon lost its humor. Darlene said that she felt panic and humiliation. "He pulled off my clothes, my nightgown, opens the curtains, and walks out. He was still laughing when he did it." Famalaro left his attractive lover handcuffed, naked, unable to move away from the window, on full display for anyone to see from the street below, or from the windows of neighboring buildings. Darlene recalled that he was gone "for hours."

Struggling with every bit of her strength in an attempt to free herself, Darlene only managed to tear and abrade her skin under the handcuffs. "One of the thoughts I had was how do I get someone's attention? And then if I do get someone's attention, what do I do when they come? I kicked the wall. I tried pulling my hands out. And I mean there were moments when I gave up."

The time for the opening curtain of the play came. And it

passed. But that was the least of Darlene's concerns. When Famalaro finally returned, and started laughing again, he unsnapped the cuffs. Darlene said she was traumatized. "I immediately went into a fetal position and wasn't capable of speech. I remember just instinctively grabbing towards the sheet on the bed, and just pulling at it and staying huddled. John was laughing and I wasn't quite sure what to do."

His next move startled Darlene even more, considering the humiliating stunt he had just pulled. "He was trying to be amorous. Kissing my back and my neck, and just kind of fondling a bit. It seemed like an eternity. He could see that I was really struggling at that point. He finally stopped behaving as if it was still play and as if it was a joke, and he actually tried to calm me down a little bit at that point. I responded to that very quickly . . . In a more instinctive way I felt that I needed to play along with this situation. The only thing I could think of was getting back to California. That was the clearest thing on my mind."

As she could best remember, Darlene "played along" with John Famalaro in order to return home safely.

When they arrived back in Orange County, she told him that she didn't want to see or speak to him again. "He was devastated. He cried. He pleaded." Darlene sought counseling from a therapist, and so did Famalaro. "He even had his therapist call mine to see if we could jointly meet and have some closure at least." Darlene refused. "I couldn't. I just couldn't . . . I believe I said goodbye in 1987 after the incident."

Even though he appeared stricken at the loss of Darlene Miller, Famalaro managed to find suitable companionship.

Kate Colby had long brown hair, a sunshine smile, full lips, and a knockout figure. She began dating Famalaro in mid-1988 and their romance grew serious enough to consider marriage. She had never heard of Darlene Miller. The timing of her entry into Famalaro's life helped salve two serious emotional wounds. It was debatable which event had hurt him most, the loss of his relationship with Darlene Miller, or the death, on Easter Day, of his maternal grandmother, upon whom he had depended so heavily for love and nurturing, and on whom he had lavished his own familial affection. Colby faced a huge task in filling both emotional vacuums. The relationship seemed to be accomplishing that, until Famalaro sabotaged it.

Accustomed to visiting the house to which Famalaro had moved, on Perth Street in affluent Lake Forest, located in southern Orange County, Kate felt completely at home. She would later admit that the relationship with Famalaro was a sexual one. Feeling frisky one April afternoon in 1989, she and John went to the upstairs bedroom, leaving a couple of his house-painting employees working in the garage downstairs. He wore work clothes, while she had on snug shorts and a light blouse. Kate recalled, "While we were upstairs, we kissed a couple of times. For some reason I was in a hurry. I don't recall why, but I needed to leave. He pushed me down on the bed." A bookcase had been placed near the head of the bed. As Kate toppled over from the none-too-gentle push, her shoulder and head struck the corner of the bookcase and she landed face up on the mattress. Dazed and hurting, she expected to be given some tender care, but felt a rush of anxiety when Famalaro lunged forward and sprawled full-length on top of her.

Somewhat surprised, but assuming that John was playing a silly game, Kate said, "Okay, I've got to go." But he maintained his full body press, holding her down. She started to struggle.

Recalling the incident, Kate said, "He put his legs, or leg, in between mine to try to pry them apart because I had held them together." As she continued to wrestle, he undid the single button at the waist of Kate's shorts, then pulled the zipper down. "He put his— he stayed on top of me on my chest, and put his knees on my arms . . . pinning my arms down."

Demonstrating her position, Kate extended her arms above her head, with her wrists crossed. Suddenly, she said, he moved so quickly she didn't realize what he was doing. "And there were handcuffs on my wrists. I don't know where they came from." She knew that he had kept a pair of cuffs looped over his bedpost. "I assume that's where they came from."

Choking in anger as she told of the struggle, Kate said, "Once the handcuffs were in place, he held my arms and was able to push my pants, my shorts, off and use his foot to get them the rest of the way off my feet. I was frightened. More than frightened. I was angry that someone was using force to do something I didn't want to do." With her face reflecting the anger, she described how Famalaro had then removed his own jeans. "There was a look in his eyes I hadn't seen before. He was looking at me with a very intense stare, but his eyes looked like he was enjoying what was happening. I wasn't."

While Famalaro held her in the helpless position, she could no longer refrain from crying out of sheer fright and anger. "I said to him, 'Go ahead and do this. But when I report it to the police it will be considered date rape.' "

Her threat worked. Famalaro wilted like a deflated balloon. With the expression of a chastened child, he removed the handcuffs. But anger took over. "His demeanor changed. His eyes changed. Instantly he jumped off of me and refastened his pants. Off the bed, he started to walk away toward the door. He yelled back things like, 'You bitch! You are the one that brought this on.' I put my clothes on, yelled a couple of things at him, and left."

Kate gave herself a couple of months to cool down, then finally accepted Famalaro's request to see her again. She wasn't sure why she capitulated. "He was a very good talker. Once I spoke to him again he said that it was just a game. He didn't expect me to take it the way I did. He said that I obviously didn't know mature sex games."

She forgave him, and brought him a birthday present on June 10. They resumed the relationship, with the sex, and talked again about marriage. When either of them traveled out of town, for pleasure or business, they would exchange affectionate letters. She even complained that they weren't seeing each other often enough. On a winter day in 1991, Kate accepted his proposal and agreed to marry Famalaro. But it fizzled and burned out by springtime. On his next birthday, Kate gave John a card expressing her sympathy because she knew he was experiencing a great deal of hurt over the breakup. Then she faded from his life.

* * *

If lost love had torn Famalaro's life again, it was soothed a couple of months later when he spotted Darlene Miller walking near a golf course. She later described the reunion. "I ran into him quite by chance in 1991. I had actually moved up to Oregon, to go to school at the University of Oregon, and I had only come back down to Orange County for the summer. I was working at a medical facility and taking a walk on my lunch break near the Mission Viejo golf course. As I was passing the corner, I heard a car honking. I didn't bother to look. And before I knew it, John was standing there. He had jumped out of the car, and said hello." She thought it happened in July, four years after their breakup.

"We initiated a dating relationship. It was very tentative on my part." Darlene wanted to take some time to reassess her feelings about John. "He seemed to be different in some way. He seemed calmer than I remembered him being." She turned down his first request for a date, but later agreed to meet him for lunch. "It was kind of a slow progression. We started meeting for dinner and then more often." She accepted an invitation to take another trip with him in early September, this time to Seattle, Washington. At the end of summer, Darlene returned to Oregon. Famalaro made several trips up there to spend time with her and to give her financial assistance.

Within a couple of months, Darlene moved again to Orange County, driven by economic pressures. She continued to date Famalaro.

He enthusiastically resumed his generous courtship. But she still noticed peculiar behavior. He rented a warehouse in Laguna Hills, near the El Toro Marine Base, for his house painting business, and eventually converted attached office space into his residence. She sometimes accompanied him there, perhaps a dozen times. He seemed extremely security-conscious, keeping it "locked up like a fortress."

The relationship progressed to mutual declarations of love. But when John suggested they move in together and get married, Darlene gave a simple, succinct answer. *"No."*

John Famalaro cried. Their life paths reached a crossroads, and they once again took different directions.

* * *

During the mid and late eighties, Famalaro focused what probably were paternal urges on his two nieces. Francine appreciated the generous time he devoted to her daughters. "It was quality time that a parent can't spend. He took them horseback riding, miniature golfing. Always had an outing planned for them. Wouldn't show up without a tropical fish for their aquarium. It was always something special. My kids related to him as a very special person in their life."

The older niece chose Uncle John to be her sponsor at her Catholic confirmation ceremony. And she confided in him. Francine told of the close relationship. "There was a lot of counseling that went on between them, things they wouldn't necessarily talk about to my husband or me. They felt free to go to John and he would help them through some of their adolescent problems."

Later, in Arizona, in early 1994, he attended the basketball championship game in which his niece played. He helped her celebrate the thrilling win by lifting her up to cut down the net. She did not try to hide the high esteem she felt for her uncle John. But the niece seldom mentioned her uncle George.

The influence of women on John Famalaro's life had been profound. Social scientists have noted that maternal overprotection and control can cause hostility toward the mother which may be transferred to women in general. Intense anger in a frustrated male who is subjugated by women can be generated from feelings of powerlessness in those relationships. Ultimately, the bottled-up fury can lead to a violent attack on a total stranger, usually a woman, in symbolic retribution against all females who have, in his subconscious mind, pushed him into a corner.

PART V
INVESTIGATION

Chapter 13

Now, the news could be released to the media.

In Orange County, C.P. (Christopher) Smith had been with the *Orange County Register* for twenty-five years, working his way up through the ranks from copy boy, to rock music editor, to entertainment editor, and finally to editing the hard news. He had watched the Huber case from the beginning, assigning various reporters, usually Jonathon Volzke, to cover the anniversaries and family developments.

Saturday, July 16, 1994, Smith and his wife planned a special celebration of his fortieth birthday. She had bought and wrapped forty presents for him to unwrap when they returned from their big night out. Because Smith loved classical music, the couple had arranged to attend the Three Tenors concert at Dodger Stadium, where he could hear the golden tones of Luciano Pavarotti, Jose Carrerra, and Placido Domingo. It couldn't have been a better birthday. And he would never have another one quite like it.

When Smith and his wife arrived home at nearly midnight, he saw the answering machine flashing with nine messages, far more than he ordinarily would have expected late on Saturday night. He knew something big was up. On the first message one of his reporters yelled, "You're not going to believe what they found!" The excited young man told of Denise Huber's nude body, kept in a freezer for three years, being located in Arizona. At the time the call was made, identification of the corpse hadn't yet been confirmed.

Forgetting all about the presents he'd planned to unwrap, Smith spent the rest of the night on his cellular phone, leaving the other line open for incoming calls, pacing back and forth in his living room, coordinating coverage of the story, dispatching reporters to Arizona, Costa Mesa, and anywhere else they might dig up collateral stories, sidebars, or anything pertaining to one of the longest and biggest investigations ever covered by the paper. Smith knew that reporter Jonathon Volzke should be notified as soon as possible, since he'd been close to the Huber family and had written most of the stories on the case. But several calls to Volzke's pager went unanswered. Other reporters, Smith decided, would have to cover the urgent breaking news, and Volzke could come in on it as soon as he could be found. Smith distributed work to Jeff Collins, Jeordan Legon, Tony Saavedra, Chris Knap, Marilyn Kalfus, Tom Berg, Laura Bleiberg, Teri Sforza, and Teresa Puente.

Smith managed to unwrap four of his presents that first night. The remaining thirty-six would take nearly a week to open.

By the time the weary editor came into his office at 7:30 the next morning, he was convinced the police had arrested a serial killer.

Volzke would have rushed to work immediately if he'd known. But he and his wife had just bought a house and tackled a major renovation project that weekend. He'd left his pager in the car. When he took a break after midnight to check on it, he found three messages, one from a detective, one from his boss, and one from Dennis Huber. "Denise found! Call in!"

Actually, Volzke had responded to a bulletin from the night editor three hours earlier. Rumors had developed about a body being found, but the corpse had been described as about five-six in height. The editor had asked Volzke, "Do you think it's Denise?"

"No," Volzke had answered. "The body is too short. Denise is five-nine."

Now, in the wee hours, it appeared that the height estimate had been wrong, and the body was indeed Denise Huber. At two hours after midnight, Jonathon checked in with C.P. Smith, then immediately called Dennis Huber. But the delay cost him the lead story, which was written by two other reporters.

The telephone woke Rob Calvert on Sunday morning, July 17. Still groggy from being out late Saturday night, he couldn't make out the caller's voice. All he heard was, "They found Denise's body. It's in the Sunday paper out on your driveway." Shocked, Calvert re-cradled the phone and headed for the front door. He would never be able to remember who had called.

He hastened outside, and saw the thick edition of the *Orange County Register* lying on the concrete. On the front page, a color portrait of Denise Huber smiled up at him. He would recall, "Sure enough, there was Denise's picture right on the front page. That was the first thing I noticed. It didn't even occur to me that they might have found her alive. My first thought was, they found her body. I was stunned, and I remained that way for a week. But I was also relieved to read that they had a suspect in custody. I hoped the Huber family could at last have some peace. And it made me optimistic that people would finally realize I had nothing to do with her disappearance. People had been giving me sidelong glances for three years. Now, they would know they were wrong, and didn't need to be suspicious of me anymore."

Remembering his fondness for Denise, Calvert said, "I always think about her and the good times we had. It's like it is finalized now." He compared the unusual circumstances of her discovery to the Jeffrey Dahmer horror. "It's bizarre. I hope that Denise didn't suffer too greatly. There are a lot of questions that need to be answered."

Tammy Brown, Denise's best friend, spent that Sunday with an acquaintance in San Diego, 100 miles south of Newport Beach. While there, she caught remnants of a radio report about the discovery of a young woman's body, but heard no name, and didn't connect it with Huber. While driving home, Tammy stopped at another pal's residence in Laguna Hills, not far from a warehouse on Verdugo Drive that had once been rented by a painting contractor named John Famalaro. Tammy called her own telephone number to retrieve messages from her answering machine. Her boyfriend had left a terse request to "Call me right away." She did, and heard the incredible news about Denise's frozen body being found in Arizona.

Trembling and near tears, Tammy immediately telephoned Ione Huber. After some words of consolation, a horrible scene played in her mind. Just as a similarly evil image had visited Rob Calvert, the cannibalistic gore perpetrated by serial killer Jeffrey Dahmer invaded Tammy's thoughts. She asked Ione, "Is she in one piece?"

Ione said as far as she knew, Denise's body was still whole.

Tammy would later say, "I didn't know if I was relieved about her being found or not. There were still so many unanswered questions." She read newspaper reports, and tried not to imagine what ghastly horror her dear friend had endured.

Nancy Streza read the articles, too, and clipped them out to eventually insert into two thick photo albums. She already had accumulated volumes of paper that filled drawers of a filing cabinet; fliers, bumper stickers, letters, and records documenting three years of work involving the search for Denise Huber. On Sunday, with several reporters in attendance, she joined Pastor Walt Shepard and the Aliso Creek congregation in prayer. They asked for justice, expressed gratitude to God for bringing Denise home to heaven, and requested strength to help the Hubers endure the forthcoming days. As Nancy prayed, she reflected on a remarkable prediction she'd heard months earlier. The religious man who drove daily past the giant banner featuring a portrait of Denise had prayed to his God for help in solving the tragic mystery and said he had been given the message that Denise would be found "in the hills above Phoenix." Nancy believed that the revelation truly had been a message from God.

The giant banner had frequently caught the attention of another sympathizer, a soft-spoken woman close to retirement age who ran a gift-card shop in Anaheim. Margie Hempstead seemed to be always smiling when she glanced over the top of her reading glasses at customers or friends. She lived near the banner, and profoundly understood the tragedy of its message. In 1989, she and her husband had rescued a stranded young woman at the same spot on the freeway. After learning of the body discovery, a deep desire to help the Huber family touched Hempstead's heart, so she put a collection bowl on the counter of her card shop with a photo of Denise, hoping to raise funds for the purpose of inscribing a photo of Denise on her headstone when the burial could finally be completed.

Hundreds of Hempstead's customers, children and senior citizens alike, dropped coins into the bowl, and many signed a giant sympathy card. She corresponded with Ione Huber, and sometimes chatted by telephone.

Photos of Denise had been published all over the country, and Hempstead admired the frequently seen portrait featuring Huber's brilliant smile. It would be a perfect tribute to have that photo etched onto the headstone, Hempstead thought. Perhaps, if she could collect enough money, it could be arranged.

The traditional day of rest, Sunday, is just another work day in many professions, including a homicide investigator's. Lt. Scott Mascher had obtained a second search warrant authorizing a hunt for evidence that might relate to serial murders suggested by the list of women's names they'd discovered earlier. He led a team of officers and volunteers, which included personnel from the sheriff's Mounted Posse, Prescott Explorers, and officers from neighboring counties, all of whom labored late into the night and the next day to remove hundreds of paint containers from the subterranean chamber. Using extreme caution, Mascher had directed the installation of red surveyor's tape to form path markers for the purpose of keeping workers from straying into other areas where a careless move might contaminate evidence.

Because of the danger that the room-sized excavation could possibly have undermined structural foundations, Mascher brought in county engineers to examine the building's underpinnings. He wanted assurance that the whole thing wouldn't collapse. After the inspection, it took all day Sunday and part of Monday to empty the underground chamber of nearly 1,800 cans which the workers carried to the backyard and stacked in an area the size of a boxcar. For records purposes, Mascher divided the emptied dirt floor into four quadrants, designated areas A through D. Two four-by-eight-feet plywood sheets, three-quarters of an inch thick, remained on the floor. Did they cover more buried bodies? With the paint cans removed, the team carried spades into the chamber to seek an answer to that question.

Determined not to overlook any possibility of other bodies being buried, Mascher decided to use search dogs to complement the human efforts. He contacted an organization called Rocky Mountain Rescue Dogs, Inc., located in Salt Lake City, Utah, and discussed the proposal with Nancy Hachmeister. The search dog expert said she thought the use of her animals would be useful, and offered some suggestions. "Evidence searching with dogs is very stressful on them," she said, "so at least two dogs will be needed, one to back up the other's alerts." Two handlers would be required. She explained that if the search was for a living person, transportation would be provided by military planes from Langley Air Force Base, but since this was a different type of hunt, the Civil Air Patrol would fly the dogs and handlers to Arizona, but would require compensation from the county.

Hachmeister agreed to bring her dog, Kallie, and her colleague Margaret Gregory would bring Ashley. Bright-eyed and alert, female German shepherd Kallie had undergone the required year of training to become a search dog. Kallie and Ashley, a regal Bouvier des Flandres, were the two most experienced animals among the twenty-five teams in RMRD, Inc. The all-volunteer organization had been founded by three Utah ski patrollers who used dogs to search for winter avalanche victims. Flushed by their success, they asked themselves, "Why not organize year-round searches?" The enthusiastic participants incorporated in July 1980. The dog owners, who work regular jobs to earn their livings, subject their canine pals to hundreds of

⊞ POLICE BULLETIN

Costa Mesa Police Dept.   P.O. Box 1200, 92628-1200   (714) 754-5255

D. L. Snowden, Chief of Police

MISSING ADULT
REWARD $10,000

DENISE ANETTE HUBER
White Female, Age 23, Date of Birth
11-22-67, 5'9", 130 lbs., Brown
Shoulder Length Hair, Blue Eyes,
Birth Mark on Right Upper Arm.

1988 HONDA ACCORD, BLUE
(Vehicle Recovered)

On Sunday, 6-2-91, Denise and a friend attended a concert at the Forum in Inglewood. After the concert they went to the El Paso Cantina in Long Beach. Denise was last seen on 6-3-91 at approximately 2:00 a.m. when she took her friend home to Huntington Beach. Denise's car was found abandoned on the Corona Del Mar Freeway, South of Bear Street on Monday night 6-3-91.

All information will be regarded as confidential — Refer to DR 91-19737.

Contact Detectives Jack Archer (714) 754-5363
Lynda Giesler (714) 754-5364
or Bob Phillips (714) 754-5120

Evenings and weekends call (714) 754-5205

This police bulletin was distributed throughout Southern California and photos of Denise Huber were distributed nationwide. (*Courtesy Costa Mesa California Police Department*)

Denise Huber was 23 years old when she disappeared, never to be seen alive again. (*Photo courtesy the Huber family*)

Ione Huber and daughter Denise in 1990 at Newport Beach, California. (*Photo courtesy the Huber family*)

John Famalaro (*right*) and his older brother George in the early 1960's. (*Photo courtesy Orange County, California Superior Court Records*)

Famalaro kissing the ring of a cardinal. All three of the Famalaro children attended private Catholic schools. (*Photo courtesy Orange County, California, Superior Court Records*)

Famalaro holding his infant niece in the late 1970's. (*Photo courtesy Orange County, California, Superior Court Records*)

John Joseph Famalaro. (*Photo courtesy Orange County, California, Superior Court Records*)

On June 3, 1991, Denise Huber's Honda Accord was found abandoned on a freeway shoulder near Newport Beach, California. (*Photo courtesy Costa Mesa, California Police Department*)

Famalaro kept the frozen remains of his victim in a stolen Ryder rental truck in his Arizona driveway. (*Photo courtesy Yavapai County, Arizona Police Department*)

Police found a locked, running freezer in the back of the Ryder truck on July 13, 1994.

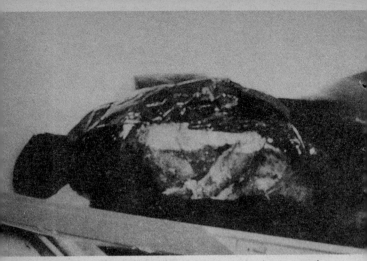

Inside the freezer was Denise Huber's body wrapped in black garbage bags.

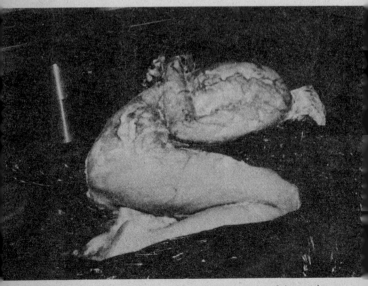

The nude, handcuffed, frozen body after most of the garbage bags had been removed.

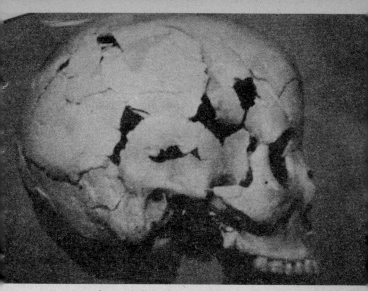

Denise Huber's skull was so severely damaged, a forensic anthropologist was required to reassemble the pieces.

One of the boxes the police found in John Famalaro's home contained a bloody roofer's nail puller, duct tape, an empty handcuffs box, and white plastic bags identical to the ones that had been pulled over the victim's head.

The bloodstained claw hammer found in Famalaro's home.

The black dress Denise Huber was wearing on the night she disappeared was found in John Famalaro's home along with her purse, shoes, and her Hawaii souvenir key ring with the keys to her Honda.

The police felt the deep scuff marks on the heels of Denise Huber's black shoes indicated she had been dragged by her killer.

Famalaro's sweatshirt was stained with Denise Huber's blood.

Costa Mesa, California
Police Chief Dave
Snowden.

Lt. Ron Smith of the
Costa Mesa, California
Police Department.

Lt. Scott Mascher of the
Prescott, Arizona
Sheriff's Department.

Orange County,
California, prosecutor
Christopher Evans.

Defense attorneys
Denise Gragg and
Leonard Gumlia.

Ione and Dennis Huber at the site of the tree planted in their daughter's memory in Newport Beach, California.

Denise Huber was buried in her father's hometown, Herried, South Dakota. *(Photo courtesy Nancy Streza)*

1967   1991

DENISE HUBER
YOU WILL ALWAYS BE LOVED

training hours in wilderness tracking, avalanche searches, and cadaver hunts. One of the hunts, which still warms the heart of Margaret Gregory, also happened in Arizona, in 1991. A two-year-old boy was missing for three-and-a-half days in the desert. She and her dog found the child, miraculously still alive, and rescued him.

The two teams arrived in Prescott about midday on Sunday, and after checking into a hotel, conferred with Sheriff Buck Buchanan and Scott Mascher. When they emerged from a police vehicle at the Cochise house, Nancy Hachmeister observed that a can of paint had been spilled in one of the areas to be searched. That would throw the dogs off any scent they needed to track, not to mention the problem of putting paw prints everywhere they walked. So Mascher brought in a hazardous materials disposal crew to clean up the spill.

Finally, in the middle of the afternoon, the dogs could begin their work. Margaret Gregory went first with her dog, Ashley, who sported the typical wiry coat, eyebrows, beard, and mustache. Gregory later reported that in the earthen room, "Ashley did not want to go into area A at all, but I made her check it out." Once she started, she showed "interest" in the corners and one wall, and in some sectors of the other three areas. To change pace, Gregory took the Bouvier des Flandres upstairs into a bedroom, where she alerted slightly. "She had no other interest in the upstairs." In the backyard, Ashley sniffed with some curiosity at a stack of boards and shelving in the middle of the side yard.

Kallie, the frisky German shepherd, worked with her handler, Hachmeister, who gave her the "body/evidence command." The dog entered the subterranean chamber and put her nose to the ground. "She wanted to go south," wrote Hachmeister, "but I called her back and directed her to section A." Kallie "alerted" at several spots, showing interest under one of the plywood sheets, "whined" as she sniffed two of the walls and scratched at the floor in section B. Leaving the basement, Kallie went upstairs, with Scott Mascher and Hachmeister following. The dog alerted at a pile of sheets, blankets, and clothing on the foot of a bed, and again under a table. She had no interest in the other bedrooms, bathrooms, or living areas.

Outside, Kallie showed some concern in the same areas Ashley had, but both dogs' jobs were interrupted when a brief, windy thundershower blew in, dampening the entire area.

The next morning, Monday, the dogs and handlers tried again. Kallie once more showed considerable interest in the "dungeon," scratching at the ground and whining. Hachmeister wrote, "Then she looked up at us as if she were saying that she had shown me what I wanted and to get on with it." In the bedroom, Kallie repeated intense sniffing in the blanket/clothing pile on the foot of the bed. She also alerted at a cabinet containing "an arsenal of guns and knives." Stacks of boxes filled the remaining rooms, crowding them to the extent that the two handlers had difficulty finding paths between the clutter. In the west corner of the garage, Kallie's ears shot up. "She alerted strongly, with such interest . . . she tried to get into the shelving area, but couldn't because of all the boxes and junk." Scott Mascher explained to the handler that boxes containing the victim's bloody clothing had been found on those upper shelves.

In a final tour of the excavated cavern, Kallie showed interest in the same areas where she had alerted before, then became weary. "By this time she was pretty burned out of searching the excavated area so many times." Outside she once again became excited near a stack of boards. Hachmeister would note, "The boards that Kallie alerted on were that of a shed the suspect had [used] in California, dismantled, and brought with him to Prescott. Why? Who knows?"

Despite the intensive search, and the dogs' enthusiasm, no other bodies were found. Scott Mascher expressed his gratitude to the volunteers from Rocky Mountain Rescue Dogs, Inc., and said goodbye to Kallie and Ashley. They and their handlers, Nancy Hachmeister and Margaret Gregory, examined the gathering storm in the desert sky, and wondered about the safety of flying home. They delayed as long as possible, and left in the late afternoon on Monday.

They made it safely home to Salt Lake City.

* * *

Another Yavapai County agency contributed a vital part of the puzzle on Friday morning, July 15. Susan Peterson of the Victim Witness Program had received a call from a woman named Jenny Redmond who claimed she knew John Famalaro about a year and had been involved with him. Redmond had also seen him knock a hole in the basement wall of his house. But, said Susan Peterson, Jenny was frightened that she might be in danger because of her association with Famalaro. The woman had agreed to come into the sheriff's office to be interviewed.

She showed up on Saturday morning, July 16, dressed in white shorts and a t-shirt. A striking twenty-eight-year-old with short dark hair, she spoke nervously to Mascher and Williamson in an interview room while a video camera recorded the conversation. They informed her that they were conducting a homicide investigation, and that Mr. Famalaro was under arrest with a $250,000 dollar bond over his head. If he somehow posted the bond, they assured Redmond, she would be immediately informed. The officers told her they would appreciate any information she might be able to contribute, starting with the background of her relationship with Famalaro.

Redmond pronounced John's name as Fahm-uh-lahro, and said she had met him through her old boyfriend, Marvin Kraft, the ex-husband of Famalaro's sister. Kraft, she said, had been helping Famalaro in his house painting business, and had gone to southern California with John to help with some employee problems in a warehouse over there.

In her relationship with Marvin Kraft, after he and Francine split up in June 1990, Redmond had often been to the house on Cochise Drive. John had left southern California, where she thought he was "one of the biggest painting contractors in the region," and moved in with Kraft in June or early July 1992. Shortly before the move, Kraft had received a call from Famalaro, frantic and upset because he "was having trouble with his workers." He'd been in the process of preparing for the move, Famalaro reportedly told Kraft, and his workers had started stealing things from him. Kraft agreed to drive over to help John, and had taken a gun along because it "might get pretty rough." So John had decided he wanted to do all the loading and moving at night. Jenny thought it sounded sort of strange, and wondered why Famalaro insisted that the police not be notified of the trouble.

Marvin made several trips to help John, she reported.

Anyway, Redmond said, John had used a Ryder rental truck to move his things from California, and it had taken several trips. She helped him unload "boxes and boxes" at the house. The assistance she gave Famalaro had indirectly led to breaking up with Marvin, Jenny explained.

"Marvin couldn't help us because he had to work, so John and I did the unloading. Marvin is kind of insecure. One day we were so busy we didn't answer the phone, so some jealousy developed. He really got upset, and said he thought John was moving in on me. That wasn't the case. But it made me see something in Marvin I didn't like, so I started the process of ending the relationship. It had nothing to do with John. I made that real clear."

Her romance with Marvin Kraft ended in September 1992. She and John remained friends. Jenny commented that Famalaro never really "settled into the house." He didn't seem to have the motivation or the time to complete unpacking all of his stuff.

Mascher asked, "Were you aware that his parents lived close by?" Jenny said she was. But she had never seen them visit John at the Cochise house. They would drive by the front and talk to him outside, but never came in. Mrs. Famalaro had dropped over a couple of times to bring him some lunch, but hadn't stayed. She added that Famalaro wanted to keep their relationship secret and that when she went to his house it would be at night. He demanded that she park her car out of sight by the side of the house.

"Did you ever notice any unusual odors?" Mascher asked.

She had, but not the kind Mascher meant. "John never used deodorant, and never opened the windows . . . they were always closed. It got pretty rank in there at times." She explained that much of his unpleasant scent probably came from the paint he used. "The sour smell from bad paint made me gag." When asked for more specifics, Jenny denied ever having noticed the odor of decaying flesh.

One of the odd things Jenny had observed was John's restrictiveness. "I never felt free to roam about the house. He kept all the doors locked, even the bathrooms. If I needed to use it, he wouldn't even hand me a key, but would go unlock it himself."

The friendship with Famalaro had been interrupted for a few months when Jenny moved to Wickenburg, Arizona, until she returned to Prescott in January 1993. At that time, they began a dating relationship. They went together about six months, during which she helped him move countless boxes into the house. A couple of them, she said, were marked "Christmas."

She also joined him in the business as a partner. He operated under more than one company name, doing house painting, general maintenance work and even carpet cleaning. Calling his companies "Masterpiece Painter," "The Maintenance Doctor," and "Restoration Company," Famalaro sought clients throughout Yavapai County and even snagged some limited work through a real estate sales group in Sedona.

"I agreed to work for him and at first I was the only one . . . I left my job, a very secure one with a good future because I wanted to help reduce his burden. As time went on, he found excuses to be gone and I'm doing it all. I needed help. I finally said, 'If you keep fooling people, I'm outta here.' I was working eighteen-hour days, plus making deliveries, driving to Sedona almost every day, one hour each way. Then he had me going out on carpet cleaning jobs. It was a neverending road with no real future."

Not only did she feel that Famalaro had mistreated her, but she began to experience some disillusionment about the way she saw him treat clients. She thought he promised his customers much more than he ever delivered, and sometimes didn't even finish the jobs he started. "I questioned his business ethics."

Mascher asked, "Did he ever mention to you anything about being in police work?"

"Yes, but as time rolled by, I started questioning everything that came out of John's mouth." She never confronted him, though. He had also mentioned being a chiropractor and a karate expert. "But he never gave me any reason to believe him."

Jenny thought that over the time she knew him, he had utilized more than one Ryder truck. When she returned from Wickenburg, she noticed that he still had one and thought it must be costing him enormous amounts of money. She never saw a chest-type freezer, but did help him move a very large upright refrigerator into the house.

She hadn't been present during the subterranean excavation work in the house, but did see a "large bone that had been brought up out of the dirt." She thought it might be a human bone.

After Redmond broke up with him, he continued to call her and beg to get back together. Asked if she had ever been frightened of him, she said, "Mad at him, yes, but never scared."

"Did you know his mother?"

"That was an odd thing. He always wanted to keep everything very secretive. Didn't want any information getting back to his mom because she might accuse him of taking me away from Marvin, and you just don't do that to your brother-in-law."

Later, Jenny Redmond would look back and realize how much the experience rattled her. "My God, you just learn that he was arrested for killing someone, who wouldn't be afraid? I just sunk inside. When you know the John I knew, you think, 'How could he do anything this hideous?' " She made it clear, though, that she had no intention of rationalizing anything Famalaro might have done. "I'm not saying I don't want to see justice, because if he did this, he should be punished. I'm just saying I don't know the killer John." The prospect of his going free alarmed her, too. "My concerns were that he would try to call me, to contact me, and I just didn't want to deal with it. Who would? It gives you a whole new look on life. If he is this person, why didn't he do anything to me?"

As the news media expanded coverage of the stunning details, readers throughout California's southland gasped over the stories splashed across newspapers' front pages. The astonishing chronicles revealed that the victim's body, found in Arizona, was still frozen after three years. Many remembered the banner stretched across the side of an apartment building adjacent to the 73 freeway, picturing a beautiful young woman named Denise Huber. Now a color photo of her dazzling smile reminded readers and television viewers of her, and brought to mind the agony her parents had suffered for more than a thousand days.

Dennis and Ione Huber gallantly spoke to reporters about the sickening news from Arizona. Ione said, "It's been a horrible three years, not knowing anything." Prayer and faith, she said, had given them some ability to hold on, and hope. "Now, at least we know. I'm very thankful that we have an answer. We needed that, even though it wasn't the answer we wanted to have." With her voice trying not to show the rage she felt at Denise's killer, Ione said she couldn't understand what kind of a person could murder an innocent victim, then keep the body in a freezer for years. "I'm very angry. I can't even imagine someone being capable of doing what he's done. I hope he gets the death penalty because of all the pain he's caused us. He just has to be so sick." After a moment of thought, she added in a near whisper, "I guess it's time for that banner to come down now that we have an answer."

Sitting next to his wife, his head bowed and his hands clasped tightly together, Dennis Huber spoke in carefully measured tones. "It's basically the best of a bad situation. We have a body with clues and someone is in custody. That's better than just finding a skeleton." It would have been even harder to bear, he said, if searchers had found nothing but skeletal remains in the mountains or desert, and could find no trace of Denise's killer. Huber recognized that the arrest of John Famalaro certainly did not end the case. Maybe the suspect didn't even commit the murder, but he certainly had kept the frozen body, which made him guilty of exacerbating the pain suffered by people who loved Denise, people who desperately needed information about her. The killer had placed the parents on an agonizing roller coaster reaching heights of hope then plunging them into the depths of excruciating pain and doubt, seemingly interminable. Keeping the frozen body, and maintaining cruel silence those three years, had compounded the crime in Huber's opinion. "It was always on our minds," he said. "You go through so many frustrations. You wonder if she's okay, and what she's going through. There wasn't a day that I didn't think about it."

Even with the passage of time, Dennis had been holding on to a thin strand of optimism. "I still had hope that we would find her alive. I didn't give that up. So, it's a big shock to know that it's over."

Of course, it really wasn't over, and Dennis realized that. He knew they faced another severe ordeal in the administration of justice. And his need for answers remained unsatisfied. "There are still a lot of questions on our minds. How did she die? How did she get into the possession of the guy they arrested? We want to know all the things that happened between the day she disappeared and when she was found."

Expressing some disdain about people who may have witnessed the abduction but hadn't come forward, Dennis commented that it was hard to believe that someone, among all those freeway drivers who passed the Honda during the critical first few minutes after Denise pulled over to the shoulder with a flat tire, hadn't observed what happened. He shook his head, saying that he suspected someone had probably seen it, but out of fear or apathy, had decided they didn't want to get involved. "I don't understand how people can be so indifferent to their fellow man."

Hastening to make certain of no misunderstandings, both Dennis and Ione expressed gratitude to the long line of friends, acquaintances, and even strangers who had supported them and contributed to the intensive efforts and expenses of trying to find Denise. Prayer and the circle of faithful believers from the Aliso Creek Presbyterian church had rescued them from despair many times.

Their faith in God had calmed the storm for them more than once. Both parents believed that divine intervention had led to the discovery of Denise's body just prior to their planned move to North Dakota, and had even delayed the move by a month. They also felt that the hand of God had led Elaine Canalia and Jack Court to report the suspicious Ryder truck. Dennis would say that it was no coincidence when the Phoenix detective pressed the rental company to double check during his inquiry to determine if the truck had been reported as stolen. The report had been made just hours prior to the officer's arrival to investigate the truck. "No coincidence there," Dennis would say. "That was guidance from heaven."

The Hubers still planned to move to peaceful North Dakota. But first, they needed to arrange a proper burial for their daughter. Both parents agreed that Denise should rest beside her paternal grandfather in Dennis's home town, Herreid, South Dakota. Once again, they received assistance to complete the task. Police Chief Dave Snowden made all of the arrangements to transport the body. He had been close to the investigation for its entire duration, and had grown fond of the parents. "It became more than a job," he said. "Everybody was touched by this case."

Reporter Jonathan Volzke, almost a part of the family by now, joined Dennis and Ione in their home. Another uncanny twist made him shake his head. His family, originally from Herreid, South Dakota, had moved to a warmer climate—Glendale, Arizona, seventy-five miles from the spot where Denise's frozen body had been found. He wrote another personally slanted story as he observed the huge volume of telephone calls Dennis and Ione answered, some from total strangers who just wanted to express sympathy. CNN and *USA Today* had given widespread news coverage to the body discovery. "I guess the story's pretty much nationwide," Dennis told Volzke. "Somehow, it's a tribute to Denise . . . she was a very good person and this terrible thing happened. People need to know that she was a total victim. That she was a beautiful person who was taken away by this animal." The police hadn't shared all the gruesome details with the parents about the condition of the frozen body, but the press coverage held back very little. Dennis commented to Volzke, "I don't know if I want any more details."

* * *

Details, though, would continue to emerge about the search as it progressed in the Arizona home of John Famalaro. In a bedroom closet, searchers riffled through neatly hung shirts and jackets. On the right end, they lifted two starched, pressed, light tan Los Angeles County Deputy Sheriff's shirts, complete with shoulder patches, name tags, and an embroidered yellow badge over the left pocket. Not everyone would recognize it as a part of a trainee's uniform. To most people, it couldn't be distinguished from a full-fledged officer's attire. Speculation started immediately about the possible use of the uniform on the night Denise vanished. Had John Famalaro worn one of those uniforms in the early morning hours of June 3, 1991, stopped to make a false offer of help to Denise Huber, convinced her that he was a deputy going home from his shift, and then abducted her after she had willingly climbed into his car? Had she been duped into thinking she was safe with an officer of the law?

Lt. Ron Smith didn't think so. He had already learned that Famalaro wore a full beard at that time. Smith always tried to keep an open mind, and not rule out any reasonable possibility. But that theory didn't get him excited. "Denise was too smart to fall for that. One thing that weighs against that theory is that it's very unusual to have a uniformed officer with such long hair and a beard."

The Los Angeles Times, in its extensive coverage of the story on July 18, carried a photo of Smith standing in front of Famalaro's house. The *Orange County Register* also included a photo, picturing him wearing jeans, a polo shirt, and white sports shoes, conferring with two other officers among the clutter being removed from the house. The reports described a search for more bodies, and quoted Lieutenant Scott Mascher's comments about the discovery of the frozen corpse of Denise. "For whatever reason, he's toted her around for three years. If he's capable of doing that, he's capable of doing who knows what else."

John Famalaro had hired a lawyer by this time. Lawrence W. Katz announced that his client had done nothing wrong, and said, "I have full confidence in my client's innocence."

Chapter 14

Even though the Hubers had offered a reward of $10,000 to anyone who provided information leading to their missing daughter, the couple who came up with the key link announced to the news media they would not accept the money. Elaine Canalia and Jack Court won the admiration of millions of readers when they declared that it wouldn't be honorable to collect payment for their deeds. "To me, it's blood money," Court said. He knew that the Hubers were not wealthy, and that donations from various individuals and support groups which would have funded the reward had been spent on costs for the long search. If he accepted the money, he knew the Hubers would have been forced to borrow it. "Absolutely not," he stated. "They've suffered enough." If the reward had been offered and paid by a deep pockets group, or a police agency, Court said, then he and Elaine would have shared it with the Hubers.

To Dennis and Ione, it was another example of the goodness in people. Under the circumstances, it would have been easy for them to slip into hateful bitterness at the entire human race, given their long suffering. Instead, finding themselves recipients of good will, help, donations, and a wide range of magnanimous gestures from generous, decent people, they experienced new insight into their fellow man. If there was a silver lining to be found by the Hubers in the tragic event, it took the form of human benevolence.

* * *

In the Cochise Drive house, Scott Mascher and his searchers added to the long list of evidence found among the jammed contents of each room. By examining huge collections of newspapers, they discovered that John Famalaro had saved several articles about the search for Denise Huber. Also, among stacks of videotapes, they located a recorded episode of *Inside Edition*, in which Ione and Dennis Huber made a heartrending plea for information about their missing daughter. Mascher had trouble containing his usual calm composure. Just how could this guy keep the frozen corpse of a missing woman concealed, and cold-bloodedly videotape a plea from her parents that was broadcast nationwide? If he had possessed one shred of decency, couldn't he have at least sent an anonymous message giving the distraught family some information?

The officers also found a pair of blood-spotted jeans and a blood-soaked white sweatshirt. Emblazoned on the front of the shirt were red letters spelling "LAKE WOBEGON" above the picture of a black and white Holstein cow standing in a green field, against a dark blue sky with puffy white clouds. Most of the blood had been absorbed into the upper right sleeve.

Behind bars, isolated from other prisoners for his safety, John Famalaro requested that he be allowed to keep a Catholic Bible in his cell. He also attended a religious gathering at which inmates chatted about their faith. Saying nothing about himself, Famalaro participated by joining in the singing of "Rock Of Ages."

Investigators breathed a tentative sigh of relief when most of the female names found in the home led not to more victims, but to stunned women who were very much alive. Two of them had no idea how they had lost credit cards and identification papers, including a birth certificate, that turned up in the house. A third woman, and her husband, had sold John Famalaro a van in 1992, and couldn't explain why the suspect had kept records with her name on them. Yet another woman, whose knapsack

had been found among Famalaro's possessions, proved to be
more elusive. When investigators located her father, he sent
pulse rates sky high by saying he hadn't seen her for several
months. A telephone call from the woman's sister, from another
state, quickly dismissed the idea that her sibling, who often disappeared for long periods of time, had met with disaster. Hearing good news that the transient was perfectly safe, Mascher
crossed her name from the list of potential homicide victims.

Other trails would be extremely difficult to follow. Many of
the women's names found among Famalaro's collection did not
include the surnames. Nevertheless, Mascher's team made every
effort to track them down, and succeeded in most cases. They
narrowed the list down to three.

Of the names cleared, one had experienced a frighteningly
close call. She had been plying her trade one night along a Phoenix street called "hooker alley." From her story, investigators determined that John Famalaro, driving a rental truck, pulled up
alongside her and asked her to join him in a local bar for a drink.
After she accepted his invitation, and had downed a cocktail, he
offered to take her to a more private place for additional drinks.
She climbed into the truck cab with him and looked him over
while he drove to a deserted nursery in the desert. A shivering
fear gradually overcame her, and she told him she wanted to leave.

Famalaro agreed to take her back to hooker alley, but first, he
said, he needed to relieve his bladder. Worried, she said she also
had to go. As he walked in one direction into the dark desert, she
headed the other way, so nervous she left her purse in the cab of
the truck. From out of the black night, she heard a piercing
scream and turned toward the source. Her "date" charged toward
her, shouting like a demon. The terror-stricken prostitute scram-
bled away in the black shadows, and managed to escape. She spent
the night huddled behind an outcropping of rocks in the cold
desert.

When investigators found the contents of her purse in John
Famalaro's house, they tracked the woman down. She told her
chilling story, but refused to press charges.

* * *

Embarrassed officials of the Ryder Company had difficulty explaining why they hadn't reported their truck stolen months
sooner. They explained that they'd sent Famalaro a letter on
January 31, 1994, demanding return of their vehicle. He had
rented it three days earlier from an agency in San Clemente,
California, not far from where he conducted his house painting
business in Laguna Hills. In the signed contract, Famalaro
agreed to bring it back on January 29, but failed to show up. So
the letter mailed to him demanded return of the vehicle and
warned, "If you do not comply with this demand . . . appropriate
legal action, both criminal and civil, may be instituted."

Why the firm never pursued the issue remained unclear, but
the agent who negotiated the agreement with Famalaro lost his
job over the original transaction. The unemployed man later
explained that he had been conned by the customer into reduc-
ing the usual deposit of $250 to a mere $100. "He was a smooth
talker. He said he was out of money and he only needed the
truck for a few hours." But the next day, the agent found a note
Famalaro left by saying he needed the truck for a few more days.
A full week later, when Famalaro hadn't shown up or called, the
worried agent telephoned George Famalaro, John's brother, who
reportedly said, "John is kind of the black sheep of the family."
He also hinted that the truck might be in Arizona. When the
agent informed his boss of the problem, and the insufficient
deposit he had allowed, the angry supervisor fired him. Not only
that, the agent later complained, they deducted $150 from his
final paycheck to cover the difference between the required deposit and what Famalaro had been charged.

While the unreturned Ryder truck sat behind the house where
John Famalaro lived, he looked out his window one day and had
a serious scare. Three young men who had previously worked
for him showed up demanding unpaid back wages. When he
failed to come to the door, they decided to seek retribution by
burglarizing the Ryder truck. Fearing what the trio might find
and take with them, Famalaro called the police. Minutes later,
two deputy sheriffs screeched to a halt next to the truck. They

corralled the trio of would-be thieves, and asked them what was going on. "He cheated us out of some money he owes us," growled the largest of the young men.

One officer stayed outside with the trio, while the other went inside to hear Famalaro's side of the story. In the subsequent police report, dated Tuesday, March 29, 1994, the deputy wrote, "I was dispatched to a burglary of a vehicle . . . Jay Samalero (sic) reported that a Ryder truck parked in his driveway was being broken into by 3 male subjects." He identified the three men, and reported, "Samalero stated the suspects should not have come to his house and was scared so he did not answer the door. Samalero at this time paid them the money he owed, and went back inside. The suspects also left. Case closed."

A hand-written postscript on the report states that, "All vehicles at this residence were checked through computer, by deputies; none were listed as stolen at this time." Scrawled just below that entry is another note. "Famalaro gave fictitious name as complainant."

After Famalaro's arrest in July, Det. Lonnie Brown discovered that trouble had again loomed for Famalaro over another motor vehicle transaction. Brown heard from a finance company in Phoenix that they'd been looking for John Famalaro since April. The painter, using a Sedona address, had purchased a van from a Chevrolet agency in Prescott but failed to make the monthly payments, so the seller repossessed the vehicle. Furious, Famalaro claimed he'd experienced serious mechanical problems with the van which, he said, gave him very good reasons not to pay for it until it was properly repaired. He found a way to rectify the repossession. On a Saturday in February, Famalaro approached an employee at a Phoenix Chevy agency, explained that his new vehicle was in the repair shop, and talked his way into driving a loaner van out of the lot. For Famalaro, the loaner turned out to be a keeper. He never returned it to the Phoenix dealer. The agency filed a stolen vehicle report with the police, but rescinded it when Famalaro contacted them by telephone and insisted he had documents to prove that the van belonged to him. Fearing a lawsuit for false charges, the dealer canceled the report.

After discovering the duplicity, the Chevy agency decided to settle the matter through civil litigation to recover their missing van. An investigator contacted Famalaro's parents, but came away complaining of their uncooperative attitude. They reportedly refused to tell him where John lived.

When Lonnie Brown obtained more details about the van, he realized that he knew exactly where it was. It had been towed from a Safeway market parking area to the Yavapai County storage lot in Prescott and impounded because someone had fired a .45 caliber weapon from inside, leaving a suspicious bullet hole in a side panel. The keys had been in John Famalaro's pocket when he was arrested.

On Monday, July 18, two detectives executed a search warrant on the 1993 white Chevrolet fourteen-foot van. In the cargo section, they observed a palm print that might have been made by a bloody hand. From among piles of paint cans inside, they seized two hammers, a hunting knife, and a black leather whip described by one of the investigators as a "quirt," black and white plastic trash bags, duct tape, and a nylon jacket. Scott Mascher characterized the bizarre collection as "an abduction kit."

Ultimately, the van and its contents proved disappointing. The bloody palm print turned out to be paint, the bullet hole was never explained, and nothing else inside the vehicle could be related to the frozen body of Denise Huber or any of the names listed as potential victims. As many other leads had, the trail of the van evaporated like a mirage in the hot Arizona desert.

It is not uncommon for avenues of investigation, clues, or leads followed by homicide detectives to come to a grinding halt in blind alleys. That's an expected part of the job. The team working with Scott Mascher had long since accepted that, but refused to allow dead ends to dampen their enthusiasm. Dan Martin, one of the two men who searched the van, found another trail that appeared to offer more promising headway. On July 19, he heard from Michael Manning, a fellow law enforcement officer in the Department of Public Safety. Manning had recognized John Famalaro from television news broadcasts, and remembered being his classmate at the Los Angeles Sheriff's Academy. They had car-pooled together from Orange County with one or two other men.

Manning reported his recollection that Famalaro had not completed work at the academy due to poor evaluations stemming from his attitude and unsatisfactory performance. Personally, Manning thought that Famalaro had not demonstrated the type of personality required to hold a job in law enforcement. As Manning recalled it, Famalaro had once boasted that he was graduating from chiropractor school and wanted to be a reserve deputy so he could earn his living as a chiropractor, but put people in jail as a sideline.

The next comment from Manning's mouth grabbed Detective Martin's undivided attention. According to Manning, Famalaro had also bragged of stalking his girlfriend because he believed that she was cheating on him. Famalaro told of borrowing a van from a friend and hiding in it while parked at the front of his girlfriend's house to watch her come and go with other men. At other times, he had also concealed himself in bushes around her house. He even admitted threatening her by saying that he would seek revenge for her indiscretions. Manning had responded to Famalaro by telling him that such conduct would not be appropriate for a prospective law enforcement officer, but Famalaro "blew off" the advice. "I just didn't like the guy," Manning told Martin.

Stalking, Detective Martin knew, was a symptom sometimes associated with men who kill women in a jealous rage. Such killers often seek out a total stranger and murder a symbolic substitute for the straying lover.

Famalaro's pattern of interaction with women came under Detective Martin's scrutiny again when another ex-classmate of the suspect called the police. The woman had been in a real estate class with Famalaro a few weeks before he was arrested. She reported that he focused his attention on her and a female friend during the entire two weeks of school. The informant said she told Famalaro that she was married but he insisted on engaging her in conversations while she waited after school for her husband. The subject of those talks disturbed her.

Martin listened to her complaint, and wrote, "On more than one occasion, Famalaro would ask her if she knew self-defense and would stress how she should watch herself when out alone." After Famalaro's arrest, the woman saw reports on television and felt goosebumps rise on her skin. Famalaro had reportedly said to her, after stressing the importance of knowing some self-defense techniques, "There's some real strange guys out there."

Just as women had so strongly influenced the life of John Famalaro, women also began contributing little trickles of information, which joined to become streams that threatened to become a river of evidence against him.

During Famalaro's tenure as a restaurant busboy in the mid-seventies, a blond waitress had noticed him. Now, twenty years later, she and her husband recognized him on television news reports when the suspect was arrested in the Denise Huber case. From their Orange County home they made a call to the Yavapai County Sheriff's Office, which put them in contact with Detective Garry J Saravo. A member of the county attorney's office's investigative branch, and a good friend of Scott Mascher, Saravo had joined the team probing the Huber case. The callers told Saravo that they had developed a deep respect for the Famalaro when he was still a bright and energetic teenager. The couple knew that he'd been to chiropractic school, and that he held a black belt in karate. The husband had once started a business, made a place for Famalaro to help promote it, and supplied the young man with a corporate credit card. When the business began to crumble and collapse, Famalaro asked permission to continue using the card in his own entrepreneurial efforts. After receiving conditional concurrence, Famalaro began charging between two and four thousand dollars monthly, making his benefactor extremely nervous. Finally, Famalaro ran the bill up to $10,300 in a single month and failed to pay it.

Detective Saravo asked to see the statements of charges, and got agreement from the informant to provide them. Adding to more comments about Famalaro, the angry husband said the painter had been using a mail drop as an address for his Orange County house painting business. The caller, though, had discovered the real location from which Famalaro operated. He said, "My son saw him driving one day, and followed him to a warehouse." The address was in a large industrial tract in Laguna Hills, Orange County, on Verdugo Drive. Famalaro, he thought, had converted an office in the warehouse to living quarters, and moved in.

The caller mentioned that they had seen several of the women with whom Famalaro had romantic relationships. He described Darlene Miller, who had gone to New York with John, and another, Kate Colby, who had been handcuffed once by Famalaro until she threatened to report him to the police.

After several attempts, Saravo finally reached Kate Colby in Orange County, and patched Costa Mesa detective Frank Rudisill in to hear the conversation. Colby told of dating Famalaro in 1991, and said she hadn't seen him for a couple of years. She still felt angry at him for two reasons. First, he had charged more than $3,000 to her credit card and had never paid any of it. Second, he had once shoved her onto a bed as she started to leave his house, and snapped handcuffs on her. When she screamed, cried, and threatened to tell the cops, he backed off. She confided that Famalaro was very secretive about his life.

Evidence mounted pointing to John Famalaro as undoubtedly the possessor of Denise Huber's body, possibly her abductor, and maybe her killer. While he sat in jail, observers expressed concern that he might be able to raise the $275,000 bail which would allow him to walk out. To prevent such a worrisome event, a justice of the peace revoked the bail, but failed to hold a hearing before making his decision. Famalaro's attorney vehemently objected, whereupon a second justice agreed to hold the hearing.

Widely divergent views of Famalaro's guilt or innocence rang through the courtroom in Prescott on July 20 during the proceedings to determine if Famalaro should kept in jail as a suspect or released on bail. Wearing a short-sleeved orange jumpsuit, bearded, bespectacled, his full hair slicked straight back, Famalaro sat with his hands manacled in front of him, not twisted behind his back as Denise Huber's had been. He silently listened to the legal volleys. No member of his family occupied any of the three dozen courtroom gallery seats.

Deputy County Attorney Thomas Lindberg, describing the killing of Huber as heinous and depraved, said, "The proof is evident and the presumption is great that the defendant is guilty of the murder and is a danger to the community." Lt. Scott Mascher took the witness stand to outline evidence against the defendant.

Famalaro's attorney, Lawrence W. Katz, who wore his hair in a ponytail as counterpoint to a sharply tailored suit, steadfastly defended the suspect. "He's a good Catholic" Katz said. In words sounding unequivocal, he declared, "There is no proof that he has ever hurt anyone, anywhere, anyplace." The circumstantial evidence being assembled by investigators, he said, proved nothing. "They haven't shown anything. They've shown there was a freezer with a dead body in it . . . He is no danger to the community." The police, he pointed out, didn't even know where the killing had taken place, and had no evidence to connect Famalaro to Huber's death.

After listening to both sides, the justice of the peace ruled that Famalaro would remain in custody, and would not be allowed to post bail. A grand jury would decide if the evidence supported an indictment of murder.

Another announcement followed the hearings. A different attorney, Thomas K. Kelly, informed observers that he had been contacted by the suspect's family and offered the job of taking over Famalaro's defense. The reasoning, he candidly said, had some relationship with religion. "They did contact me and part of the rationalization in hiring me is that I am Catholic." Lawrence Katz was Jewish.

Not hiding his consternation, Katz put his disdain in succinct terms. "Mama wants a Catholic. No Jews allowed." Warming to his subject, he reinforced the idea that Famalaro's mother had been the driving force in making the change. "I've never heard of such a thing in my life. I put my heart and soul into this case. I liked him. I looked at him as the guy next door type who needed a real aggressive defense. We got along well. I don't know what the hell she did, but John was not a factor in that decision. It was her . . . she has him gripped like a vise." Financial matters may have influenced the change as well, he acknowledged. "What happened here, I think, is that they wanted somebody cheaper."

Twenty-four hours later, the Yavapai County grand jury listened to testimony from Lt. Scott Mascher and Det. Lynda Giesler in a secret, two-and-a-half hour hearing. Evidence presented by the two officers convinced the jury to issue an indictment against John Famalaro of first degree murder in the killing of Denise Huber. They also charged him with grand theft of the Ryder truck. The murder, they proclaimed, was "heinous and depraved," which made it possible under Arizona law to allow prosecutors to seek the death penalty against Famalaro. But no one knew yet whether he would be tried in Arizona or California. That would be decided according to the evidence still being collected. A spokesman for the Yavapai County Attorney's Office said, "We will try the case in the jurisdiction where there is most likely to be a conviction." He added that it would depend largely on evidence to show where the victim actually died.

The investigation team had not yet determined, either, whether Famalaro was the only suspect in the case, or if others might be involved. A Southern California psychic, who had provided the Hubers with his insights early in the case, called the Costa Mesa PD to announce his certainty that at least one accomplice had been part of the abduction and killing. To give credence to his theory, he reminded anyone who would listen that he had predicted the body would be found in some type of container within a storage area.

Even without the psychic's help, investigators had certainly not ruled out the possibility of involvement by an accomplice or the likelihood of more victims. Lt. Ron Smith told reporters, "Because of the nature of this crime, we still have the possibility of other victims. If somebody can do this once, what would stop them from doing it again, once they cross that threshold?"

At least one clue of another victim had been eliminated. Famalaro's ex-girlfriend who had observed the digging underneath the Cochise Drive house had reported seeing a bone pulled from the dirt. About eighteen inches in length, it might have been human remains, she thought. But another witness reported that the bone also had a hoof attached, and probably belonged to a deer. Nevertheless, the search for a possible co-killer and more victims would continue.

In Newport Beach, still in preparation for moving to North Dakota, Dennis and Ione Huber reacted with enthusiasm to the grand jury's indictment of Famalaro. "I think it's great," Dennis said. "One jury at least thought he was worth holding. With all the evidence they've got, it should have been pretty cut and dried."

Events that had taken place in Orange County, California, seemed to be assuming major importance in the investigation. Detective Saravo asked Lynda Giesler and Frank Rudisill if, when they returned home, they could pick up the credit card billing statements the ex-waitress and her husband had dug up. Saravo also suggested a visit to the warehouse on Verdugo Avenue in Laguna Hills. Giesler had already heard of the Verdugo address, from papers found in the Cochise Drive house. A search warrant would be arranged.

Everything looks new in south Orange County's Laguna Hills. There are no aging industrial sections or dilapidated residential neighborhoods. More "estates" than homes fill the lots in gated communities. The broad avenues winding through the rolling terrain are landscaped with green belts, and modern industrial tracts appear to be designed by Frank Lloyd Wright or I.M. Pei. Not far from the I-405 freeway, a development of business buildings occupies several blocks around Verdugo Drive which can be accessed a short block from Moulton Parkway in Laguna Hills. In the 23000 block of Verdugo Lane, behind a dozen towering eucalyptus trees rooted in a well-manicured sloping lawn, a clean one-story building, painted off-white with gray wooden trim, looks more like an office complex than a warehouse. Inside, though, are cavernous storage and work areas; four units measuring about 4,500 square feet each. John Famalaro had operated his house painting business out of unit B in 1991 and part of 1992. On one side of him, in unit A, a limousine service provided luxurious rides to affluent Orange County business leaders. On the other side, in units C and D, an energetic, trim young man named Steve Parmentier ran a garment manufacturing business. His workers cut patterns from huge bolts of cloth imported from China, to be turned into fashionable clothing.

Parmentier and John Famalaro became acquainted during Famalaro's one year of occupancy in unit D. The manufacturer often gave his painter neighbor boxes of cloth trimmings rather than sell them or toss them in dumpsters located at the rear of the building. Famalaro gratefully accepted the scraps of cloth and made use of them as cleanup rags in the painting operations.

In his 4,500 square feet, Famalaro stored hundreds of paint containers, scaffolding, ladders, tarps, and the paraphernalia of the house painting business. He constructed a pair of storage sheds inside the warehouse, and converted office space to a bedroom, next to a restroom. Just outside the office/bedroom, he installed a row of cabinets, a sink, and a large refrigerator. Always a private, somewhat secretive person, he kept all doors to these private quarters securely locked, as well as the cabinets and refrigerator, and made certain that his employees, who could only enter from the back alley through large roll-up doors, kept away from his personal areas.

When Famalaro moved out in 1992, with the help of his ex-brother-in-law, Marvin Kraft he took everything, including the dismantled interior storage sheds and his refrigerator. Steve Parmentier took over unit B to expand his garment business.

Chapter 15

During the stay in Arizona by Ron Smith, Lynda Giesler, and Frank Rudisill to work with the Yavapai County team, other officers in Orange County picked up the ball and carried it to the warehouse on Verdugo Street in Laguna Hills.

Detective Jack Archer, who had originally worked with Giesler on the case, rejoined the investigation to lead the Orange County team. He drove to the warehouse with Crime Scene Investigation Supervisor Bruce Radomski, whose duties involved running the crime lab's photography section, diagramming the layout of evidence, and overseeing the work of criminalists who collect evidence. The usual routine followed by detectives during the initial steps of processing a homicide case started with arrival and examination of the crime scene, then contacting Radomski to outline the need for specific follow-up by specialists. Giesler said about Radomski, "Detectives tell Bruce what they want, and he sees that it's done. He's very good at it. I wouldn't want to work a murder investigation without him." She emphasized that the boss-subordinate interaction is downplayed, that a homicide investigation is always a matter of efficient teamwork.

Accompanied by Radomski, Archer arrived at the Verdugo Drive warehouse and met Steve Parmentier, the clothing manufacturer who had been Famalaro's neighbor. Parmentier said the painter had moved out in August 1992, allowing him to take over the space Famalaro had occupied almost two years ago. Archer asked if they could look around the place, and Parmentier cooperated fully, even to the extent of hiring workers to move the hundreds of clothing racks to give the investigators easier access.

The officer's request was not a random one. Jack Archer already had a pretty good idea where to look. In previous interviews with several men who had been temporary employees of Famalaro, one of the workers told of being ordered to clean the floor during the process of Famalaro's moving out. The employee had pulled a hose into the building and sprayed a strong stream of water on multicolored paint spills stuck to the concrete floor. He had tried in vain to wash away the stains, but most of them stubbornly adhered to the floor.

From this description, an idea formed in Archer's mind. He asked the worker if all of the splattered paint had remained on the concrete, or if possibly one or two had washed away under the water pressure. "Oh yeah," the employee answered enthusiastically. "Right over here. There was a big brown spot." He led officers to the southwest corner of the unit, and declared, "The stain here washed right out."

Spilled or spattered paint would not easily succumb to water spray, Archer figured, but dried blood would dilute and drain away. At least most of it would. He knew that Radomski had a way of making the remaining stains show up. Luminol is a chemical that reacts to blood and literally causes bloodstains to glow in the dark. A pigment in blood, known as heme, reacts to Luminol and creates a luminescent glow. To be more certain that the tested material is blood, an additional test is usually applied. The criminalist swabs the material with another chemical, leuco malachite green (LMG). If the tested substance is blood, it will turn green.

That night, Monday, July 18, Archer and Radomski summoned Criminalist/Crime Scene Investigator Laurie Crutchfield to the warehouse corner where the employee had pointed out his successful cleaning efforts. A dark room was necessary for more successful use of the process. Crutchfield opened her Luminol kit and sprayed the chemical where the worker had pointed, then switched off the lights. She and two detectives held their breaths, but not for long. An eerie blue glow virtually lit up the corner. A great deal of blood had been spilled on that spot.

Much of it had apparently drained underneath the baseboard. An application of LMG confirmed the find.

Using cutting tools, the officers carefully removed sections of the wood framing and drywall, plus the soaked baseboard, and placed them in evidence containers. Crutchfield would recall, "There was an area of thick deep maroon color between the concrete and the wood board." Blood cannot be scraped from concrete, so she used moist swabs to lift samples, and took the collected materials to the Orange County Crime Lab for additional testing.

Just to play it safe, Crutchfield and Radomski sprayed Luminol throughout the warehouse to see if any other bloodstains would show up. They found nothing more. If a victim had bled profusely inside that building, it had been in one isolated spot only.

Buoyed by the discovery of blood in the Verdugo Drive warehouse, Det. Jack Archer expanded the probe in Orange County. It didn't take him long to discover that John Famalaro had apparently needed more storage capacity than the Laguna Hills facility provided, so the painter had rented space in other self-storage units. The trail led to a facility in San Clemente, a picturesque oceanside city about twenty miles from the warehouse. In the same city, Famalaro had rented, and failed to return, a Ryder truck.

The commercial storage manager spoke to investigators. Famalaro, he said, had contracted for seven of the units, starting in July 11, 1992, and ending on February, 5, 1994, and kept a big freezer in one of them. One peculiar requirement on which Famalaro absolutely insisted struck the manager as somewhat peculiar. "The whole time the freezer was here, he wanted twenty-four hour electricity." Ordinarily, the manager explained, the business provided electrical power only twelve hours a day, from 7 A.M. to 7 P.M. "People here thought it was very odd that he needed round-the-clock electricity. It's written right on the contract. Twenty-four hours."

When it came time for Famalaro to haul his property away from the storage unit, according to the manager, he asked for help from employees to lift his freezer into a truck's covered cargo bed. The painter seemed to be in a big hurry. "He said he had a generator on his truck that would keep the freezer running while he was driving. But the main thing was, he wanted it loaded real quick."

Detective Archer obtained from the Arizona team the charnel freezer's serial number, 10C-01352, and traced the Signature 2000 brand appliance to a Montgomery Ward store in Orange County. John Famalaro had bought it there on June 10, 1991, one week after Denise Huber vanished. He used an American Express credit card, to which was charged $562.49, and asked that it be delivered to the warehouse in Laguna Hills. Famalaro had apparently kept the freezer in the Verdugo Drive warehouse for eleven months, then moved it to the San Clemente storage facility until February 1994. Five months later, it turned up in Arizona in the back of a Ryder rental truck.

When he drove the truck to Arizona carrying the morbid load, he reportedly stopped at several gas stations along the way where he asked for and received permission to plug in his freezer for an hour or so, giving the reason that he didn't want the meat inside to spoil.

One witness revealed to Scott Mascher in Arizona a disturbing account of how Famalaro had recruited him to help move the freezer into the house on Cochise Drive. The two men had carefully measured the bulky appliance, then grunted and strained in efforts to manhandle it through the doorways. But no matter how they angled it, it wouldn't fit, so they laboriously hefted it back into the truck bed. During their struggle, the freezer remained unplugged, but not long enough to allow significant thawing of the contents.

The Arizona team interviewed Famalaro's ex-brother-in-law, Marvin Kraft again, and learned that he had helped the painter build cabinets in the Laguna Hills warehouse before Huber disappeared. He had seen a large, upright, almond-colored refrigerator/freezer in use there while Famalaro occupied unit B. The appliance had later been moved to the Cochise Drive house. One of the investigators would later theorize that Famalaro had kept the body of Denise Huber in the large refrigerator from the night she vanished, June 3, until he acquired the large freezer on June 10. In order to squeeze the body into the limited interior of the refrigerator, it would have been necessary to fold it into the tuck position and force the head down onto the chest. That theory could account for the cramped position of the body, the way officers found it, inside a spacious freezer that would have accommodated a more natural position.

Among the tons of painting supplies, appliances, and personal possessions Famalaro had moved to Arizona, he also hauled the dismantled storage sheds he'd removed from inside the warehouse. When Scott Mascher heard this, he realized why both Kallie and Ashley, the Rocky Mountain Rescue dogs, had shown consistent interest in the piles of wood at the side of the Cochise Drive house. The wood was from the storage sheds, which had been close to the spot where blood had pooled on the warehouse floor and seeped under the walls.

From all indications, Famalaro had lived in the converted office space of the warehouse from February or March 1991, until he relocated to Arizona in August 1992. Tracing backwards, detectives learned that he had earlier shared a house rental with an elderly man on Perth Way in Lake Forest, from August 1989 to March 1991. It was in an upstairs bedroom there, according to his one-time girlfriend, Kate Colby, that he snapped handcuffs on her and pinned her to the bed, causing the relationship to be interrupted for many months. When he surreptitiously moved out of the home on Perth Way one night, he owed the landlord for several months of unpaid rent. The landlord took the debt to court and won a judgement in April 1991, ordering Famalaro to pay her $6,100.

Financial woes piled up on all sides of John Famalaro in the spring of 1991, in the months before Denise Huber vanished.

* * *

By July 23, 1994, Denise's body would soon be ready for ship-
ment to Herreid, South Dakota, to be interred next to her grandfather. The Hubers planned to have a closed casket funeral for
her in the small community. First, though, the faithful friends
and acquaintances in Orange County wanted to say goodbye to
Denise in an appropriate way. On a sun-swept day, when Pacific
breezes cleared the air, they all met at the Mariner's Church in
Newport Beach.

Over 700 mourners came to pay their respects and celebrate
the life of Denise Huber. They came from northern California,
Tennessee, Canada, and all across the southland. In the modern
interior of the church, they quietly nodded recognitions, shook
hands, gazed at a photographic collage picturing Denise in various phases of growing up, then silently filled the rows, trying to
hold back tears even before the ceremony started. Colorful floral
arrangements decorated the podium. Mounted on a tripod, a
large, luminous portrait of Denise smiled brilliantly down on the
congregation.

Soft piano music acted as a soothing balm to the assembly, as
Jack Hafer, assistant pastor of the Aliso Creek Presbyterian
Church stood to offer words of welcome, followed by prayer, and
a short recitation listing high points in Denise's life. The Reverend Walt Shepard, who had been personally involved in organ-
izing help for the Hubers and constantly supportive of them,
spoke words of inspiration describing how prayers from all over
the world had helped the family survive three years of strife and
relentless horror. Shepard's fourteen-year-old daughter, Eliza-
beth, sang, "His Eye Is On The Sparrow," a long-time traditional
at funerals in Ione's family.

Debbie Detar Scott stepped up to the microphone and reminisced about her days at Covenant College as Denise's inseparable roommate and how people thought they were sisters except
for their noticeable difference in height. Scott dressed in black
and wore her long dark brown hair in an exact duplicate of the
style shown in Denise's tripod-mounted portrait. Speaking
quickly and dabbing at her nose with a tissue, Scott recalled the
school days and the more recent years together in Newport
Beach. She concluded by addressing the parents seated in the

front row. "Dennis and Ione, you raised a very special daughter. Denise has brightened and influenced many lives. You must be very proud to have had such a daughter. I wish I could have been more like her. Denise, we will always be thinking of you, always treasuring the time spent together. Never will I forget your smile. Thank you for being such a good friend. I really, really miss you. I will always hold your memory close to my heart and one day I will see you again in heaven. So walk with God, my dear friend, and smile down upon us, and you will continue to brighten our days. I love you."

A young man in a suit and tie replaced Scott at the lectern. Alan Thompson had been a buddy of Denise's in junior high school and in a church group. He recalled that Denise had never been in a bad mood or angry and was everyone's friend. She had loved the L.A. Kings, he said, and was the best water skier he'd ever seen. He brought subdued laughter to the crowd by recalling that "I'd sometimes have to drive the boat crazily to make her fall so the rest of us could ski." He admired her energy, her fun-loving attitude, and her devotion to the Bible. "I'm sure we all know that she is spending eternity with her Father in heaven."

Andrea Ludden, Denise's closest friend from the seventh grade through high school, wore a dark green floral patterned dress with a white yoke collar as she spoke. "Losing Denise was the hardest thing I've ever gone through in my life." She recalled summer camp, when Denise "always managed to step in the stinging nettles" and the joy they shared during a trip they took together. "I'll always miss her and I thank God that I got to be a part of her life."

Music had been a big part of Denise Huber's life. The next few minutes in the church memorialized that love with a remarkable tribute; a song written for Denise by Nancy Streza. "It was from my heart," Streza would later explain. "I had a picture of her in mind, walking on the sand in Hawaii, with that golden sun tan, smiling like sunshine."

At the keyboard sat a professional musician and close friend of Streza, John Andrew Schreiner. He bore a striking resemblance to Elton John, both physically and in his voice. He played and sang:

HER MEMORY

Five foot nine, eyes of blue
Oh Denise, we love you!
She went to a concert on a casual date,
said goodbye to her friend
And drove home real late.
What happened next was a mystery
Someone took her away,
Left us just her memory.

Bright eyes and laughter; a heart full of love
A trusting faith in her God up above
She loved music and dancing
Was a loyal Kings fan,
Walked on the beach with her golden suntan.

Three years of praying,
Three years of fright
But I know in my heart
Everything is all right.
In living and dying, she's safe in God's hands
The same Lord who loves us has her best in his plans.
He'll bring us together for eternity
They couldn't take her soul or her memory.

Bright eyes and laughter, a heart full of love
A trusting faith in her God up above
She loved England and dolphins
Was a loyal Kings fan,
Walked on the beach with her golden suntan.

Though it's still a mystery
We have her memory.

(Nancy Streza, July 1994)

Three more speakers filed up to the podium. Dave Nieuwsma, Denise's cousin from Canada and a youth pastor, said, "I'm from Vancouver, Canada, and I did not share Denise's enthusiasm for the L.A. Kings." His tenderly delivered words brought more gentle laughter. He reflected on his younger days when he lived in Modesto after the Hubers moved to southern California, and how he loved traveling south so he could visit Denise and swim in their pool. Speaking of the pain the family had experienced in losing their beloved daughter, he reminded the congregation how faith could help them survive.

Next came Claudia Moreland who had been Denise's baby-sitter and later her teacher in the fourth and sixth grades. Moreland recalled Denise's love for dogs and desire to be a veterinarian, her love for frogs, and the time Denise had lived with Moreland while the rest of the Huber family moved to Texas. "Today I share these details of her life hoping that you will leave here with her memory etched in your heart . . . We miss her." Acknowledging Denise's deep faith in the Lord, Moreland said, "We know that one day we will see her smile again."

Dick Streza, Nancy's husband, noted that he'd known Denise from the time she was twelve years old at Calabasas Presbyterian church. In prayer, he recalled, Denise always wanted to ask the Lord to give special attention to her grandfather. Now, she and her grandfather were together, Streza said. He concluded by speaking of Denise's strong faith in God.

Following the singing of a hymn, Jack Hafer paid tribute to the press and the police, commenting that some of them would have been at the services, but couldn't because they were in Arizona working the investigation. He then introduced Costa Mesa Police Chief Dave Snowden, as "one of the guys who has become very special, along with all of the officers, to the family."

Powerful emotion clearly reflected in his face and his voice, Snowden said about Denise, "I'm not surprised that she has touched our lives, because contrary to the image usually portrayed in motion pictures, cops can't turn the switch off when they go home, and forget the caseload they've had." Describing the pain that police see on a day-to-day basis, he cited a proverb in which it is said that a piece of the cop dies every time a young person is seen dead at the hands of a criminal. His officers felt that way. Denise, he said, had truly touched the lives of everyone in his department because working such a case involved the intricate study of the victim's life, and hers was "an exemplary life in an exemplary family." After learning everything about Denise, including her favorite songs, what food she liked, what she did for entertainment, Snowden said, he actually found himself rooting for the Kings one day. "Her picture has become my constant companion, on my desk, on the visor of my car, and even on our dresser at home . . . Dennis and I have become pretty close friends over our breakfast meetings to discuss the case." Through the incredibly complex investigation, he said, he directed his people to treat it as if Denise was their daughter, and they all came to feel that she was, indeed, their daughter. When he'd heard the news of her frozen body being found a few days earlier, he said, "I went back to the office pretending that allergies were causing my eyes to puff up and turn red." He apologized to the church for saying, within those hallowed walls that he hoped the killer would not be on this earth very long.

"There have been only two cases that have touched me this deeply," Snowden said, his voice trembling. "The other one was a twelve-year-old-girl who died on my birthday in 1982. . . ." Snowden paused, his swelling vocal cords betraying him, and clenched his jaws. His eyes moist, Snowden choked out the words, "I can tell you, you'd better hold your kids close to your breast." He wavered again, and managed his final words. "Dennis said it so aptly, 'Parents should not live to bury their children.' Thank you." Dave Snowden held his head high as he walked back to his seat.

"Near the Cross," followed, sung by John Andrew Schreiner. Dr. Henry Wabbendam, a professor at Covenant College, Chattanooga, Tennessee, rounded out the presentation with a final brief talk.

The photo collage of Denise included a snapshot of a present she had given to her parents. It was a simple piece of fabric upon which she had embroidered the words, "Life is fragile: handle with prayer."

* * *

From behind her windows in Prescott Country Club, John Famalaro's mother watched officers come and go at the Cochise Drive house. She expressed frustration and anger at the constant activity. News reports especially agitated her by quoting neighbors' comments characterizing the Famalaros as secretive or bizarre. "A lot of people are doing a lot of lying," she protested to an interviewer. "It is unbelievable what they are saying. This is killing us."

If a stranger who had never met the mother wandered into town, he would probably assume from her appearance—the gray, neatly coiffed hair, simple but stylish housedresses, spry movements—that she was a kindly grandmother who would welcome anyone into her home. Her political activism, in which she had worked hard against allowing gambling and pornography interests to lodge a foothold in the county, and her ability to flare in anger, might come as a surprise. She had also established a reputation as a shrewd real estate investor. But the pressure and pain of the investigation seemed to be wearing her patience razor thin.

Calling her son John "a very hard-working man," she commented that she had seldom seen him in recent weeks. "I hardly knew what John was doing or where he was going. He would leave early in the morning and return late in the evening. He worked so hard last year that he came down with pneumonia." Bitterly, she complained about all the public statements detailing her son's life. "Everybody else seems to think they know what he was doing. Those people all want their fifteen minutes of fame." Mr. Famalaro, she said, was very ill. The word had been spread that he suffered from Parkinson's disease. "He's not doing very well. This is hurting him."

Coming to grips with allegations that she had been a powerful influence in her children's lives, she said, "Sure, I ran a tight ship. But if I were a liberal and my kids got into trouble, people would have said that it was because I was a liberal. Since I am a conservative Christian, they are making me out to be a domineering mother." She strongly objected to suggestions that she had been overly protective about keeping her sons away from females. "Where do they get that stuff? That's just not true. For anyone to say that is just wrong."

Tilting her head in the direction of the house where investigators continued to probe for evidence, and neighbors seemed all too willing to criticize the Famalaros, she said, "I see them over there, leaking information to reporters all the time. They are trying to build a case any way they can. Maybe it's because I've been involved in politics . . . You know all the suffering that Jesus went through? That's what's happening to me now."

She'd heard that defense attorney Lawrence Katz had informed reporters he'd been dismissed because of his Jewish faith, to be replaced by a Catholic lawyer. Shaking her head, Mrs. Famalaro argued that religion had nothing to do with the decision to fire Katz and hire Jim Kelly. Kelly, she said, "offered me a hand when I needed one."

"I'm telling you," she growled, "I think the end is coming. There are bad things happening out there. I am counting on Jesus to bring our family through this."

Another member of the Famalaro clan, in Orange County, had different concerns. John's brother, George, said that he hated to see the family name dragged through the mud again. He complained that just when he thought it was finally safe to use his own name, after his own bout with the law more than a decade earlier, "They are dragging up all my stuff again. When is it going to end?" His mother, he said, just sits and stares, saying, "Pray for me."

"My father is dying of Parkinson's disease and trying not to understand any of this. It's going to push him over the edge."

Claiming that he hadn't even seen his brother for nearly five years, George Famalaro spoke of John. "When I talked to detectives, I just wanted to tell them that I knew my brother as a sweet, lovable guy. I don't know nothin' about nothin'." After a short pause, he added, "Buying that freezer, renting that storage space, dragging it all over the country was like he was saying, 'Please catch me'. . . . Someone's got to get him some Valium and get him to start thinking."

* * *

On the subject of George Famalaro, a Costa Mesa police spokesman said, "He's being interviewed as to his brother's movements." John Famalaro's brother was not considered a suspect in the case.

Chapter 16

For Arizona officials, the question loomed like a gathering desert thunderstorm—would John Famalaro stand trial in Yavapai County or be extradited to California? County Attorney Tom Lindberg summarized the status in late July. "Right now, the evidence indicates that the truck came from California. The freezer was purchased in California and brought . . . to Arizona. It was kept plugged in while it was in the truck. Is that enough to push the case back to California? I don't know. A blood match would make a stronger case for California jurisdiction."

The same day, an announcement came from the Orange County Crime Lab that preliminary tests of the blood sample taken from the Laguna Hills warehouse showed similarities to samples taken from the body of Denise Huber. More sophisticated DNA tests would be conducted to determine if conclusive results could be obtained.

Dennis and Ione Huber wondered if it would be better for Famalaro to face a murder trial in Arizona. Justice in California often seems to creep along at an infuriatingly slow pace. When judges sentence killers to death, Californians just shake their heads with cynical disbelief. In 1994, nearly 400 murderers languished in San Quentin's death row, and only two executions had been carried out in thirty years. Could the state logically claim to have a real death penalty? Residents had overwhelmingly mandated by ballots, twice, their approval of capital punishment. But somehow small activist groups, along with a clogged labyrinth of appeals and legal issues, kept the will of the people from being carried out. Maybe, the Hubers hoped, Arizona could do a better job.

"I'd like to see the death penalty in this case, and I'd like it carried out," said Ione, still packing in Newport Beach. "My fear is that it might not happen in this state."

Dennis agreed, but expressed hope that if the evidence brought the Famalaro trial back to Orange County, justice would prevail. "I feel there's still enough good people here that we can still get a conviction, despite the justice system." Shifting to the subject of his daughter's death, Dennis thought the available facts indicated she had been killed in the Laguna Hills warehouse, and that she had not suffered over a period of days or weeks. "It would make sense . . . that's where it happened. I want to believe it happened quickly that night . . . I want to believe it was swift. It's important to me that it was swift."

John Famalaro's new defense attorney, Tom Kelly, hoped for a trial in California because he thought laws there would make it tougher to seek the death penalty. "In my opinion, it's best to have this matter tried in California. I don't think it's any secret that Arizona has some of the toughest criminal statutes in the country." If the two states agreed to move the trial out of Arizona, Kelly would be forced to hand over the defense to someone else. He held no license to practice in California.

The parents had planned for Denise's body to be shipped to South Dakota for burial by the end of July, but heard that it would be delayed another day so the defense team could conduct their own, independent autopsy.

Moving a deceased person from one state to another is not an inexpensive process. Once again, compassion for the Huber family by a generous Samaritan, who had never met them, would rescue them from bearing the expenses. Police Chief Dave Snowden, acknowledging that the death of Denise had been extremely emotional for him, had been actively involved in not only the investigation, but also in giving his personal time and effort to aid the Hubers in the three-year search. He had recruited a close friend of his, Robert R. Risher, president of an ambulance and mortuary business in southern California, to attach bumper stickers to a fleet of vehicles used in his ambulance business.

Now, Risher volunteered more help. Through his contacts, he arranged for the transportation of Denise Huber's body to Herreid, South Dakota, at no expense to the family. And in another gesture of extreme generosity, he provided the casket and burial. Risher said, "I know how much this case meant to Dave, and I wanted to help in any way I could. This is a difficult time for people. I have a twenty-two-year-old daughter and can only imagine how they feel. You've got to look at it from that point. It's not often that a loved one is found after such a long period of time. We just want to help put the body to rest and bring the family some peace."

Twenty years earlier, as a rookie cop Snowden had met a young ambulance driver, Risher, and formed an enduring friendship. During the long association, Risher developed a profound respect for police personnel and sympathy for the tragedies they face. When two cops died in a crashed helicopter, in 1987, he paid for their burials.

Elated by Risher's generosity toward the Hubers, Snowden praised his close pal. "He's a compliment to the human race. I love him to death . . . He's an incredible guy."

In the ongoing struggle to determine where John Famalaro would face trial, the issue of extradition complicated the problems. Even if investigators concluded that the murder took place in Orange County, and Arizona officials agreed, they couldn't simply transport the suspect across state lines. If he and his attorney chose to fight extradition, the process could drag on for months.

First, Orange County D.A. Mike Capizzi would be required to convince a superior court judge to issue an arrest warrant for Famalaro. In Arizona, Famalaro would be faced with the decision to go without a fight, or to use the legal system in an all-out effort to prevent his transfer. His determination to fight the move would require Orange County to present the facts to Governor Pete Wilson, who would in turn, contact Arizona Governor Fife Symington. This would set in motion yet another hearing to give an Arizona judge the opportunity to rule on the extradition request. If the judge gave court approval, Famalaro could finally be transported to the Orange County Jail to face arraignment, followed by either a preliminary hearing or a grand jury indictment, and endless hearings on legal motions to dismiss or reduce charges. Each step, like a grueling obstacle course, contains pitfalls that could at any point along the way allow the defendant to walk. Contingent upon prosecutors avoiding legal traps that could set Famalaro free, he would face trial, in which he could be ruled mentally incompetent and sent to an institution until psychiatrists declared him well, at which time he could walk out, free and unfettered. Or a jury might find the circumstantial evidence against Famalaro inadequate to prove guilt beyond a reasonable doubt, in which case he would still walk out, never to be tried again for Denise Huber's murder.

Constitutional guarantees in the United States are rigidly imposed on the basis that it's better to set a guilty person free than to convict an innocent one. It's not a perfect system, but until the human race finds something better, it is all we have. Murder cases in which the prosecutor has nothing but circumstantial evidence, with no corroborating witnesses or hard evidence, metaphorically called "a smoking gun," are often the most difficult to try.

John Famalaro, by law, was innocent until proven guilty. Convincing a jury of that could be an extremely difficult task.

Three days before the end of July, the announcement came. John Joseph Famalaro would be tried in Orange County, if he could be extradited.

Christopher Evans, the deputy D.A. who had spent two weeks in Arizona conferring with county attorneys and observing the investigation, drew the duty of prosecuting Famalaro, and got the word while still lodged in Yavapai County. D.A. Michael Capizzi had virtually given him carte blanche to build the case.

Born on Long Island, New York, not far from the birthplace of John Famalaro, Chris Evans grew up in awe and admiration

of his father. The senior Evans fought in WWII with the 2nd
Marine Division on Guadalcanal, Saipan, Tinian, and Iwo Jima,
and returned safely to become a lawyer in Connecticut. "He is
why I became a lawyer," Evans says. "He was a Renaissance man
and I wanted to be just like him. He taught me the importance
of humility, and when I speak to a jury, I can still remember the
importance of that. He was my hero."

When Chris reached the age of twelve, the Evans family moved
to southern California where he completed high school and enrolled at Cal State University, Long Beach, next to the pounding
waves of the Pacific Ocean. "I was born in a seaside town, and
I've spent most of my life close to one ocean or the other. I feel
a very strong attachment to the sea, both physically and emotionally." He finished his academic years at Western State University, Fullerton, where he earned a law degree in 1982. The
years in school were not indolent, carefree days at the beach.
Evans worked as a fireman and paramedic for twelve years, much
of it while in school. The experience would turn out to be valuable for him in his work as a lawyer, particularly in understanding
pathology and physiology, not to mention the corollary exposure
to police agencies where he learned "cop talk" and enforcement
procedures.

After passing the exam, he joined the D.A.'s office in Riverside
County, where he worked in the desert community of Palm
Springs. It didn't take him long to figure out that well-known
organized crime figures from cold eastern climates liked to
spend winters in the warm desert air. It took courage when he
faced several of them in court cases. One in particular had been
frequently acquitted of various charges. Evans, though, convinced a jury to send the guy to prison.

After two years in Palm Springs, Evans joined the D.A.'s staff
in Orange County. One day he accepted an invitation to take a
tour of a state prison. He asked a guard who was acting as a
guide if any famous inmates occupied the cellblock. "Yeah," said
the guard, and named the man Evans had sent up. A few minutes
later, while seated in the cafeteria, Evans spotted the notorious
con, who instantly locked eyes with the worried prosecutor.
Evans' pulse quickened when the guard beckoned the stern-

faced tough guy. Trying to keep his heart from banging too loud, Evans watched the steely-eyed thug march over to his table. Wondering what it would be like to be murdered right there, Evans waited. The con stood in front of him, jabbed out a thick paw in offer of a handshake, grinned, and growled to the guard, "If my lawyer was as good as this guy, I wouldn't be here."

One bit of information passed on to Evans by his father, and later by colleague Bryan Brown, would serve him well in a number of cases. "There are unpleasant things that will happen in trial that you cannot predict. Some will catch you completely off guard. When that happens, you must not show emotion." From those wise mentors, Evans learned what to do. "When I feel the heat rising from an unexpected turn of events in trial, with my face feeling that hot red, I go to a calm place in my mind. I look calm. When that pressure comes, it is best to ask myself, how can I make this work for me?" Over the years, Evans had used the lesson countless times.

Off the job, Evans often found peace on the ocean sailing his thirty-two-foot vessel along the coast, or across the channel to Catalina Island. When time allowed, he would also join three other prosecutors to don wetsuits and ride surfboards at several southland beaches. One of his fellow surfers, Evans found out, had attended a Catholic high school. The colleague recalled a classmate of his, an odd kid named John Famalaro.

In the middle afternoon of July 29, Chris Evans telephoned Dennis Huber to inform him that Orange County would try John Famalaro for murder. But, of course, they had to extradite the accused killer first. Reporter Jonathon Volzke happened to be sitting in the Hubers' living room when the call came. He saw Dennis give the thumbs up sign halfway through the conversation with Evans. The settlement of the trial venue was only half the news. The other half was that all autopsy work had been completed, and the body of their daughter could now be sent to South Dakota for burial.

Slumping into an easy chair, Dennis said to his wife, and to Volzke, "This is the end of a chapter. Not the end of the book, but the end of a chapter." He allowed himself a big sigh and expressed relief that they could have the funeral as planned. "There's a finality to it."

Jonathon Volzke traveled to Herreid, South Dakota, with the Hubers to attend the funeral and to become acquainted with his own family's roots. The Aliso Creek Presbyterian pastor, Walt Shepard also made the trip, as did Police Chief Dave Snowden.

The white steel casket containing the body of Denise Huber arrived in a black hearse with a white top on Monday night, August 2. Dennis, Ione, and Jeff stood close to their beloved Denise that night for the first time in more than three years. The casket remained sealed. "It was like being hit in the face with a snow shovel," Dennis told reporter Volzke.

Clouds drifted across the broad Dakota sky on the next morning as nearly 250 people crowded around the small, brown, wood-frame First Reformed Church to attend services for Denise. The crowd represented approximately half of the town's entire population. Because the church pews could accommodate only a fraction of the assembly, attendants set up two television monitors, one in the basement and one outside in the shade of a giant cottonwood tree. In a prominent spot close to the entrance stood a tripod displaying the same photo collage of Denise that mourners had admired at the Newport Beach services.

One of Ione's nine siblings, Bob Vandenburg, wiped away a tear and said, "Denise has touched more people today than if she'd lived to be one hundred years old."

Inside, the white casket, decorated with a spray of red and white carnations, stood on a gurney behind the smiling portrait of Denise. For the last time, "His Eye is on the Sparrow" was played for her. Walt Shepard delivered words of faith and several friends and relatives eulogized the beautiful young woman whom they missed so much. Dave Snowden spoke emotionally again, saying, "When I took the oath of a police officer many years ago, I didn't know what to expect. No one prepared me for the hurt, the pain, the anguish of a case like Denise's disappearance." He described the closeness of sitting with the Hubers the previous evening, and the uplifting beauty of watching the sun set across the western plains while visiting the grave of Sitting Bull. "When we began this investigation three years ago, we did not know that Denise's longest travel would be from the arms of her family to the cemetery here in Herreid."

Eighty-degree temperatures, made even warmer by the sweltering August humidity, didn't bother the mourners as they gathered at the Herreid cemetery that afternoon. A red canopy shaded the white casket. Ione, wearing a black and white striped jacket, red belt, and black skirt, stood holding Dennis's hand, as they both bowed their heads in grief and prayer. Other family members stood with them while Walt Shepard led them in prayer. He observed that, "Denise . . . is no longer wandering, lost in our imagination." At the end of the ceremony, before the casket was lowered into the earth where Denise could at last rest beside her grandfather, a flotilla of multicolored balloons ascended into the cloudy sky.

At a potluck supper afterwards, Dennis watched his granddaughter, Ashley Denise, not yet two, toddle across a lawn. Trying to contemplate the reasoning for his daughter's death, he said, "I don't think I could ever begin to figure out why. She was a beautiful, wonderful person who deserved to be in this world, but I guess God wanted her up in heaven more than He wanted her here."

Ione commented, "I can't find the words to describe her. She was just a beautiful person and she should not have had to leave us the way she did."

Usually silent, Jeff couldn't contain his anger about the accused killer. "I'd love to confront him with my bare hands. And you can put that in quotes. Her death makes you appreciate your loved ones when you've got them. It makes you realize just how temporary life is."

In the cooling twilight of that evening, Jonathon Volzke strolled the length of the quiet farm and cattle town, three whole blocks of tree-lined streets, widely spaced wooden buildings, with one bank, a small cafe, the Huber motel, the hardware store where "Tuffy" Volzke had supplied farmers, the school where a young Ione had taught, and no traffic lights. Peace reigned over the tiny German-Russian community, where doors remained un-locked. The fliers asking "Have you seen Denise?" had at last been taken from store windows, replaced by affectionate posters such as, "Love and prayers to the Huber family." He tried to picture the buildings in wintery blizzard conditions, and in the imminent fall season when leaves would cover the broad yards. In the quiet dusk, he could almost hear music from the six churches.

Volzke hoped that the Hubers could, indeed, find peace when they moved to Mandan in a few weeks, up by Bismarck, and escape the painful memories of Orange County.

PART VI

JUSTICE

Chapter 17

On the day after Denise Huber's funeral, the State of Arizona made an official motion to drop the murder charges against John Famalaro.

The move wasn't as drastic as it sounded. Since Orange County had filed murder charges against him, on the basis that Huber was killed in California, Arizona had no reason to pursue the action for the same crime. They would, however, keep intact the allegation of grand theft related to Famalaro's possession of the Ryder truck.

In Prescott, Ron Smith, Lynda Giesler, and Frank Rudisill helped load a seventeen-foot rental truck with stacks of boxes and the now-empty freezer. "We had nothing against the Ryder Company," Giesler would later say, "but we chose a different agency to rent our truck." Nearly exhausted, the Costa Mesa team dreaded the long drive across the desert to Orange County. They had been working fourteen to sixteen hours each day, and not eating dinner until late at night, before collapsing in the historic Hassayampa Inn, where Tom Mix, Clark Gable, and Carole Lombard had once stayed.

For the trip home, Giesler and Rudisill drove the truck, and Smith caught a commercial airline flight. He carried with him a suitcase full of key documents assembled during the investigation.

An eight-hour drive across the Mojave Desert in August is no picnic, and the two detectives couldn't help but envy the lieutenant. His flight took less than one hour. Their drive would last more than eight hours. It didn't help when a tire blew out near the halfway point, and surrounded by sand, creosote bush, and cactus, and whipped by blistering wind, Giesler and Rudisill had to mount the spare.

Newspaper photographers surrounded by reporters greeted them in Costa Mesa and took snapshots of eight men off-loading the big freezer. Ron Smith updated the news media on details of the case against John Famalaro. "We're pretty confident that he was in the Orange County area during the 2nd and 3rd of June, which is when Denise disappeared. But we're looking for any kind of receipt, phone bill, letter, canceled check, anything that would give us a time and a date and a location . . . anything that would somehow connect him with Denise before the disappearance." Smith explained that it would help considerably to find evidence to explain the alleged encounter between Famalaro and Huber on the freeway that night. "Is it just chance that her tire goes flat and he happens to be driving by? Or had he been following her?"

The huge volume of material brought back from Arizona in the rental truck, Smith said, might take months to sort and classify.

As had been expected, the Arizona attorney, Tom Kelly, passed the baton to new defense counsel in California. Because John Famalaro claimed to be near bankruptcy, the Orange County Public Defender's Office would assume the task of protecting his legal rights before the trial and later in court. Leonard Gumlia accepted the challenge.

Well known in southern California for his defense in several high profile cases, Gumlia had a reputation for thorough research, rapid-fire speech in his detailed court presentations, and powerful tenacity. Light complected with blue eyes and an unruly mop of reddish brown hair parted at mid-scalp, standing a little over six-one and slim at 185 pounds, Gumlia's penetrating, bespectacled countenance gave him the look of an intense intellectual. The first child born to his parents in 1956, in Crookston, Minnesota, Gumlia turned out to be the only son in a family of three children. His mother owned a farm just across the western Minnesota border, in North Dakota, less than 200 miles from the region in which both Dennis and Ione Huber were born. Gumlia's father worked as a plumber, then later as a potato broker.

Gumlia attended St. Olaf High School in Northfield, Minnesota, the site of the disastrous raid by Jesse James and his gang on September 7, 1876. Gumlia's intellectual skills showed up early, and he earned acceptance into Stanford University where he took a degree in political science in 1978. To study law, he migrated south to U.C.L.A., and graduated three years later. The Orange County Public Defender's Office added him to the payroll in 1982.

Taking time out, Gumlia joined the 4th District Court of Appeals in the late eighties to become an appeals research attorney, where he gained valuable knowledge that would put him head and shoulders above many of his colleagues in his eventual courtroom work.

Few lawyers attack their work with more energy or dedication than Leonard Gumlia. In 1992, he wholeheartedly believed that his client, Cynthia Lynn Coffman, had not willingly participated in two shocking murders of young women, one in nearby Huntington Beach and the other in adjacent San Bernardino County. For the latter killing, Coffman had already been sentenced to death for joining her lover, James Gregory Marlow, in sexually assaulting and killing the innocent twenty-year-old victim, then burying her in a deserted vineyard. Charged with a similar murder in Orange County, Coffman faced a trial that might result in another death penalty. James Marlow had already been convicted and sentenced to death a second time.

Gumlia spent months researching the case, and formed the opinion that Coffman had been an unwilling partner who felt compelled to stay with Marlow out of deep love and overwhelming fear which resulted from his threat to harm her young child if she left. After a hard-fought trial, Gumlia reeled with disappointment when the jury found his client guilty of murder. But he rebounded with a concerted effort to save her from a second death sentence. When the jury announced their verdict of life without the possibility of parole, he shot his fist into the air in a gesture of relief and triumph.

Shortly after the dramatic finale, Gumlia married Kristen Widmann, the paralegal who had assisted him with research and logistics. She, too, was an employee of the public defender's office.

Several elements of Gumlia's reputation brought admiration from his colleagues. He showed no fear of tackling the most difficult cases, and fought each one with the determination of a tiger. His fierce will to defend his clients with every resource available left little time for off-duty activities, but he still managed to support the Stanford University athletic department, and to study the Civil War and the eastern front battles of World War II.

As soon as his boss assigned the Famalaro case to Gumlia, he and his wife-assistant, Widmann, accompanied by an investigator, flew to Arizona to meet the new client and the attorney, Tom Kelly. Afterwards, they visited the house on Cochise Drive, and began to identify boxes of material that might be useful in the defense case. Just as the Costa Mesa team had done, Gumlia rented a truck to haul the boxes to California. Widmann and the female investigator drove it across the desert.

Gumlia subsequently visited the Costa Mesa PD to inspect the load of evidence Lynda Giesler had transported from Arizona. Widmann spent weeks photocopying every document. Examination and analysis of the combined piles of evidence would take months. Also, using a Rolodex file found in Famalaro's possession, Gumlia began contacting hundreds of people who potentially might provide exculpatory testimony. Those contacts branched to other names, and yet more contacts.

During visits to Famalaro in the Yavapai County Jail, the attorney listened patiently to his client. From years of experience, Gumlia knew that accused killers often have preconceived notions about what might be important in the defense case, and are usually wrong. But out of a sense of duty, and the responsibility to learn as much as he possibly can, an attorney must listen and weigh each comment.

A matter of major concern to Gumlia became apparent with the probable transfer of Famalaro to the Orange County Jail. From comments by other defendants being represented by public defenders, Gumlia learned that inmates had made threats against Famalaro. Angry prisoners had allegedly said, "This Famalaro guy is in real trouble when he gets here." Gumlia publicly theorized that the threats may have been generated by the extraordinary publicity the case had received, which had resulted in widespread sympathy for the victim, Denise Huber. He probably also realized the warnings could have emanated from the low status held in jails and prison by certain criminals. Child killers, rapists, and men who savage women are considered scum in the peculiar code of the incarcerated. In any case, Gumlia requested of jail administrators that if Famalaro wound up in Santa Ana's county jail, extra precautions be taken to protect him.

After a one-month skirmish, Famalaro gave up on the battle to fight extradition and signed a release that would allow his transfer to Orange County. Standing before a judge who asked if Famalaro was prepared to return to California, he answered, "I am, Your Honor." The governors of both states promptly signed the order.

As authorities prepared to move Famalaro into the state, Dennis and Ione Huber prepared to move out. By the end of August, they released an open letter.

> "As we are now preparing to leave California, we would like to take this opportunity to thank the people of the community for their support and for the many cards and kind words expressed to us during these past few weeks. We are grateful for the prayers and words of encouragement from so many people. We also want to thank the Costa Mesa police, the concerned people who have called to help, the apartment owners and Baker Plywood for displaying the banner. It has helped to ease our pain to know there are so many caring people in the community."
>
> Dennis and Ione Huber

They moved to a modern new home in a spacious, quiet neighborhood of Mandan, North Dakota, across the Missouri River

from Bismarck. Later, they also bought an older home to fix up
and sell. In the clean, quiet, low-crime environment, they would
await the trial of John Famalaro. Nothing could keep them from
traveling back to Santa Ana and sitting through every minute of
it, determined to see their daughter's killer brought to justice.

On the day before little Ashley Denise Huber celebrated her
second birthday, the man accused of killing the aunt she had
never seen arrived in Santa Ana. Dressed in a green shirt and
brown pants, with belly chain and manacles, he was flown in
Yavapai County's four-passenger Cessna 182 under the close
watch of guards to Orange County. His attorney, Leonard Gumlia, reiterated apprehension about Famalaro's safety in jail. "I
am very concerned. You just look at the enormous amount of
publicity surrounding the case, the popularity of the victim in
Orange County. You can't help but be concerned."

Expanding on that theme, Gumlia dropped the first hints that
he might seek a change of venue for the trial—to have it moved
to another county where prospective jurors hadn't been exposed
to the barrage of news coverage. Worried that prosecutors might
succumb to public pressure to seek the death penalty, Gumlia
said, "We have fears that publicity may put extra pressure on
them."

Within a few weeks, Famalaro appeared in court to enter an
official plea. Shielded by a glass partition from spectators or possible assailants, in a Newport Beach municipal court Famalaro
stood shifting his weight from foot to foot. His attorney listened
to a formal reading of the charges, murder and kidnapping, and
entered a plea of not guilty.

Both the defender and prosecutor Chris Evans said they expected the trial to commence within a year, and estimated that
it would last about forty days. Rather than a preliminary hearing
to bind Famalaro over for trial, a grand jury would hear the
evidence and issue an indictment, just as had been done in Arizona. Bail would also be denied.

The estimate attorneys made would prove to be extremely
inaccurate. Even a revision, in which Leonard Gumlia told a

judge that the huge volume of documents and evidence he needed to analyze, more than sixty-five boxes, would postpone the trial until the summer of 1995, would be far too optimistic.

Due to the extraordinary volume of material to be processed during preparation, along with endless delays, motions, hearings, and conflicts in the schedules of lawyers, the trial would not begin until the spring of 1997.

One of the major issues to be resolved first was the question of finding an unbiased jury in Orange County. Convinced that the vast amount of publicity in newspapers and television in southern California had irrevocably prejudiced the majority of the population, Leonard Gumlia presented a request to change venue, to transfer the trial to another county where a more objective jury pool might be found. In his written motion, Gumlia included the results of a poll he had arranged which "reveals that eighty-three percent of prospective jurors recognized this case . . . and based on publicity alone, six in ten of all prospective jurors believe both that Mr. Famalaro is guilty and should receive the death penalty." He also wrote, "It is just as much our position that the disappearance of Denise Huber was such a deeply felt experience for Orange County . . . that there is no chance of a fair trial."

Attempting to head off anticipated arguments that Famalaro had been living in Arizona for several years, thus would not be very well known in Orange County, and that years had passed since the crime, Gumlia wrote: "It is hard to pigeonhole Mr. Famalaro in this scheme. On the one hand, he is clearly a non-resident, having been arrested at his home in Arizona. On the other hand, he is a former resident of Orange County. Where do *former* residents fit in the law? To the extent his residency is a factor, however, perhaps the newspaper articles establish the salient point: Mr. Famalaro is described in the headlines as an 'obsessive loner . . . ' a 'misfit' and 'shyster,' the brother of a convicted child molester . . . The publicity has repeatedly tied Mr. Famalaro to his mother and a very, very conservative Catholic religious conviction. While recognizing Orange County is a conservative area, there will be those who are offended by the family's and the defendant's extreme views."

Responding to the motion, prosecutor Chris Evans argued that other highly publicized and emotional cases had been fairly tried in the county, including the notorious "Freeway Killer," William Bonin (who was one of three men executed since reinstatement of capital punishment in the state). Also, said Evans, publicity had tapered off sharply in the months following Famalaro's extradition. Besides, newspaper reports certainly carried nothing as inflammatory as they had on Bonin, who had publicly confessed to twenty-one killings.

Charles Manson, according to Evans, had been the subject of a barrage of publicity, yet his Los Angeles trial was not subjected to a change of venue. The prosecutor pointed out that Orange County contained the third largest population in the state with over 2.5 million residents, making it larger than seventeen other entire states. Surely, argued Evans, an objective, unbiased jury of twelve people could be found.

No change of venue, ruled the judge, would be necessary.

If prosecutors chose to seek the death penalty, they would base it on the special circumstances of kidnapping and sodomy. Leonard Gumlia felt strongly that the evidence would not support a verdict beyond reasonable doubt that Denise Huber had been kidnapped or sodomized. What if she went willingly with the man who killed her, he asked? What if she, in a state of fright, accepted the offer of a ride to safety from her stranded car? Under the law, Gumlia argued, that would not be kidnapping. Citing evidence presented to the grand jury, Gumlia wrote, "The evidence . . . supported an inference that the defendant and the victim went to the defendant's warehouse and that the victim was killed there. However, it did not support any inference that the victim was taken to the location by force or against her will. Therefore, the special circumstance allegation charging that Ms. Huber's death was the result of murder accomplished in the course of kidnapping should be dismissed."

By California law, kidnapping is defined: "Every person who forcibly, or by any other means of instilling fear, steals or takes, or holds, or detains, or arrests any person in this state, and carries the person into another country, state, or county, or into another part of the same county, is guilty of kidnapping." And, Gumlia emphasized, kidnapping need not involve physical force. The law also spells that out: "The requisite force or compulsion [for kidnapping] need not consist of the use of actual physical force or express threats; the taking is forcible where it is accomplished through the giving of orders which the victim feels compelled to obey because he fears harm or injury from the accused, and his apprehension is not unreasonable under the circumstances."

Gumlia wrote, "In the case at bar, there were no facts presented to the grand jury which would support an inference that Denise Huber was taken from the site of her disabled car by force. There were no signs of violence at the scene, and no way of telling whether the injuries she ultimately incurred were inflicted during her journey to defendant's warehouse or after her arrival. Neither was any evidence presented that Ms. Huber resisted transportation at some point before arriving at the warehouse.

"At best, the evidence showed that Ms. Huber ended up at a location that was foreign to her. It also showed that she had been drinking that evening, and that her car was not driveable. There is thus no evidence that makes it more likely that she was transported to the warehouse by force than that she was transported to the warehouse by deceit. If she was tricked into going to the warehouse, then no kidnap was accomplished."

Regarding the special circumstance of sodomy, the law defines it as: "Sodomy is sexual conduct consisting of contact between the penis of one person and the anus of another person . . . any sexual penetration, however slight, is sufficient to complete the crime of sodomy."

To deal with that issue, Gumlia wrote: "There was evidence presented to the grand jury that Ms. Huber had spermatozoa in her rectum at the time of her autopsy. There was no evidence as to the source of the spermatozoa. Nor was there any evidence of trauma to the rectal area. . . .

"In the instant case, the evidence presented certainly supports an inference that Ms. Huber engaged in anal intercourse with somebody. The elements missing are; 1) that the intercourse was forcible, and 2) that the intercourse was with the defendant . . . There is not evidence that the defendant was the person responsible for the deposit of spermatozoa." At best, Gumlia insisted, the evidence presented to the grand jury supported an inference that Denise Huber had engaged in anal intercourse "with someone."

Such suggestions enraged Dennis and Ione Huber. Of course, no parent knows complete details of the sexual conduct of his or her offspring, but the Hubers would have bet their lives that Denise was certainly not engaging in such activities. They knew of her moral sense and believed wholeheartedly that her sexual experiences were very limited.

Gumlia did not include in the motion the problem faced by the prosecution, that the so-called spermatozoa found in Huber's body were not in adequate condition to reach reliable conclusions from DNA testing.

Chris Evans argued before Superior Court Judge Kathleen O'Leary that both kidnapping and sodomy had indeed taken place, and cited law cases to support his position.

Regarding the kidnapping, he agreed with the defender that no kidnapping had occurred *if* Denise Huber had consented to go with the defendant of her own free will. But, he said, "Let's talk about what the free consent would be by way of law . . . To consent, a person must act freely and voluntarily and not under the influence of threats, force, or duress, and must have knowledge of the true nature of the transaction involved." The individual must also possess sufficient mental capacity to make an intelligent choice whether or not to do something the other person proposes. In Chris Evans' view, Denise Huber would, under no circumstances, have gone anywhere near Laguna Hills with John Famalaro if she had been conscious. She would have fought, struggled, argued, and perhaps tried to leap from his car, even if she had climbed in voluntarily, which was also quite unlikely in Evans' opinion.

Judge O'Leary listened and weighed both attorneys' arguments. In making her ruling, she commented that she was not certain that the evidence supported the special circumstance of kidnapping, and had very carefully considered throwing it out, but would let a trial jury decide the issues.

Evans knew he faced a formidable mountain. With only circumstantial evidence to place before a jury, it might be exceptionally difficult to convince all twelve people that Famalaro had killed Denise Huber. It could be a nearly insurmountable task to prove the special circumstances of kidnapping and sodomy beyond a reasonable doubt.

Chapter 18

Still digging for more convincing and substantial evidence that might convince a jury of John Famalaro's guilt, Chris Evans suffered a setback that made him wonder if his whole case would crumble.

The killer of Denise Huber had twisted her arms behind her back and snapped handcuffs on the wrists. Two of John Famalaro's ex-lovers informed investigators of incidents in which he had suddenly bound them with handcuffs during sex play, and frightened them out of their wits. In one of the boxes searched at Famalaro's home, investigators found an empty handcuffs box which apparently contained the ones used on Huber. Evans planned to use the testimony of the two ex-lovers to make it clear to the jury that Famalaro was the killer who had bound Denise Huber with the manacles.

Also, other items collected during the search might lend additional credence to the probability that Famalaro harbored a lingering interest in sexual bondage and domination. Lt. Scott Mascher and his team found an assortment of pornography ranging from *Playboy* magazines, advertisements for stores offering sexual paraphernalia, dial-a-porn numbers, to hardcore bondage publications. He and Evans were convinced that Famalaro had ordered the handcuffs through one of the publications.

In addition to the lascivious material, videotapes and articles about murder turned up in the house searches. All of the material involving sexual deviance, Evans figured, could strengthen his argument that Famalaro had acted out of lustful urges for sexual dominance of Huber, and had committed the murder to either prevent her from going to the police, or because she tried to reject or resist him. The collection of smut might also be useful in showing a consciousness of guilt or at least an unhealthy interest in the subject. Of course, Evans realized, any number of ordinary people might keep tapes or articles about sex and murder as a general interest. But those folks do not keep nude, frozen bodies of murder victims in storage. The publications containing details of notorious crimes became significant only in combination with other evidence.

Evans wrote, "The newspaper articles reveal Famalaro's long-standing fascination with homicide and sexual homicide. The articles he collected include one about the so called 'Barbie-Ken' murders in Canada. This infamous case included a couple of people who engaged in sexual homicides including sex with a dying or unconscious victim. Other articles contained stories on infamous serial killers, with maps and photos. Defendant also collected articles regarding theft of human remains by a satanic cult, the Manson killings, notorious sexual-serial killer Henry Lee Lucas, and the Orange County 1993 Stuart Tay homicide, where the young victim was buried in a shallow grave in a backyard. Famalaro's fascination also [dwelled on] human remains. The article collection featured a story about human remains found hanging in tree by a noose. The defendant also kept articles on forensic pathology in Orange County, the MacDonald's massacre in San Ysidro, California, and various other homicide articles."

Along with these "souvenirs" of murder, Evans said, Famalaro kept three articles about the Denise Huber disappearance, and he specifically recorded a television piece on the case.

Pornographic material, Evans argued, "displays defendant's motive and intent in sexual contact with young women . . . Unlike most everyone else, he kept the victim and instrumentalities of his crime, just like he kept his magazines, photos, and articles."

Acknowledging that the prosecution would depend entirely on circumstantial evidence, Evans wrote, "There will be no direct evidence presented by the People regarding the murder or the sexual assault of the victim. The newsclips and . . . the pornography are links of circumstantial evidence that tend to prove motive and intent for the murder, and that the sexual assault occurred—a fact the defendant, no doubt, will strongly contest. Although evidence will be presented that the victim's body contained two spermatozoa deep in the rectum, it is anticipated that the defense will dispute this evidence or contend that the defendant was not the source of it."

Defender Leonard Gumlia, vehemently arguing against the inclusion of sexual material or articles about murder found in the possession of Famalaro, pointed out that items the prosecution sought to introduce into evidence were a very small part of the massive volumes of publications kept by his client. Famalaro had been charged with sodomy, but none of the sexual material portrayed that particular sexual act, Gumlia said. And the wide variety of articles about homicide simply showed an interest in the subject, not that he had committed a crime. Gumlia asked, "Is the prosecutor asserting that the presence of this material creates an inference that the defendant intended to kill Ms. Huber?" If so, Gumlia countered, another question must be asked. "Does that mean that the presence of his collected articles on diamonds create an inference that he intended to buy her a diamond? Or, does the presence of his collected political articles create the inference that he intended to discuss the issues of the day with her? As absurd as these assertions are, they are of no greater logical weight than the argument put forth by the prosecution."

To allow such irrelevant evidence into the trial, Gumlia argued, would waste a great deal of time, would be of "minimal probative value" and would be outweighed by its prejudicial effect on the jury.

Giving special mention to the videotape Famalaro had kept of *Inside Edition,* in which the parents of Denise made a nationwide plea for information about their daughter, Gumlia admitted that it fell into a different category. But, the defender protested, it could not be shown to the jury in its entirety. He wanted certain portions excised, including tape sequences of Denise during her life, statements by her father expressing his personal feelings, information Gumlia termed "false" about the flat tire, and conclusions from an investigator that there had been a kidnapping.

To the dismay of Chris Evans and several outraged cops, a judge agreed with the defense and ruled in their favor. The evidence about Famalaro's collections of sexual material, literature about murder, and much of the *Inside Edition* tape would not be allowed in the upcoming trial.

Round one went to Leonard Gumlia, and took some of the sting out of punches Evans planned to throw.

During the ongoing battle over what evidence a jury could hear in the murder trial, the Huber family set in motion a separate issue very important to them. Along with legions of Americans, the Hubers had heard stories of convicted killers profiting from their crimes by selling their stories to magazines, books, or movie producers. Dennis and Ione decided to block that eventuality before it could happen by filing a lawsuit against John Famalaro. From their new home in North Dakota, they asked prominent Orange County attorney Jeoffrey Robinson to initiate the civil action.

Robinson explained the reasoning, pointing out that the Hubers had anguished long and hard over the decision. Based on the charges against Famalaro, he said, the Hubers "will not rest until their every legal right is exhausted. Even if they don't collect a dime, it sends a message to him reminding him of what he has to face."

In January 1996, while snowdrifts covered the eighteen-month-old grave of Denise Huber, an Orange County judge awarded her parents a judgement against John Famalaro of $1,000,000, plus $10,000 in damages. As Robinson had said, the Hubers would probably never collect one single dime of the money.

* * *

The Hubers' move to North Dakota provided some of the expected relief, but not as much as they had hoped. Selling computer software to mortgage bankers, Dennis experienced moderate success, while Ione fared reasonably well in the real estate business. They purchased a 1916 vintage home in Bismarck and embarked on the hard work of restoring it to its original luster, with plans to move in and sell the newer house. It closed escrow on November 12, 1996, their late daughter's 29th birthday.

Haunting pain, though, did not fade away with the relocation. "I don't know if these days are any different," said Ione. "Sometimes I get angry why it all had to happen. You kind of go through different phases, mood swings." Now and then, they would catch sight of a rental truck, and a terrible thought would plague them. *Is that the one in which Denise was found?*

The growing popularity of cellular phones acted as a reminder to Dennis. "I know if she would have had a car phone, she'd be alive today." He also wondered if he had taught Denise how to continue driving on the rim in case of a flat tire, would that have prevented the tragedy?

Memories of Denise came to mind frequently. "I think of her many, many times every day," said Ione. "I always think of the good times. She was a likeable person and a joy to raise. I miss her a lot . . . We're struggling. It's never going to go away."

Ione's eyes glistened with moisture. "I will always remember the last time we saw Denise. She was happy. She stuck her head around the corner and said, 'I love you, Mom and Dad.' "

A visitor cheered them in September 1996. Nancy Streza, with Jeff's permission, brought with her little Ashley Denise Huber. For years, Nancy had been not only a dear friend, but a spiritual inspiration for them. They took her and the child boating on the Missouri River and spent the fall evenings reminiscing about the good times. After a week, Nancy returned to Orange County, but the granddaughter stayed longer.

Interminable delays in establishing a trial start date kept the Hubers in exasperating suspense. After being told that it had a good chance of starting in November 1996, they made plans to travel to California. Once again, a postponement forced them to cancel the arrangements.

Prosecutor Chris Evans kept in close contact with Dennis and Ione as officials repeatedly entered new trial dates on calendars, then marked them out. He patiently explained the cause of each delay. Jeff Huber still lived within a short drive of Orange County, and Evans also spoke with him frequently. Evans' own father, whom he had admired so deeply, had passed away in 1993, making the prosecutor even more aware of the bond between parents and offspring. With Jeff, Evans established a rapport that transcended the upcoming trial. Both men had strong interests in music. In his own youth, Evans had played the guitar and trombone. The urge struck him to renew and hone his guitar skills, so he consulted Jeff, who went with him to offer guidance on the purchase of a Gibson brand instrument. Huber even threw in a few lessons, and Evans attended some of Huber's gigs. By this time, Huber had adopted the shoulder-length hairstyle of young men in the music business, with matching blond chin whiskers and a light mustache. He too anxiously awaited the upcoming trial.

Because of the huge volume of evidence and the complex legal wrangling, the Orange County public defender followed the usual policy of assigning two lawyers to difficult cases. An intelligent, dedicated and experienced attorney, who shared the same given name as the victim, joined Leonard Gumlia early in the process to help analyze evidence and plan court strategy. Denise Gragg had fought tenaciously against the death penalty throughout her career, consistent with her firm belief that no one has the right to kill people, other than in self-defense, not even the state.

In contrast to the tough, emotionally draining arena of criminal trials, Gragg's second-floor corner office reflects her romantic side. Posters of *Gone With The Wind* along with life-size cutouts of Clark Gable as Rhett and Vivien Leigh as Scarlett, and a Scarlett doll, decorate her workplace. As a youngster in the sixties, she loved taking a bus from Orange County to L.A. to visit a great aunt who would take her to the ornate old movie palaces in Hollywood, sometimes two or three a day. "I've lost count," she says, "of how many times I've seen *Gone With The Wind.* But my favorite actor was Jimmy Cagney and my second favorite movie is *White Heat.*"

A native Texan, Gragg became a Californian early when her father, a U.S. Naval ROTC officer, moved to Palo Alto to become a computer systems analyst. They soon gravitated to the southland where Gragg attended school in Yorba Linda and Fullerton, then Pomona/Claremont College. To obtain her law degree, she returned to the San Francisco Bay area and matriculated at prestigious Boalt Hall, University of California, Berkeley. She passed her bar exam in 1981. Her partner for the Famalaro case, Gumlia, expressed the greatest respect for Denise Gragg. Once, upon hearing someone compliment his intellectual abilities, he pointed to Gragg, and said, "There's the intelligent one. She's so bright it's scary."

Asked how she can rationalize putting intense effort into defending beasts who have committed heinous crimes, Gragg thoughtfully responded. "You know, I really haven't met any client I would regard as a true beast. Some of them have done beastly things, but each and every one of the defendants I've met also has a human side." If people accuse her of resorting to technicalities or trickery to get criminals off, Gragg rejects the notion. "I do not say anything in court that is untrue, and when I walk out of there, I have a perfectly clear conscience. Just because the state brings charges against a defendant, it does not mean the person is guilty. Without people like me, our system would fail. We would have kangaroo courts like some other countries. The founding fathers didn't put those guarantees into the Constitution because they liked crime."

In her role as supervisor of writs and appeals in the P.D.'s Office, Gragg has convinced more than one courtroom opponent that she knows the law and can present it effectively in court.

Recognizing that the Famalaro trial could be extremely emotional, during which the jury could probably be brought to tears more than once, Gumlia and Gragg filed a motion to disallow so-called victim impact testimony. Such testimony is applicable only if the defendant is found guilty of murder and the trial goes into a penalty phase to determine appropriate punishment. The issue had been controversial for years. California, and several other states, had passed legislation allowing victims' families to tell juries how much the loss of their loved ones negatively impacted their lives. The California law, though, had been written five months after the murder of Denise Huber.

The U.S. Constitution forbids the enactment of *ex post facto* laws, which means that it precludes, for the most part, retroactive application of new laws. So, reasoned Gragg and Gumlia in a fourteen-page motion, victim impact testimony by the Hubers should not be allowed in the pending trial of John Famalaro, in case it advanced to a penalty phase. Noting exceptions to *ex post facto,* the judge denied their motion.

The delays, motions, and conflicts of schedule had stretched the patience of Orange County residents long enough.

Chapter 19

Nearly six years after someone bludgeoned Denise Huber to death, and almost three years after Yavapai County officers found her frozen body, a pool of prospective jurors assembled in the eleven-story Orange County Superior Court building. The modern structure stood at the center of a high-rise local government complex in Santa Ana, less that one-half mile from the Victoria Drive home where an introspective, frail child named John Famalaro had once lived.

Ione and Dennis Huber planned to make the trip from Mandan, North Dakota, and stay for the full trial no matter how long it took, but they would wait until the start of actual testimony. Once again, generous benefactors would help fund their trip and their living accommodations in Orange County. A woman who had lived close to them near Vista Grande would give them the full use of her recent model Buick for the duration of the trial.

Superior Court Judge John "Jack" Ryan inherited responsibility for the Famalaro trial. A twelve-year military veteran as a sergeant in the U.S. Marine Corps before obtaining his law degree, Ryan had also served as an Orange County prosecutor for nine years. First donning the robes of a municipal court judge in 1981, he was elevated to the Superior Court three years later. Known for balancing a sharp sense of humor with tough insistence on following correct courtroom procedure, Ryan commanded respect from both sides. Leonard Gumlia said, "I like him very much, personally. I didn't agree with his calls on the change of venue motion or the victim impact issue, but I think he certainly conducts fair trials."

Chris Evans agreed with the compliments paid to Ryan. "I was happy to hear that he would be the judge in this case. He knows the law better than most attorneys, is very even-handed and fair, and has strong control of his courtroom. He hasn't lost touch with the blue-collar guys in this world, and uses common sense. And most important, he doesn't tolerate a lot crap from either side."

To be certain that the jury would be selected from a fair cross-section of Orange County residents, Judge Ryan requested a jury pool of 1,200 candidates. The crowds of prospective jurors, wearing visible numbers on their chests in place of name tags to insure anonymity, assembled and were given the opportunity to tell the court if a protracted trial would impose unusual or financial hardships on them. It didn't take a genius to realize, from the very size of the group, that something important was brewing.

Several hundred reluctant members of the assembly presented acceptable reasons to be excused, so were thanked and sent back to be considered for shorter trials. In shifts, the remainder occupied the 123 seats in Ryan's courtroom on the eleventh floor, and filled out multi-page questionnaires inquiring about their personal views related to the justice system. "What are your general feelings about the death penalty? Do you have any religious convictions about the death penalty? Do you feel the death penalty is used too often? Too seldom?" The form gave candidates the opportunity to say whether they would automatically rule out or impose capital punishment, and if they could be impartial in their findings. It asked if they had formed any preconceived notions about the defendant's guilt or innocence, and what information they had learned about him through news media or any personal contacts. Space was also provided for the answer to an essay question: "Please summarize in as much detail as possible all that you have heard or read about this case, Denise Huber and her family, and the defendant John Famalaro."

Gradually, over several laborious days, more prospective jurors were weeded out before the commencement of *voir dire*, the questioning by attorneys and the judge. One man was overheard saying, "I don't want to sit up front and look at that piece of scum," referring to John Famalaro. It didn't take long to eliminate the speaker as a possible juror. About 200 candidates remained.

Days before the scheduled trial kickoff, an understandable and short delay occurred when defender Denise Gragg learned that her sister, who had been suffering through a long illness, had succumbed to it.

As the process resumed, one of the jury candidates, Bonnie Snethen, number 384, laughed at the idea of becoming a juror on a major homicide case. The slim, attractive blonde, smartly attired, knew that of all the people jammed into the courtroom, she would probably be the least likely to be selected. After all, her ex-husband had been a deputy D.A. They'd been divorced sixteen years, but she still maintained contact with him. Not only that, she had brushed shoulders with Judge Ryan at several social functions, while he was still a deputy D.A. "I'm outta here," she figured.

Prior to receiving the questionnaire, when the judge outlined general facts about the upcoming case to the room full of curious candidates, Snethen at first didn't recognize the name Famalaro. Then she vaguely remembered having heard something about the crime, and her breath caught in her throat. She realized it certainly would be a major trial. The victim, she recalled, was in her early twenties, and Snethen could understand the parents' horror, since she had a daughter close to the same age.

Serving jury duty on such a case might be interesting, Snethen mused. She had left a job in the finance business a few days earlier, and had been considering relaxing on the beach or perhaps taking an extended cruise for a couple of months before taking new employment. Then came the jury summons. Several valid reasons to request hardship dismissal entered Snethen's mind, but she didn't feel that such an escape would be honorable.

On the second day in the crowded gallery section of the courtroom, Snethen completed her questionnaire, turned it in to the bailiff, and sat quietly.

"Hello, Juror 384, how are you doing?" came the judge's voice.

"Well," Snethen replied, her expression signaling that she was doing fine, "I need to address the law enforcement issue. My father is a retired Long Beach Police Officer. On my questionnaire, I did make a note that my former husband is a Senior Deputy D.A. And I am—I do personally know Judge Ryan." Even though she addressed her remarks to the judge, she referred to him in the third person as a sign of respect. After a moment of hesitation, she added, "And I am currently dating a retired Long Beach Police Officer who is now employed as a special investigator for the city of Long Beach."

Snethen almost rose from her seat, fully expecting orders to leave immediately. But the judge waited expectantly, so she continued to talk. "As far as being a fair juror, I think I could be. I certainly am aware of the system. I've been exposed to it all my life. I understand the death penalty or life without the possibility of parole. Basically, the way I feel is that someone who commits a crime such as this should be removed from society. I don't really care what the penalty is as long as we're guaranteed the criminals are not back on the streets and an active part of society. So I could go either way on the penalty without a problem."

A hint of recognition seemed to show in Judge Ryan's face, Snethen thought, but she couldn't be certain. He asked, "You could vote for death if you were satisfied the aggravating factors were so substantial in comparison with the mitigating factors?"

"Absolutely."

"Or you could vote for life without the possibility of parole?"

"Absolutely."

"How about law enforcement? Could you be objective in evaluating a police officer witness?"

"I believe I could . . . All things being equal, I would like to think I could be objective."

Leonard Gumlia asked Snethen a question he wanted every prospective juror to hear. "In your experiences with law enforcement or with your former husband, did you ever . . . discover that someone who had been arrested really was just not guilty in terms of the proof of evidence, but was innocent of the charges?"

"Not to my knowledge."

"Is it possible the system can make a mistake?"

"Absolutely."

To the next question about her ability to presume innocence, Snethen answered, "I don't have a preconceived notion or feeling that Mr. Famalaro is guilty. I would have to hear the evidence before I could make that decision."

Following more interrogation about her objectivity, Gumlia scanned her questionnaire then asked, "You had a close friend who was murdered?"

"Yes."

Gumlia wanted to know if the emotional experience of knowing a murder victim, even though it had happened nine years ago, would cause Snethen to give extra weight to victim impact testimony. In her response, Snethen said, "No, I don't think so. This young man I had known since he was five years old—I'm very good friends with his mother—and it was a horrible thing. But I don't think that would influence me, although I did want the court to be aware of it."

Gumlia sat down and Chris Evans stood. In the same manner he would use in chatting with a group of friends in front of a cozy fireplace, he said, "Hi, 384."

"Hi."

"Let me ask you this question to start. Do you understand that the impact of the victim's death on the family is one thing you *can* consider as part of the factors and circumstances of the crime in this case, as an aggravating factor?"

"Yes."

"You can give that the weight of an anvil or a feather, or anywhere in between. You do understand that?" Both Evans and Gumlia, in questioning each prospective juror, used carefully chosen words to not only elicit an answer from the individual, but to also educate the other jury candidates. Snethen gave another affirmative reply. The prosecutor briefly queried her regarding the commitment to being unequivocally fair to both sides if she acted as a juror on the case, then turned toward the judge.

Judge Ryan summoned Evans, Gumlia, and Gragg to a sidebar for a whispered conference. Gumlia had reserved a decision whether or not to use one of his peremptory challenges to excuse Bonnie Snethen, so Ryan asked him if he wanted to be heard regarding a motion to have the court dismiss her "for cause," meaning that she was legally unqualified to serve as a juror on this case. In a hushed tone, the defender spoke. "To be honest, I don't believe she's given an answer that disqualifies her." He expressed his opinion that publicity about the case to which Snethen may have been exposed plus her ties with the justice system might invalidate her, but could find no solid legal grounds for the court to dismiss her.

Judge Ryan observed that her divorce from the deputy D.A. had been a long time ago, while Gumlia noted that she kept ongoing ties to law enforcement. The judge smiled and said, "If we had to excuse everybody who seemed to be pro law enforcement, we'd be in real trouble."

Conceding that Snethen's death penalty views seemed moderate when compared to opinions stated by many of the jury candidates, Gumlia said, "I'm worried about what she knows that may come into play . . . Her familiarity with the system could be dangerous." He agreed, though, with Ryan that Snethen's former husband had moderate views that probably would not have influenced her to be biased one way or the other. After Ryan denied Gumlia's motion for the court to dismiss her, the defender requested the judge to ask Snethen a few more questions about her acquaintances in the district attorney's office.

Ryan turned toward Gumlia and Denise Gragg. "The next peremptory is with the defense." Bonnie Snethen and the majority of the prospective jurors fully expected Gumlia to thank and excuse juror number 384. Muffled expressions of surprise rumbled through the room when he announced, "I'd ask the court to thank and excuse the juror in seat ten, juror number 162."

Bonnie Snethen wondered if her survival was only temporary. She knew that, with several days of jury selection still ahead, she could be excused and replaced at any time.

Another young man sitting in the crowded courtroom had a gut feeling that he would definitely be selected as one of the jurors. David Reyno, age thirty-six, a native of Leonard Gumlia's home state, Minnesota, had quietly observed three days of the selection process. The soft-spoken man with brown eyes and neatly trimmed black hair kept his smoothly handsome facial features in a calm, contemplative expression. He later described his reaction when called to jury duty in early April 1997. "There was a huge crowd when I was sent upstairs to the eleventh floor. I knew it had to be a big case, and wondered what it was about. In the courtroom, when Judge Ryan told us it was the people versus John Famalaro, it still didn't click. But when he said the defendant was accused of killing Denise Huber—wow! It hit me. And right then, I had the gut feeling that out of all those hundreds of people, I would land on that jury.

"When they called me up to the jury box, about halfway through the proceedings, I did feel some doubts and thought they might release me. I told them that I'd kept track of the news at the early stages when Denise disappeared. I live in Costa Mesa and was raised just a few miles from where she was abducted. I felt identification with her because I have friends and a sister her age. During those years she was missing, I sort of lost track of it, but heard the news when they found the body. She was in cold storage all that time. You just wish that somebody would have found her in that freezer much sooner. I was relieved when they finally did discover the body, for her parents' sake.

"At first, when I saw the way the defense lawyers looked at me, I thought that I was going to be released. But suddenly that gut feeling came back, and I knew I was going to be one of the jurors."

David Reyno and Bonnie Snethen watched other prospective jurors take seats in the box and answer endless questions. Some were dismissed within minutes, others lasted for hours thinking they had been accepted, then looked startled when either the prosecutor or a defense attorney thanked and excused them. For the most part, jury selection is a tedious process, but now and then the atmosphere becomes heated and electric. Juror number 410, a tall woman who might have been a model, dressed in white pants and a white blouse, told the court that she wouldn't be a good candidate because she was too emotional. Evans asked her if she could look John Famalaro in the face and vote for the death penalty. She answered by glaring at the seated defendant and in a the low growl of a lioness, with her teeth clenched, snarled, *"Yes!"* Leonard Gumlia excused her.

A priest answered when the court clerk called his number, and surprised the assembly by saying he could vote for the death penalty if aggravating circumstances warranted it.

During the questioning process, Denise Gragg emphasized at one point that a vote of not guilty would not be a vote "against the Hubers. We will not ask you to vote against the Hubers."

Prospective juror number 381 explained that he may have been emotional when he filled out the questionnaire because it was done just twenty-four hours after a nephew had killed his own girlfriend, then committed suicide. The defense team excused number 381.

The unexpected can happen, and did. In the late afternoon of May 7, with the lawyers and all participants virtually exhausted, twelve jurors and four alternates had been finally accepted by the prosecution and the defense. Grateful and relieved, the judge had started to thank the remaining prospects for their patience when one of the seated alternates, number 200, raised her trembling voice. "Your Honor . . ."

Judge Ryan asked, "Did you have something to say?"

Seeming close to an emotional breakdown, the woman groaned, "I don't think I can do this!"

"You don't think you can sit?" Ryan patiently asked.

"No, I don't. I really apologize . . . This has been getting worse as I sit here. I'm not truly sure I can be fair." With the court's permission, Chris Evans asked her if she could expand her explanation. The woman fought back tears and said, "I'll be

honest, I'm having a hard time even looking at the defendant."
She just couldn't give him a fair trial, she confessed.

Ryan commented, "That's why we ask these questions. Some
can sit and some can't."

Embarrassed, the woman glanced toward the sparse crowd of
weary prospective jurors who now would have to continue the
grueling selection process, and uttered, "They are going to mug
me in the parking lot."

Gumlia and Evans both quickly agreed to stipulate the woman
should be excused. Ryan informed the remaining sixty-plus candidates not to leave. The process would have to begin once more.

The loss of the one alternate threw off the carefully worked
out balance the defense and prosecution had sought. As new
prospects came forward, and were accepted or bumped, each
side sought to restore the equilibrium. The afternoon droned
on into evening. At 5 P.M., the air conditioning was shut down,
and the room became sultry. Impatience and fatigue caused
groans when either Gumlia or Evans excused a juror. Twenty
candidates came forward, answered questions, and twenty were
dismissed. Through the giant west-facing windows of the courtroom, the assembly could see the sun dropping close to the Pacific horizon ten miles away. They sweltered in the stuffy room.
One man called out loudly, "Hey judge, how about sending out
for some pizza?"

A dozen more prospects endured interrogations, until at last,
at 6:30 P.M., both sides announced their acceptance of the im-
paneled jury.

David Reyno's prescience about becoming one of the jurors
turned out to be accurate. Both he and Bonnie Snethen survived
the harrowing process. They, plus eight women and two men,
and the four alternate jurors, were sworn in to hear the evidence
in the case of the People vs. John Joseph Famalaro.

Chapter 20

On the initial day of trial, Thursday, May 8, 1997, the first witness waited nervously while Leonard Gumlia made an impassioned appeal. Clarence Darrow would have been impressed. Gumlia did his best to persuade Judge Ryan that pretrial publicity had negatively influenced enough of the prospective jurors that the entire process should be repeated, preferably in another county. Furthermore, he said, the *voir dire*, in which prospective candidates were questioned in open court, with the entire jury pool listening, caused additional contamination. And he complained about an incident during that process, in which the assembly had laughed out loud when one panelist muttered that the defendant should "fry" for the crime.

In rebuttal, Evans argued that nothing had happened to cause an unfair trial and that the so-called laughter wasn't a reaction to something funny, but more a nervous reaction to a shocking statement. Judge Ryan agreed and denied the motion.

Most of the 123 seats in the eight-row gallery filled with silent, rapt spectators. Ione Huber sat beside her son Jeff in a corner at the back of the room, her husband absent. Dennis wouldn't arrive from North Dakota until the weekend, but planned to attend every subsequent day of the trial along with Ione. So would Nancy Streza, their loyal friend from the Presbyterian Church. During the entire trial, other friends, relatives, and supporters dropped in periodically, including Pat and Gillian Fay, Pastor Walt Shepard, and Police Chief Dave Snowden. In regular attendance, Margie Hempstead, who had collected money in her gift-card shop for a headstone, watched quietly. She beamed with pride at her accomplishment of providing money to pay for the laser imprinting of Denise's portrait onto the black granite stone. Dennis Huber marveled at how Hempstead's contribution had covered the cost within a few pennies.

Fascinated with the trial process, astrologer Dana Holliday attended most days, even at the cost of renting a hotel room to avoid the forty-mile commute from her Los Angeles home. An intense student of criminology, she had acquired details about every major killer in recent decades, and had worked up astrological charts on them. Holliday reached interesting conclusions about the patterns of such killers. For example, she discovered that most serial murderers fell under the signs of Gemini and Sagittarius. Many of them, she noted, committed murders close to their own birthdays. It was no accident, she said, that Denise Huber had died on June 3, and John Famalaro's birthdate was June 10.

Toward the back of the courtroom, close to the windows, newspaper reporters Greg Hernandez from the *L.A. Times* and Stuart Pfieffer of the *Orange County Register* listened intently while hurriedly scribbling notes for their daily articles. Jonathon Volzke, the reporter who had become a *de facto* part of the Huber family, had been promoted, but would still manage to visit periodically. Acclaimed mystery author T. Jefferson Parker would also make an appearance. For the first dramatic day, and in subsequent key moments, television reporters and video camera operators lined up near the jury box, steadfastly observing orders not to photograph the judge, witnesses, or jurors.

Most of them did not recognize the tidy, gray-haired woman wearing a simple floral-patterned housedress, seated all alone toward the rear of the room, on the eastern aisle. John Famalaro's mother sat quietly, resting her cheek against her right fist. That opening Thursday would be one of very few days she would attend.

At 2 P.M., Prosecutor Christopher Evans stood to deliver his opening statement to the jury. He courteously greeted the jurors and said, "This is my opportunity to get up here and tell you a little about what I think the evidence is going to show you in this case." The witnesses might not be called in chronological order, he warned, and he might not mention all of the evidence they would hear. It was more important that they hear the evidence from the witness stand, not from him. With that, he made an easy transition into a brief outline of events in the case.

"On June the second, 1991, which is where this case is going to start, Denise Huber was living with her mom and dad in Newport Beach . . . The defendant was living in a warehouse in Laguna Hills. He had a painting business, and he had a little bedroom set up in there." Using a chart and maps, Evans illustrated the distances between the sites. As Evans spoke, it soon became clear that he had a knack for speaking to each juror as if he had known them for years. He genuinely liked people, and they could sense it in his honest face, eye contact, and the way he leaned forward from the hips, towards his audience, when he wished to emphasize an important point.

He told of Denise getting dressed to attend a concert at the Forum in Inglewood with her pal, Robert Calvert, who was a friend, not a romantic partner, and of their evening at the event, then later at El Paso Cantina. Knowing full well that the defense planned to make an important issue of the alcohol Denise consumed that night, Evans acknowledged that she and Rob had a few drinks plus some beer before she took him to his home.

"The evidence will show," Evans said, "that she wanted to go home . . ." and that she had a habit of removing her stockings to be more comfortable while she drove. The thigh-highs had been found on the passenger seat of the Honda.

Pointing to a map, Evans traced Huber's freeway route, the 405 to the 73 where she had a flat tire at approximately 2:30 in the morning. Pausing momentarily, he scanned the jurors' attentive faces. Articulating each word, he said, "That flat tire cost her her life."

Picking up speed, Evans said, "Along comes the defendant, Mr. Famalaro." The prosecutor described the freeway shoulder where Denise was stranded as "well-lit with a lot of potential help all around," and explained that emergency call boxes stood only yards away. Apartment buildings could be reached down the slope across Bear Street, and pay phones were accessible within a five minute walk. So was an all night convenience store. "The evidence will show that she had a wallet full of credit cards and an AAA card that she never got out, was never able to use . . . because she ran into John Joseph Famalaro that night."

Leaning from the hips toward the jurors, Evans said, "The defendant knew what was going to happen next. You will see from looking at the evidence in this case that Denise Huber did not go easily . . . that at some point, the defendant dragged her. You are going to get a look at a picture of the shoes she was wearing that night, with medium-high heels of leather . . . and the leather is stripped all the way off the backs of both those shoes right down to the white plastic underneath it. The heel cap is missing from one of the shoes." His description created a mental image of the victim being dragged, and the backs of her heels being scraped along a rough surface such as concrete or asphalt pavement.

In the gallery, chairs stopped squeaking, and the usual coughing or whispering among spectators ceased as Evans spoke. "The evidence will show that the defendant was concerned that Miss Huber would be able to identify him, or be able to see where he was going to take her . . . that he blindfolded her so she wouldn't know where they were going . . . The defendant knew exactly where they were going . . . in the opposite direction from Denise Huber's home." The route, Evans said, took Famalaro and his captive through Irvine, past U.C.I., the university where Huber had graduated, twelve miles to Laguna Hills, winding up at a warehouse in an industrial site.

"That is where the defendant was living, and he took her there for the purpose of sexually assaulting her in a place of privacy." Famalaro, he said, removed Huber's clothing, gagged her, and bound her wrists behind her back with heavy metal "police-type" handcuffs. "The defendant sexually assaulted her that night. He wanted sodomy. He decided that Denise Huber would not be allowed to live. The evidence will show that he knew what was going to happen . . . he knew how he was going to do this. After he decided she would not live, he got a white plastic bag with yellow drawstrings, placed it over her head, and cinched it down. He knew he was going to make a mess of her head, and he knew he would have to control the bleeding."

Creating horrific word pictures of the murder, Evans told the jury that Famalaro had pulled two more white bags over the victim's head, and pulled the drawstrings tight. "Then he looked for his weapons, which were a nail puller and a hammer . . . The evidence will show that he picked one of the tools up, raised his hand, and struck her as hard as he could on the head. The wounds are fierce and devastating." In painstaking detail, Evans described how Famalaro wielded the hammer then struck the victim repeatedly with the nail puller, shattering the girl's facial bones and skull with at least thirty-one devastating blows until gray matter from the brain began oozing out of the wounds. "The beating occurred with such ferocity that it drove pieces of those plastic bags into her skull. The evidence will show that Denise Huber never came home . . . She died at that point."

Sitting in the back of the room, Ione Huber held her breath and her eyes misted while Jeff clenched his fists. For the first time, muffled sobs escaped her lips.

When Dennis Huber later heard the prosecution's theory of the deadly blows, he hoped it wasn't entirely accurate. He had developed a personal theory that Famalaro must have struck his daughter a blow that rendered her unconscious within moments after encountering her on the freeway. Maybe, Dennis thought, the assailant had knocked her out with the hammer to make it easier to drag her into his vehicle. In the father's scenario, Denise never regained consciousness, so she never suffered. He figured that after knocking her out, Famalaro took her to the warehouse, satisfied his obscene lust on her unconscious body, decided to kill her so she could never go to the police. That's when he used the nail puller to bludgeon her to death.

No, the suffering father rationalized, Denise never felt the pain or humiliation. She must have been unconscious during almost all of the ordeal.

* * *

Continuing with his riveting presentation of what the trial evidence would show, Evans told of the parents' pain during a long, futile search, and of Famalaro's decision to keep the body, all the clothing, the contents of Huber's purse, and even the bloody weapons he had used to end her life. Indignation showed on the prosecutor's face as he mentioned Famalaro's purchase of a freezer, into which he placed the naked, handcuffed body. Keeping her head encased in white plastic bags, Famalaro covered the body, which had been forced into a tight tuck position, with larger black trash bags. Eventually, Evans said, the defendant moved to Arizona and took his charnel freezer along with him.

Fast-forwarding to July 1994, Evans took the jury through the stunning discovery in the cargo section of a Ryder rental truck which was parked in Famalaro's driveway. Investigators, he said, observed the long extension cord and large variety of containers, which made them wonder if they had encountered a drug lab. But what they found in the freezer was far worse.

Through fingerprints, he said, they identified the remains of Denise Anette Huber, who had been missing since June 1991. With search warrants, the officers entered Famalaro's home and found evidence that he had kept her clothing, personal possessions, and identification documents. The trail led back to Orange County, where criminalists used Luminol in the warehouse in which Famalaro had lived and conducted business. They found blood that turned out to be from Denise Huber's body.

Because the body had been frozen, Evans said, sperm deposited in her rectum had been preserved, but had deteriorated enough that it could not be conclusively identified as belonging to Famalaro. Why did the defendant keep the body? Evans suggested one possible motivation. "The evidence will show that he kept it as a perverse trophy to remind him of the success he had on that June 2 night, 1991, into the morning of June 3."

Winding down with his half-hour opening statement, during which the jury clung to his every word, Evans said, "Finally, ladies and gentlemen, the evidence is going to show that the defendant collected newspaper articles and a videotape about Denise Huber's disappearance. That is what I expect the evidence to show in this case. Thanks for your attention."

Gallery observers finally exhaled. The presentation by Evans, ringing with sincerity, clear in its understandable language, and punctuated with the body language of an honest man, drew rave reviews in whispered conferences.

Leonard Gumlia and Denise Gragg reserved the right to present opening statements at a later time, if they wished.

"You may call your first witness, Mr. Evans," announced the judge.

"Thank you your honor. The people call Robert Calvert."

Rob Calvert entered the southeast corner of the room, walked briskly up the west aisle, through the swinging double waist-high doors, and stopped inside the low divider that separated the gallery from the court proceedings. He raised his right hand, listened to the oath recited by court clerk Terri Walsh, and swore to tell the truth, the whole truth, and nothing but the truth.

John Famalaro, now thirty-nine, sitting stone-still at the defense table between Gumlia and Gragg, wore a gray patterned sweater and dark slacks. His full brown hair parted in the middle and his beard neatly trimmed, he showed no interest in the witness and simply stared in the direction of Judge Ryan, who towered over the room from his elevated desk. Calvert glanced in the defendant's direction, but Famalaro didn't seem to notice.

Before Chris Evans could get a single question out of his mouth, Leonard Gumlia asked for a quick sidebar. Judge Ryan had a reputation for trying to keep such whispered meetings at an absolute minimum.

In the huddle behind Ryan's desk, Gumlia asked the judge to disallow any questions from Evans seeking Rob Calvert's opinion regarding the possible alcohol-induced impairment of Denise's ability to drive on the night she vanished. Gumlia intended, though, to raise the issue of her sobriety. He planned to extensively air it with detailed cross-examination. "We will be arguing—we have her blood alcohol level around .08 . . . just above the legal limit. And if she thinks there could be a problem with police, our argument will be she is less likely inclined to use a call box. That is going to be the argument, and it is a valid one."

Evans spoke up to say that he understood that no valid blood alcohol level could have been taken from the body fluids in the freezer. "There were indications it might have been roughly .07, but—"

Gumlia interrupted. "We are going to do it two ways . . . on just the drinking pattern and we are going to do it with the bloody fluid." Judge Ryan agreed that the witness was not qualified to give an opinion about Huber's ability to drive a motor vehicle unless a legal foundation could be laid.

When the questioning began, Evans elicited from Rob Calvert that he and his friend Denise had gone to the Morrissey concert on the night of June 2, 1991, in her car, which she drove. They'd stopped on the way to buy a small bottle of vodka, orange juice, and pretzels which they consumed while parked, prior to entering the Forum. During the performance, they drank some beer. Later, while spending more than two hours at the El Paso Cantina, Calvert said they'd danced and sipped more beer. Evans asked if she was intoxicated at approximately 2 A.M. when they left the restaurant/bar. Calvert unequivocally answered, "No." At his house, he'd said goodbye to Denise, and never saw her again.

Hoping that he had defused the defense's planned attack on Huber's sobriety, Evans changed the subject. He now wanted to be certain the jury would reach a conclusion that the spermatozoa found in Denise's body came from no one but John Famalaro. The prosecutor asked Calvert, "Did you ever have vaginal sex with Denise Huber?"

"No."

"Did you ever have anal sex with Denise Huber?"

"No."

Preparing to introduce Denise Huber's bloody clothing into evidence, Evans asked if Calvert had looked carefully at Denise that night. "Yeah," he said. "When you are with someone as pretty as Denise, you know, it is pretty much looking at her from top to bottom was the norm." And he'd held her close while dancing. Evans showed Calvert a series of photos depicting the gory apparel, and asked if he recognized the garments. Calvert confirmed that he'd seen the black dress, jacket, purse, shoes, and her key ring from Hawaii. Evans even established that she had not hobbled or limped, knowing that the nine women on the jury would realize that if the heel cap on her damaged shoe had been missing before the abduction, it probably would have shown up in her walk.

The two defense attorneys, Gragg and Gumlia, planned to take turns in cross-examinations. Gumlia questioned Calvert regarding the time of arrival at the Forum by referring to different estimates the witness had previously given to investigators and to the grand jury. Opening the door to the issue of sobriety, the defender drew from the witness the size of the vodka bottle they'd purchased and the quantity of beer Calvert and Huber drank. Observers mentally speculated about the defense apparently attempting to show that Huber had consumed enough booze to make her reluctant to call the police after she was stranded on the freeway.

Regarding the shoes she wore, Calvert said that he had seen them over a period of several months. That comment might blur the picture of them being damaged as the result of being manhandled by an abductor, since the shoes could possibly have been previously scuffed.

After three-quarters of an hour on the stand, Calvert appeared weary and relieved to be finally excused, subject to recall.

A short break gave spectators the opportunity to buzz excitedly, after which Lt. Ron Smith settled into the witness chair, impeccably dressed in a suit and tie. On maps, he established exactly where the abandoned Honda had been found and the existence of several emergency call boxes and pay telephones within close proximity. The Costa Mesa Police Department was actually within a brisk twenty-minute walk of the site. Access to the apartments or phones on Bear Street, he said, would require passage through an opening in the chain link fence down the slope from the car.

Denise Gragg conducted the cross-exam and wanted to know

if the route to the fence opening would have required walking through a rocky, gravelly area. Smith said it might. The possible inference would be that such a walk would have damaged high heels, if Huber had attempted it. Gragg's next few questions brought out some details about the visibility of pay phones.

Smith left the stand a little after 4 P.M. to be replaced by Denise's long-time friend, Tammy Brown.

Prosecutor Evans took Brown through her years of close companionship with Denise, then the shock of hearing that her friend was missing, and Tammy's discovery of the Honda. Yes, Brown said, Denise often removed her "thigh-high" hosiery to be more comfortable while driving. Responding to Evans' gentle questioning, she described Denise as a very neat dresser, especially when going out. Evans held up an enlarged photo of Denise's black 9West pumps as they were found in Famalaro's house, and brought attention to the scuffed heels. Tammy recognized them and indignantly asserted that Denise would never have worn shoes in that condition.

On cross-examination, Denise Gragg reviewed the events in which Brown found the Honda, then inquired about the last time she had seen Denise actually wearing the black pumps. Probably several weeks before Denise vanished, the witness said. Brown's time on the stand lasted only eighteen minutes. To her, it seemed like hours. She would later say about her testimony, "I was a nervous wreck. I was Denise's best friend so I didn't want to make her look bad by sounding like an idiot. I wanted to be clear. I guess I was, because Detective Lynda Giesler told me that I did an excellent job."

Judge Ryan used Fridays to conduct other court business, so excused the jury until Monday morning. He cautioned them not to watch news reports, read about, or discuss the case, and said, "Don't do silly things like riding down the 55 or 73 or 405. It is all right to be on those freeways if that is on your way home. Don't go down there for taking measurements or looking at signs or lights. That is improper. You have to base . . . every decision you make in this case upon what is given to you here in this courtroom." He bid them a nice weekend, after which one of the alternate jurors asked to stay for a minute. When the others had filed out, the juror advised Ryan that his job often took him close to the warehouse in Laguna Hills, and he was concerned that it might look improper for him to be in that vicinity. Ryan thanked him, and sagely advised that the juror's presence in the region was no problem if the man didn't conduct any sort of independent investigation.

Reporters surrounded the lawyers as they left the courtroom and in the hallway. Evans, Gumlia, and Gragg treated the news media reps with courtesy, but couldn't say much about the trial.

During an earlier break, Stu Pfieffer and Greg Hernandez, the two reporters, asked Mrs. Famalaro for any comments about her son's trial. The gray-haired woman simply raised her hand to inscribe in the air the shape of a heart, and said, "I have a broken heart."

As Jeff Huber left the courtroom, he told Pfieffer and Hernandez that at first, he had experienced almost uncontrollable fury toward Famalaro, and would like to have confronted the killer one-on-one. But more recently, Huber said, he had been dealing with the anger better. "But I still want him to face justice for killing Denise. He took her life and he should have that taken from him."

Ione Huber dreaded Monday morning, when she was scheduled to testify. But at least, she thought, instead of looking at the back of John Famalaro's head, she would have the opportunity to look into his eyes. From the witness stand, she would be facing him, and she hoped she could see some sign of understanding about the horror he had perpetrated.

Chapter 21

"You may call your next witness," announced Judge Ryan, looking in the direction of Chris Evans shortly after nine on Monday morning.

"Thank you, Your Honor. The people call Ione Huber." A soft, sympathetic rumble came from the gallery. The jurors, who had been hearing about the daughter's death, now got their first glimpse of the parents as Ione stood, let go of Dennis's hand, and stepped through the swinging half-doors.

As she settled into the witness chair, Ione fixed her gaze toward the defense table, trying to make eye contact with John Famalaro, but he carefully avoided facing her, preferring to stare down at his hands or straight ahead.

"Good morning, Mrs. Huber," Evans greeted, genuine courtesy in his tone.

"Good morning."

"Mrs. Huber, are you related to Denise Huber?"

"Yes. She was my daughter." An empathetic silence gripped observers. Easing into the difficult subject, Evans took her back to the morning of June 3, 1991, and heard Ione say that her daughter had never returned home from a night out at a concert. The prosecutor introduced some photographs, and asked Ione to identify them. She looked carefully at the first one and said, "I see Denise's keys, her shoes—those were Denise's. I recognize them by the Hawaii key chain. And those *are* her shoes." Speaking in a firm, even voice, Ione said the pictured items belonged to her daughter; a purse, checkbook, credit cards, a list of phone numbers in Denise's handwriting, and her wallet.

Her voice caught momentarily when the next photos came into view. She recovered quickly, and said they depicted a black dress with matching jacket that belonged to Denise.

Answers came easier to questions about the location of the Huber home on Vista Grande, the site of the Honda, and the university where Denise graduated in 1990. Evans guided the witness back into a discussion of how Denise had dressed, listening carefully to responses from the mother about shopping with Denise for clothing, which gave her a clear understanding of the importance her daughter placed on personal appearance.

Regarding the photo of the damaged 9West shoes, Evans asked, "Do you recognize those shoes?"

"Not the way they are there," Ione said, leaving no doubt about her convictions. Even with the scuffed heels, though, she did recognize them as shoes her daughter had worn.

"Did Denise have the habit of going out of the house wearing shoes in that condition?"

"No," Ione snapped. "Never."

"Thanks very much. Nothing further."

It is not easy for a defense attorney to question parents of a murder victim. A fine line must be walked to garner information while treating the witness with care, both from a personal desire to avoid exacerbating the hurt, and to refrain from alienating the jurors. Denise Gragg understood the problem, and formed her questions as gently as possible. Slowly, she established that Denise had lived with her parents and would probably have worked Monday, June 3, at one of her two places of employment, The Cannery Restaurant or the Broadway department store in the Fashion Island mall.

Getting around to the shoes, Gragg asked, "The kind of damage in the photograph . . . on those heels—when you said that she wouldn't go out with damage like that, are you referring to the tearing on the back of the heels?"

"The tearing and the fact that one tip is off."

"So you don't think she would go out—"

Ione interrupted, "No, never, absolutely not. She would not do that."

Shifting quickly to the Honda, Gragg drew from the witness that she had opened the passenger door and looked inside. There were no keys in it and Ione couldn't recall the lighting conditions. After a few more inquiries about work, and about a private eye the Hubers had contacted, Gragg announced she had no more questions.

Sixteen minutes on the stand passed quickly. As Ione rose, she once again looked in the direction of Famalaro, but he still refused to face her.

Surprised observers whispered in disbelief when they learned how the next witness fit into the developing story. The attractive, stylish woman with dark brown hair and a trim figure identified herself as Kate Colby and walked to the stand with the grace of a model. Chris Evans asked, "Have you ever dated a man by the name of John Joseph Famalaro?"

"Yes, I did." At Evans' request, she pointed out the defendant. A few raised eyebrows and low gasps in the audience reflected a question on most observer's minds. How could this guy attract such a woman?

"Back in June 1991," Evans asked," do you know where Mr. Famalaro was living?"

"Yes, I do. In a warehouse in Laguna Hills." She had been with him there on a number of occasions and easily identified a photo of the building. "There was a large warehouse portion, and then an office portion with two rooms. One of the rooms was set up as his office, and the other was his bedroom. There was a door leading to it that was padlocked."

Her direct testimony turned out to be startlingly brief. After she told Evans that the interior of the warehouse had a dirty floor, he abruptly said, "Nothing further. Thank you." Observers hoping to hear some juicy details of the relationship felt disappointed.

Questions put to Kate Colby by Denise Gragg established for

the jury that Famalaro operated a painting business out of the warehouse, employed several helpers, and drove a white Nissan pickup registered in Colby's name. The defender returned the witness back to Evans, who asked if Famalaro drove other vehicles too, and sometimes rented cars. Colby said he did.

The ensuing short bursts of questions and answers began to look like a volleyball game. Gragg got from Colby a statement that the defendant rented cars to take her on dates. To Evans' inquiry, she said that Famalaro rented luxury cars such as Infiniti and Lexus sedans to drive for social occasions. Gragg drew focus back to the white pickup, getting agreement from the witness that Famalaro drove it most of the time. Evans wouldn't allow that statement to end the volley, so asked if Colby had seen Famalaro driving the other cars, too. She had. Denise Gragg let the game end. It lasted a total of six minutes.

A tall, well-tanned man with movie star good looks took the oath next. Joseph Michael DiGiacomo told the jury that he was the twenty-year veteran Yavapai County deputy sheriff who responded to a radio report of a possible stolen Ryder truck in the Prescott Country Club on July 13, 1994. He said he found the vehicle backed into the side driveway of a house on Cochise Drive, but the license plate didn't match the report. Later he checked the vehicle identification number, which matched. Because of the large cans stacked around the area, he wondered if he had stumbled on a drug lab. "Arizona has a lot of what we call mobile labs . . . It is not uncommon to find vehicles used to manufacture methamphetamine, which is the drug of choice right now for users. It is easy to rent a vehicle of this type, manufacture the drugs, then abandon it."

With narcotics officers present, DiGiacomo said, he observed a locksmith open the cargo compartment of the truck, and saw a sealed freezer. "There was a long extension cord running from it and over the back fence."

When one of the investigators opened the freezer, according to DiGiacomo, a foul smell drifted into the air. His next comments caused observers to twist uncomfortably in their chairs and grimace. "After the freezer was completely opened, one of the officers physically placed his hands inside it, and felt around, felt the object inside, and quickly looked over at me. He said, 'I feel what appears to be a shoulder and possibly some metal, something metal.' " The witness told of stopping the investigation at that point, placing crime scene tape, and calling Lt. Scott Mascher, who was in charge of criminal investigation. When Mascher and Det. Lonnie Brown showed up, DiGiacomo said, he briefed them on what he had found.

The cross-examination conducted by Leonard Gumlia lasted only two minutes. He verified the truck had been stolen in Orange County, asked a few questions about paint cans around the truck, its visibility from the street, and got agreement from the witness that no drug lab had been found. After some inquiries about the desert countryside in Yavapai County, and confirmation that the freezer was running, Gumlia sat down. Evans had no redirect questions.

During a twenty-minute break, Chris Evans stepped into the gallery's first row, leaned over, and whispered to Ione and Dennis. "How are you doing?" he asked.

Both parents said they were holding up okay.

"I just wanted to let you know," said Evans, "that you may not wish to stay for the next witness. I'm going to have to show some pretty gruesome photos." His face showed deep concern. But the Hubers said they had traveled a long way, and endured a lot of pain already. They would stay.

After the recess, Evans called Lieutenant Scott Mascher. Well tanned, dressed in a crisp white shirt and tie, and sharply creased slacks, the articulate young officer could have been selected from an imaginary catalogue of perfect prosecution witnesses. Evans was delighted with Mascher and most of the individuals he would call to the stand. Wholesome, clean-cut, with honest faces—the kind of people a jury would probably admire and believe.

Mascher had shot up through the ranks of the Yavapai County

Sheriff's Department. His admirers predicted that he would one day run for, and win, the office of county sheriff. The affinity between Mascher and Chris Evans could easily be seen. They had worked together in the investigation, during which a strong mutual respect developed.

The first few answers to Evans' questions established that Mascher arrived at the Cochise Drive house along with Det. Lonnie Brown, and were directed to the freezer by Deputy DiGiacomo. Brown, clad in protective gear, had lifted the freezer lid and began cutting away layers of black plastic.

Mascher described to the jury the grotesque sight: "I began to see a shoulder . . . some ice-like frost had been building up on the body. I could tell it was a body by then. I could see some decomposing flesh with the ice crystals, the frost buildup, and I saw hands behind the back. And there were steel handcuffs attached to the wrists."

In the first gallery row, Dennis Huber leaned his head forward and placed cupped hands over his face. Ione dabbed at her eyes with a white tissue, and Jeff clenched his jaw muscles. Nancy Streza, sitting with them, silently sobbed, as did other relatives.

Evans asked, "When you saw the handcuffs, what is the next thing you did?"

"I think we opened the bags a little bit more. I didn't see any clothing. It appeared that the body was nude, and I sorta hoped to get some I.D. or something."

As the prosecutor had warned Dennis and Ione, he brought out a folder of eight by ten-inch photographs. They depicted full body shots of the frozen victim, Denise Huber. The first few revealed little detail, with mostly black plastic bags visible. But with each successive photo, more of the whitish body came into view, until the entire figure, curled into a tight tuck position, could be seen, but only by the witness. Mascher described the grim contents, saying that in the picture, the victim's head remained obscured by white plastic bags. Evans handled the photos with extreme care to prevent flashing them to gallery observers, especially family members in the front row.

Some photos investigators had taken would never be introduced into the trial. Evans had viewed shots of the victim's head, but decided they were too hideous to allow anyone to see. Even if he had, the judge would probably have ruled them out as too inflammatory or prejudicial. The prosecutor even dreaded using pictures of the reconstructed skull, but felt it would be necessary to demonstrate to the jury the ferocity of the lethal attack inflicted on Denise.

Testimony by Mascher chilled the audience. Evans handed him a photo and asked him to tell what it depicted. Mascher said, "This is the freezer . . . Looking down into it on the left side are the plastic bags, cut open. You can see the right arm, a portion of the back. You can see the ice crystals and frost that has accumulated on the body . . . and the apparent blood and body fluids that are frozen in the bottom."

One of the most dramatic moments of the entire trial came next. Evans asked, "Would you be able to come down here and with the court's permission, demonstrate the position of the body?"

Removing his jacket, Mascher moved to an open space in front of the jury box. Each juror stood to get a better view of the lieutenant. Members of the audience craned their necks to see him. Evans said, "Can you describe for us the position of the body as you get in that position?"

"Yeah," Mascher replied, as he kneeled on the floor. On his knees, he curled into a tuck position, stretching to put his head down as far as possible, and placed his arms behind his back. He explained, "It appeared that the body was in a kneeling position. The back of the freezer where the hinges are would be where I am facing . . . The feet were straight out. The arms were behind the back with the right arm on top. Palms were out, I remember. The handcuffs were on the wrists, and the body was curled with the head tucked way up under the chest and sort of bent way down. I don't know if I can get my head in that position because it was sort of crammed in there. But the head and neck were bent way down up against the back side of the freezer."

* * *

Silence reigned in the big room, even as Mascher stood, donned his coat, and returned to the witness stand. Jurors settled back down into their chairs, faces grim.

Mascher said that he ordered the freezer closed and sent to a crime lab in Phoenix.

Switching gears, Evans next explored the multiple searches of the house on Cochise Drive beginning on July 14 and ending on July 26. Among the hundreds of items seized as evidence, Mascher said, were two cardboard boxes, designated as items 212 and 213. Each box had been inscribed in red letters, possibly printed with a felt tip marker, with the word "Christmas." Also on the exterior of both boxes, investigators had noticed address labels. At one time, the containers had been shipped to a clothing manufacturer who occupied two units adjacent to Famalaro's in the warehouse on Verdugo Drive in Laguna Hills.

For the next half hour, Chris Evans asked Scott Mascher to examine photographs of the contents in boxes 212 and 213. The litany of items stored in each container shocked jurors and observers. How could the defendant have kept such a gory collection? And, for God's sake, why?

Using the stack of photos, Mascher reported that box 212 contained the wadded, blood-spotted black dress and black jacket Denise had worn. One of the spaghetti shoulder straps on the dress had been pulled apart, and the right side of the garment torn. Smaller boxes inside 212 contained her driver's license, credit cards, checkbook, auto club card, black purse, underwear, compact, car keys on a key ring bearing the word "Maui," and the black pumps. Several of the items, including the key ring, shoes, and clothing had been spotted with blood.

Mascher said he recognized a photo of the shoes because he recalled "the drag marks." Leonard Gumlia objected, calling the comment a conclusion, and asked that the remark be stricken from the record.

"Sustained," said Judge Ryan. "The answer is stricken. The

jury is ordered to disregard the last answer." It would soon become apparent that Gumlia planned to vigorously attack the theory that Denise Huber's shoes had been scuffed during a struggle or while someone dragged her.

Continuing with the inventory of material found in box 212, Mascher told of retrieving a pair of stone-washed jeans, size 32 waist, 32 length, with apparent blood on one of the legs. Other pants found in Famalaro's closet, apparently belonging to him, were the same size. Mascher had also pulled from the box a sweatshirt, imprinted with the red words "Lake Wobegon," which had been soaked with large smears of blood.

An additional item from box 212, described by Mascher, at first puzzled gallery observers. The witness called it, "A cluster of cloth materials, sort of all gobbed together and . . . looks like fused together from an apparent blood soaking and then drying." It would later be revealed that the cloth "cluster," almost the size of a baseball, had been jammed into the victim's mouth before the killer sealed her lips with duct tape. Famalaro had saved the loathsome wad.

Dried bloodstains also marked a wooden-handled claw hammer found in box 212.

Box 213, said Mascher, even had apparent bloodstains on the interior side of the cover flaps. The contents included an empty handcuffs box, a roll of silver duct tape, a blood-spotted roofer's nail puller, and white plastic bags with yellow drawstrings. Evans made certain in his questioning that the jury understood the bags were identical to the ones that had been pulled over Denise Huber's head. The duct tape appeared to be the same type as the strips someone had placed over her eyes and mouth.

Also from the box came a rolled up five-by-fifteen-foot tarp splattered with dried blood.

Asking Mascher to slip on a pair of white latex gloves, Evans handed him two objects, separately wrapped in white paper. The witness carefully unwrapped each one and held them up for the jury to see. He had previously identified photos of the hammer and nail puller. Now he held the actual murder weapons, according to the prosecution, in his hands. Most of the jurors hurriedly took notes on pads the bailiff had provided. Gumlia leaned over and whispered to his co-counsel, Denise Gragg. At Evans' request, Mascher meticulously rewrapped the two tools. Two simple tools, used universally by workmen. But now, weapons that sent chills down the spines of everyone who gazed on them.

Next, Evans held up another ordinary item. "Showing you a copy of a videotape. Did you have occasion to look at it prior to court today?"

"Yes, I did. I obtained this from Detective Lynda Giesler from the Costa Mesa P.D." It, too, had been found in Famalaro's house. Mascher had reviewed the tape again that same morning, and told the jury that it was a copy of an *Inside Edition* television show profiling the Huber disappearance. He didn't mention that it showed the Huber parents begging for information about their daughter. They would see a portion of it later.

Countless newspapers had been found in the Cochise Drive house. A few of them became evidence. Evans asked the witness to withdraw two sections of the *Orange County Register* from protective plastic bags and read the headlines aloud. He complied, reading in a clear, firm voice, "Hubers Refuse to Stop Hoping for Return of Their Daughter," and "Family of Missing Woman Gets Solace from Faith and Friends." The papers bore dates of Friday, June 14, 1991, and Wednesday, July 3, respectively. According to the witness, the two papers had been taken from a six or seven-inch stack in an upstairs bedroom of Famalaro's home. Mascher mentioned they "were being saved up in a closet."

Gragg spoke up. "Object to the word 'saved'. Move to strike it."

Judge Ryan agreed. "The objection is sustained. The answer is stricken."

Two more newspapers, also editions of *The Register,* became part of the evidence. One, with a June 7, 1991, headline said, "Newport Woman Still Missing, Officers Stymied, Family Offers $5,000." The other, from June 4, 1992, featured a photo of the Huber family in front of the banner that had been seen by millions of motorists, and contained a headline reading, "Painful Anniversary."

With those images in the jurors' minds, Evans turned the witness over to the defense.

Chapter 22

With a half hour remaining before the lunch break, Denise Gragg stood to question Scott Mascher. More than one listener cupped hands behind ears to hear Gragg's soft voice which lacked enough timbre to carry into the back reaches of the big courtroom.

She first wanted to know if she should address Mascher as investigator or detective. With barely concealed amusement, and courteously calling her "ma'am," he said, "Right now, it's Lieutenant Mascher." Gragg smiled, too, then asked him a couple of questions about the frozen body, the house search, and if the other end of the extension cord from the truck, strung over the fence, terminated in the yard belonging to Famalaro's mother. Mascher's answer cleared up a misconception. "There was an extension cord that went from his backyard over to his mother's yard. Initially it appeared that it was plugged into the freezer, but it wasn't." The freezer, he said, actually was connected to power from the Cochise Drive house. The cord had probably supplied power to the freezer for a short time, but had subsequently been disconnected.

Forming her inquiries in a manner to demonstrate that the newspapers in evidence had been culled from huge numbers of publications Famalaro had saved, Gragg spent considerable time on the issue and got agreement from Mascher that his team had sifted through thousands of papers in various parts of the house. She intended to show that Famalaro's possession of the articles about the Huber family were nothing more than a small portion of many newspapers he'd saved. Refining it even further, Gragg drew out the information that Famalaro had kept the whole papers, not clipped out specific articles. To observers, it didn't matter how many rooms full of paper the defendant had collected. He still possessed articles all the way from Orange County about the parents of the frozen corpse he'd kept for three years.

The videotape, too, had been one of more than fifty Famalaro owned. Mascher commented that many of them contained scenes of actress Suzanne Somers. Gragg may have regretted asking if the tapes were scattered throughout the house, or all in one place, when Mascher said, "Most of the tapes were in a box. The Huber one was on a shelf in the office, so it was like separate."

The evidence in box 212 came into focus again with Gragg's questioning. Some of the material hadn't been clearly visible when investigators had first opened it. Inside, the witness said, "There was a knapsack on top of a black garbage bag, a big one like the ones in the freezer. And inside of that bag were the boxes, and the dress, and the hammer, and the car keys, and the credit card, and the Levi's and the sweatshirt." When he'd first opened the black bag, a foul smell came from it.

Regarding the hammer, Mascher couldn't be sure that he'd seen dried blood on it, but on the nail puller, he said, he saw something in addition to blood. "I sort of thought it was tissue, more like human tissue than blood."

Winding up the morning with a few questions about the Ryder truck and the paint cans in the yard, Gragg suggested a break for lunch.

During the ninety-minute recess, reporters cornered the Hubers. Popular television personality Vicky Vargas from KNBC Channel Four interviewed them in the hallway. Patiently, and with remarkable dignity, they answered all questions.

In a subsequent conversation with a friend, Dennis described his feeling that morning when he had first laid eyes on John Famalaro. For years, he'd been extremely angry at the abductor of his daughter, and didn't know how he would react when he sat in the same room with the man accused of killing Denise. "I was a little surprised. My gut didn't boil the way I thought it would." But he certainly felt no sympathy for the defendant.

When the court reassembled at 1:30 P.M., before the jury came in, Denise Gragg, the movie buff, made a request for the judge to give some special instructions to the jurors. "It's come to our attention that there's a movie called *Breakdown* starring Kurt Russell which apparently opened a week ago. I've not seen the movie, but my information is that it centers on the abduction of a woman near a broken-down car, that the victim in the movie is placed at one point in a kneeling position not unlike the position of the alleged victim in this case, and that there's even some scene or point having to do with a freezer. Out of an abundance of caution, it's the defense's request that the court perhaps ask the jury not to see the movie while the case is presented."

Frowning, Judge Ryan asked, "It's not based on this case, is it?" Gumlia chimed in to say they didn't know. Ryan retorted, "Well, somebody would know."

"You'd have to ask the screenwriter . . . if he drew any inspiration from it," said Gumlia.

Gragg added, "It's not based directly on this case. Kurt Russell [in the role] is the husband of the abductee, but there does seem to be some plot elements that are very close to the facts in this case." Chris Evans, given the opportunity to comment, said he'd never heard of the movie, but didn't object to an admonition to the jury. Gumlia volunteered that the defense would rent it for the jurors to watch after the trial. Spectators weren't sure if his comment was a rare outburst of humor or if he meant it.

Ryan agreed to tell jurors not to watch the movie, ordering them to avoid seeing *Breakdown* until after the trial concluded. Juror 384, Bonnie Snethen, raised her hand and reported having already seen it the previous weekend. So Ryan amended the order. "Dismiss whatever you saw in the movie and do not confuse it with this case. It's not about this case . . . If you have a problem with that, I expect you will tell us and we'll talk about it." Snethen said she understood.

* * *

Once more, using photos of stacked newspapers, Denise Gragg emphasized that her client collected countless publications. Mascher agreed that many other cardboard boxes had been found in addition to 212 and 213, but none others marked "Christmas."

Touching on many topics over the next twenty minutes, Gragg asked if procedures had been followed to avoid contaminating evidence, which Mascher confirmed. On redirect, Evans sought to establish that the critical newspapers came from a small stack in the upstairs bedroom. After a short re-cross by Gragg, Scott Mascher stepped down.

Because of his deep involvement, Mascher wanted to stay in Orange County for the remainder of the trial, but duty called, and he returned to the high desert of Yavapai County.

A tall, slim blonde woman took the stand next, and observers wondered if she was another of Famalaro's strikingly attractive girlfriends. Far from it, Laurie Crutchfield opened her testimony by telling the court that she worked for the Orange County Crime Lab, assigned to crime scene investigation as a forensic scientist. She described conducting the Luminol tests at the Verdugo Drive warehouse which revealed the presence of probable blood in the southwest corner. She and the investigators had removed parts of the wall, where it made contact with the concrete floor, for further testing.

Evans held up the nail puller and asked the witness if she had also taken samples of what appeared to be blood from it. She had, and explained that it was done by using a cotton swab soaked in distilled water to dilute the dried stains and take samples. She had repeated the process with the hammer, which also yielded blood from the dried spots.

More blood came from Crutchfield's tests of items found in the "Christmas" boxes, including a tarpaulin and the Lake Wobegon sweatshirt. She said she had sent all of the samples to another scientist at the Orange County lab named Mary Hong.

Leonard Gumlia stepped up to conduct cross-examination. After verifying the exact spot in the warehouse where blood had

304   Don Lasseter

been discovered, he asked if human tissue had been found on the nail puller, as Scott Mascher had suggested. Crutchfield said she hadn't seen any, but reiterated that blood had been verified on both the nail puller and the hammer. The sweatshirt, she thought, had been folded inside the tarp, and had stuck to it when the blood dried. Gumlia quickly asked, "You're not offering an opinion that the blood was deposited to the shirt other than from the tarp?" Crutchfield admitted that she didn't know how the blood got on the shirt. With that small victory, Gumlia sat down. After Evans confirmed again that blood had been found on both the hammer and the nail puller, the witness was excused.

Suspense gnawed at spectators. All that blood—on the warehouse floor, on the hammer, the nail puller, and on clothes that must have been worn by Famalaro—could it be proved, after three long years of storage, that it conclusively came from Denise Huber?

Lab specialist Mary Hong took the stand at 2:30 that Monday afternoon. She told Evans that her duties included examining evidence for biological fluids and DNA typing of those fluids. He asked, "In this case were you involved in sampling a board from a warehouse for DNA analysis?" Yes, she said, she had performed the tests and had examined the scrapings for DNA.

Mary Hong, reduced the explanation of DNA to simple terms that took no more that an hour to cover.

First, she cleared up one mystery that had puzzled observers. It had been mentioned that some sperm had been found in the body of Denise Huber. If DNA tests could show that sperm came from John Famalaro, there would be very little doubt that he had perpetrated the crimes of which he stood accused. But a simple statement from Hong destroyed that possibility. "My results essentially were inconclusive as to the DNA type of the sperm donor."

It appeared to be good strategy by Chris Evans to dispose of that issue first, so jurors wouldn't be breathlessly waiting for those results. Now, he could concentrate on the blood. Hong's next comments, though, seemed to deflate the hopes that she could say the bloodstains on the hammer, nail puller, and clothing, belonged to Denise Huber. Without that, the case might evaporate. The witness worried the Hubers and their friends by saying, "Sometimes, you're dealing with samples where you might get some DNA but it's too degraded. What I mean by that is DNA degrades when it's been subjected to time or heat or bacteria. It's chopped up into smaller and smaller pieces and if those pieces are too small . . . we couldn't do the typing. So in those cases, we get no results."

DNA samples collected in many locations of the U.S. must be sent to independent labs for analysis. Orange County, however, built its own lab in 1990 and gained nationwide respect for reliable DNA work. Mary Hong had been part of that since its inception. Guided by questions from Evans, she explained the fundamentals of DNA, how it works, and how the lab handles it. When Evans asked if Hong had received a sample of cells from the body of Denise Huber, Leonard Gumlia quickly offered a stipulation that the samples were, indeed, from Huber. That would prevent a long, laborious process of proving the fact.

To keep it clear for jurors, Evans introduced a chart showing the distinct numerical marker differences between DNA from Huber and DNA from John Famalaro. Using it, he referred to the bloodstained board taken from the warehouse, and elicited from Hong the statement, "The bloodstain on the board could not have come from Mr. Famalaro, and it could have come from Ms. Huber."

Samples of blood from the nail puller, she said, produced the same results. Likewise, the stained Levi's found in Famalaro's possession, which were his size. The hammer, however, produced no identifiable DNA.

Unlike the astronomical numbers often heard in other trials, in which the likelihood of identification numbered one in more than six billion, suggesting that the DNA "donor" was the only human on earth who could have left the blood, figures in the Famalaro trial were far lower. Hong said, "These types . . . occur approximately one out of every hundred individuals." So, she said, all of those samples "could have" come from Denise Huber.

Additional testing came up with the same results for tiny blood spots on Denise Huber's Hawaiian key ring, wallet, the 9West pumps, her purse, the roll of duct tape, on empty white plastic bags, the handcuff box, and the Lake Wobegon sweatshirt. On several of the items, though, the probability the blood belonged to Denise dropped to one in twenty-three or one in thirty people. The jury would have to decide the usefulness of such statistics. Did the DNA results help corroborate other circumstantial evidence, or were the probabilities too low to be of any decisive use?

Cross-exam by Leonard Gumlia drew from Hong even lower stats for parts of the DNA results, dropping them to only one in ten probability.

Following an afternoon break, during which Hong prepared a chart for Gumlia, he resumed his questioning. By having her explain the chart, he reaffirmed the conclusion that sperm cells found in the body of Denise provided no DNA conclusions regarding the possible donor. He also laid foundation for his planned attack on the very existence of sperm cells. One of Gumlia's key objectives in the case centered on creating doubt that his client had sodomized the victim.

Trying to re-support the areas Gumlia had undermined, Chris Evans asked Hong if it was her job to look for sperm. No, she said, someone else in the lab would do that, a specialist named Lisa Arnell.

Day two of trial testimony came to a close just prior to 4 P.M. In two days, Chris Evans had gone through eight witnesses. He had only seven more to prove his case of first degree murder with special circumstances of kidnapping and sodomy against John Famalaro. Taking care to avoid being overheard by jurors, spectators quietly chatted about it while waiting for the elevator. Some even began making bets that the defendant would walk. Others thought at best, the jury might not be able to reach a verdict.

* * *

Day three started at 9 A.M. sharp, with a senior forensic analyst taking the oath while John Famalaro, dressed in a light tan and bright blue sweater, more appropriate to a ski resort than a courtroom, sat unmoving. Daniel Gammie eased into the witness chair. A criminalist with the Orange County Sheriff's Department for thirteen years before leaving to become a forensic analyst with a private firm, Gammie had traveled to Arizona with Chris Evans and pathologist Dr. Richard Fukumoto in 1994, only to be turned back by a jurisdictional problem. Later, though, after Lynda Giesler and Frank Rudisill drove the evidence to California in a rental truck, Gammie's expertise became most useful. Many of the photographs Chris Evans had introduced into evidence were snapped by Gammie. And he had lifted blood samples from most of the items found in boxes 212 and 213, then sent the samples to Mary Hong. Evans ran Gammie through each one, galvanizing the gory clothing and bloodied possessions of Denise Huber in the minds of each juror.

During Denise Gragg's cross, she established that stains on the wallet had been transferred there from another bloodied object, but no information came out to reveal the source. She also asked if Gammie had found any grass on the shoes. The witness answered, "Yes, I have a record that I did discover a blade of grass on the right shoe." Gragg could possibly find that useful later in the trial.

Blood on the jacket Denise wore did not show up to the naked eye, Gammie said. He drew a diagram of the jacket, extremely neat as if he'd been trained as a professional cartoonist, and demonstrated how he used a high intensity light to identify blood. His efforts were hindered by an excessive growth of mold on the garment. He told how he finally got positive results for blood around the neckline and shoulders. In his examination of the jacket, he'd also found a piece of chewed gum stuck to the back neckline, and a package of gum in the front pocket. The enigmatic bit of evidence would never be entirely explained. Observers could only guess that Denise had been chewing gum that night, and it had probably fallen from her mouth during the attack. How it became stuck to the back of her neckline would remain a matter of speculation.

The black dress, Gammie said, was also moldy and badly degraded. The left shoulder strap was torn, and still hanging on
by a thread. Gragg asked him if he was able to make a determination how the damage had happened. Gammie answered, "I
wasn't able to form an opinion. It didn't necessarily look like it
was cut. It had a frayed appearance."

Regarding the Lake Wobegon sweatshirt, Gammie did form
an opinion. "On the right sleeve, particularly up near the shoulder, bloodstains appeared much more diffused, almost dilutant."

"Was that consistent with someone mopping up blood with
it, or putting the shirt into a quantity of blood?"

"It appeared as though water had been added to it." Some
of the blood also appeared to have been transferred onto the
fabric, not splattered on it. Gragg's questions suggested that
smears on part of the sleeve might have happened from folding
the shirt, thus transferring the gore from one spot to another.
Her questions seemed designed to create doubt that the killer
had actually worn the shirt during the violent bloodlust inflicted
on Denise Huber.

DNA specialist Mary Hong had skimmed the surface of the
treacherous topic on Monday. Now the prosecutor needed to
visit the subject again, so he called forensic scientist Lisa Arnell
to the stand. She was well-known to court officers, but under her
maiden name. Ever courteous, Chris Evans commented on still
thinking of Arnell by the former name and offered congratula-
tions on her recent marriage. Getting down to business, he drew
from her that she performed DNA and sexual assault analysis.

The blood-soaked warehouse board which had yielded simple
DNA results for Mary Hong had also been examined by Arnell.
Her testimony included a simple explanation of a more sophisticated procedure recognized by experienced trial watchers because it produced results resembling a bar code. Jurors leaned
forward during Arnell's crystal clear explanation, appearing to
be fascinated. Gallery spectators gave credit to Evans for his clear,
fundamental questions.

Many of his inquiries necessarily dealt with the unpleasant

subject of collecting tissue and liquid from a murder victim. Arnell described the procedure for obtaining oral, vaginal, and rectal samples with the use of long cotton swabs. Spermatozoa, she said, could be collected and identified in such a manner by placing the sample under a microscope and staining it with "Christmas tree stain," so named due to the red and green dyes involved. The magnified sperm cells will turn red, separating them from other cells mixed on the swab.

Referring to rectal samples collected from the body of Denise Huber, Evans asked, "When you did this examination of these swabs, did you find any spermatozoa?"

"Yes, I did."

"How many spermatozoa did you find?"

"I found one on one slide, and one on the other slide."

At the defense table, Leonard Gumlia appeared to be making copious notes. From a front row vantage point in the gallery, some observers could see that many of his notes consisted of squiggles, geometric patterns, and doodles. Considering his extraordinary IQ and memory, he probably didn't need written reminders of questions he planned to ask in cross-examination.

Chris Evans brought out more color photographs and asked Lisa Arnell to identify images of "ovoid, dark reddish" sperm cells. The prosecutor had to use extreme caution in pointing to various hues in a photo, since he was color-blind. Arnell detailed the shape of a sperm cell. "I suppose you could compare it to a tadpole. It has got an ovoid body, and if the sample is fresh . . . you may see the tail on the end." The tails, she said, commonly drop off but the cell can still be identified as "apparent sperm." That single word, "apparent," would give defenders ammunition for a major counterattack on the existence of spermatozoa in the samples taken from Huber. No sperm, no sodomy—a finding which would eliminate one of the special circumstances that might send Famalaro to death row.

"Hold on a second," Evans said in a seldom raised voice. "I don't want to get confused here. Spermatozoa was detected in this case, wasn't it?"

"Yes. In certain slides, yes." She agreed that the photos she held depicted sperm cells, but in her notes she had written "apparent." Evans' questions took her through detailed explanations of sperm cell identification procedures to bolster her opinion. Sperm cells found in the rectal environment, she said, can last from hours to days. "The temperature of the body is very important as well."

Arnell had delivered the samples in question to another expert analyst, in a different county, for verification of her findings, she said. Spectators realized who the next witness was going to be.

The defense team huddled during a morning break, after which Leonard Gumlia began his cross-exam. His approach contrasted with Evans' in its cool, clinical appearance. While Evans made eye contact with the witness or jurors, Gumlia tended to look away, as if in deep concentration. To question Lisa Arnell, he chose to remain seated where he had reference material assembled at his table.

Within the first few questions, he spotlighted the word "apparent." He also drew an admission that "Christmas tree" staining might color other material in the sample a reddish color, thus the determination that a cell is sperm required other subjective interpretation, taking into consideration the shape of the red object.

"Did you tell the grand jury that based on everything you knew and had read, that sperm could not survive in a deceased person beyond a week?"

Arnell didn't bite on that one. *"No.* Those references were to living individuals."

"Are you familiar with the concept of contamination between the vagina and rectum?" Arnell said she was. Gumlia said, "There are studies that show in a large number of cases, even where the only sexual assault that is reported is rape, penetration of the vagina, that small amounts of spermatozoa are in fact detected in the rectum because of maybe drainage or the way bodies were positioned at the times, things like that." His voice inflection made the statement a question. Arnell agreed that literature to that effect had been published. She suggested that the absence of sperm in the vaginal swabs might contradict that theory in this case, but couldn't completely rule out the possibility that such drainage had taken place.

Juror Bonnie Snethen reacted negatively to the implication of drainage from one bodily cavity to the other. She would later say she thought the theory was ridiculous.

Returning to the examination of cells, Gumlia asked if the tail of a sperm cell had dropped off, could the remaining shape resemble a yeast cell? Possibly, Arnell acknowledged. Could it resemble other waste product cells? Arnell said she couldn't comment on that.

Introducing one more possible doubt that the two cells in question were sperm, Gumlia asked the witness if she knew that another laboratory, the FBI, did not allow scientists to draw a conclusion that a cell was sperm if the tail was missing. Yes, Arnell said, she knew the FBI applied that rule. For some reason though, the FBI would not allow its scientists to testify in courts regarding that opinion. Arnell expressed her view that the Orange County Lab protocol rightfully allowed the conclusion that cells without tails could be called sperm.

Did the witness know, Gumlia asked, the volume of sperm in male ejaculation? Yes—a range of 50 million to 150 million spermatozoa. The defender pummeled Arnell with a series of technical questions that reflected his own detailed research and excellent understanding of the science. After one hour of questioning, he turned her back to Chris Evans.

The prosecutor, too, had done his homework, and allowed Arnell to clarify several points. She reiterated her doubt about drainage of sperm from one body site to another, agreed that freezing had probably helped preserve the sperm cells, and reasserted that at least two of the cells appeared to be spermatozoa.

In a volley of cross-exam and redirect, the lawyers brought out issues of sodomy causing physical injury, that most labs allow identification of sperm cells even if the tail is missing, how long sperm can exist in hostile environment, and the effect of freezing on such cells. Gumlia at last said, "I think we have exhausted the issues," whereupon Judge Ryan excused the witness.

* * *

As expected, veteran criminalist Edwin Jones from the sheriff's office in Ventura County, 125 miles north, strode forward after the noon recess. Judge Ryan asked about the difference between a criminalist and a forensic scientist, to which Jones answered, "I think they are synonymous."

Sorting through the photos of microscopically examined cells, Evans heard Jones identify seven of the forms as spermatozoa. Gumlia made little headway in attacking the conclusions. He seemed somewhat angry when he asked, "Do you know why it is our nation's leading forensic laboratory [FBI] would not yet advance to the point that you have advanced to in your ability to discern sperm?" Ryan sustained the prosecutor's objection. Questions about sperm cells plowed the same ground again until Jones was excused a half hour later.

Jurors, spectators, and the Huber family girded themselves for the most stressful part of the trial, when Dr. Ann Bucholtz took the stand to tell about the autopsy of Denise Huber's body.

Chapter 23

Prior to the testimony of Dr. Bucholtz, Judge Ryan called for a ten-minute break. When he declared court back in session, but with the jury still outside, he held a note one of the jurors had sent him. Ryan told the attorneys that Denise Gragg had been observed wearing a shoe with the heel cap missing. The victim's damaged shoes had also been missing one heel cap. Was this some subtle demonstration that the problem is common and not necessarily the result of being manhandled by an abductor? The judge asked if any of the lawyers wished to comment. Evans had nothing to say. Denise Gragg, apparently distressed and embarrassed, said, "Well, I would like some statement from the court that I wasn't attempting to tamper with the jury. I have been known to lose those heel things off my shoes all the time. I certainly never intended to have a pair of shoes with a missing heel [cap] yesterday. I can't even guarantee that won't happen again. I lose those heels often."

Flustered, Gragg continued, "Obviously, my concern is [that] anybody would think I wore a shoe purposefully with a heel cap missing. You guys know me. I would assume you wouldn't think that."

Ever the gentleman, Evans chimed in. "I don't think that." Judge Ryan said he didn't either. He called the jury in to deal with the matter. "I just wanted to comment on a note. Some of you will understand what I am talking about. Others will not. What the attorneys wear in court is not evidence. What was observed,

I believe it was yesterday . . . was not done on purpose, okay? And
that is the end of the discussion."

No one would have guessed the profession of Dr. Ann
Bucholtz. Slim with good-looking, delicate features, conserva-
tively styled brown hair, and tasteful apparel, she might have
been an accounting executive or a young college professor.
Somehow, she just didn't fit the image of a person who dissected
the bodies of murder victims for a living. She had been employed
as a medical examiner in Phoenix for years and had conducted
more than 2,000 autopsies.

Answering the prosecutor's questions, Bucholtz led listeners
on an unsettling tour of an investigative procedure few people
would ever want to witness. Killers make it necessary to subject
human remains to a series of final indignities. After the body of
Denise Huber had been thawed with the help of hair dryers,
and sexual assault swabs taken, Bucholtz had carefully removed
the jewelry, she said. Evans inquired about the head injuries and
asked her to diagram them at an easel.

In the front row, Dennis Huber wept silently. Ione cried, too,
but continued to watch. Periodically, both parents stared at the
back of John Famalaro's head, unable to comprehend how or
why this brutal crime had happened.

For the next ten minutes, the witness reeled off descriptions
of mind-boggling injuries to the face, scalp, and skull of Denise
Huber. Juror Bonnie Snethen would later say, "The most dramatic and hardest part of the trial for me was when Dr. Bucholtz
testified. She was the best witness they had, impeccable credentials, so well-spoken and intelligent. The subject matter was so
gruesome. I wondered why the Hubers were sitting there, day
after day. It had to be so horrible for them, reliving this. Then
I knew. They were there for Denise."

With carefully selected questions, Evans made certain the jurors understood that the massive skull injuries had apparently
been inflicted by the hammer and nail puller he had earlier

introduced into evidence. As he had done previously, the prosecutor carefully kept ghastly photographs from being seen by anyone but the witness. The jury would be able to examine them later, during deliberations. Soft groans could be heard in the audience when the doctor described gray matter oozing through cracks in the skull, and the work of stripping flesh from the head so the myriad of skull fragments could be reassembled and glued together. "We got a few missing pieces that we could not put back in. Either they wouldn't fit, or they were lost."

Viewers had difficulty even imagining what kind of an enraged frenzy drove the killer to continue hammering at a beautiful young woman's head the way the killer had. Dr. Bucholtz referred to the injuries in an unusual way. "We look at the *insult* to the top of the head—that is a term of art, an insult in describing injuries." Little bits of plastic, she noted, could be seen clinging inside skull fissures, and hair had been imbedded into the bone from the force of powerful blows.

The victim's mouth and eyes, according to the doctor, had been covered by duct tape which had slipped down as skin decomposed. Removal of the tape revealed the mouth had been frozen into an O shape. Apparently, a wad or cloth had been shoved inside and taped over. When it was removed, it left her mouth in the form of a silent scream.

No serious injuries were found on the body. Evans asked if all sexual assaults resulted in trauma to the various orifices violated. No, said Dr. Bucholtz, not always.

Cross-examination by Leonard Gumlia emphasized that no serious injuries had been inflicted below the victim's neck. While this may have mitigated, to some degree, the mental picture of the killer's actions, it ironically helped the parents' state of mind. The absence of any defensive wounds, along with the knowledge that the handcuffs had not dug deeply into the flesh of Denise's wrists, provided some relief to Dennis Huber. It reinforced his belief that Denise had probably been unconscious soon after the abduction, and had not suffered prolonged torture.

After a long series of questions about the victim's bleeding, the collection of swabs, and the plastic found imbedded in the skull, Gumlia asked, "Is there any way you can tell us—if this jury finds there was sperm—can you tell us whether it was placed there pre- or postmortem?"

"I don't know," the witness answered in candid simplicity. No evidence could be offered that might reveal if Denise had been sexually assaulted before she died or afterwards. One question may have backfired on the defense. To Gumlia's inquiry about the probability of anal trauma resulting from forced sodomy, the doctor replied that she had seen many cases of sexual assault, but had seldom seen lacerations in either of the assaulted orifices.

Final questions by both lawyers focused on the body's state of decomposition. Bucholtz offered the opinion that the frozen corpse, at some time during the years in the freezer, had partially thawed, allowing fluids to drain to the floor of the appliance. Later, the body and the fluids had solidified when re-freezing took place. Decomposition had occurred and advanced to the point where skin had started to slip. With that ghastly mental picture hovering over the courtroom, the elegant doctor stepped down and made her exit, leaving a late afternoon crowd of appalled, queasy observers.

Michael Winney, who had taken Denise Huber's fingerprints during the autopsy completed the day of testimony. He also revealed that he had saved the white plastic bags removed from the victim's head, and during his steps to preserve them, a blood-soaked wad of cloth had fallen out of one. The ball of fabric had apparently been stuffed in Huber's mouth.

At 4:30 P.M. Denise Gragg announced that the defense had no questions for Winney.

As the crowd filed out, Dennis and Ione again answered questions for reporters Stu Pfiefer and Greg Hernandez. About the damage to his daughter's skull, Dennis said, "It was so terrible. You wouldn't do that to a dog. Have you ever heard of anybody doing that to an animal, let alone Denise?" Explaining his staring at the back of Famalaro's head, the upset father said, "I wanted to see his reaction. I wanted to see if it hurt him, too."

Denise Gragg also spoke to the reporters, and asserted that the testimony did cause distress to Famalaro. "He was bothered by it. He was fighting back tears. But he's been told not to express any emotion."

On day four, Wednesday, Chris Evans called the first of his final two witnesses. Jason Snyder, the man who had been dating Huber but arranged for his friend, Rob Calvert, to accompany her to the last concert she ever saw, took the stand. He answered a couple of brief questions about his relationship with Huber before Evans got to the main reason for Snyder's appearance. The lawyer wanted to show that Denise had not engaged in any sex prior to her abduction, so any sperm in her body must have been put there by the killer.

Evans asked, "During the course of your dating relationship, did you have vaginal intercourse with Denise?"

"No, I did not."

"Did you have anal intercourse with Denise?"

"No, I did not."

"Thanks very much. Nothing further."

Denise Gragg established that the witness had received a telephone message from Huber on that night inviting him to meet at the El Paso Cantina. Gragg, in an earlier hearing, had warned that she would inquire about Huber's sobriety. She asked, "How did Miss Huber sound to you on that message?" Snyder said that Denise sounded like she was having a good time. Digging for more specifics, Gragg garnered information about the platonic relationship and asked if Snyder had seen Denise when she'd been drinking. He had. "So you knew what she sounded like when she was under the influence of alcohol?" The witness agreed that he had.

Gragg asked if the tape message sounded like Huber was drunk. But Snyder simply repeated, "It sounded like she was having a good time, and maybe had a couple of drinks." Gragg reminded him of a statement he'd made to the police describing her as sounding "buzzed." The witness admitted using the term, but added, "She was articulate, not slurring her words or anything like that." Determined, Gragg handed him a police report and asked if he had used the words "pretty well buzzed." Snyder said he had.

Reminded of speaking with Rob Calvert about that night, Snyder denied that Rob had said Huber was drunk. Once more, Gragg handed him the police report from 1991, but he replied that he had told the police he couldn't remember, and he still couldn't recall using the word drunk.

Evans took over and worked on softening the assertion that Denise had been "buzzed." He got from Snyder that the word meant to him, "Maybe a couple of drinks, happy person, not slurring words . . . She was not drunk on the telephone." A volley of questions from both sides never moved the witness far from his definition.

The final witness for the prosecution was Steve Parmentier, the owner of the garment business in the Laguna Hills warehouse. He described the relationship he'd had with his house-painting neighbor John Famalaro six years before. Evans asked if Parmentier had ever given Famalaro certain items. "Yes. We would give him . . . rags. After we cut our garments, there would be leftover pieces we'd give him."

Producing photos of cloth fragments, Evans asked if it depicted rags the witness had given Famalaro. Parmentier recognized distinctive markings and answered in the affirmative.

"Were they decomposed like that when you gave them to him?"

"No."

The witness also recognized the cardboard boxes, marked "Christmas," as containers that had been mailed to him from a supplier.

Observers concluded that the grisly fabric ball apparently

stuffed in Huber's mouth came from the rags given to Famalaro by a friendly neighbor.

A brief cross-examination by Gragg revealed nothing new.

At 9:48 A.M., prosecutor Chris Evans stood to announce that pending the admission of exhibits into evidence, "I rest my case in chief."

Judge Ryan excused the jury and ordered them back on Thursday to hear the defense's case. Before the Hubers could leave their first row seats, Leonard Gumlia made an admirable gesture that must have been difficult for him. He approached Dennis Huber, offered his hand, and commented that his efforts to defend Famalaro were not meant in any way to degrade Denise. Taken by surprise, Dennis shook hands with the lawyer, and let his heart guide his answer. "Everybody has a job to do," he said, "even if it's a crappy one." There would be no more exchanges between the two men.

Before the Hubers left, they formed a prayer circle with Nancy Streza, family members, and other friends to request heavenly guidance for the jury.

The trial had progressed with dazzling speed. Spectators wondered if the prosecution had presented enough evidence to convince the jury of guilt beyond a reasonable doubt, and how much of it the defense could refute. Several observers speculated that even if jurors did come in with a guilty verdict, the special circumstances of kidnapping and sodomy would not hold up. So Famalaro would get a prison sentence that allowed a good chance of parole.

The opportunity to present opening statements by attorneys provides them a forum to lay out before the jury a plan of where they are going with evidence in the case. What the lawyer says is not evidence, but sometimes it can make an indelible impression on the minds of jurors. That is why it shocked observers to learn, on Thursday, that neither Leonard Gumlia nor Denise Gragg would make an opening statement before launching their case in chief to defend John Famalaro. They had declined to speak at the outset and they would not speak now. So Judge Ryan invited them to call their first witness.

A powerful-looking man with a shaved head and a mustache drooping over the corners of his mouth strode forward and took the oath. When court watchers learned his identity, they wondered how he could serve the defense case. The witness spelled out his name, Thomas Coute, of the Costa Mesa P.D., and said had been one of the first patrol cops to arrive at the abandoned Honda. Denise Gragg's questions made it clear that Coute had been called primarily to establish that no evidence of a struggle had been seen by police near the Honda.

Evans, now in the role of cross-examiner, asked the officer if he been looking for tiny scraps of leather, perhaps one-eighth of an inch in size. No, the officer said, nor had he crawled around on his hands and knees trying to find other minuscule bits of evidence.

After Gragg had asked Coute if he'd seen any blood or drag marks, Evans retorted by inquiring if the witness would have any idea what a leather shoe drag mark would look like on dark asphalt. No, he said, he wouldn't.

No one recognized the next witness, a young woman who said she was Cynthia Brown. No relation to Huber's friend, Tammy Brown. The witness had been employed by the *Orange County Register* back in June 1991, delivering papers in Costa Mesa. On her way to work one morning, just before 2:30 A.M., she had spotted the Honda parked on the 73 freeway shoulder, with its emergency blinkers flashing. But, she told Gragg, she hadn't seen anyone nearby. Evans made the point, through her, that the flashers were probably turned on to indicate a need for help.

The defense team's first two witnesses used only 23 minutes of court time.

Witness number three would consume only twenty more minutes. A spry man for seventy, small, with full black hair looking very much like Ronald Reagan's, he had utilized the services of house painter John Famalaro in June 1991. A verbal agreement had been reached between the painter and the client on June 1, after which painting supplies were delivered to the customer's home on June 2, and the contract was signed on Monday, June 3, the same morning that Denise Huber vanished. On that day, the witness said, Famalaro seemed normal in his demeanor and mannerisms, but three or four days went by before he saw Famalaro again. When the painter showed up on June 8th, "He looked very ill. Said he was ill and looked ill." Famalaro told the client he had been in bed sick with pneumonia.

Chris Evans asked, "He didn't tell you about anything he may have done wrong, did he?" No. The client had seen Famalaro paint several houses in the neighborhood during the following weeks. The sprightly little man seemed glad to be finished with his day in court.

Another Costa Mesa police officer was called as the defense's next witness. Sgt. Burton Santee had been dispatched to the Honda at 11:45 P.M. the night it was found on the freeway. He arranged for it to be towed to an impound lot. He had spent over two hours at the scene, walking in all directions. Denise Gragg asked him if he'd seen any blood, clothing, drag marks, or signs of a struggle that night or the following day when he returned to the scene. No, Santee said, he hadn't.

The first question from Chris Evans neutralized any impact the answer might have made. "When you say you saw no signs of a struggle, you are not telling this jury that a struggle never took place in that area, is that right?"

"That is right." Like Officer Coute, Santee hadn't been down on his hands and knees looking for little bits of leather that had been scraped from a pair of high heel shoes.

A few minutes after 11 A.M., Santee stepped down. On his way out, he nodded and smiled at Ione and Dennis Huber, whom he had met many times as a member of the Aliso Creek Presbyterian Church.

A balding, bespectacled forensic scientist from the Orange County Crime Lab answered the next call. On July 21, 1994, he said, he examined a white pickup truck that had once been driven by John Famalaro but was registered in Kate Colby's name. It had been turned back to a finance company in late 1991 or early 1992 and subsequently used by other owners. A presumptive blood test in the vehicle interior turned up nothing. Neither did tests of the truck bed.

By 11:30, the defense had used up all of its witnesses for the day. Judge Ryan excused the jury for the weekend.

Leonard Gumlia and Denise Gragg spoke to reporters on their way out of court and astonished listeners by their comments. Virtually, they were conceding the guilt of their client, but planned to fight tooth and nail to prevent the imposition of the death penalty. Gumlia would give no details of what he might or might not know about how Denise Huber had been killed. But he said, "There was no captivity, no longevity. She died within an hour."

Both attorneys insisted that no kidnapping had taken place, implying that the victim went willingly with Famalaro, and that no sodomy occurred. Their informal capitulation in the guilt phase made it clear why they had chosen not to deliver an opening statement. Of course, the trial would proceed, because the jury could not be informed of the impromptu comments.

Regarding the illness of Famalaro during the first few days Huber was missing, Gumlia said, "Something happened that affected him. He was sick to his stomach at what happened."

Chris Evans, taken aback by the remarkable words from his opponents, condemned their actions as inappropriate and unethical, and criticized their out-of-court discussions.

* * *

Day six of the trial opened on Monday. Famalaro entered the courtroom through a side door leading from his holding cell, wearing a dark gray patterned sweater, navy blue slacks, and light brown shoes. He glanced toward the gallery and nodded to his mother, making one of her few appearances. The two defense attorneys left him at the table, and walked back to the seated, gray-haired woman. They both knelt and held a whispered conference with her. Mrs. Famalaro would later be overheard saying that she was there "to support the real John Famalaro, not the one you see here in court."

A few technical matters occupied the first hour, during which Gumlia announced that he would probably conclude the guilt phase on the next day. The Huber family and spectators couldn't believe it. At one time, it had been expected that the defense would call at least forty to sixty witnesses. Now, after the testimony of only five, the defenders planned to wind it down.

At 10:10 A.M., Christine Wong, senior investigator for the public defender's office, sat in the witness chair. She told of visiting the site where the Honda had been found, three years ago, to photograph the surrounding area, then repeating the process just one week ago. She had walked down the slope and measured it as sixty four feet from the car site to the bottom. Wong also had traveled to Arizona in 1994 to inspect Famalaro's house, where she counted more than twenty stacks of newspapers.

Focusing on the site of the Honda, Evans noted that she hadn't taken pictures of an asphalt berm, or low curb. He asked her why. She just hadn't thought to take such a picture, she said. A few observers wondered if Huber had been dragged over the rough curb, damaging the backs of her shoe heels.

If it had startled the gallery crowd to see Costa Mesa PD officers summoned by the defense, they were stunned to see the next witness called by Gragg: Detective Lynda Giesler. She had retired in December 1995, but had been retained by Chief Snow-

den on a contract basis to manage the room full of records related to the case.

Starting with questions about the *Inside Edition* video, Denise
Gragg elicited from Giesler that the same tape also contained
several other segments of general television programming. After
hearing the witness say that "a number" of news clips had been
found in the house, Gragg said she had no further questions.

To Chris Evans, Giesler pointed out that the video segment
on the Huber case, the only portion of *Inside Edition* recorded
by the defendant, could be seen at the very beginning of the
tape. Giesler's entire testimony lasted a total of eight minutes.

The guts of the defense case, according to Gumlia and Gragg,
hinged on overturning the charges of sodomy and kidnapping.
Both lawyers felt that the evidence of sperm cells found in
Huber's body was weak. With their next witness, they intended
to cast even more doubt on that issue.

Charles A. Sims might have been a senator with his thick white
hair combed low over the forehead, ruddy complexion, and
heavy face. He told the jury that he was a pathologist, had done
medical work two decades earlier, and had started a sperm bank
in 1977. Sims said he had examined photos of the alleged sperm
in this case, and had visited Lisa Arnell to personally view the
samples. Asked by Gumlia if he had reached any conclusions,
Sims announced, "It's my opinion I could not conclusively identify sperm."

A detailed description of his analysis followed, after which
Gumlia asked, "Could you advise anyone that those slides you
saw contain spermatozoa?"

Sims chose to answer metaphorically. "If it was an airplane, I
wouldn't fly it."

Evans stood, his eyes sparkling, and began cross-examination
by asking, "Are you a pilot, sir?" It brought grins in the gallery.
Sims said he had been at one time. Evans pursued it. "So you
wouldn't get in an airplane and fly it because you're not a qualified pilot?" The matter of qualification set the tone for the prosecutor.

"Are you a forensic pathologist?"

"No."

Demonstrating a remarkable understanding of science and terminology, Evans gradually established that Sims's experience in dealing with sperm in dead bodies, or in cavities other than reproductive organs, was limited. The short exposure the witness had in such matters had occurred in the sixties and seventies. Nor had Sims viewed any other rectal swabs, for clinical or forensic purposes, in two decades.

With the precision of a surgeon, Evans dissected each statement made by the witness. When Sims suggested that frozen crystals of matter might look like sperm, Evans asked, "Could you direct us to a particular case that I could verify by making some phone calls . . . where this ice crystal phenomena has produced something that looks like a sperm?"

"No."

Question after question regarding Sims' expertise resulted in the same answer. Polite and incisive, Evans never raised his voice or appeared cynical. Twenty minutes into the session, he handed the witness a photo and asked, "When you look at this, you're not saying that's not a sperm, are you?"

"That's correct. I'm not excluding the possibility that any of these are sperm." Several of the jurors reached for their notepads. The defense made little headway in efforts to repair the damage.

Before the defense would rest, they questioned two more witnesses. On Tuesday morning, May 20, Gordon Zelinski took the oath. Short, heavyset, balding, dressed like a successful executive, Zelinski's soft facial features relaxed into an expression of supreme confidence.

If jurors had lost credence in the previous expert's testimony because he was not a forensic scientist, they might listen more attentively to Zelinski, who said, "I am a criminalist and a consulting forensic scientist." The credentials he presented, including a stint as director of the Phoenix Crime Lab, seemed impressive.

Spieling off a technical explanation of spermatozoa analysis, with considerable detail about identifying cells with no tails, Zelinski said he, too, had visited Lisa Arnell at the Orange County Crime Lab and inspected the evidentiary slides. Presenting photos to the witness, Gumlia asked if any of the specimens pictured could be conclusively identified as sperm.

"No," Zelinski stated. He did, however, say that some of the cells might be consistent with characteristic of sperm.

"Sir, are you a doctor?" Evans asked.

"No, sir."

"What was your master's degree in?"

"I don't have a master's degree . . ."

Leaving the education behind, Evans asked if Zelinski was being paid to testify. Yes, he said. He would charge $130 per hour for research and court time. He couldn't remember how many hours he had already charged to the case. And he hadn't written a report. Evans wondered aloud if that was a deliberate oversight so the prosecution couldn't examine his findings through discovery laws. The witness denied it, and countered by expressing surprise that Evans hadn't asked to interview him. Each time Zelinski spoke, he looked in the direction of the jurors, and often let his lips turn up in a complacent smile.

The reason for the obvious relaxed confidence demonstrated by Zelinski became clear when Evans revealed that the witness had testified hundreds of times and actually taught defense attorneys how to cross-examine experts.

Maybe Zelinski had too many credentials as an expert. Evans asked him if he also claimed expertise in shoe and footprints comparison. Yes. In car tire tracks? Yes. Tool mark comparisons? Yes. Alcohol level interpretation? Yes. Determination if someone is impaired by drugs? Yes. Dramshop evidence (liability of a bar when a drunk customer drives and causes injury)? Yes. Poisons and alloy substance exposure? Yes. Fingerprints? At last, Zelinski said no, and explained that he only develops and chemically processes fingerprints. Evans reminded him that his resume included fingerprint evidence examinations, then continued the roll call of Zelinski's expertise. Firearms evidence? Yes. Bullet comparisons? Yes. Gunshot residue? Yes. Technical photography? Yes. Automobile headlights and taillights functioning involved in accidents? Yes. It sounded as if the witness was a jack of all trades.

Having worked at turning Zelinski's long list of expert qualifications against him, Evans asked, "When was the last time you did bench work on sperm identification?"

Zelinski couldn't remember, but recalled doing some in Phoenix in 1962 or 1963. Then he recalled doing some sperm identification in the nineties, but said they weren't criminal cases, just government internal affairs stuff. He declined to name the cases. And he couldn't recall how many such investigations. Now twisting in his chair, he suggested that Evans was playing a "lawyer's game."

"I'm sorry, Mr. Zelinski," Evans said with calm dignity. "Did you say that was a lawyer's game?"

"Sure," the witness snapped. "Was it less than ten, more than six? And if you don't have any memory, you are guessing. And I am not going to guess."

Maintaining perfect courtesy and voice control, Evans asked, "And did you say it was a lawyer's game to make you say something that was untrue?"

"Absolutely."

"All right," said Evans, "I would like to ask you a question that is designed to get the truth from you," and again asked Zelinski how many sperm identification cases he had worked on. "Was it under five?" No matter what number Evans posed, Zelinski couldn't remember. Squirming and becoming more frustrated, Zelinski finally blurted out that he had never done full time bench work on sperm identification.

Pressing harder, but still polite, Evans asked for any specific cases in which the witness had done sperm identification work. There was one in Texas, said Zelinski, and some other criminal cases. But claiming that he did not have an "encyclopedic memory," he couldn't recall names. Evans also elicited an admission that Zelinski had received no recent training in microscopy and spermatozoa. Nor had he published any papers on the subject.

Perhaps even more impressive to observers than Evans' remarkable knowledge of the specialty were his easy to understand, logical questions. Some attorneys make the question so complex, they lose the jury.

Winding down, he got agreement from Zelinski that he hadn't done any postmortem cases in the last ten years, and that most labs allow for identification of sperm cells without tails. Zelinski's frequent trial testimony, he admitted, was always for the defense.

Before releasing the witness back to the Gumlia, Evans put the photos in front of him again and got an admission that at least one of the pictures portrayed possible sperm.

Leonard Gumlia had only one question on redirect involving proficiency tests. Zelinski knew nothing of such tests. He stepped down at 11:33 A.M. Chris Evans had clearly won the battle of experts.

The final witness was Beth Goss, senior investigator for the public defender. She showed the jury a pair of 9West brand pumps, similar to those Denise Huber had worn. The witness had purchased the used shoes from a thrift shop for an experiment. Paralegal Kristen Widmann, who had been assisting the defense, and who also happened to be Leonard Gumlia's wife, had gone with Goss to the Honda site. Wearing the shoes, Widmann had walked around the area and climbed down, then up, the slope. Now, in court, the defense presented those shoes. Scuff marks could be seen on the heels.

Criticizing the experiment as decidedly unscientific, Chris Evans made his skepticism obvious. First, he asked about the difference in size between Kristen Widmann, five-six, 135 pounds, and Denise Huber, a much taller five-nine, and five pounds lighter. Goss agreed, but said Widmann was the only person close to that size she could find. The prosecutor inquired if Goss had any preconceived notions about how the test shoes should appear after the experiment. No. He did get her agreement that the test shoes did not show as much damage as Huber's shoes. Evans just shook his head, glanced at the jury, and said, "I have no further questions." Neither did the defense team.

Leonard Gumlia stood to announce, "The defense rests."

At this stage of any murder trial, the prosecution has the option to call more witnesses to rebut the defense evidence. Chris Evans decided he would forego presenting a rebuttal segment.

Now, it was time for the summations by the lawyers. They would take place the next day, Wednesday, May 21.

Chapter 24

"Good morning, ladies and gentlemen," Chris Evans said, scanning the twelve jurors and the four alternates. It is a universal fact that jurors, without ever being trained to do so, adopt poker faces during a trial. Famalaro's jury had been quite successful in showing little emotion, shock, revulsion, or other facial responses in response to the spectrum of testimony and evidence they had endured. But few of them could hide the admiration they felt for the prosecutor. It showed in their eyes.

Evans would present his version of what the evidence inferred, followed by Denise Gragg, then Leonard Gumlia arguing their points of view. Evans would be entitled to the final turn, since the prosecution bore the burden of proving the case beyond a reasonable doubt.

"This is the time in the trial . . . where I get to tie some things in for you," Evans said. "A lot of evidence that has been admitted . . . photos, exhibits, and things you haven't yet examined, weave into the fabric of this case. It's going to take a while, so get comfortable." For the next several minutes, he explained legal definitions of the charges against Famalaro, first degree murder and the special circumstances of kidnapping and sodomy. Intent to kill had to be shown, he said. "Picking up that nail puller and striking the victim at least thirty-one times in the head is just about as clear an expression of intent to kill as you and I will see in our lifetimes."

Striding back and forth in front of the jury box, making eye contact with the jurors, using hand gestures, and leaning forward from the hips, Evans spoke intently, giving examples and explanations. Kidnapping, he said, meant unlawful movement of a person by force or means of instilling fear, a substantial distance, without the victim's consent. "I would submit to you, ladies and gentlemen, that the movement of Denise Huber was unlawful and it was done by force or means of instilling fear . . . When you look at the distance in this case, whether you assume that Denise Huber was taken from the car or she was dragged, kicking and screaming from the defendant's truck or vehicle and dragged that last one hundred feet into the warehouse, that distance is substantial." If consent to movement by the victim is induced through deceit, fraud, force, or fear, it is not kidnapping. Evans emphasized that even if Huber had entered the killer's vehicle voluntarily, kidnapping could still be found if the jury believed that during the ride, it became against her will because of force, threats, or duress.

The other special circumstance, sodomy, he explained, according to definition must be perpetrated against a living human being. "There is a ton of evidence in this case on that issue. She was handcuffed. You don't handcuff a dead person . . . You don't blindfold a dead person . . . You don't gag a person who can't speak . . . if you want to perform sodomy on a dead person."

Breaking down the long, complex jury instructions the judge would soon read aloud, Evans worked to simplify them. He explained how circumstantial evidence may be used to convict a defendant. Famalaro, he said, was caught red-handed with a murdered body that had been stripped, blindfolded, gagged, handcuffed, and bludgeoned to death. And he was caught with murder weapons and the victim's clothing in his house. That was why, Evans announced, the defense would concede guilt on the murder. Several jurors' impassive expressions gave way to raised eyebrows.

"The trophy—that is what that body was. That is what Denise Huber's remains became. A trophy. That is one of the reasons he kept her. We know she was a true trophy because he kept the clothes, too, and all her identification."

Speaking now with righteous indignation, Evans reminded jurors that within hours of the abduction, Famalaro was callously talking to his customer about the virtues of various paints. Repeatedly, Evans used the phrase "caught red-handed."

Which vehicle Famalaro had used on the night Denise vanished had never been clarified. During that period, he had been driving several different pickup trucks. A red vehicle had been mentioned repeatedly, and a white one had been unsuccessfully searched for evidence. Evans said, "Well, if that is not the truck that has anything to do with this crime, then who the heck cares? Nobody. Just like any car he might have rented, or any other vehicle he *didn't* do this crime in. Who cares?" Maybe it was the red pickup the client had seen, which had never been found, suggested the prosecutor.

So, said Evans, if the defense planned to concede murder, the important issues were sodomy and kidnapping. Sodomy. In the one day of Denise Huber's life, the last day of her life, was there an incredible coincidence? "Here is the day she is taken, the day she is handcuffed, duct-taped over the eyes, had her clothes removed, her shoes beat up. The day all this happened, is it a coincidence that is the day we find sperm in her rectum?"

Regarding the experts called by the defense, Evans shook his head in disbelief "The two guys they called to talk about sperm were just awful witnesses . . . That is a real problem for the defense in this case. Let's talk about Dr. Sims because he is easier to talk about for me. Dr. Sims is an honest, nice person, who almost admittedly had no business being here. His honesty revealed his lack of qualification." And Sims did not rule out that samples were, indeed, sperm. "I am not saying that he recanted his testimony, or like Perry Mason I cracked him on the stand and made him cry and admit that he killed Denise Huber . . . That didn't happen. He was a cooperative witness. He was just honest."

Pointing out that the prosecution witnesses who identified the samples as sperm were far more qualified as a result of working daily in the lab, Evans said, "Let's now talk about the strange case of Mr. Zelinski. The guy was a joke. He was an expert in *everything.*" Evans ran down the long list. "He got a little upset with me, didn't he? That tells you about his attitude." Recapitulating Zelinsky's testimony, Evans didn't try to disguise his hostility toward the witness's arrogance, evasiveness, and unresponsive answers. "What about cases with sperm and microscopes? That was like pulling teeth. He couldn't name them. You know, the closest we got was some supposedly secret cases. 'If I tell you, I would have to kill you.' He didn't really say that. He said he was doing some civil work involving misconduct by police officers, and examining sperm. I guess he is referring to police officers raping people. I had this vision of hundreds of police officers raping people in the back of their cars." Evans asked if this type of attitude gave the jurors confidence in the witness. Mr. Zelinski's testimony, Evans said, should be "given the weight of air."

After a short break, Evans resumed his talk with, "I sure appreciate the attention you have given me so far." Jurors smiled.

Reminding the jurors of the blood found in the warehouse where Famalaro had worked and lived, the newspapers he'd kept about the case, the videotape of *Inside Edition*, Evans said these were not coincidences.

With the judge's permission, Evans stopped talking long enough to put the tape into a video machine and show the jury a few seconds of the TV show in which the Hubers begged for information about Denise. Observers shook their heads about the convoluted justice system which allowed only snippets of the tape to be viewed. Wouldn't it be closer to the truth to show all of it?

Appealing to jurors to use common sense, Evans returned to the issue of kidnapping. "Folks, she was headed home. She was not going down to Laguna Hills. She was not looking for somebody like Mr. Famalaro. She was not looking for anything but to go home and get in bed at her mom and dad's house." He pounded home the point that Denise didn't plan to go anywhere else that night.

Blood spots on Huber's car keys gave an indication of what happened, Evans said. "You can picture it for a moment. She was not abandoning her car to go off and have a couple pops with Mr. Famalaro down in Laguna Hills. She is holding her keys . . . probably when she got hit. The purse is a little bit bloody. The wallet is bloody."

Help was within a short walk. Huber had an auto club card, credit cards, and the phone number for a cab company in her wallet. "She never made it. We know she didn't spend a lot of time around that car because of the timing of witnesses. She put on her four-way flashers. That was a beacon for that guy." Evans raised his arm and pointed to John Famalaro. "And it would have been a beacon for the highway patrol. She was not hiding from the cops. I will pull over and put my four-way flashers on. There is a great disguise!"

Evans paused to take a breath and scan the jurors' faces. "Ladies and gentlemen, Denise Huber did not go voluntarily past all this help. That didn't happen, not in this case, not in this lifetime, not on this planet. This is an area that she was intimately familiar with. This triangle of U.C.I where she went to college, her house, the location of the car, and Rob Calvert's house . . . She didn't go past all those convenience stores, pay phones, all those lit areas. She didn't go past her college campus, not knowing where the heck she was."

Scorn appeared on Evans' face as he brought up Denise's damaged shoes. "I am going to call that test they offered the great shoe fiasco. If that test showed anything, it is extremely beneficial to the prosecution's case. It clearly shows that when you walk down that hill, and up, your shoes aren't going to be damaged like the victim's shoes were . . . And the only person they could come up with to wear the shoes was the defense attorney's wife?" Highly critical of the experiment, Evans said it would be impossible to reconstruct what had happened that night to damage the victim's shoes. "Was Denise Huber running for her life down that slope with a head injury? There is no evidence she went down the slope, and there is certainly no evidence of how she might have done it if she did."

Building on the theory that Huber had been forcibly abducted at the site of her Honda, Evans said, "Do you blindfold somebody after they have had a good chance to look at you and after they have taken you to their hideout? Does that make any common sense whatever? Do you blindfold somebody after they have taken a leisurely ride down to Laguna Hills for help? No. That doesn't make sense."

Glaring first at John Famalaro, then turning toward the jury
with a pained expression, Evans said, "I have to apologize to
you. I don't want to have to show you these pictures that I now
have to show you." With that, he held up three photos. The first
was of Denise Huber's body, frozen, blindfolded, nude, curled
into a tuck position. The second depicted her mouth. "It shows
her mouth in the position that was consistent with that rag." He
referred to the ghastly wad that had been stuffed into her mouth.
The third showed her wrists handcuffed behind her back. Evans
carefully handled the photos, tilted in a manner to prevent the
parents in the front row from catching an accidental view of
them.

Ione and Dennis both sat with their heads bowed, tears in
their eyes. Judge Ryan kept a careful watch on them.

Evans continued. "I didn't cause this. But when you look at
these pictures, you are going to see—" He stopped. "I am going
to ask you if you can look at these pictures when you get back
there." He nodded toward the jury room.

Listing a few anticipated statements that might be made by
the defense, Evans put a negative twist on them, making them
sound ridiculous.

Denise Huber's body was found completely nude. Evans asked,
"Why on God's green earth does he have to remove her underwear if not to do a sexual assault? Is it an enormous coincidence
that beyond reasonable doubt there is sperm in her rectum? It
is not."

Explaining the well-known term used in mystery cases, "red
herring," Evans said, "When they used to hunt foxes in England,
they would try to make it sporting by tying decomposing herring
fish in trees to throw off [a hound's] scent of the fox. In the law
business, it becomes known as a red herring. Designed to throw
off the scent." The defense had used a red herring, Evans said,
with the suggestion that sperm had drained from the vagina to
the anus. He asked incredulously, "Was there any evidence of
vaginal sex in this case? No."

Concluding his one-hour talk, Evans said, "I am not asking
you to convict based on any one of these things. I am asking you
to put them all together and consider them as a whole. The

defense can give you their version of reasons for every one of these things. But they can't do one thing. They can't give you a reason why each one of these, in total, should be excluded. That is because it is very clear that this defendant did what he has been charged with. Thank you very much for listening to me and I will talk to you again later."

During a lunch break, *L.A. Times* reporter Greg Hernandez spoke briefly with Famalaro's mother. She told him that listening to Mr. Evans' words was like "open heart surgery without the benefit of anesthesia."

At 1:40 on that warm May afternoon, Denise Gragg faced the jurors. "Good afternoon, ladies and gentlemen." She reminded them that in the very beginning, during juror questioning, they had been warned that it would be an emotionally upsetting case in which they would feel great sympathy for the victim and her family, and that they were going to see horrifying things. "You now have a task and a duty far harder than the task of any attorney standing up here, and that is you have to be able to put those emotions away and look at what was proven in this courtroom." Each of them had promised to do that, Gragg reminded.

As anticipated, Gragg did not deny that Famalaro had caused the death of Denise Huber. "I agree with Mr. Evans that at the end of the arguments, you will come to a determination that Mr. Famalaro is responsible for the death of Ms. Huber. That is not the end of your decision-making process." She urged the jurors to remain loyal to their oath, and make decisions based only on what the evidence had shown beyond a reasonable doubt.

Gragg promised not to talk about the sodomy charge, since Leonard Gumlia would discuss that later.

The inferences in the case, she said, would lead to five conclusions. "Number one, that Ms. Huber's assault did not occur where her car broke down on the freeway. Number two, that Ms. Huber joined Mr. Famalaro voluntarily, without force. I don't mean she went off on a date with him or anything like that. I just mean that the facts are going to show that she did not get into the car under force or threat, she got in voluntarily. Number three, that the first violence in this case happened at the warehouse. Number four, that Mr. Famalaro's intention on the first encounter with Ms. Huber was not to hurt her or rape her or sodomize her or to kill her or any of those things. The violence occurred because of events that developed during the course of their encounter. And number five, it's going to show you that the killing occurred at the warehouse not as the result of some preexisting plan, but with what was at hand because of what preceded it.

"The evidence is going to show you that Ms. Huber was unconscious from the first blow. It's going to show that she was handcuffed after that first blow. It will show that she was gagged after that first blow, probably, or at least that's the most reasonable inference. She never woke up again and its going to show she was killed when she was in that state."

With that chilling prologue, Gragg segued into an explanation of circumstantial evidence. "If you have two interpretations and they are both reasonable interpretations, you must choose the one that points toward innocence."

Jurors and spectators alike listened attentively when Gragg said she would explain about the encounter that brought Huber and Famalaro together. "Well, one piece of evidence is that Ms. Huber had been drinking that night." Gragg commented that she didn't bring it up to dirty the reputation of Denise Huber, and that drinking was no justification for what happened. Its relevance was to show Huber's state of mind and that alcohol can affect the judgement. The victim was not "rip-roaring drunk," but possibly had impaired judgement. Huber had to make a choice after being stranded after 2:15 in the morning on a nearly deserted freeway. "We can draw an inference that she wouldn't want to involve the police," said Gragg, because of the earlier drinking. She had a shot glass in her car and probably smelled of beer. "It's reasonable to assume she would look for help that wouldn't involve the call boxes . . . and to assume that if she could get help without waking her parents, she would just as soon do that."

Explaining that because Huber switched her flashers on, and took her purse and keys, it appeared that she left the Honda in quest of a phone or for help to change the flat tire. The unlocked doors may have been left that way to allow access by a tow truck driver she might call using her auto club card. And Huber was not near the Honda when the newspaper delivery woman drove by at 2:25 that morning.

Putting those assumptions together, Gragg presented a scenario in which Huber walked to the break in the fence, trod through it over rough pavement, down the gravelly slope, through green grass, perhaps to seek help at a business on the street below.

Attentive spectators wondered if Gragg's theory of Huber walking down to Bear Street was correct. It might have been easier at the bottom of the dark slope for Famalaro to accost and subdue her there.

Defending the experiment with the shoes, Gragg noted that Huber's shoes were not new and had been worn previously, making them more vulnerable to damage such as a lost heel cap. She chided Evans for not clarifying his theory of where the victim had been dragged, on the freeway or at the warehouse. Besides, Gragg said, if dragging had occurred, there probably would have been more damage, or the shoes would have slipped off Huber's feet. The damage looked to Gragg like it was caused by walking through stones with sharp edges that made upward indentations in the leather.

Arguing about the prosecution's theory that blood had spattered on Huber's keys while she held them and was hit, near the Honda, Gragg disputed the idea. If that's where the first bloody blow happened, then why didn't investigators find blood on the ground near the car?

Possibly, observers thought, that point supported further the idea that Huber had walked down to Bear Street, and was slugged there. Police couldn't have examined every inch of ground in the area. But Gragg suggested, "The only possible interpretation of all this evidence is that there was no struggle at the car . . . Ms. Huber got out of her car, turned on the flashers, took her purse, and walked." It would take only minutes to reach the 55 freeway on foot. "The rational inference is she's already walking down the 55 at the time Cynthia Brown drives by, at about 2:25 A.M. . . . and it's equally reasonable that she met Mr. Famalaro there."

What facts inferred that Huber entered his vehicle consensually? Gragg said, "It's almost 2:30 in the morning. If Mr. Famalaro is out that night with the thought, 'I'm going to find somebody that I can sodomize and kill,' then the last place he would be is on the 55 freeway at 2:30 in the morning." Not many prospects on the freeway at that hour. And, asked Gragg, "If he encounters a woman who is walking down the side of the road, what is the evidence that he approaches her with the idea he's going to hurt her some way?"

Perhaps realizing what answer might be forming in jurors' minds, Gragg quickly stated, "Well, the only evidence of that is what happened at the end, and I will grant you, a reasonable interpretation is that she gets killed at the end, is a thought he had formed from the get-go, but it's also reasonable to assume . . . that it wasn't the first thing he thought of when he saw her." In the defender's scenario, Famalaro stopped and initiated an encounter with her "for less sinister purposes."

Offering more support for her theory, Gragg pointed out that the murder weapons were tools, not guns or knives. No blood was found in any vehicle. The white pickup he used most often was tested and showed no signs of blood. Certainly, she said, if Famalaro had spilled Huber's blood in the red pickup, as implied by the prosecution, he wouldn't have taken the elderly customer for a ride in it the next day.

Still chopping away at the theory of forcible kidnapping, Gragg reminded jurors that no noticeable injuries had been inflicted on Huber's body below the neck. Gragg challenged two prosecution assertions that Huber was forcibly kidnapped during the initial encounter. First, if the victim was knocked unconscious at that point, there would be no need for a blindfold. Second, if Huber resisted at the scene, and was forced into the car, then blindfolded, how was she restrained?

Spectators mulled that over. Threats? A knife at the throat?

Famalaro was supposedly an expert an martial arts; could he have subdued her that way? Maybe he had a gun at that point.

Gragg said, "We know the handcuffs didn't occur in the car because we know the handcuff happened after the clothes were taken off. The clothing isn't cut and it's difficult to see how you would take a jacket and dress off intact if she was handcuffed. Inferentially, that happened at the warehouse."

Gragg continued supporting her theory. "We also know that she had her clothes on when she was hit for the first time."

That made sense, considering her bloody clothing. Gragg said, "If it happened at the scene, and she's unconscious, why blindfold her?" And if he blindfolded her because she regained consciousness on the way to the warehouse, then why no evidence of a struggle in his truck? Grabbing one of Chris Evan's assertions, that the warehouse was a secluded place of privacy, Gragg said that fact supported the theory that Famalaro took Huber there to seduce her, not to sodomize and kill her. The blood was found on the floor and wall close to the office he had converted to a bedroom. If he planned to kill her, why would he take her to a place where his employees would be arriving in a few hours? He could have taken her to any number of isolated wilderness sites in the county.

Much of the blood on her personal items, Gragg asserted, was transferred there from other bloody items.

Denise Huber, said Gragg, was alone, stranded on the freeway. "You must also take into account her nature, which was not shy or timid, but friendly and outgoing—as well as what effect the alcohol may have had on her judgement."

To be certain the jury understood the definition of kidnapping, Gragg gave several examples, then said, "You may decide that . . . Ms. Huber might have gotten nervous depending on what was happening as she went to the warehouse. Unless there's some evidence that force was used on her to keep her in the car, the fact that she ended up at the warehouse doesn't mean this was kidnapping. There is no evidence of force being used on her, other than the fact she ended up in a situation she didn't want to be in."

Alluding to the fact that the bottoms of Huber's feet were soiled, Gragg suggested that at some time she had been unrestrained in the warehouse, which had a dirty floor, perhaps walking inside to use a phone, fully clothed. If the jacket had blood on it, it happened in the warehouse. "She's hit because she is running from him or resisting a sexual pass."

The first blow no doubt caused unconsciousness. Gragg postulated that it was from a hammer blow, and the rest of the devastating wounds resulted from repeated blows with the nail puller. To the defense, that evidence supported a finding that Famalaro had not planned to kill, or he would have been equipped with a more conventional deadly weapon. The attack, then, was spontaneous. Some time passed between the two attacks. Subsequently, he used the second tool to finalize the death. The absence of abrasions from the handcuffs inferred they were snapped on her after the clothing was removed. "That first blow made her unconscious. Now he takes off her clothes, he puts on the handcuffs. He puts on the gag which we know she doesn't have from the first blow because gum she was chewing came out of her mouth, and puts on the blindfold. Why does he do these things to someone who is unconscious? The rational explanation is that he doesn't know if she's dead or not dead, and he's waiting for her to come to so he can do what he wants to do with her . . . she's not going to be able to move or scream. Why blindfold her if she's already seen him? Well, the only place she's seen him is in the dark, getting in the truck, driving along. Maybe he's sort of closing the gate after the horse has gone through, but he blindfolds her while they are in this warehouse. Maybe he couldn't look her in the face."

Denise never recovered consciousness, Gragg said. "Famalaro decided to kill her probably because he realized . . . it's getting late, workers are coming, and now he's in serious trouble. He has a wounded, naked, handcuffed woman and has to do something."

From there, Gragg's account created a petrifying spectacle of gore. Famalaro's Levi's and Lake Wobegon sweatshirt were splat-

tered, not soaked with blood. Famalaro, she said, must have been
hitting Huber and placing successive plastic bags on her head.
The blows made slits in the bags, and blood flew through them
onto his jeans and the shirt. That would explain no blood on
the handcuffs, which were behind her back. Blood was also on
tarps, which are commonly found in a painter's warehouse. More
blood finally soaked the right arm of the shirt, "like someone
just moving a bloody body, particularly if the arm is under the
head where the injuries are."

Breathless, and perhaps emotionally drained from her own
narrative, Denise Gragg asked to take a break.

When Gragg continued twenty minutes later, she revisited the
definition of kidnapping, emphasizing the importance of trans-
porting the victim a substantial distance. If it had been only the
last one hundred feet in the warehouse, she said, that was not
a substantial distance.

Gragg discussed her client's actions after the killing. "There's
no argument that he knew he killed somebody, nor that he did
not turn himself in. That's not a point at issue." She relied on
the dates Famalaro ordered and received the freezer, more than
a week after Huber was killed, to bolster the defense theory that
he hadn't planned in advance what he would do with a dead
body.

Famalaro had taken "hideous risks" by retaining all the evidence and the body, which Gragg didn't think supported the
concept of keeping a trophy.

"Everything in this case happened in an unplanned manner,
at least in terms of the steps that finally led to the killing of Ms.
Huber," Gragg declared. "The weapons were tools that were
lying around the warehouse. There is no reason to believe that
Mr. Famalaro would expect to meet someone on the freeway at
2:30 in the morning. This was not some preplanned kidnap,
sodomy, murder." Denise Huber, she said, was "a young woman
who made a mistake, an innocent mistake . . . a mistake out of
misplaced trust. That mistake led to her death . . . because of a
series of events that started out as a friendly, consensual encounter."

Without looking at her client, Gragg said, "Mr. Famalaro . . .

is guilty of murder. He's guilty of murdering Denise Huber, but he did not kidnap her and any fair-minded assessment of the facts will indicate there is no evidence that supports an interpretation that he kidnapped her."

Exhausted, Denise Gragg seemed relieved to let Leonard Gumlia replace her at the lectern.

Chapter 25

"Good afternoon," Leonard Gumlia began at almost 3:30, P.M. addressing jurors whose eyes had started to glaze with fatigue. "It's hard to argue this late in the day, especially since you've been listening all day . . . I'm going to talk primarily about the evidence on sodomy, but I did make some notes as Ms. Gragg spoke and as Mr. Evans spoke, and I want to go over a couple of things related to the case, the special circumstances."

Several observers glanced at each other in confusion. Hadn't they just heard a one-hour discourse on kidnapping? Chris Evans appeared concerned, too, and objected about the announced intent to retread the same subject. Agreeing, Judge Ryan said, "I'm assuming he's not going to do that."

"May I have five minutes?" Gumlia pleaded.

"Don't take more than two minutes repeating anything Ms. Gragg has already so eloquently stated," ordered Ryan.

Nodding his assent, Gumlia said, "Unless Ms. Huber was dragged unconscious into a car, it would have been impossible to hold her in that car. A man cannot drag a person into a car. If he goes in first, he can't shut the door behind her. If he pushed her in and goes around to his side, then she can get out. If she's dragged into that car, she has to be unconscious and he would have had to go back and get her shoes." Speaking in his usual rapid-fire delivery, the defender evoked a series of animated mental images similar to fast-forwarding a videotape—difficult to keep up with. He quickly added that the massive head injuries would have left blood at the scene. Without directly saying it,

Gumlia seemed to be telling the jury that Huber had willingly entered Famalaro's vehicle. Pacing, then standing with feet wide apart and using generous arm motions, the defender worked hard to assure that the jury stayed with him.

"The final point I wanted to make on the kidnapping is that, no doubt, Ms. Huber became concerned during the drive." Responding to the description by Chris Evans of a "kicking and screaming" victim, Gumlia suggested that Famalaro may have given Huber a "song and dance" about taking her somewhere, at which she became concerned. But, he declared, a woman who becomes apprehensive in such circumstances isn't necessarily going to kick and scream. If she's unsure about the man's intentions, she will not necessarily provoke him. "The prudent course is to wait and see, until you can get to a place where you can safely leave the car . . . With that, I want to go into the sodomy charge."

Conceding that sexual assault had certainly occurred, but denying it was sodomy, Gumlia complained that the only evidence the prosecution had used to support the charge was the questionable presence of sperm. Evans, he said, had "made fun" of the defense's expert, Mr. Zelinski, but had failed to bring in a medical doctor to affirm the presence of sperm. "We know that the FBI, the leading forensic laboratory in the country is not convinced, based on science, that these could be called sperm cells." In a federal court, he added, an FBI expert would testify to that. The training of law enforcement criminalists, the defender said, was fallible.

The prosecutor, said Gumlia, had obscured the issue by attacking the credentials of defense experts as clinical rather than forensic scientists. Referring to the color photos of microscopic cells, Gumlia challenged prosecution opinions that they were sperm.

Famalaro, sitting motionless at the defense table, appeared to be in a daze.

"If there was sperm in this case . . . there should have been DNA. I know the prosecution has tried hard to explain that away." Comparing the analysis of the cell samples to a diagnosis of cancer, Gumlia asked the jurors if they would be willing to undergo major surgery, such as a mastectomy or removal of the colon, based on such doubtful identification of cells. "If you are convinced on their testimony and on the state of what we know, then you should convict Mr. Famalaro of sodomy." But, he warned jurors, if they agreed there should be more confirmatory tests, "then you have a reasonable doubt." Gumlia spelled it out again, "I submit to you, nobody can know that is sperm, ever."

After a quick whispered exchange with Denise Gragg, Gumlia announced, "I have nothing else to say specifically about the evidence related to sodomy." But he wanted to comment on the subject of reasonable doubt. The ghastly photos, which the jurors would soon have an opportunity to examine, would be difficult to look at, he said. But he appealed to each person to "pull back" and make decisions based on logic. "You twelve . . . are the ones we chose, and you all said you could, and we are asking you to do that."

Reasonable doubt, Gumlia said, is a serious business. He expressed hope that each juror would make an unemotional decision, for both the kidnapping and the sodomy special circumstances, based on standards they would expect for themselves. "You never want to second guess yourself," he cautioned. Gumlia advised the jurors to imagine meeting Denise Huber someday in another place, and asking her what happened in her encounter with Famalaro. "Where did you meet? What was said? Where was force first applied?" If jurors had those questions in mind, Gumlia said, "then you're having the doubts based on the evidence."

Sounding drained, he said, "I'll finish with this thought: We hope the prosecution at least tells you exactly what happened, exactly where it happened, and why. Why? How do you know the force was applied here? How do you know that is really sperm? How do you know whether it was applied premortem or postmortem? How do you know these things? I hope you hold them to that, so they can tell you . . . because they have the burden of proof, and they should answer those questions for you." Speculations and "maybes" would not suffice, he said. "Thank you."

Not wishing to waste usable time, Judge Ryan turned to Chris Evans and said, "You may make your rebuttal argument."

After his customary courteous greeting to the jury, Evans scratched his head. "I'm not very sure what the defense attorney said . . . I'll call it comments about reasonable doubt. I couldn't follow his reasoning, about meeting Denise Huber somewhere and asking her, 'Hey, what happened?' I don't even know how to respond to that kind of talk. It isn't contained in the jury instructions." No court procedure, Evans said, alluded to meeting the victim somewhere and asking what happened. And no rule existed requiring the district attorney to explain everything that had happened. "I don't know how to respond to that, so I won't. I'm just standing here speechless on that."

In listening to the defense arguments, Evans said, he wondered why they hadn't sworn an oath on the Bible, because their words sounded more like testimony than summation arguments.

Asking the jurors to use common sense and to weigh the evidence, Evans spurned Denise Gragg's suggestion that the victim's judgement had been impaired. No evidence or testimony, Evans said, supported that. And he resented the appearance of blaming the tragedy on Denise Huber's "mistake" or faulty judgement. "Ms. Gragg said the only possible inference . . . is that Denise Huber didn't want police involvement." Explaining that an inference is a conclusion stemming from a verifiable fact, Evans demanded, "Tell me where the initial fact is to prove that one. Where is it? Was there any testimony about that? She didn't want police involvement." Sounding like actor Jimmy Stewart, Evans said, "Hey, quite the gosh-darn contrary. You have to be kidding me. It's two-thirty in the morning. She wants to go home. She's alone. She wants help, police notwithstanding." The same logic, he said, applied to the faulty notion that Huber didn't want to wake up her mom and dad. Evans glanced at the parents in the front row, and several jurors followed his lead.

Huber had parked her car, switched on the flashers, taken her keys and purse out, and closed the doors. Then, said Evans, pointing an accusing finger at the inert defendant, "along came trouble." She'd left her car unlocked, and defense counsel implied that it was to allow easy access for the auto club. Evans used that implication as an example of defense speculation unsupported by testimony or evidence. "It's more reasonable," he said, "that she was just in a hurry."

Still incredulous about the "shoe fiasco," Evans commented that the unscientific test had backfired on the defense, since it demonstrated little damage to the pumps used. "They want me to tell you where Denise was dragged. Don't you think if I knew, that I would have told you by now? Come on. Where does it say that I have to do that?"

Countering the comment made by Gragg that if the victim had been dragged, her shoes would have come off, Evans asked, "Says who? What if the fight lasted four seconds and Denise was struggling to keep her shoes on?" He accused the defenders of defying the laws of physics. No signs of struggle had been found in Famalaro's white pickup. "I guess that means that every time there's a struggle in the world, there's physical evidence of it. I guess that's an immutable law of physics. And I guess it's another law of physics that all high heels dragged on asphalt or concrete will leave marks." Blood on Huber's keys? Gragg had said it must have been transferred from some other bloody item. Evans pointed out that no other bloodsmeared item had been close to the keys in the storage box.

Other "bad inferences" drawn by the defense, Evans said, included the assertion that Huber had walked up or down the slope, walked to the 55 freeway, that she had encountered Famalaro there, that he wouldn't have been searching for a victim to sodomize on the freeway at 2:30 in the morning, and that he was driving the white pickup. No facts supported any of those, he said. And if Famalaro had assaulted Huber in the red pickup, the defense had said, it would have been dumb to take a client for a ride in it the next morning. Dumb? "No dumber than having her dead body in a freezer in his driveway."

Assailing Leonard Gumlia's summation, Evans referred to the defender's observation that it would have been difficult for Famalaro to restrain his captive inside the car. Allowing himself a tiny sneer, Evans asked, "How about crippling, paralyzing fear as a restraint? How about some handcuffs?" And the claim that the handcuffs went on after the clothes came off; "You know, obviously you can't take clothes off with cuffs on. But you can injure someone and take the cuffs off, or cripple someone with fear, and remove the cuffs to take clothes off."

Judge Ryan interrupted to call for the evening recess. Evans would conclude his final arguments on the following morning.

Before Evans could resume his presentation on Thursday morning, Judge Ryan summoned him, along with Denise Gragg, into chambers, where Leonard Gumlia already sat. Gumlia said, "Judge . . . I was told by two people in the courtroom, and I could not witness this myself, that during parts of Mr. Evans' argument, the Hubers were either nodding in approval or disagreeing, shaking their heads negatively. It could be a natural reaction. I am not here to impugn their motives. But it related to things about whether Denise [Huber] would have done certain things. So I believe it could be construed, if it is true, and I have no reason to disbelieve the people who saw it, it would be a form of testifying. I don't want to publicly scold the Hubers. I was going to ask that Mr. Evans speak to them and request them not to do anything like that. I would ask that the court admonish the jury that audience sounds or movements or expression from anyone are just not to be considered as evidence. I don't know how else to handle it. I could ask for a mistrial, I suppose."

Denise Gragg corroborated Gumlia's concern. "When Mr. Evans said something about Ms. Huber would not go voluntarily, or something about what Ms. Huber would do, someone was either nodding or shaking their head vigorously in agreement with what he was saying, in full view of the jury."

Evans added, "I don't know who was sitting in the front row yesterday. I know Mr. and Mrs. Huber were . . . I will speak to them, and if that is going on, I will make sure it stops."

Judge Ryan was openly skeptical. "That is not going on. Mr. Huber put his head down when pictures were being shown to the jury. That was obvious . . . There was a lady next to Mrs.

Huber who was moving her head. I saw this. Had absolutely no significance as to agreeing or disagreeing to what Mr. Evans was saying. She was nodding over towards where Mrs. Huber was sitting. I am observing, you know. I am making sure the jurors are awake, and I am looking out at the audience." He noted that he'd recently had to scold a family in another trial, and hated doing it. The head movements he'd seen yesterday, he said, were nothing like the descriptions given by the defenders. However the judge agreed to tell the jury to ignore such activity.

Juror Bonnie Snethen would later say that Judge Ryan was correct. She hadn't noticed anything in the audience, and felt certain other jurors hadn't either. "So much was going on in court. We didn't have any time to watch the audience."

With court called to order, and the jurors seated, Judge Ryan informed them that they would begin deliberations on Monday, then added an admonition that they must not read anything into any activity by people in the audience. "Your decision in this case must be based on evidence and the law." With that, he invited Chris Evans to conclude his rebuttal argument.

Expressing his appreciation to the jury for patience and for listening to him, Evans brought them back to the issues by pointing to a photo he held of the freeway site. The flat tire marks on the concrete could be clearly seen. Evans used them as more evidence that Denise Huber's judgement had not been impaired, and that she had not been affected by the drinks she'd consumed, as seen by the way she had safely slowed from freeway speed and pulled the car to the shoulder.

Recapping some of the argument from Wednesday, Evans brought up the red pickup truck again, in which the defender had said it would have been "dumb" for Famalaro to take a client riding if he had used the vehicle to abduct Huber just a few hours earlier. Something had bothered Evans about that, he said, so he had checked the trial transcripts. And he'd caught the error. The client had testified that, "We didn't go in

Famalaro's car on the ride. We went in my car. We didn't go in the red truck."

Also, the prosecutor had thought over the inference, suggested by the defense, that Famalaro wouldn't have taken Huber to his warehouse office/bedroom to kill her because employees would be arriving there within a few hours. But, said Evans, that room was kept locked, and employees not allowed to enter it. It was the most logical place to take her.

He also took issue with the theory that much of the blood on Huber's personal possessions had been transferred there from other bloody material. It could have happened during the killing. "This was a bloodbath. There is blood everywhere. Blood on the wallet." Maybe the killer's bloody hands had dripped on her things if he opened her purse to look for identification of the person he had murdered.

Evans resented the reference to Denise's friendly and outgoing personality to support an inference that she had willingly gone with Famalaro. Even if she had accepted his offer of help, which was unlikely, at some point the encounter had turned into a kidnapping. "Because if it starts out as lies and a trick to get her in the car . . . along the way Denise Huber has a lightbulb that goes on in her head as she is passing the turnoff to her house. All those lights, all those pay phones, the twenty-four-hour convenience store, as she is leaving Costa Mesa, Newport Beach, driving through Irvine, past her college, in an area totally the wrong way, at 2:30 or 2:45 in the morning, to drive out into the darkness of an industrial park . . . no one is there at night, if her lightbulb goes on and she stops the consent, and it becomes force, of course it is a kidnapping."

Defense lawyers had implied that dirt on the bottom of Huber's feet suggested she had walked unfettered in the warehouse. Evans couldn't disguise his indignance. "Maybe I just missed that day in court. Dirty feet! Do we know where that came from? No. Could it have come from her car? She removed her stockings. Maybe she drove without her shoes on. Who knows? Could it have come from the way her body was stored, in those days before she was stuffed into a freezer? Who knows?"

It had been implied that Huber willingly accepted Famalaro's offer to take her to a telephone. "Are they telling us that she wanted to ride twelve miles in the wrong direction to make a phone call to get her car fixed that was three miles from her house? I wonder if you can accept that."

Softening his tone, Evans explained that he had no desire to impugn the integrity of counsel in any of his statements. "I don't do that. I want to talk about the quality, intellectually, of their argument." But, on the other hand, he said, he read the daily transcripts and listened to the defense. "I am not a potted plant over here. I am going to remind you of discrepancies."

The first blow with a hammer must have taken place in the warehouse because that is where hammers are kept? Evans shook his head. "Of course, a hammer would never be in his work truck, would it?

More animated now, Evans excoriated the defense for repeatedly using the term, "The only possible inference is . . ." There were usually several possible inferences from facts. He particularly didn't like the only possible inference that Huber must have been unconscious when the killer gagged and handcuffed her. "You don't gag somebody [who is] unconscious. You don't handcuff somebody [who is] unconscious . . . And the supporting factor they gave you for that was . . . he couldn't look into the face of the victim. You have got to be kidding me. This guy can't look into the face of the victim? This guy that can bash her head in at least thirty-one times, this guy that can put bags over her head, this guy that can cuff her, this guy that can put his erect penis in her rectum, this guy that can take her off the street, this guy that can collect those articles, this guy who can read about the Hubers still keeping hope? This guy can't look into her eyes? Not on your life."

Another ridiculous assertion, Evans said, was that Famalaro had blindfolded her at the warehouse because Huber had only seen him outside at night when it was dark. Certainly, said the prosecutor, she could have seen him at the well-lighted freeway or at any time along the twelve-mile drive.

To make a finding of kidnapping, the defense had said, required that the victim had been transported a substantial distance, and if it was only the last one hundred feet in the warehouse, that wasn't substantial. Evans bristled. "Was that one hundred feet trivial? Not in Denise Huber's life. That is probably the last one hundred feet she ever moved."

The whole attack had been spontaneous as described by the defenders. "They said it was not planned. Well, maybe. But you have to overlook the handcuffs, the tape, the gag, and the bags."

"Counsel told you that this was just really a case about a young woman who made a mistake. Wow! This is not a case about that. Denise Huber—you didn't make a mistake, Denise. You didn't make a mistake. You got murdered. You got kidnapped. And you got sodomized. It is not your fault."

The sperm evidence occupied most of Evans' remaining time in front of the jury, during which he recapped the testimony and evidence that supported the existence of sperm in the victim's body.

"And finally, ladies and gentlemen, thankfully, I am done . . . It is time for me to put the case in your hands, and I am going to do that. When I look at the twelve of you, I know that you will be able to make a decision. I know you will. And I know that what you do will be justice in this case. Thanks very much for listening to me."

Judge Ryan read the long, dry, convoluted instructions legally required, and clerk Terri Walsh swore in bailiff Roger Hilton to take charge of the jury. The nine women and three men filed into the jury room at 11:30 A.M.

In the middle of the afternoon, the jury sent a note to Judge Ryan asking for clarification about the crime of sodomy. He convened court and read to the jury the legal definition, after which they resumed deliberations.

Most observers thought it would take at least a couple of days, *if* the jurors could reach a decision at all.

In the northwest corner of the eleventh floor, with a beautiful view of Santa Ana and Mount Baldy in the distance, twelve jurors became much better acquainted. They sat in twelve office-type

armchairs with orange padding, around two tables pushed together to form a square. Two copper-colored thermal pitchers
sat on a tray in the center, for coffee or water. A couch offered
more comfortable seating at the east wall.

Bonnie Snethen later recalled her reaction. "God, we could
finally talk. We had so much inside us about the case, and we
could finally talk about it." Each of them had religiously followed
the daily admonitions from Judge Ryan not to discuss it with
anyone, including their own families at home.

David Reyno had avoided much social contact with the others
during the trial, to prevent the appearance of discussing the
case, but later said that he bonded closely with them during
deliberations. In the first meeting, "We chattered for a little
while and then went to lunch."

After eating, they gathered again in the sunlit cubicle, and
tackled the problem of electing a foreperson. Reyno recalled, "I
thought I would make a pretty good foreman, because I oversee
a team on my job and I have a leadership role in my church. If
no one else wanted it, I would have agreed to do it." Another
juror turned to one of the group named Bill and said she thought
he would be a good foreman. "No, not me," he replied.

Snethen had served on a jury five years earlier, and recalled
that the choosing of a foreperson had been "annoying and
clumsy." In that case, no one would volunteer, and they took
forty-five minutes to finally choose a leader by ballot. Now, she
thought, "Here we go again." So, to avoid repetition of that
experience, she spoke up. "If no one else wants the job, I don't
mind doing it. I'll be glad to serve." They elected her unanimously by voice vote, everyone saying, "Great!"

Under her guidance, the twelve agreed to hold a roundtable
discussion before doing any voting. "We talked first about
whether Famalaro had committed the murder and all agreed
that he had." They discussed it even further. "We wanted to get
past even a chance that he didn't kill her." Once more, none of
them had doubts on that issue. "So, we moved on to the kidnapping, and discussed that." They examined maps in evidence
to look at the most direct route from the Honda site to the
Laguna Hills warehouse. "Even if Denise had agreed to get in

his car," said Snethen, "it couldn't have taken her very long before she knew she was in trouble." The group figured that a hammer blow had probably been struck to Huber's head in Famalaro's vehicle. "We felt she struggled when she realized she was going in the opposite direction she wanted to go. It was probably, 'Hey, let me out of here,' and he restrained her or struck her. We weighed other scenarios within context of the evidence. We used maps. Maybe she was forced into the car and tied in."

The juror named Bill sat next to Snethen. He carefully examined the shoes Huber had worn, and said, "He's dragging her and she catches her heels on that asphalt berm." Bonnie, too, looked closely, and agreed. They read the jury instructions again, and erased all doubt whether Huber had entered the killer's car willingly or by force. At some point it became kidnapping.

David Reyno recalled going through the evidence, piece by piece, and encouraging his colleagues to do the same.

If the jurors could not reach a decision that day, they would be required to wait over the long weekend before resuming deliberations. Each person expressed a willingness to work as long as they needed to, whatever it took to reach an appropriate decision. So, just in case, they asked permission to work late that evening.

Next, they grappled with the charge of sodomy. "The defense team," Snethen said, "kept alluding to sperm with no tails. At one point, I considered asking for a reading of the transcript to verify that one of the experts we discussed had, indeed, said the cells were sperm." They read the instructions several times, which they thought were rather complex.

In David Reyno's recollection, "We had all agreed there was definitely a kidnapping. There was no way she would have gone willingly with that guy. On the sodomy charge, we got stuck for a little while on the question of when it happened. And we had some confusion on the instructions."

Finally Snethen sent a note to the judge asking for clarification. All of them felt satisfied with the result.

After one more time around the table, giving each juror a

chance to discuss any issue, they agreed to take a vote. They chose to do it by voice rather than secret ballot.

They went around one time only. All twelve voted unanimously after less than six hours of deliberating. Bonnie Snethen summoned the bailiff.

Chapter 26

Dennis Huber had a hunch the jury wouldn't be out long, so he and Ione, along with a few relatives and friends stayed close to the court, hanging around the third floor cafeteria for a while, then watching another trial. After 5 P.M. they waited in the hallway, knowing that the jury was still in session.

When Judge Ryan heard that the jury had reached a decision so soon, he quickly arranged for the bailiff to summon the lawyers and Famalaro. Ione, Dennis, and their entourage sat in the front row.

"My clerk will read the verdict and findings," said Ryan.

Terri Walsh spoke aloud. "Case number 94ZF0196, Verdict: We the jury in the above-entitled action, find the defendant, John Joseph Famalaro, Guilty of the crime of felony, to wit, Violation of Section 187 of the penal code of the State of California, murder in the first degree." Her clear voice continued with announcements that special circumstances of kidnapping and sodomy were true.

Judge Ryan ordered the jury to return in one week to begin the penalty phase, in which they would hear evidence of aggravating and mitigating factors to help them decide on a recommendation of life without the chance of parole or the death penalty for John Famalaro.

To reporters, Dennis Huber said, "Justice is finally here. We've waited for this day for a long time. It's been our goal for six years. The truth came out. It's a tremendous help. It's not going to bring Denise back, and it's not closure—"

Ione interrupted, "But we're glad justice has been served. Thank God. He answered our prayers."

They, along with Nancy Streza and the rest of their loyal group, went to a restaurant that evening and raised glasses of champagne to Chris Evans, the jury, justice, their prayers that had been answered, and to Denise.

On Thursday, May 29, the temperature would reach ninety-three degrees in Santa Ana, but air conditioning kept Judge Ryan's courtroom comfortable as Chris Evans addressed the jury once again. Promising to keep his portion of the penalty phase short, he said, "If you blink your eyes, you may miss it." It wouldn't be that brief, but his five witnesses, including Dennis and Ione, would complete their testimony before the sun set that same day.

Leonard Gumlia, sounding much more chipper than expected, said, "Hi again, everyone. I will go a little longer than Mr. Evans." His witnesses, he said, would include Famalaro's brother George, sister Francine, their mother, and several women with some remarkable comments. The defender hoped they would provide the jury with enough sympathy and reasoning to reject the death penalty. He would even present, he said, a PET (positron emission tomography) scan of his client's brain to show that he had "extra activity in the temporal lobe associated with basic emotions, basic instincts involving sex and violence." The jurors took notes.

The gallery stirred when Darlene Miller stepped forward to take the oath as the first prosecution witness. Stunning in her white jacket, navy skirt and gold chains, which matched her shoulder-length blond hair, it seemed inconceivable to many viewers that she had been a serious romantic partner of John Famalaro.

On the Independence Day weekend of 1987, Miller said, she

and Famalaro had flown to New York to celebrate her birthday by attending some Broadway plays. But it had turned traumatic for her. Answering Chris Evans' questions, Miller described how he had handcuffed her, naked, in front of a window and left her for three hours. Completely traumatized by the time he returned and released her, she curled up on the floor in a fetal ball. She'd broken up with him over the incident, and hadn't resumed the relationship for a long time.

Prosecutor Evans felt comfortable that he'd shown the jury Famalaro's pattern of using handcuffs during sexual encounters, just as he had used on Denise Huber.

Leonard Gumlia handled the cross-exam with clever dexterity. He spent some time on developing information about the relationship and Famalaro's work, personality, and behavior, then showed her a series of family photographs, asking her to identify the people in them. Taking on a deadly serious tone, Gumlia asked, "The time he put handcuffs on you, was that the first time you had seen the handcuffs?"

Miller answered, "That was the first time I had seen them."

"And had you ever, at any time, either before or after that, had handcuffs on with Mr. Famalaro in a consensual manner?"

"Never!"

"That Sunday morning in New York would have been the only time you ever had handcuffs on in Mr. Famalaro's presence, is that correct?"

"That is correct."

"Isn't it true that the reason the handcuffs were on you that morning is that you had engaged in consensual sex with handcuffs on?"

"No, that's not true."

Gumlia commented, "That's fine," then handed her a color photograph. Darlene Miller immediately blushed crimson. "Is that you handcuffed at the window in New York?"

"Yes, it is."

"Do you recall Mr. Famalaro taking a picture of you at that time?"

"No, I don't."

Handing her another photo, Gumlia asked, "Is that you in the picture with the handcuffs on?"

"Yeah, I would say that does look like me."

"And just so it is clear, you are handcuffed in your front and you seem to be fondling a penis in that picture?" Gallantly, the attorney made no reference to the big smile on her face in the photo depicting her full-length nude body, apparently lying on her back and sexually fondling a man. If the man was John Famalaro, he apparently held the camera while standing and looking down at Darlene Miller, whose facial expression suggested enjoyment of the sex play.

She choked out a barely audible, "Yes," but said she couldn't recall when the picture was taken. To his subsequent questions, Miller claimed to have blockages of memory due to the trauma.

Chris Evans had never seen or heard of the photos. Caught totally by surprise, he could feel the hot blood rushing to his face. From somewhere deep inside him, though, he summoned the advice from his father and other mentors—*Don't show emotion during a trial crisis.* Clearly, the jury could now regard the witness as untruthful. Evans found a calm place in his mind, and mulled over a question. *How can I turn this into an advantage?*

On redirect examination, Evans referred to one of the explicit photos, tagged as defense exhibit PP, and asked, "When Mr. Famalaro first put the handcuffs on you, were you sure that this was a joke, or did you know?" Miller said she wasn't sure. Evans followed up with a question that reminded jurors Miller had already admitted some fondling activity in that hotel room.

The mortified witness said, "I do remember him trying to initiate sex," and recalled some fondling "to a small degree." Evans wondered aloud if the photos depicted intimate activity before Famalaro had left the room with her cuffed and exposed at a window. Miller again wasn't sure.

"In any event," Evans said, "however it happened, did you tell him it was okay to leave you by that window for three hours?"

"Absolutely not."

The prosecutor, feeling that his point about Famalaro's use of handcuffs on women remained intact, completed his inquiries of Darlene Miller by changing to other areas of her past relationship with the defendant. It included her recollection of his red pickup, which Famalaro claimed had been stolen. Gumlia completed re-cross with no further references to the humiliating pictures. When Darlene Miller walked out of the courtroom, every eye focused on her.

Handcuffs took center stage again with the next witness, Kate Colby. Another beautiful ex-romance partner of Famalaro, she told of the bedroom incident in which he had pushed her onto the bed, snapped manacles on her wrists, and attempted to pull her shorts off. "There was a look in his eyes I hadn't seen before . . . a very intense stare, like he was enjoying what he was doing." Rather than curling up into a helpless ball, Colby snapped back at him, threatening to tell the police. It apparently cooled his ardor, because he backed off and released her.

Following Colby, Evans put a woman on the stand who said she had seen Colby's wrists after the incident, and described them as "skinned, red, and raw."

The final two witnesses for the prosecution would present victim impact testimony that Leonard Gumlia had fought to keep out of the trial. Chris Evans leaned over the rail dividing the court from the gallery and whispered to the parents, "Are you ready?" They both nodded.

Ione Huber courageously walked to the witness chair. Evans asked, "Can you tell the court and the jury . . . what your life was like from the night Denise Huber disappeared to the time Mr. Famalaro was arrested on July 15, 1994?"

Her voice steady at first, Ione said, "Well, initially I was very much afraid. I panicked. We were frantic with worry when she didn't come home. We didn't know what had happened. Then later that evening when we found the car I just felt like I had been kicked in the stomach. I was shocked. Couldn't eat or sleep for several days. It was a very helpless feeling. We didn't know what had happened. We didn't know if she was being tortured.

We didn't know if she was alive, if she was being held somewhere. My world turned upside down. As time went on we did everything we could to try to find answers. We sent fliers out to lots of business places. We sent them to newspapers all over the country. We had lots of interviews on television shows. I couldn't go back to work. I went back probably after about four months, but only on a part-time basis and this was very difficult and painful. I just felt that I could never be happy again."

Evans asked, "What things during that period of time caused you the most pain?

Her voice now cracking noticeably, Ione answered. "Well, we had a lot of things to deal with. First of all we didn't know anything, so we had to decide what do with Denise's room. We walked by it every day for three years. We didn't know anything and her things were there. Her clothes were there. All her belongings. She had a car, you know. We didn't know what to do with the car. Her birthday came and Thanksgiving like all in the same week. That was very painful because she wasn't there. Then Christmas came and I couldn't put up a Christmas tree. We didn't buy any Christmas gifts that year. It was just a hollow feeling. In fact, for three years I didn't have a Christmas tree. Then another painful thing, we went to several weddings during that time, and to see these young ladies walk down the aisle, and we'd think about would Denise ever be able to do that. Would we ever see her do that?"

Choking sniffles could be heard from the Hubers' friends and from spectators. Tears ran down the faces of several jurors, including men. Dennis held his head in his hands, his eyes red.

Giving Ione a brief opportunity to pause, Evans asked, "Finally, can you tell us how her death has impacted your life?"

"I'll try, but there's no way to really adequately describe that because it's impacted us more than anything. When I found out she'd died, so many of my dreams for her died. She had dreams of her own, too, and one of the things I brought with me, in 1995 her class had a reunion and they sent us a pack of materials, and one of the things that was in that packet was a letter, and just before her graduation all of the students wrote a letter to themselves that they would receive on their ten-year reunion—"

Denise Gragg spoke up. "Your honor, we'd object to the letter." Judge Ryan sustained the objection.

Evans advised Ione not to read it aloud, and asked, "Is there anything about that letter—or, in answer to the original question that I asked you how her death has impacted your life, you'd like to tell us without reading from the letter?"

Now wiping away tears, Ione said, "I just wanted to share that Denise had dreams for her life, that she had written this letter and some of the dreams were that she would be married one day, that she would have a career, she would have a family, and she was never able to do those things. I have a lot of memories of Denise that are things that we did together and can't do anymore. We used to go out for lunch. We used to go to the beach, to the pool. We liked to cook together. We had a special meal we cooked, chicken chow mein. She had her part and I had mine and we always enjoyed doing that. And her death just devastated us so much emotionally, physically. Even to a point I had several surgeries in the past years, including cancer surgery, and I feel the stress that I've been under has really contributed to that. Our lives will never be the same. I know you've seen pictures of Denise but I want to show you a picture of the real Denise." Ione held up an enlarged color photo of her daughter, wearing a cap and gown, smiling radiantly. "This is my daughter with her smile, her sense of humor. She brought so much joy to my life. I don't have that joy anymore. Denise was sensitive, caring, and compassionate, and I miss her companionship and laughter. I miss everything about her and there's no way I can really just adequately tell you. I think I've only just touched on what impact that has been on my life, but I know my life will never be the same again."

Evans tenderly thanked her. "No further questions."

The defense wisely announced they would not ask Ione Huber anything.

As Ione made her way back to the first row, Dennis rose and donned his suit coat. When he settled into the witness chair, Evans said, "Mr. Huber, I'm going to ask you two questions. What was your life like between June 3, 1991, when Denise disappeared, and July 15, 1994, when you finally learned what had happened to her?"

The father's faltering voice betrayed his emotion, but he managed to speak clearly. "Well, my world was totally turned upside down that night when we realized she wasn't there. The person that I loved so much was not there and we did not know where she was. We went three years and we did not know what had happened to her. We looked for her but she just wasn't there. One of the things is the feeling of somebody—my wife described it as being kicked in the gut and I really have written the same thing. It was like somebody standing there—all the time you couldn't even get a breath. I couldn't eat, couldn't think of anything but Denise. And sometimes that feeling got worse. It was worse every time a body was found, or bones, or something. You just got sicker. You never got well. You were just always sick. I remember in the fall I think it was that somebody said, why don't you relax, and go to Palm Springs and get away from it, just not look so hard. We worked so hard to try and find out what happened to her, so we drove to Palm Springs.

"The first thing that hit us was there was a body found there in the desert. Immediately we called the Palm Springs Police Department and they had no identity on the body. It was like that same kick in the gut. We turned around and we drove back . . . maybe being home was better than being away. There's no way you could enjoy it. I felt like I couldn't breathe for that weekend because I was just sure it was her. And we did not know until Monday, and you take a weekend and think about that, how long that time can be. It's just unreal. The stress, the stress was so tremendous. Two of my doctors just described me as a walking time bomb. There were a lot of health problems. I believe due to stress. I think that can kill you. That can make you old. I'm certainly not anything like I used to be. The day she disappeared was the day that I was supposed to open my own business and obviously, I didn't. It's hard to figure out—I've not had focus for six years. Every day I think of Denise. And I can't think of business. I can't think of a lot of things but that. But that three years of not knowing was just—I can't describe that to you."

Evans quietly inquired, "Finally, let me ask you this. How has her murder impacted your life?"

Throughout the courtroom the emotion hung like a dark cloud. The sounds of open weeping punctuated Dennis Huber's heart-wrenching words. "Well, when her body was found—all hope went out. There was absolutely no hope. This was somebody that I loved so very much and Denise's friends would say—they would tease me that she was daddy's little girl. Daddy's little girl was never going to come home. It was final. It was over. There's a bond between a daughter and a father . . . And some of the things about her life and mine flash, the old saying, before your eyes, but I remember the night in November, that night when she was born, it was our first born and I was so happy. I looked down and there was that immediate love and I was so proud and I had so much hope and that hope was gone. It was gone forever. I remember when she played softball and I was her coach, things like that, the growing up. The one thing I will remember and will never forget when she was in junior high I was doing a lot of travel for business and was on the road a lot and we sensed, and maybe—Ione says, you know, get it back together. Well, we did. We sat down and every Friday we set a date for breakfast. Denise and I would go to breakfast. Jeff wasn't there, Ione wasn't there. It was us. We'd go an hour before and sit and talk about things and I will never forget that hour. This went on for years with the quality time that we had and the bond, and that's broken. Denise had the ability to cheer me up even on my worst days. She was that type of person. She was happy but her smile and her 'Hi, Dad,' and it was better. The last thing I can remember that she wrote to me was probably a day or two before her disappearance and it was stuck on my computer screen at home, I had set it up in my office. She just said, 'Hi, Dad. I love you. Have a great day. Love, Denise,' and a nice happy face which she always signed. That was her signature then. I wouldn't take a million dollars for that little two-by-two piece of paper. I'll guarantee you that. I'll cherish that always. I have a feeling inside of me that there's like this hole and I don't think that's ever going to get filled up. It's just that pain. It's there. We inscribed on her headstone in South Dakota, we put there, 'Denise, you'll always be loved,' and that's true."

Chris Evans thanked Dennis Huber. Again, the defense showed admirable restraint in not questioning the broken-hearted father. He stepped down.

Tear-stained faces turned toward the prosecutor as he announced, "Your Honor, the people rest our case in chief."

Judge Ryan instructed the jurors to return on Monday, June 2, to hear the defense portion of the penalty phase. They would begin trying to save John Famalaro's life on the sixth anniversary of Denise Huber's last night of life.

Chapter 27

John Famalaro hobbled into the courtroom on Monday morning, June 2, on crutches, his left foot in a rubber thong shoe. In the gallery front row, someone jokingly asked Dennis Huber if he'd made a visit to the jail over the weekend, and put some hurt on Famalaro. The disability turned out to be a foot infection.

Before calling his first witness, Leonard Gumlia asked the judge for a short hearing. Still wrestling to have victim impact testimony eliminated, and laying groundwork for future appeals, he said, "We wanted to put on the record that four of the jurors were openly crying during the testimony of the Hubers." Chris Evans said he hadn't heard any crying in the jury box.

Stern-faced, Judge Ryan said he had noticed tears, but no outright sobbing. "There was no crying. There were tears, and I believe there was tearing in the audience." Gumlia conceded that he would accept the characterization of "tearing." Ryan added, "The jurors were saddened . . . but there were no outbursts, no nudging, no handkerchiefs, nothing out loud." The defender had made his point, so Denise Gragg called her first witness.

A middle-aged woman told the jury she had been a neighbor of the Famalaros in Santa Ana in the sixties and seventies. She recalled some friction with Mrs. Famalaro regarding building permits and other misunderstandings. The witness seldom had contacts with the three Famalaro children.

Witness number two said she had also lived on Victoria Drive and had been a classmate of John Famalaro up to the third grade. She'd noticed the boy was a quiet loner. Mrs. Famalaro had once scolded the witness for allowing a pet to urinate on the sidewalk. "She told me I needed to clean that up, so I had to go home and get a bucket and broom, come down and clean the sidewalk." Evans asked if she'd ever seen young John being picked on or beaten up. No, the woman said, she hadn't.

A third woman testified that she had been at the same school as John, but didn't know him very well. When she'd seen the family in church, she said, they appeared very "focused."

A fourth Victoria Drive ex-neighbor from the early sixties testified that she'd seen Mrs. Famalaro upset a couple of times over minor incidents. She'd had little contact with the boy named John, but recalled he was quiet.

One more childhood classmate of Famalaro, a male, characterized him as studious, awkward, kept to himself, and was the object of teasing by other kids. Evans asked if the witness had ever seen Famalaro beat up at school. No, he hadn't.

The five witnesses used only forty-five minutes of court time. After a break, the seventy-one-year-old, gray-haired mother of John Famalaro made her way to the witness chair, smiling, then turned toward her convicted son and gave him a wink. Dressed simply in a light violet jacket, white blouse, dark skirt, wearing a double strand of pearls and her ever-present glasses, she seemed jocular in her first few answers to Denise Gragg. Unable to recall if John was born in 1957 or 1958, she said didn't want to bore the jury. "I am embarrassed they have to listen to all this stuff."

Her perception of home life during John's childhood evoked a tight-knit family involved in wholesome activities. She recalled reading books to her children and taking them and their little pack of friends to Knott's Berry Farm, Disneyland, and movies. The older son and sister had done so well in school, she said, that it broke her heart when John was expelled from St. Joseph's, but she didn't ask administrators for the reasons. The child did seem sulky and moody to her at times. Mrs. Famalaro's own mother, she said, had singled out John for special love and attention.

Their lives went well, she said, with regular attendance at church and healthy family activities, until "everything exploded." Saying that she'd been "overly absorbed" with her offspring, the witness wondered what went wrong. "At the risk of being laughed at, which won't be the first time. I have found out since that you don't save anyone's soul. The person has to save their own soul. I thought that by getting them involved in speaking, reading books, getting superlative at their studies, they wouldn't get into areas that were no good." Denise Gragg asked if "no good" meant sinful areas. "Yes," the witness asserted. "Some of their contemporaries were doing things that I knew were not right, and I was trying to protect them from that."

At one point, Mrs. Famalaro said, she became politically active. "May I tell you how it started? I didn't know our country had a problem. I mean, I am raising this family. We are getting this house built, and oh boy, here we are in Santa Ana doing all these wonderful things, right? So I was invited to go to the Ebell Club to hear the father of the Polaris missile speak. And he said some startling things, which we won't get into here, because it is very political. And I went home and I said, 'Oh my gosh, Dad, do you realize these things are going really bad? We're losing our country.' He didn't believe me." The speech she'd heard had centered on federal reserve problems, the budget, and stripping down the military. "Well, I was very impressionable, at age thirty. Those things knocked me out." So she invited the speaker to share his message with 500 guests in the Famalaro home. "Well, I became a real advocate. Here I had these three kids, and I am going to save the world for all these people. I am Joan of Arc."

In the courtroom, spectators glanced at each other with puzzled expressions. The witness continued. "I thought I could straighten things out. All of these entities, all of these infringements, not a two-party system, twiddle-de-dee and twiddle-de-dum, everyone working to one end. I got very concerned . . . So what happened then I realized crime was a very serious thing, so I got on [Sheriff] Brad Gates' bandwagon, helped him get elected. Then I would go to [District Attorney] Michael Capizzi's

courtroom and [Judge] Chatterton's courtroom, and follow what
they would do and try to bolster them. And then I threw my hat
in to try to become a councilwoman in the city of Santa Ana . . .
Then, on the same front page with my candidacy being announced, here is my firstborn in terrible trouble." She referred
to the legal problems faced by her chiropractor son, George,
when he faced charges of sexual misconduct with his minor patients. "You don't win a campaign with your firstborn in deep
trouble . . . But I thought maybe there were enough people out
there who would have realized I was being sincere. I ran that
whole [fight against] Mitchell brothers pornography, that terrible theater . . . I would have 400-500 pickets out there fighting
pornography, and I thought those people would elect me, and
I could eventually straighten a lot of things out."

Denise Gragg, encouraging the long, impassioned soliloquy,
asked if one of Mrs. Famalaro's concerns included Communism.
"Absolutely. But I can't get into that too deeply because I found
out that communism wasn't really it. Communism was just one
of the 'isms' and it is something we should have been fighting.
It was an orchestration when it fell and it is an orchestration
today that we are getting along so well with . . . I found out that
I did make a lot of converts as I went along. A lot of those people
are journalists, they are on radio, very many people who knew
that I was right . . . May I add something?" The witness said that
her daughter and older son had helped her at that time. But,
she said, "It is only since then they have become so sophisticated
and they have gotten out into the world and the world has shown
them that their mother was wrong." Sarcasm dripped like sap
from a poison tree.

John, though, "Helped me out of sincerity, and really wanted
to do it. I had a thousand people picket against abortion over
in front of the Anaheim Convention Center. And of course, I
know that his picture wasn't shown in this courtroom, or anyplace else, that he was fighting for life because this is a death
culture here. He was fighting for life. He had saved the un-
born . . . on the front page of the *Register*. He did that out of his
heart. He didn't do it because I wanted him to." The elder two
children, she said, never did anything she wanted.

Stunned silence filled the courtroom. Dennis and Ione sat dazed. No one had heard such a speech since Humphrey Bogart, as Queeg in *The Caine Mutiny*, rolled steel balls in his hand as he sat explaining that his disloyal officers had betrayed him causing all the problems on the ship he captained.

Mrs. Famalaro explained how she had tried to prepare her children for a possible foreign country invasion by saving food. She had also spent a great deal of money arranging for lecturers to inform the public of dangerous evils. "I see it as a Christianity problem. The assault on Christianity is terrible today." Her children, she said, had gone along with that until about the age of fifteen. "And then I found out that the hormones click in and . . . mom becomes very irrelevant. Mom was okay until then, and then I am irrelevant." She denied using any corporal punishment on them, saying she had simply been trying to inculcate her children with moral values. That way they would know the evils of sex and pornography. Good people were being hurt by it, she proclaimed, even the President. "[Ted] Bundy said before he died that it was pornography got him into it . . . I submit that pornography is getting everyone into this. Pretty soon, all of you will be up on the stand. No one is immune from this. I am up here brokenhearted. I am up here broken in every kind of way . . . And the ironic angle is, I am the one down there at the Mitchell brothers picketing them for days, giving up all this time, and pornography got into my family. It hit me with my own bullet."

More than one observer wondered if this obviously intelligent, articulate woman, was putting on an act designed to persuade the jury that John Famalaro had been subjected to a bizarre childhood which twisted his psyche and sent him into uncontrollable rages against women. Or was this witness unaware of how she sounded?

Answering Gragg's questions while her son sat hanging his head, the animated mother discussed the backgrounds of her three children, the problems with George, how Francine had become alienated, and what John planned to be when he grew up. "He had about twenty goals. He was going to be a chiropractor. He was going to be a journalist. He was going to be a mortician. I think I put that in his head. I said, 'George will treat the patient, and you bury them.' Big joke. He really meant well."

Regarding her ill-fated trip to live with her daughter at college in Iowa, Mrs. Famalaro called it the most embarrassing thing in her life. "That blew up within six months. No mother should go to school with her daughter."

According to Mrs. Famalaro, when John's girlfriend, Helen Lyons, gave birth to his baby but wouldn't allow him access to it, a court hearing had ensued. The mother claimed she had peeked through a little window into the room where her son sat appealing for custody. "I saw John was sobbing on the stand, begging for the baby—begging! They ruled against him." She offered him money, she said, to seek out and gain custody of the child. "This is the story that changed his life. He was never decent after that. He was muddled, confused, always thinking, 'Where is this baby? Why did this happen to me?' It just wasn't the same. It was over then."

When the witness dabbed at tears in her eyes with a tissue, the jurors faces' remained impassive.

As Mrs. Famalaro spoke about never seeing her grandchild and complained about unfair adoption practices, the judge sustained Evans' objection. She appeared upset at being interrupted, ignored Gragg's next question, and combatively asked, "Is it possible for me to finish that statement in a different way? I've seen questions asked here all the time that they are done in a different way."

Evans calmly objected again, and was sustained. In answering another query, the witness said, "I'm trying to tell the jury something, but I guess I'm not allowed. Right?" More sustained objections curbing her gratuitous speeches appeared to irritate Mrs. Famalaro.

Finally, Judge Ryan addressed her personally. "Mrs. Famalaro, you're telling the jury lots of things. You have an excellent attorney up here. She knows how to ask questions. We don't generally in this business tell people, 'I want to tell you this or this.' We just tell them to listen to the question, and you'll be allowed to answer."

"Sure," the witness shot back. Her answers became short and

monosyllabic, until Gragg asked why she and her husband had moved to Arizona. Becoming agitated again, she said, "Number one, I was sick of trying to save the world because the world doesn't want to be saved. And secondly, the thing with George just about put me in a state of collapse. I thought I'd like to get away and just be quiet. That's why we went, to get me away . . . from the embarrassment."

Gragg posed several questions about George and his marriage, prompting more sustained objections from Evans and escalating frustration in the witness. Asked if she had expressed anger about George's wedding, she retorted, "Is it all right to answer? I'm getting a little confused. This morning, everything was okay. This afternoon—"

Judge Ryan cut her off with his own quip. "Wait until tomorrow."

Not to be outdone, the witness turned toward him and sweetly said, "You have a good sense of humor, Judge." Ryan allowed himself a little smile.

Back to Gragg's question, Mrs. Famalaro explained that she wasn't angry with George about his wedding, but about his previous "free loving."

"Was there an occasion when . . . you found out that George was free loving with some woman in a motel?" To the affirmative answer, Gragg asked, "What did you do about that?"

Her pale face flushing pink, Mrs. Famalaro snorted, "You are really trying to make me look like a fool." Angrily, she answered, "Well, I went to the motel and I walked in the room. I might not have caught him the night I went in the car, but there they were. And of course George double talks everything, but couldn't double talk that . . . So I took a clock and banged it down. I thought time might stand still that way." She had no recollection of attacking the small, thin woman she confronted, but did recall that police were summoned, and rationalized, "They had enough conscience to tell the police I didn't do anything."

Another traumatic split with George had taken place in Arizona, after his divorce, Mrs. Famalaro said. "We had been meeting with him in Phoenix, and he would bring our little grandson. We were going to meet on Easter, and he said to me on the phone, 'We'll be there.' So I says, "Who is we?" Well, his lady friend. His lady friend and he were going to sleep in the same room as the baby, as that little boy. So I hung up on him, and that was the last hangup I ever made on George." The lady friend, Mrs. Famalaro said, was a woman who, accompanied by her husband, had frequently visited George while he was "in jail."

While John had lived next door, at the Prescott Country Club, he frequently took his mother to visit Mr. Famalaro, who was hospitalized. The witness recalled, "The last day John visited my husband, whether he had a premonition, whatever it was, he wrote him a beautiful love letter telling him how much he cared for him, and he brought this beautiful plant. That day he drove away from the hospital, with me, to never be with my husband again. Every sheriff's car in the county pulled him out and took him away from me as they left me standing in the middle of the street not able to drive a car."

According to Mrs. Famalaro, John had asked permission to dig under his house to make a paint storage space because neighbors were complaining about so many containers stacked in the yard. Her son looked very tired and haggard during that period, she said.

Denise Gragg flashed back to another issue. She asked when Mrs. Famalaro had stopped bathing her children. At about age five, she said. Had she ever told them there was a difference between good sweat and bad sweat? No. "So you don't recall telling them they only had to bathe once a week because they were only getting good sweat?"

"God help us," the witness groaned. "This is foreign to me. I knew this wouldn't be a picnic, but this is a lulu. I've told you everything from A to Z in my life. Why would I hide that? Sweat . . ."

"Did you wash your hands obsessively?"

"No. I didn't have blood on my hands. Just dirt."

"Did you ever go into the boys' rooms to make sure their hands were up on top of the covers so they wouldn't be able to masturbate while in bed?"

Her face wrinkling in bemusement, she answered, "I don't

know this one. No. I didn't have those kinds of thoughts. I mean I had other kinds of thoughts about what they could do, but I didn't think about that."

"Did you ever tell either of the boys that masturbation would cause nosebleeds?"

"No. I told them it would make them go crazy because that's what I heard all my life . . . that masturbation can make you go mad. Maybe we have some evidence of it all around town."

"Did you ever, when commercials came on that had scantily clad women, put your hands over their faces?"

"I might have . . . How about more like turned it off. That would seem more like me."

"Did you want the world to know that you were a good family?"

"Sure. And I wanted me to know, and first of all . . . I wanted Jesus to know . . . A lot of people may doubt that. Well, I mean it with all my heart. I've given my life working for Jesus and will continue to do it."

After a break, Chris Evans stood, with his usual aplomb and dignity, to cross-examine Mrs. Famalaro. Apologetically, he said, "You know this is a difficult thing for me to do?"

She responded, "No one should be in this position. No one." Agreeing, Evans drew from her that John Famalaro hadn't lived at home with her, basically, between ages thirteen and seventeen while he was at boarding school. Only on weekends, she said.

At the time of the murder, asked Evans, he was grown man who had not lived in her home for many years? True, she agreed.

"Your daughter was never accused or convicted of hurting or killing anyone, was she?"

Waspishly, she said, "I don't think so, Mr. Evans. Not that I've heard of."

"And George was convicted of molesting, but did he kill anyone?"

"Mr. Evans, you know he didn't. Is this like the word trophy?" Her feisty retorts were not well received in the gallery. And the message being sent by Evans was clear. If the influence of John's

upbringing had driven John to eventual murder, why not the
other two siblings? Evans knew when to stop. "Thank you," he
nodded. "I have nothing further."

A brief volley of questions finally ended the session at 3:15.

One last witness consumed six more minutes during which
the man said he'd known Famalaro as a child, but not intimately.
Judge Ryan sent the jurors home at 3:30.

On Tuesday morning, an elegant woman nearly six feet tall,
with long, dark auburn hair, wearing a white suit with a gold
patterned bodice and pearls, answered questions posed by
Denise Gragg. The witness told jurors that her name was
Francine Kraft and that John Famalaro was her younger brother.
Three years separated their ages. She had tried to act as his
protector during their early childhood. George, she said, had
been their mother's favorite, while John was a weakling. "My
mother was the dominant force in the family." And George had
been tough on his kid brother. In the mother's testimony, she
hadn't recalled using corporal punishment, but Kraft said a belt
had been used to spank the boys.

Kraft took listeners through a complex childhood, her relationship with her brothers, George's attempt to fondle her, and
her move to an Iowa college, accompanied by her unwelcome
mother.

Religion, Kraft said, was a powerful influence during their
upbringing. But regarding her mother, Kraft said "I know now
that what she [was] is not religious. She was an eccentric religious
person." In retrospect, she felt like her mother had monitored
the boys to prevent masturbation.

John, she said, had a hard time with interpersonal relationships at school, and his classmates made fun of him. She rode
the bus with John to keep kids from picking on him. Away from
school, he spent as much time as he could with his grandmother,
who later lived with him.

The emotion of such recollections brought tears to the wit-

ness, and to her convicted brother as well, who sat sniffling at
the defense table. His infected leg, Gumlia had told the judge,
was growing worse.

Kraft revealed that her daughter, now a teenager, dearly loved
her uncle John, who was the youngster's godfather. Through
most of her testimony, Kraft managed to make eye contact with
Famalaro, and gave him a smile now and then.

She drew a chuckle from the jury when Gragg asked if
Francine had reported to her parents the alleged attempts of
sexual fondling by George. "Never! Oh my God, no!" In answering another question from Gragg, Francine started to reveal a
different incident. She said that John had called her in June
1991, the same month Huber had been murdered, and while
crying told her that George had sexually molested him when
they were children. But Judge Ryan wouldn't let the jury hear
it.

Eventually, the witness said, John moved to Arizona to live
with Marvin Kraft after Francine had moved out. She saw her
brother periodically during that time, during which he looked
ill and unkempt.

After dredging up extensive history of the defendant's family,
Gragg turned the witness over to Chris Evans.

Beginning with his gratitude for Kraft's cooperation, Evans
inquired if Famalaro had been known to hit other children in
school. She didn't recall, and couldn't verify that she had told
an investigator of such incidents. Nor did she have any recollection of him being expelled from St. Joseph's parochial school.

Through a series of questions about Famalaro's day-to-day life
as a child, Evans worked to paint a picture of a relatively comfortable existence with no more trauma or negative influences
than most children experience. And the defendant's relationship
with Kraft's daughters was loving and normal. Francine Kraft left
the courtroom with her dignity intact.

An even more dramatic witness stepped up next. Velma Finch,
George Famalaro's former girlfriend who had been traumatized
by the motel encounter with his mother, told of the long, rocky

relationship. She recounted the frightening event in graphic detail, and said she really believed she was going to die that night. "I felt an emotional terror that remains today." Observers wondered who was on trial, George or John Famalaro, or maybe their mother. What did this woman's testimony have to do with mitigating or aggravating factors related to John Famalaro's crime? The judge excused her, and called for a lunch break.

Only one witness showed up for the afternoon session, a middle-aged blond woman who spoke with a German accent. She had been a waitress in Anaheim in the mid seventies, and had known the teenaged John Famalaro who worked part-time with her as a busboy. He was a hard worker, she said, and was full of fun and laughter. He and his grandmother had even lived with her for a short period of time, and she had helped him find an apartment in Glendale. Later, the waitress had also met the young woman, Helen Lyons, with whom Famalaro had fallen in love.

When the witness stepped down, observers scratched their heads again. What did this woman's testimony prove? That Famalaro was a hard-working kid who loved his grandmother. Maybe that was all the defense wanted to show. Maybe such a portrayal would make jurors reluctant to send such a nice guy to death row.

Tuesday's session ended early. On Wednesday, they would hear from the killer's brother, George Famalaro, who had experienced his own troubles with dark urges and the law.

Chapter 28

Word quickly spread on Wednesday morning that John Famalaro had been hospitalized overnight due to his inflamed foot. Speculation buzzed among the gathering court watchers, but it was soon quelled with the announcement that the defendant would show up. Bailiffs brought him in at 10:40 A.M., in a wheelchair.

A few minutes later, his brother George took the oath to tell nothing but the truth. Shorter than John, George's dark brown hair, thinning on the crown, tumbled in curls on his forehead. He wore a well-tailored suit, red tie, and white shirt. It soon became obvious that he would rather be anywhere else.

Beginning with a perfunctory greeting, Leonard Gumlia asked George to give some basic background about himself, his education, and his profession, then got directly to the point. "In 1980, were you arrested and ultimately convicted for molesting a ten-year-old boy and unlawful intercourse with a seventeen-year-old girl?"

"Yes."

"And specific charges were oral copulation involving the boy?"

"Yes, those were the charges."

"As a consequence of that conviction, were you sentenced to any particular location?"

"Patton State [Hospital] in Riverside, Ontario area."

"Was that a commitment for what was formerly known as a

mentally disordered sex offender?" Yes, the witness said. "How long did you spend there?"

"Two and one half years."

Verbally recognizing how difficult this was for George Famalaro, Gumlia asked for his feelings about his parents. The witness said he'd been very close to his father and felt sorry for his mother. Her intentions, he stated, were always good and she had tried to do the best she could. But he no longer had any contact with them. "They moved away. No phone number, no address, no nothing. They just disappeared."

Demonstrating an impressive speaking voice and excellent vocabulary, he spoke of his early home life as "insulary, a test tube environment" with an "overly conservative" dominating mother and very strict religious influence. Her method of instructing her children, he said, was "hysterical manic . . . there was a lot of internal pressure."

How did your brother and sister cope with that, asked the defender. "Francine withdrew . . . and did the best she could, at least externally. John seemed to go the other way and try to do what I did, which was to perform to please . . . he saw that my methods didn't work, and he saw Francine's methods didn't work, so I am sure he was struggling to find his own way."

Sex, he said, was never talked about. If it came up, his mother would become "real uncomfortable and squirmy." Regarding baths, "It seemed like I was pretty old to be bathed by Mom." When she washed his genitals, "her breathing changed, it was kind of escalated. Looking back now, it just felt like an energy surge of some kind."

Because he felt that his mother wanted him to be a priest, Famalaro said, he entered a seminary. "I lasted two years and damned near had a nervous breakdown. I had to get out." His mother "pulled back emotionally and never was the same with me."

The witness capsulized the treatment of each sibling. "When I got to puberty, I got ostracized as the black sheep for not becoming a priest. Then the focus was on Francine and when [Mrs. Famalaro] followed her to college. When that didn't work out, then John . . . was on the conveyor belt the longest. He was in the incubator, taking all of what he took from Mom." Continuing about his kid brother, he said, "John had a tough road to go. He was ill with something all the time. Things were coming slower to him. He got the wrath of my mom."

John Famalaro, sitting in his wheelchair at the defense table, apparently overcome with emotion, openly wept. Most of the jurors could see him, his chin quivering, wiping tears away. Their faces remained blank.

To Gumlia's inquiry about how George treated John, he said, "I might have teased him or picked on him a bit." He denied ever beating John. The relationship was always "superficial" and the two siblings were never "buds."

"Have you ever called your brother a pansy ass wimp?"

"Probably . . . There is not a lot of anger in that."

Interaction between the two brothers tapered off when George went to college, he said. He met John's girlfriend, Helen Lyons, and recalled the devastation when the relationship ended. He observed that in John's business enterprises, the younger Famalaro was "powerhouse, working for days on end, not stopping to eat, high energy, excited, euphoric." And, in his relationships with women, John was "very generous with his spending habits."

At the other end of John's emotional spectrum, according to George, he was, "just barely able to breathe or keep his eyes open . . . worn out, frazzled, not taking care of himself, scrawny, and just not there."

In John's relationships with women, "What I saw was an initial excitement—wooing, pursuing, and getting. Then once that happened, almost sabotaging . . . work, work, work, and not nurturing the relationship."

Gumlia asked, "At some point, did you start to notice there was a sexual aspect to John that you had not seen before?"

"Yes. It changed from what I had seen early on." From an early shy reluctance to mention sex, John had metamorphosed to flamboyance. "Off-colored jokes, sexual books, sexual gag gifts. Very open about sexual comfort." After tagging the bases on several other of John Famalaro's personality and behavior traits, Gumlia released George to the prosecutor.

* * *

Evans asked, "Whatever happened at your house on Victoria Drive, whatever kind of childhood it was—you would probably say it really wasn't that horrible, wouldn't you?" George Famalaro agreed with that, especially in the early part of his youth. But there was a shift during the teenage years. Pursuing that point, Evans got agreement that John may have been more influenced by his grandmother, and his two siblings more by their mother. Recalling their adult years in Orange County, George pictured John as hard-working, happy, successful, bouncing back and forth between gregarious and shy. George also thought that John had learned proficiency in martial arts.

One by one, Evans enumerated the wholesome activities George and John had experienced as children, unconditional love from their father, their mother driving them to school, no physical beatings. The witness affirmed them. About George's mother bathing him, Evans asked if he had told an investigator that she ceased doing it when he reached age ten. George said he wasn't quite sure when it ended. And he absolutely denied ever sexually molesting his little brother.

Openly answering Evans' questions, and admitting his problems relating to the sexual offenses with his young patients, George Famalaro appeared to be a candid and honest witness.

Evans asked him, "With those two patients, you didn't kill them, did you?"

"No."

"Why not?"

"That is not what was going on with me at the time. Killing wasn't—it wasn't about anything like that."

"Thanks very much." Evans sat down.

With a new energy in his step, Leonard Gumlia approached the witness and handed him an envelope. It contained a card George had sent to his father. On the envelope, he had inscribed the words, "Call 1-800-RYDER" and "Maytag, your first name in freezers." Gumlia wanted to know what that meant.

"I was just trying to lighten up something that was just devastating for my father."

At Gumlia's instruction, the witness extracted the card and read the note he'd written. "Hey Dad, can't believe you wouldn't and didn't call me. What a loser. I know you were under the control of the She Devil, but this is ridiculous . . ."

"This is the father you loved and respected, right? This is the father who is dying of Parkinson's disease?"

Now subdued, the witness replied, "Not at the time . . . he didn't seem like he was dying to me."

"I thought you didn't know where they were? Does 'Call 1-800-RYDER' refer to the Ryder truck involved in this case?"

"Yes. And I didn't know what was going on with any of that."

"This was 1995. And you had been interviewed by police and investigators by then?"

"Correct."

"The part on the Maytag and freezer, what was that referring to?"

"What John was accused of doing at the time." Trying to explain was obviously not easy for the witness. His previously well-organized sentences became garbled.

Gumlia, now sounding angry, didn't equivocate. "You had contempt for the same pansy ass wimp brother?"

"I wouldn't say contempt." Even if George wouldn't say it, his brother apparently felt it. John sobbed openly, tears and fluid from his nose running down his face.

"This is the pansy ass boy you used to take down to this abandoned warehouse where you stored your *Playboys*, right?"

Trying to maintain his calm, Famalaro said, "You mean the one incident with the house?"

"The one incident, you went to the house more than once?" Bristling, Gumlia referred to an abandoned house not far from Victoria Drive.

"Not with John."

"And did you have a *Playboy* stored there, or did you take them with you when you would go there to masturbate?" Wide-eyed gallery spectators waited for objections.

"No, I had them in a little closet."

"Now, you have your pansy—"

"Objection, argumentive," Evans calmly protested. Judge

Ryan sustained it. George Famalaro admitted taking his brother and his sister to the empty house, but just once, and there was no sexual activity. Gumlia asked where he obtained the magazines, and he said he rummaged through neighborhood trash cans to find them.

When Famalaro characterized his sibling relationship as "superficial," Gumlia wanted to know what caused it to be that way. The witness blamed it on the incident at the motel, when his mother had confronted Velma Finch. "I should have stuck by my mom no matter what she tried to do to Velma. I think I was really ostracized after that."

Gumlia asked for clarification. Famalaro, struggling, said, "We became less close after that."

"Were there times when John openly hated his mother?"

"We all did."

Becoming even more aggressive, Gumlia probed the incident for which George Famalaro had been arrested. "Did you testify in the trial and swear to God that it wasn't true?"

Famalaro nodded. "Uh-huh."

"Because it wasn't in your interest at that time?"

"No. I was in complete denial, and the very problems that led up to that were still present then until I got help." Gumlia's ensuing questions suggested that George had agreed to confess and undergo counseling in order to avoid doing prison time instead of incarceration in a state hospital. Famalaro disagreed.

Turning to more recent events, Gumlia asked George if he had visited John since his arrest. Yes, one time, and he'd brought along a girlfriend.

"Didn't you bring her as a witness to see if you could talk to him about whether he is going to ever say he was molested, isn't—"

His voice loud and trembling, Famalaro interrupted. "Excuse me! If I could say what?" Furious, he said that he had never even heard the accusations of molesting his brother until recently. Asked if he'd since received a letter from his brother, George said he had.

"What did it say?"

Looking toward the ceiling to remember the contents, George quoted his brother's words. "Thanks for coming to visit me. It was good to see you." Toward the end of the letter, he said John had written, "If you are okay with it, sometimes I would like to talk about whatever happened between us when we were younger."

Gumlia asked, "Did you ever go back to your brother and ask him, 'John, my brother, what is this all about?'"

"I don't think so. It was a cue for me that something was really wrong and I didn't know where John was going with that."

"Were you worried at any time since John Famalaro's arrest that you might have had any psychological contribution to the crime that he ultimately committed?"

His jaw muscles flexing, and face tense, the witness considered his answer, then spoke. "If anything, not from these new claims that I am hearing, but more from when my crime happened, that threw John into some sort of tizzy. I want to come up with some sort of a thing that, you know, what could have happened differently with all the family, myself included. But it wasn't about things that aren't true."

For the next few minutes, Gumlia asked questions about the witness possibly fearing the effect this case might have on his personal life. Of course, George Famalaro said, it gave him some concern.

Following increasingly combative exchanges between witness and lawyer, Judge Ryan asked the jury to take a five-minute break. Out of their hearing, he turned to the defendant. "Mr. Famalaro, your attorneys have informed me that you wish to waive your presence for the remainder of your brother's testimony?"

In a quavering voice, John Famalaro said, "Yes, Your Honor." He declined the judge's offer of an audio hookup in the holding cell. "I don't want to hear it." Ryan granted the request.

With the jury re-seated, Gumlia announced he had no more questions. Chris Evans made a few perfunctory inquiries, after which Ryan excused the witness, and the jury, for the day.

The drama of the penalty phase had ended. The defense called ten more witnesses over two days, all of whom testified that John Famalaro had been a nice guy, a loner, a hard worker, had once acted heroically in chasing a mugger, was saddened over a lost love, followed religious principles, and was a terrific uncle. But the heart of the matter had been presented. Several days passed with no court sessions.

It didn't surprise anyone that John Famalaro did not testify in his own behalf, since the defenders had hinted several times that he wouldn't.

On June 12, before noon, Leonard Gumlia announced, "The defense rests."

Four days later, Chris Evans greeted the jury one last time. "I don't apologize for having brought you here," he said. Pointing to John Famalaro, now recovering from his infection, Evans said, "Because it was his conduct, June 3, 1991, that brought you here." The prosecutor would speak nearly one hour to explain why the jury should return with a penalty of death.

He could not apologize, either, for displaying the ghastly photos of Denise Huber. "These are pictures you will never forget."

After explaining the legal guidelines the jurors must follow, Evans began summarizing the evidence. Chiding the defense for failing to produce elements they had mentioned in opening statements, Evans asked, "You didn't hear the testimony of a forensic psychologist in here talking about a diagnosis of a mental disorder, did you?" No evidence of a PET scan had been brought to court, either.

Famalaro had shown a clear lack of remorse, Evans accused, and his treatment of two women with handcuffs demonstrated a foreshadowing of the future. His retention of the body and murder artifacts equated to keeping a trophy of his crime.

The defense had tried to portray an abusive childhood. On the contrary, said Evans, Famalaro's life was filled with opportunities. He had a loving grandmother who bonded with him and a grandfather who called him "Honey boy." His affectionate sister tried to protect him. A waitress had given him friendship and help. Several women had loved him. He'd thrown away opportunities to be a chiropractor, a sheriffs deputy, and to obtain college degrees. Seeing his brother's troubles gave him the chance to avoid similar problems.

Evans rejected the allegations of a terrible childhood. "We all have some problems." If Famalaro had hated his so-called abusers, why did he reach out to kill an innocent stranger, not people who allegedly mistreated him? Regarding Famalaro's unusual mother, Evans pointed out, "She doesn't get mom of the year. She was a bad mother in many respects. But she didn't teach the defendant to hurt people. She didn't instruct him to kill."

Should the jurors give the defendant any sympathy? "Sympathy," Evans said, "given appropriately, is beauty." But given when it was not deserved was not good. How much did Famalaro deserve? Had he already used up his allotment when he snatched Denise Huber, when he took her to the warehouse against her will, when he handcuffed and blindfolded her? When was sympathy exhausted? When she was screaming, when he stuffed a ball of rags in her mouth, when he struck that first blow to her head, or the fifteenth, or the thirty-first? "I will submit to you that the defendant has used up all the sympathy he deserves."

The jury and audience sat riveted to every word from the prosecutor, in awe of his sincerity and ability to connect with his listeners. He continued. "Let me tell you something you don't want to hear. I am uncomfortable telling you about it. That crime was done for several reasons and one of those was his pleasure." Evans described in graphic terms the excitement and sexual pleasure Famalaro had derived from using his handcuffs and carrying out the forced sodomy.

Victim impact evidence was twofold, he said. The impact on the victim and on the survivors. The victim, Denise Huber, had a life of promise ahead of her. What did she die for? For the defendant's brief moment of selfish sexual pleasure. "I am terribly sorry to tell you. That was the value that night of Denise Huber to him." The prosecutor wanted the jury to understand her death. ". . . With unimaginable terror. As she realized she was being caught by this guy capable of karate, imagine the terror she felt. The helplessness as the handcuffs went on her. Imagine the fear and terror when she was taped. Imagine the feeling of impending doom as that gag went in her mouth. 'I can't even scream any more.' It is unimaginable."

And the impact on the family. Evans quoted the gut-wrenching words of Ione and Dennis in their statements to the jury. Dennis wound it up with the inscription on her headstone. "Denise, you will always be loved."

"Human life on June 3, 1991, had zero value to this defendant. Ironically, through his lawyers, he is asking for life. He will ask for your mercy, your sympathy, your compassion . . . Ask yourself what consideration and sympathy he showed Denise Huber on the freeway that night. Ask yourself what mercy he showed as he beat the life out of her with his nail puller and hammer. Ask yourself that."

Expressing confidence that the twelve jurors would make the right decision, Chris Evans thanked them a last time for listening to him.

Denise Gragg and Leonard Gumlia would both plead with the jury for John Famalaro's life. Gragg went first.

Acknowledging that "There is no limit to the compassion the Hubers should have," she said, "No one can imagine what they have gone through." However, Gragg said, "That doesn't mean that it is wrong or immoral to feel some compassion for the person that John Famalaro became, and how he got that way." The penalty phase was not a game that the Hubers would lose if the jury sent Famalaro to prison for life, or would win if he received the death penalty.

Famalaro, she said, had two sides. The person on the outside was attempting to be successful, to have a life, a job, a place in society, and attempting to feel good about himself. And then there was the wretched John Famalaro who never got there, no matter how hard he tried. "It is that second, secret side . . . that resulted in what happened to Ms. Huber."

Citing philosophies about application of the death penalty, and reasons it should not apply to Famalaro, Gragg turned to Evans' treatment of the word "sympathy." She pointed out that sympathy is "not forgiveness." No one was asking for forgiveness. "He is responsible for what he did . . . but we are talking about what sentence he should get." Gragg gave theoretical examples of the same crime committed by a person with no criminal background and one with a long history of criminal activity. There should be a difference in the sentences they receive. "The act is the same, the responsibility for the act is the same. It is only that the punishment is dependent upon more than just responsibility."

Spectators and court officers alike welcomed the ninety-minute lunch break, grateful for the opportunity to temporarily step away from the dramatic proceedings.

When Gragg resumed her passionate appeal, she told jurors that Famalaro had been subjected to emotional abuse, intellectual abuse, and abnormal sexualization as a child. "He had a dark, frightening, unloving childhood in which he never had a safe haven at home." She spoke of the destructiveness perpetrated by the mother. "This woman had the time to organize political rallies, to hide in the back of George's car, to assault his girlfriend, to go to college with her daughter. But her youngest child gets kicked out of school and she doesn't find out why."

The childhood was abusive, Gragg asserted. "Not abusive like someone getting whipped once a day, but destructive the way water on a cliff can erode the face of it. All of these things that we have talked about day after day resulted in this wretched, scared, sad, withdrawn child."

Was his rearing an excuse for the crime? "It doesn't make what he did right. Doesn't make what he did excusable. But it is a reason not to kill him, and that is why we brought that evidence to your attention. And I am going to turn it over to Mr. Gumlia now."

Leonard Gumlia, for his last turn at the lectern, picked up where Gragg left off, discussing Famalaro's childhood by characterizing the mother as frightening. Disputing the prosecutor's portrayal of the defendant as both good and evil, Gumlia said,

"The other side is not evil John Famalaro, it is wretched John Famalaro."

To illustrate the defendant's story, Gumlia borrowed from his own small son. "My son likes Lincoln Logs." Pointing to a pair of miniature log cabins, which he planned to use as metaphors representing a normal childhood and a wretched one, he said, "My wife and I—she is the one you heard about in the guilt phase with the shoes—we put this together." Each log symbolized contributions made by the parents in nurturing the child, adding up to a solid structure or one with an unstable foundation that can crumble.

John's foundation, Gumlia declared, was built on evil, warped religion, paranoia, on being told the world is bad, and on anger. It resulted in an obsessive compulsiveness, pack-ratting habits, and an abnormal sexuality.

Relying heavily on the journal Famalaro had written in the mid seventies, Gumlia stressed that his client wanted to be normal. The prosecutor had criticized Famalaro for so many blown opportunities. "These are not blown opportunities," Gumlia insisted. "These are a person trying, who desperately wants to be normal, and to succeed. But he can't."

His client, Gumlia said, used coping mechanisms, including immersing himself in work. Expressing Famalaro's thoughts, he said, "If I am busy enough, I don't have to stop and think about all the wretchedness."

For the vast majority of his life, Gumlia said, Famalaro had basically decent and generous instincts. But, "as a child he has no control. He has been totally dominated by a woman and is being sexualized, everything is sex, either pro or negative. Is it such a surprise that out of sexualization would come desire for control? In this case the handcuffs ultimately became the tool."

Neither the frozen body nor the artifacts Famalaro kept were trophies, argued Gumlia. The prosector, he said, had tried to support that theory with a false example of trophies, the nude pictures of Darlene Miller in New York. How could those photos be trophies? With a verbal flourish, Gumlia snapped, "That roll of film wasn't even developed until recently!"

After a break, Gumlia removed his coat and made an interesting comment about himself. When he spoke to people, including juries, he said, "Sometimes it's hard for me to look directly in the eye, because when I look at someone directly in the eye, I lose track of what it is I want to say." It was a courageous bit of self-analysis, explaining why he sometimes gazed into the distance or stared at the ceiling while speaking.

Now, one of his two Lincoln Log houses stood intact, while the other had collapsed in shambles. To Gumlia, the broken one represented how his client's life had been shattered. Famalaro's self-imposed control had snapped. "Intellectually, his life was devoted to not harming people. And somewhere, that control snapped . . . When your own life has no value; your own life is worthless to you . . . it is hard to see value anywhere. That is why historically people have done crazy things in depression, even evil things, which this was." He pointed at the little collapsed log structure. All of the negative pressures in Famalaro's life, Gumlia said, "Every one of these things works its effect, the eroding effect, and finally causes this to collapse in a heap. And that is what happened to Mr. Famalaro on June 3. He collapsed in a heap and Denise Huber was the victim."

Denise had not suffered for a long period of time, Gumlia said. "Certainly, it was terrible for her, but death did happen quickly. There was nothing prolonged about it."

Growing hoarse after putting every fiber of his emotion into the plea, Gumlia tapered toward his close. "In the end, remember that the death penalty is reserved for a very, very, very small group of irredeemable people who commit murder. It is for those who kill and enjoy it, not for those who become sickened by their own actions . . . John Famalaro is still a human being. The State has asked you to kill him. We respectfully argue to you that there is both an intellectual and emotional reason that life without parole is the appropriate penalty in this case.

"I thank you very much."

Judge Ryan read the legal instructions to the jurors. Now all the pressure would rest on the shoulders of the twelve people who had easily reached a verdict that John Famalaro had com-

mitted murder with special circumstances. Could they now u-
nanimously decide if he should spend the rest of his life in
prison, or be sentenced to death?

In the jury room once more, on Tuesday, June 17, the responsibility loomed over the nine women and three men. Bonnie
Snethen acted as foreperson again, and they agreed to keep the
same roundtable discussion procedure. One juror expressed sympathy for both the Huber family, and the Famalaros. "If I weighed
sympathy on a scale, it would be even. But when I add in the
brutality of the crime, and how he kept the frozen body for three
years, it's like adding a bowling ball to one side of the scale."

As each member contributed opinions, thoughts, and weighed
the testimony, Snethen began having doubts they would be able
to agree on a verdict.

Photographs played a big part in their discussions. On a cork-
board, they posted the pictures of Denise Huber's body to be
sure they kept in mind the horror of her death. Juror Anna
Brown later said, "It helped remind us of how brutally she
died, while John Famalaro went on with his life for three years."
She felt confident that God would lead them to the right decision.

The grisly photos also touched juror Kris Gundel. "They are
something I will never erase. It was gut-wrenching for me, and
I think it was gut-wrenching for everybody."

The snapshots of Darlene Miller sexually fondling Famalaro,
Bonnie Snethen said, did reduce some of the woman's credibil-
ity, but it was undeniable that handcuffs played a part in the
defendant's mode of interacting with women.

When it came time to analyze the remarkable testimony of
Famalaro's mother, a few of the jurors had to fight off the urge
to laugh. They had seldom heard anything so strange. "If she
was my mother," said David Reyno, "I would have run away."

Laurie Vance contributed her view. "His mother is a big part
of who he is, but he was an adult when he committed this crime."

"Yes, his childhood was messed up," observed Kristen Gundel.
"He was really neglected. But sympathy can only go so far."

Some of the panelists seemed swayed by the psychological impact of Famalaro's upbringing. But Anna Brown noted, "They never proved it. They never brought in anyone to testify that he had mental problems."

Bonnie Snethen pointed out that in Leonard Gumlia's opening statements, he had talked about a PET scan to give evidence of possible neurological imbalances in the brain of his client. But no such evidence had been produced.

They broke for the night, but few of them had very much sleep. Snethen sat in front of a mirror at home, and asked herself why she was on that jury. She wondered if divine intervention had placed her there because she had some understanding of the legal system, and could help the panel avoid pitfalls and assure they made decisions entirely consistent with the law. She would be especially cautious, she decided, to prevent any stubbing of toes on innuendos, and to keep focus on what was presented in court. She said, "The law will lead us in the right direction and we will know what our responsibilities are in weighing aggravating versus mitigating circumstances."

David Reyno felt a close bond to his fellow jurors. The lawyers, he thought, had done a terrific job of selecting a balanced and fair panel. During deliberations, he made a point of saying they were after justice, not vengeance. Personally, he accepted that John Famalaro had grown up in peculiar circumstances, but he thought that many people had experienced far worse and hadn't turned to murder. In examining the photo of Denise Huber's body, he had nearly gagged. It bothered Reyno deeply that "Famalaro had snatched a person off the street who had done no harm to anyone." He'd had a difficult time keeping back the tears when Dennis Huber had spoken about never seeing Denise walk down the aisle at her wedding. "I am such a believer in the family unit and marriage." The emotion was so thick, he said, it just reached across the room.

During the testimony of the brother and sister, he had noticed John Famalaro's crying, and felt some sympathy. "I am affected by emotions. Even in him."

The sobbing by Famalaro had also been observed by Snethen, during the testimony of his sister. But while the brother spoke, the defense attorney blocked her view of Famalaro. One of the jurors noticed that he "had stuff from his nose on his face."

Mrs. Famalaro's testimony had struck Reyno as "odd." To Gundel, "His mother was a freak. There's no other word to describe that woman."

The personal journal Famalaro had written which chronicled his loss of Helen Lyons had been introduced into evidence by Leonard Gumlia. The jurors read segments of it aloud, and felt sorry for him. One of them pointed out, though, how long ago that had been. The murder was committed years later.

As the morning wore on, stress and emotion filled the little room. Several of the jurors cried. They broke for lunch to get some air and ease the tension.

In the early afternoon, all of them seemed to feel hesitant, just sitting quietly, some still wiping at tears. Snethen inquired, several times, if they wanted to discuss anything else. Short bursts of conversation ended quickly, Finally, Snethen asked if they were ready to take a vote. They were. This time it would be on written ballots. She tore pieces of paper from one of the notebooks, and passed them around. Each person entered their verdict, and handed the folded slips back to her.

Snethen unfolded and read them aloud, one at a time. Death. Death. Death. When she held up the twelfth ballot, "You could have heard a pin drop."

"Death."

No one knew what to say. More tears. One of them asked, "Shall we offer a prayer?"

Dave Reyno said, "I would be glad to lead us in one." They all joined hands and bowed their heads while Reyno asked for a heavenly blessing that they had reached the right decision. He also asked God's help for the Huber family and for John Famalaro. Amen.

Bonnie Snethen summoned the bailiff.

Epilogue

Judges in California murder trials have the option of rejecting juries' recommendations to send convicted killers to death row. If the judge believes the facts of the case warrant a lesser sentence of life in prison without the possibility of parole, he or she holds the legal power to order the reduced punishment. A special hearing to announce the sentence is usually held within a few weeks after the verdict.

Judge John Ryan set September 5, 1997, to conduct the sentence hearing for John Famalaro.

The courtroom gallery filled again on that Friday morning with reporters and court watchers. Ione and Jeff Huber sat in the front row, with family and friends occupying the seats close by. Dennis remained in North Dakota to wrap up important business affairs. He had hoped that John Famalaro would make a statement, perhaps expressing remorse for the crime, but was informed that the convicted killer would remain silent.

None of John Famalaro's relatives found any reason to attend the hearing.

The convicted killer sat stonily at the defense table, now dressed in orange coveralls instead of the slacks and sweaters he'd worn during the trial.

Leonard Gumlia spoke up to voice a complaint about a cartoon that had appeared in editorial section of the *Orange County Register*. "It ridiculed the defense as the jury was deliberating."

He included it in a packet of other documents to support a request for a new trial, largely based on previous motions to change venue due to heavy local publicity about the case.

Judge Ryan saw no harm in the cartoon or other news coverage. "This court believed after the *voir dire* that not one of the sitting jurors had any knowledge about this case which would interfere with their ability to render a fair, impartial verdict . . . The evidence as to Mr. Famalaro's guilt was just overwhelming. Nothing concerning publicity before, during, or after the trial indicates that any juror was improperly influenced."

Other issues raised by the defense, in requesting a new trial, were based on their opinion that no kidnapping or sodomy had been proved. The so-called sperm found in the victim's body, they asserted, could not conclusively be identified. Judge Ryan unequivocally disagreed. "It was sperm. Evidence proved that quite satisfactorily in my opinion . . . I had no question. That was my view and is my view. I went through all of the evidence . . . the handcuffing, the gagging, the blindfolding, the strip—the taking off of Ms. Huber's clothing, and the finding of spermatozoa in the rectum. The reasonable inferences include the fact that this victim fought as hard as she could. The restraints had to be applied while she was still alive. Mr. Famalaro had to have forcible sex in mind. He moved this woman to his warehouse where no one else was around, in the middle of the night. Just no reasonable doubt as to what he had in mind, what he did and how he did it. That is the sodomy aspect. Those same factors go to the kidnapping.

"The evidence proves that this lady would not willingly get into a stranger's car when she was so close to help. It is unreasonable to believe as the defense suggests that she had a fear of police because she had been drinking alcohol that evening. Even if . . . she got into that car voluntarily, she would not have accompanied Mr. Famalaro to the warehouse; would not. She gave Mr. Famalaro a hard time . . . and the evidence later on proved that he could get the handcuffs on quite easily without the other person being aware. In this court's mind, Ms. Huber was forced and restrained long before she got to that warehouse. There is no reasonable doubt as to either special circumstance."

Ryan denied the motion for a new trial.

A short discussion ensued with the lawyers, after which Judge Ryan explained the mitigating and aggravating circumstances he had weighed in reaching a penalty decision. "I found there were some mental and emotional scars from Mr. Famalaro's mother's behavior during his childhood. Her control over her children was not normal or healthy. Her view on sex, pornography, and politics were just off the board."

On the issue of aggravating circumstances, Ryan commented on the brutality of the crime. "Just imagine what was going through Miss Huber's mind during the ride from Costa Mesa to the warehouse, then being stripped of her clothing. She had to be making noise, or Mr. Famalaro thought she was, so she was gagged. A rag was shoved in her mouth and then masking tape placed over that . . . You have to think about the mental anguish, the physical discomfort, the things going through her mind . . . It is reasonable to assume that the numerous blows to her head were because Mr. Famalaro was enraged . . . induced by her resistance."

Victim impact evidence, Ryan said, was quite substantial for both parents. "They made extraordinary efforts to locate their daughter. They had difficulty with their work, eating, sleeping, but they always had hope. They went through years of not knowing, years of worry and hope. That is certainly aggravating."

Before pronouncing sentence, and over objections by the defense, Ryan allowed brief statements from Ione Huber, Jeff Huber, and the reading by Nancy Streza of a letter from Dennis Huber.

Jeff spoke in a clear, firm voice, tinged with anger. He noted that he had seen the effect on his parents, aging them "twenty or thirty years in the last five or six years." Little Ashley Denise, a week away from her fifth birthday, Jeff said, knew almost nothing about her late aunt. "Someday, I am going to have to explain to her what she has to look forward to growing up and having to deal with people like Mr. Famalaro over there." Jeff raised his arm and pointed as if he wished it were a rifle. "When she goes out on a date, I am going to be sitting there saying, 'Oh man, I hope she doesn't get a flat tire. You never know what kind of gutter slime you are going to encounter in this world." The whole experience, Jeff said, had given him a bad taste "for my fellow mankind."

* * *

Ione Huber stepped to the lectern one last time. Recalling detailed chronology of the excruciating trauma, and the hours after Denise vanished, she said, "I cannot adequately describe the pain, agony, and helplessness that I experienced for the next several days, which turned into weeks, then months, and years." She recalled the pleas she had made through the media for information, met only by the killer's silence. "At times, it was more than I could bear. Not knowing where she was, if she was dead or alive, or if she was being tortured . . . was by far the worst thing I have ever experienced."

The move to North Dakota to escape and start a new life, Ione revealed, hadn't worked very well "because we have been devastated financially as well."

When the terrible discovery of the frozen body was made, "I knew then all hope was gone, and I would have to face the reality that we would never see our beautiful, loving daughter alive again . . . She would have been the delight of any parent. She was robbed of her life and future at such a young age . . . John Famalaro took all that away. He robbed her of her future husband and children, and future grandchildren for me and my husband. I miss her more than words can describe and my heart aches because of the horror that void has left in my life.

"I still have many questions that this man knows the answers to but hasn't revealed to us. I wish he would have gotten on the stand and told us the truth. These unanswered questions continue to haunt us. I have seen no compassion and no remorse from him. And I agree with the jury's recommendation that John Famalaro be given the death penalty. Anybody who can murder a beautiful, young, innocent person and then compound that crime by keeping us suffering through more than three years of total silence doesn't deserve to continue his life."

Nancy Streza introduced herself and read a statement from Dennis Huber. In it, he noted that his life had been put in limbo when his daughter vanished. When she was found, he wrote, it was better to know but, "Inside, I hated it because all hope was gone. My life will never be the same. I feel like there is a big hole in me that will never be filled. I hate going to weddings and seeing fathers walk their daughters down the aisle because I will never be able to do that. I will never know the grandchildren Denise may have given us . . . All I have is a grave and a headstone to visit and talk to."

He reminisced about all the fun he had experienced with his loving daughter. He spoke of the health problems he and Ione had experienced from the stress. Famalaro, he said, had more than one victim. "Some of us are still walking around." Dennis, too, approved of the jury's verdict of death for the killer. "I ask for justice."

In a deadly quiet courtroom, Judge Ryan spoke. "John Joseph Famalaro, it is the judgement and sentence of this court that for the offense of murder as charged in the indictment of which you were found guilty . . . that the appropriate sentence is death, and it is the order of this court that you shall suffer the death penalty. Said penalty to be inflicted within the walls of the state prison at San Quentin in the manner prescribed by law . . . at a time to be fixed by this court in the warrant of execution."

Before the end of September, John Famalaro joined the 475 other men condemned to death, held in San Quentin on a peninsula of San Francisco Bay a few miles north of the Golden Gate bridge. He will not face lethal injection, now used by California, for many years, if ever. Quite a few of the men on death row have been there for nearly two decades. Scores of them haven't even started the long process of appeals, which are automatic for convicts sentenced to death.

Leonard Gumlia and Denise Gragg express confidence that appeals courts may overturn the death sentence for Famalaro.

They are opponents of capital punishment and work vigorously to defend against its inappropriate use.

Chris Evans doubts that Famalaro's penalty will be reversed, believing the verdict was lawful and based on reasonable evidence. Evans continues as one of the most effective prosecutors in Orange County. He hopes one day to write books about his experiences, and to marry the "incredibly intelligent, sensitive, beautiful, and spiritual" woman who is the great love of his life.

Lynda Giesler revels in her retirement, with her dogs, enjoying visiting relatives, and keeping contact with her lifelong friends in the Costa Mesa Police Department.

Scott Mascher shot up through the ranks of Yavapai County Sheriff's Department, and now accepts even more responsibility as commander of patrol operations for the eastern half of the county. His admirers predict that he may one day run for, and win, the office of county sheriff.

Elaine Canalia married Jack Court shortly after Famalaro was convicted. They sold their paint business in Phoenix and realized their dream of moving to Fiji in the Pacific to own and operate a tropical resort hotel.

Bonnie Snethen and David Reyno are proud of the jurors with whom they served on the Famalaro case, hailing the complete fairness and objectivity of the group.

In October 1997, Ione and Dennis Huber sold their homes in North Dakota and moved back to Orange County. She made the move first, while he finalized the sales. Ione found a job teaching third grade. Before Dennis could join her in California, to work in the mortgage banking software business, he faced one more painful decision. He had to say goodbye to Sam, the faithful dog who had loved Denise. Dennis believes they are romping together in heaven, free of earthly pain.

AUTHOR'S NOTES AND ACKNOWLEDGMENTS

Researching and writing a true crime story can be an emotionally wrenching exercise. I sat next to the Huber family during the trial, chatted with them, dined with them, and felt the pain with them. As I learned about the life of Denise Huber, I posted photographs of her around my word processor, and grew to know her. The loss, by brutal murder, of such a wholesome, responsible, and decent person is inexplicable. To ponder why she crossed paths with a man who committed the horrible abuse, then took her life, is frustrating. And to make sense of it in a book is impossible. I've done my best to report the facts, according to the trial, scores of interviews, public documents, and my observations. Even though portions of dialogue are re-created from interviews, there are no fictionalized parts in this book. To the best of my knowledge, the events as I have reported them are true. To protect the privacy of certain individuals, I have changed their names.

I cannot adequately express my gratitude to the long list of people who generously provided assistance in this project. Chris Evans used many of his off-duty hours to help me understand the legal complexities. Dennis, Ione, and Jeff Huber shared their lives with me, along with joy and grief related to loving and losing Denise. Leonard Gumlia and Denise Gragg sat generously and courteously for interviews. Scott Mascher made my visit to Arizona a rewarding experience. Elaine Canalia and Jack Court are two of the friendliest people one could ever meet, and I hope to be a guest in their Fiji hotel soon. Tammy Brown brought photocopies of her mementos to our meeting, and Rob Calvert talked with me about his affection for Denise. C.P. Smith of the *Orange County Register* was an extremely valuable source of information. Chief

Dave Snowden, Ron Smith, and Lynda Giesler patiently answered my endless questions. Gillian and Pat Fay made me comfortable in their home and let me borrow videotapes of their vacations with the Huber family. It saddened me in February 1998 to learn that Pat had succumbed to a long bout with cancer. Nancy Streza also loaned me tapes, and allowed me to quote the touching song she wrote in memory of Denise. Dana Holliday, a real true-crime buff and astrologer extraordinaire, provided fascinating input, as did Margie Hempstead. Bill Hamilton, of The Cannery restaurant, not only helped remember Denise, but provided dinner for the Hubers and this author at his establishment.

Only one request for information during my research went without answer, and probably for very good reason. I wondered why Denise's Honda could sit on the freeway approximately twenty hours, with emergency blinkers flashing, and not come to the attention of the California Highway Patrol. My inquiry to their headquarters in Sacramento was met with courtesy, but eventually a choice by the commander not to make a statement. I realize, of course, that I put him in an awkward, no-win position. Obviously, if officers had overlooked the vehicle, or ignored it, the commander would prefer not to publicly say so. I prefer to think that the unit in charge of that region was short-handed or busy on urgent pursuits that night. Certainly, if one of them had stopped to check out the Honda, it would have made no difference in the outcome of the case.

Finally, I want to thank the newspaper reporters with whom I chatted nearly every day of the trial. I sincerely admire the work of Greg Hernandez of the *L.A. Times,* Stu Pfiefer and Jonathan Volzke of the *Orange County Register,* as well as Chris Goffard of the *Daily Pilot.*

No non-fiction author can survive without the unselfish contributions of many people. Eventually, one person decides if the mountain of work will culminate in a book. Paul Dinas of Kensington Publishing gave the green light to my literary agent, Susan Crawford, and allowed me to tell this story. Karen Haas helped polish the final product. It is my sincere wish that, as a team we have honored Denise Huber and her parents with this chronicle.

A memorial scholarship has been established in Denise Huber's name at:

Covenant College
14049 Scenic Highway
Lookout Mountain, Georgia
                30750
706-820-7209